THE TĀRĪKH-I-MUBĀRAKSHĀHĪ

THE TĀRĪKH-I-MUBĀRAKSHĀHĪ

YĀḤIYĀ BIN AḤMAD BIN 'ABDULLAH'
SIRHINDI

Translated into English from the Original Persian with Textual Notes and Index
by

H. BEVERIDGE

MANOHAR
2026

Due to the academic and scholarly importance of this volume, we are reprinting/republishing it from the original source without any modifications or changes. Therefore, some misprints and errors may occur.

Reprinted 2026
First eBook edition 2026

ISBN 978-93-7451-588-4 (Hb)
ISBN 978-93-7451-290-6 (eBook)

Published by
Ajay Kumar Jain *for*
Manohar Publishers & Distributors
4753/23 Ansari Road, Daryaganj
New Delhi 110 002

Printed and bound in India

CONTENTS.

PAGE

ABBREVIATIONS.

Aḟif—Shams-i-Siraj Afif, Tarikh-i-Firozshahi (A.S.B , 1888–1891) and also Elliot (Translations of Extracts from Afif).

B. De—English Translation of Tabākāt-i-Akbari (A.S.B., 1913).

Badaoni—Muntakhab-ul-Tawarikh (A.S.B.).

Cam. Hist.—Cambridge History of India, Vol. III. By Lt.-Col. Sir Wolseley Haig, K.C.I.E., etc., Cambridge University Press, 1928.

Elliot—Sir H. M. Elliot, History of India. Trübner & Co., London, 1872.

Ferishta—J. Briggs, History of the Rise of the Mahomedan Power, R. Cambray, 1908.

Howorth, H. H.—History of the Mongols, 4 vols. Longmans Green & Co., 1876.

Ibn Batuta—Travels of: (*a*) Translated by Lees, 1829; (*b*) The Broadway Travellers, Ibn Batuta, Travels in Asia and Africa, 1325–54, G. Routledge & Sons Ltd., London, 1929.

Indian Ephemeris—By L. D. S. Pillai, published under the authority of the Government of Madras, 1922.

Ishwari Pd., Dr.—History of Mediæval India, Indian Press, Allahabad.

J.A.S.B.—Journal Asiatic Society of Bengal.

J.N.S.—MS. of the Tārīkh-i-Mubārakshāhī belonging to Sir J. N. Sarkar, Kt., C.I.E.

J.R.A.S.—Journal Royal Asiatic Society.

MBL—MS. of the Tārīkh-i-Mubārakshāhī in the Bodleian Library (MS. Fraser, 150).

MBM—MS. of the Tārīkh-i-Mubārakshāhī in the British Museum Library (MS. no. 41057).

Ranking—G. S. A. Ranking, English Translation of Badaoni (A.S.B., 1898).

Raverty—H. G. Raverty, English Translation of Tabāķāt-i-Nāṣiri (A.S.B.).

T.A. or Tab.-i-Akb.—Tabāķāt-i-Akbari of Nizām-ud-din Aḥmad (A.S.B.).

Thomas—Chronicles of the Pathan Kings of Delhi.

The Tārīkh-i-Mubārakshāhī.

THE AUTHOR'S INTRODUCTION.

IN THE NAME OF ALLAH, THE COMPASSIONATE, THE MERCIFUL.

Infinite praise be solely to God, the Creator of the angel and the mankind, Who with the assistance[1] of the equity of the emperors, the defenders of the Faith,[2] elevated and established the foundation of the Islamic Religion in a manner that it might not be endangered "*till then when those in their graves would be taken out*"; and unlimited thanksgiving be to the Eternal[3] and Sole Lord, Who by the awe-inspiring sword of the emperors,[4] devoted to the Faith, razed to the ground and destroyed the foundations of the infidels so that they could not construct their edifices "*until the Day of Resurrection!*" "*In the words of the Prophet, upon him be peace, the Faith and the Country are like twins.*"

Increasing benedictions and pious salutations be upon the chosen among the created beings, the abstract of the existences, the best and the greatest among the men, the chief of the descendants of Adam, Muḥammad bin 'Abdullah bin 'Abdul Muṭṭalib bin Hāshim bin 'Abd Manāf;[5] and peace be upon the "*followers and descendants of the Prophet that are pure, holy, and righteous*"; especially, upon the four friends, the chosens of the Omnipotent God, and the true Caliphs; upon him, the best among the companions and the associates, Amiru-l Mu'minin Abu Bakr al-Ṣidīķ, *May Allah be pleased with him!* whom[6] He has honoured

[1] MBM and MBL read استمادت.

[2] MBL reads دین داران.

[3] Text reads صمد, which literally means "in want of nothing" (بی نیاز).

[4] MBM reads ملت صلابت : MBL reads ملّتِ کفر از صلابت شمشیر شهریاران.

[5] MBL reac ، قاتل مشرکان دیار عرب و کفار after عبد مناف, but MBM omits it.

[6] JNS begins here.

by saying that, *he was the second among the two who took shelter in the cave*;

upon him, who was the crown among the just and the selected, whose action is a proof positive of (the existence of) God, who was befriended by Allah, the Bestower of gifts—Amir ul Mū'mīnīn 'Amr ul Khaṭṭāb[1]—*May Allah be pleased with him!* whom He has honoured by saying, "*He is severe upon the infidels*";

upon him, who was the greatest martyr in the cause of Allah, the chief among the saints, who put into shape the Ḳorān—Amir ul Mū'mīnīn Osmān, the son of 'Affān, *May Allah be pleased with him!* with regard to whom he has said, "*The most compassionate among them*" (followers of the Prophet);

upon him, who was the last of the (four) Caliphs, the helper of the weak, the victorious lion of Allah—Amir ul Mū'mīnīn, 'Ali-bin-Abi-Ṭālib, *May Allah be pleased with him and May He honour him!* with regard to whom He has said, "*Thou seest in him one bowing and performing Sijdah and praying for the grace and glory of Allah*";

upon them, who were the two pieces of the Prophet's body, the apple of the eye of Zuhrā Batul (daughter of the Prophet)—"*the pupils which gave sight in both her eyes*"!—Amir ul Mū'mīnīn Al Ḥasan and Al Ḥusen—*May Allah be pleased with them and may they remain contented with the decree of Allah*, and *May He* (*also*) *be pleased with all the companions of the Prophet, with those who came after them, and with the Imāms, who were shown the proper path and were satisfied with the decree of Allah—those who pronounced judgment with honesty and administered justice with equity*, every one of whom (companions and *Imāms*), was the leader of the Religion and believer in the Religion, according to the saying of the Prophet, "*My companions are like stars, whomsoever you follow, you take the proper path.*"

It is represented by Yāḥiyā, the well-wisher of all Muslims,[2] the humblest slave of the Omniscient Lord[3] and the son of Aḥmad bin 'Abdullah[4] of Sirhind[5]—*May God help him to be devotional*

---

1 JNS reads 'Amr bin-ul Khaṭṭāb, but MBL and MBM read 'Amr ul Khaṭṭāb.

2 MBM reads كافه اسلام : MBL reads كافۀ اهل اسلام : JNS كافه انام.

3 MBM and MBL ملک علّام : JNS ملک غلام

4 JNS reads ابن احمد عبد اللّه.

5 MBL السیرندی : MBM السیهرندی : JNS السرهندی.

and May He free him from sin! that, when the Great and Glorious God granted the rein of sovereignty over Hindustan[1] to Mu'izzu-dunyā-wa-ud-dīn Abu-l-Fateḥ Ḥaẓrat Mubārak Shāh-ul-Sulṭān[2] *May Allah perpetuate his kingdom, his sovereignty and May He increase his dignity*—the powerful lord of the universe, the ruler over the sons and daughters of Adam, the lord of the Persian and Arabian Kings, the potent royal personality befriended by the Merciful, and the son of Naṣir-ud-daulat-wa-ud-dīn Khiẓr Khān, the great and the bountiful and of revered memory—*May his tomb be sanctified, and May he dwell in paradise*—and He installed him upon the throne of the capital city, Dehli, which had been the chief seat of many a great and noteworthy ruler, the world and its denizens, owing to the immense benignity and justice of the heavenly-exalted king, were honoured with the gift of law and order; moreover,[3] the recalcitrants and the infidels for fear of the sharp edged sword and the vast army (of His Majesty) walked into the corner of misfortune,[4] and remained sick, distressed and ruined. [*May God, the Great and the Glorious, cast perpetually till the continuance of the progeny of Adam, the shadow of the imperial umbrella—the shadow of God in the universe*[5]*—upon the world and its denizens, and May He, under His own shelter and defence,*[6] *protect it from misfortunes and disasters of the final day.*

Verse.

O! that thou mayest avail yourself of the throne,
fortune, prosperity and youth,
As a good king, thou mayest scatter wealth according
to your desires!

---

[1] MBL زمام سلطنت و قوام مملکت هند و سند : MBM and JNS read زمام سلطنت مملکت هندوستان.

[2] MBM has no "ul-Sultān" after Mubārak Shāh : JNS agrees with MBL.

[3] MBL and MBM read مگر : JNS omits مگر.

[4] MBL در کنج : MBM در کنج ادبار : JNS در کنج ادیار.

[5] MBM ظلّ اللّٰهِ في الْعَالَم ; MBL reads العالمين instead of العالم : JNS agree with MBM.

[6] MBL gives در پناه و عصمت خویش جای دهد : MBM reads خویش نهد JNS agrees with MBL but omits جای.

On the whole, this well-wisher (*i.e.*, the author) had the intention of being honoured by kissing the ground of His Auspicious Majesty,—*May Allah, The Most High, ever make him supreme !*—but owing to the dearth of any suitable present worthy of the royal dignity, let him narrate the history of the late emperors[1]—*May Allah shed lustre on their demonstrations !*—who obtained under the custody of Allah, The Most High ! the guardianship over events (*i.e.*, whose period of sovereignty is reminiscent of various events). The facts (of this work) have been gathered from various histories and recorded up to the coronation of the powerful Firoz Shāh—*May Allah shed light on his tomb !*—the deceased (Emperor), and after that event whatever was witnessed[2] (by the author) has been related.[3]

Verse.

What gift can the Earth make to the Sky ?
What service can a beggar[4] render to the King ?

This book has been called, "*The Tarikh-i-Mubārak Shāhi*" If it be accepted by His Majesty, it is hoped that the slave (the author) will be sufficiently pitied for and sympathised, and that the head of his prosperity will touch the sky of beatitude and felicity. *God Is The Helper !*

An account of the deceased pardoned martyr Sulṭān Sa'iyid[5] Mu'izzu-duniya-wa-ud-din Muḥammad Sām Ghuri,[6] May the blessing of God be on his tomb, and May he dwell in paradise !

As Islām was established in Dehli and the countries of Hindustan by the late pardoned martyr Sulṭān Sa'iyid, we begin with his account.

Sulṭān Sa'iyid, the great and powerful emperor, was the son of

---

1 MBL قصۀ سلاطین ماضیه : MBM adds ضابط بوده اند after ماضیه : JNS agrees with MBL.

2 MBM روات ثقات هر چه : MBL روات و ثقات و هر چه : JNS agrees with MBM.

3 در این سطور مسطور گردانیده : JNS omits سطور.

4 MBL خدمتی گدا : MBM خدمت گدا : JNS agrees with MBL.

5 MBL سلطان سعید : MBM and JNS سلطان السعید.

6 MBM محمد بن سام : JNS agrees with MBM : MBL محمد سام.

Bahā'-ud-din Sām [1] and the nephew (brother's son) of Sulṭān 'Alā'-ud-dīn Jāhān-soz. When after the demise of Sulṭān Saif-ud-dīn, son of Sulṭān 'Alā'-ud-dīn Jahān-soz, the sovereignty of Ghur was vested on Sulṭān Ghiās-ud-dīn Muhammad, the elder brother of the Sulṭān Sa'iyid, he bestowed the fief of Tīgīnabād [2] upon Sultān Mu'izz-ud-dīn.[3]

Parentage of Muhammad Ghuri.

On the first year (of Ghiās-ud-din's reign), Sulṭān Sa'iyid raided Ghaznīn from which the tribe of Ghuzz had brought out by force the late Sulṭān named Khusru Malik, the daughter's son of late Mahmud Ghāzī. In 569 H.[4] (1173 A.D.), Sulṭān Ghias-ud-dīn drew his force from Ghur and marched to Ghaznīn. The tribe of Ghuzz who were the masters of Ghaznīn, having lost all strength for opposing the invader, made off, perforce, to their own country. Ghaznīn fell to Sulṭān Ghias-ud-dīn, who conferred it upon the late Sulṭān Sa'iyid (Mu'izz-ud-dīn) with the title of Sulṭān, and himself turned back towards Firoz-koh,[5] his capital.

Raid of Ghaznīn by Muhammad.

The same year, the late Sulṭān Mu'izz-ud-dīn brought the vicinity of Ghaznīn under his jurisdiction. On the second year, 570 H. (1174 A.D.), he conquered the *aktā'* of Gurdez.[6] Next year,[7] he led

Mu'izz-ud-dīn's campaign agst. Uchch, Bhati and Multan.

---

[1] MBL and JNS read Shihāb-ud-din Sām : MBM, Bahā'-ud-din Sām : Ferishta gives the name as Bahā'-ud-dīn Sām and relates that 'Alā'-ud-din appointed his two nephews, Ghiās-ud-dīn and Mu'izz-ud-dīn, to the government of the province of Ghur called Sunja, but as the revenue of the province did not support them in the style they wished they made encroachments on their neighbours for which 'Alā'-ud-din confined them in a fort of Jooristan (Tab-i-Nas. Wajiristan). But when Saif-ud-dīn, son of 'Alā'-ud-dīn, ascended the throne he released his two cousins from their confinement and again conferred on them the Government of Sunja.

[2] MBL and MBM. Taknabād (تكناباد) : JNS agrees with them : Tab-i-Nas. Tīgīnabād : Dow calls it Tunganabād and places it in the province of Khorasan. The city of Taknabād or Tiginābād was situated between Ghaznīn and Ghur.

[3] Tab-i-Nas. says that he became *Sar-i-Jāndār* (the chief armour bearer).

[4] Ferishta writes 567 H. There is discrepancy among writers with regard to the date of the capture of Ghaznīn. Some say 567 H.; others 569 H. and 570 H. See Raverty, p. 449, f.n. 8.

[5] MBM فرز كوه : MBL and JNS فيروز كوه.

[6] MBL and MBM read كرديز : JNS كرديز : Tab-i-Nas. and Badaoni (p. 4 Bib. Ind.) Gurdez : Acc. to Raverty it is the name of a valley with hills on two sides, belonging to the tribe called the Tājiks. اقطاع—(*iktā'* or *aktā'* literally means, assignments of land; feudal lands; cuts, etc., *iktā'* is the plural of *kit'*).

[7] Ferishta writes 572 H.

his army towards Uchch,[1] Bhati,[2] and Multān. The Bhati tribe shut themselves up in the fortress of Uchch and showed opposition; but after a few days' lighting, by the aid of Allah: The Most High, the fortress was taken.[3] Having placed the *aktā'* of Multān[4] and Uchch in charge of *Sipah Sālār* 'Alī Karmākh,[5] Mu'izz-ud-dīn returned to Ghaznīn.

Mu'izz-ud-dīn's march against Gujrāt via Multān and Uchch.

In the year 574 H. (1178 A.D.), Mu'izz-ud-dīn marched towards Gujrāt *via* Multān and Uchch. Rai Bhim Deo,[6] the accursed chief of Gujrāt, who had a large number of elephants and an immense foot and cavalry, gave him battle; after a severe struggle the Muslim army was defeated, and the Sultān retired[7] without any success.

Mu'izz-ud-dīn marched to Furshur and Lahore.

In the year 575 H.[8] (1179 A.D.), the Sultān marched against Furshur[9] and conquered it. Next year,[10] he successively despoiled Lahore; neither could Khusro Malik resist the invader in the open

---

1 It was situated on the east bank of the Panjnad, 70 m.s.s.w. of Multan. It was here that Alexander was severely wounded and he narrowly escaped with his life.

2 MBL اچه و ملتان : JNS اُچّ و تهته و ملتان ; MBM اچ : Bhatia a strong fort of this name is situated between Multan and Alor. Ferishta writes Multān and Oocha, and makes no mention of Bhati. Tab-i-Akb. and Badaoni refer to Bhati. The tribe of Bhattis whose name has been variously spelt were previously in possession of a great part of Sind.

3 The translators of Ferishta incorrectly relate a story how owing to the treachery of the Queen the place was reduced. For full particulars see Raverty, pp. 449–51, f.n. 2.

4 Tab-i-Akb. (Bib. Ind. 36) writes that Multān was conquered from the schismatics known as the Ķirāmitah.

5 MBL علي كرناخ : Badāoni (Ranking, A.S.B., p. 66) Ali Kirmaj : Ferishta-Ali Kirmany. Tab-i-Akb., 'Ali Karmākh.

6 MBL بهوچديو : Tab-i-Akb., Ferishta and Badaoni have Bhim Deo: JNS راى بهلم : Ferishta writes that Rai Bhim Deo was the lineal descendant of Brahma Deo, who opposed Mahmud of Ghazni. Some writers call him Bhoj Deo.

7 The Sultān suffered many hardships on his way to Ghazni. (Ferishta.)

8 The authors disagree in date. Some say 575 H., others 576 H., the majority 577 H., and Badaoni 580 H. MBM read خمس و سبعين

9 The MSS. read فُر شور : The place may be identified with Peshawar.

10 MBM and JNS ديگر متواتر : MBL سال ديگر متواتر.

field, nor did he dare come outside the fortress. When the invader neared Lahore, Khusro shut himself up in the fort, and at last, made a presentation of an well-equipped elephant as a tribute.[1] The late Sulṭān then returned to Ghaznīn from that place.

Mu'izz-ud-dīn marched against Lahore and founded Sialkot.

In the year 580 H.[2] (1184 A.D.), he again advanced to Lahore, sacked and plundered it. On his return-journey he laid the foundation of Sialkot[3] between the two rivers, the Ravi and the Jilum; appointing Ḥusen Kharmil[4] as the warden of the fort, and giving him munitions of war, the Sulṭān returned to Ghaznīn. After some time, Sulṭān Khusro Malik with a group of his partisans and the Khokhar tribe laid siege to Sialkot; but the prosperity of Maḥmud's descendants[5] having come to an end, the invader failed to conquer it, and had to withdraw.[6]

Mu'izz-ud-dīn invades Lahore.

In 582 H. (1186 A.D.), the Sulṭān again invaded Lahore. Khusro Malik shut himself up in the fort, and put forth battle. Failing to defend himself, he was compelled to seek an interview and was taken with the Sulṭān to Ghaznīn.[7] On the death of Sulṭān Khusro Malik the same year, the *aktā'* of Lahore was placed under the charge of *Sipah Sālār* 'Ali Karmākh.[8] the commandant at Multān.

---

1 Tab-i-Nas. (Raverty. 452), Tab-i-Akb. (37) and Ferishta say that Khusro sent also his son. and Ferishta gives the name of the son as Mullik Shāh.

2 Tab-i-Nas. gives 581 H.

3 Yahiya like Nizam-ud-din Ahmad (Tab-i-Akb. 37) says that Sialkot was founded by Mu'izz-ud-dīn. whereas the author of Tab-i-Nas. (trans., p. 453, f.n. 4) and Ferishta say that the Sultān only restored or repaired it. As a matter of fact. this was one of the ancient forts founded by Hindu rulers but had become dilapidated.

4 Tab-i-Akb. Ḥusen Kharmīl: Ferishta. Hoosein Firmully: Tab-i-Nas. Ḥusain. son of Khar-mīl.

5 Khusro was the descendant of Sulṭān Maḥmud of Ghaznīn.

6 Badaoni writes that in 581 H., the Sulṭān marched against Diwal (Thatha) and plundered it.

7 Tab-i-Akb. says that he was afterwards sent to Ghiaṣ-ud-dīn at Firoz-Koh. Ferishta writes that Khusro and his family were confined in a fort in Jooristān (Tab-i-Nas. Gharjistan) where they were some time after put to death.

8 Badaoni علي كرماج : MBL كرناخ. JNS and MBM read علي كرماخ

In the year 587 H. (1198 A.D.), the Sulṭān drew up his forces and proceeded against the fort of Tabarhindah.[1] Having conquered it and handed it over to Malik Ẓiā-ud-dīn Tulaki,[2] and placing under him 1,200 selected and brave warriors of note, made his return. After having made necessary provisions for the upkeep of the fort, when the Sulṭān was about to depart, he received information of the approach of the accursed Pithor Rai[3] with his numerous cavalry, foot and elephants against the Muslim army. The late Sulṭān went forward to meet that wretch with his own equipage in the vicinity of Tara'i near Sarsuti, in the village of Tara'in.[4] The two forces faced each other, and on the day following, both drew themselves up in battle array. Although the Muslims displayed great valour and failed not to expose themselves to the (enemy's) dagger, yet by the aid of the Almighty Allah, the detested unbelievers were crowned with victory and the Muslim army was defeated. When the Sulṭān saw this, he spurred on his charger[5] against Govind Rāi,[6] the ruler of Dehli and the brother of Pithor Rāi, and who was mounted on an elephant, which was always in the front line of the army, and smote him on

Mu'izz-ud-dīn to Tabarhindah; battle with Pithor Rai: former's defeat.

---

[1] Tab-i-Akb. (138) Fort of Sirhind: Ferishta (Brigg. I. 172) Bitunda. MSS. read تبدهند.

[2] All the three MSS. read تو کلي: Badaoni reads Tukili: Tab-i-Naṣ. Tulaki: Ferishta Toozuky: The correct reading is Tulaki. Ẓiā-ud-dīn was the Ḳāẓī of Tulak, a town near Herat.

[3] MBM نتهور راى: JNS reads پتهور راي: Tab-i-Naṣ. "Rāē Kolah Pithora" (for explanation see Raverty. P. 458, f.n. 6). Ferishta calls him Pithow Ray.

[4] در حوالی ترائي خطهٔ سرستي موضع ترائين: MBM صرستي: MBM and MBL read ترابن: JNS نرائين: Ferishta (Brigg. I. 172) writes that the Sulṭān encountered the enemy at the village of Narain, now called Tirowry, on the banks of Sarsuti, (14 m. from Thaneshwar and 80 from Dehli). Cunningham is of opinion that the exact site was on the banks of the Raukshi river, 4 m. south of Tirawri, and 10 m. to the north of Karnal. Raverty (Tab-i-Naṣ. Trans. 459, f.n. 1) identifies Tirawri with Talawari. Sarsuti is a sacred river of the Punjab rising in Sīrmor State, passing by Thaneshwar, Karnal and Patiala joins Gagger.

[5] MBL اسپ بر کوفت: MBM reads بر گوفت and omits اسپ: JNS agrees with MBL but it omits اسپ:

[6] MBL and MBM read کند هرا راى: JNS agrees with MBL and MBM. Tab-i-Akb. (Bib. Ind. 38) کهاندى: Tab-i-Naṣ. گوبند راى: Ferishta calls him Chawand Rai. Badaoni agrees with Tab-i-Akb. Chand, the Hindu bard calls him Rāi Govind.

the face thereby breaking the teeth of the accursed chief. The Rāi, in return, struck the Sulṭān on the arm with his lance and wounded him.[1] The Sulṭān was about to slip out of his stirrup when a dexterous Khalji foot-soldier[2] immediately mounted behind him and supporting him in his arms rode hard out of the battle field.[3] The army of Islām was defeated and they retreated to a place safe from the attack of the unbelievers. The tumult which had commenced with the disappearance of the Sulṭān soon subsided with his safe return in the army.[4] The army was then set at rest. With successive marches the Sulṭān took his way to Ghaznīn via Multān and Uchch. Failing in his pursuit of the fugitive, Pithor Rāi marched against the fort of Tabarhindah which was defended by Ẓiā-ud-dīn Tulaki, and invested it for thirteen months. At length, supplies of fodder and of the new recruits failing, Ẓiā-ud-dīn, perforce, sought for negotiations and evacuated the fort.

Mu'izz-ud-dīn marches against Hindustan

In the year 588 H. (1192 A.D.), the Sulṭān having enlisted a big force moved towards Hindustan.[5] Pithor Rāi who, too, was prepared for action hastened to Tara'in, and drew up his men as he had

---

[1] MBL and MBM read از زخم نیزهٔ گذارد کرد : JNS. از زخم نیزهٔ زد : Tab-i-Akb. (*ibid.*, 38) بر سلطان نیزهٔ زدهٔ.

[2] MBM and JNS read خلجي پيادهٔ : MBL. خلجين : Tab-i-Akb. agrees with MBM and JNS.

[3] Badaoni (Ranking. P. 69) writes—"The Sulṭān got off his horse, and taking up his son Khilji upon his horse and mounting behind him took him off the field."

[4] The author of Habibu-s-Siyar, contrary to all other authorities, writes that Mu'izz-ud-dīn, after the wound that he had received, fell from his horse and lay upon the field among the slain at night: and in the dark, a party of his own body-guard returned to search for his body, and carried him off to his camp.

[5] Ferishta says that the Sulṭān's army was composed of 120,000 chosen horse, composed of Turks, Tajiks and Afgans, many of whom had their helmets ornamented with jewels, and their armours inlaid with silver and gold.

[6] Acc. to the Rajput version, a hostility arose between Pithor Rāi and Jai chandra, Rājā of Ḳanauj, respecting the Ḳanauj princess. Having learnt the state of Pithor Rāi's affairs, the Sulṭān made preparations to avenge his previous defeat. Bijoy Dev, Rājā of Jamūn, despatched his son with a body of forces to help Mu'izz-ud-dīn and Jaichandra. The latter had been in communication with the Sulṭān, and had made up his mind to humiliate Pithor Rāi. During the encounter it was decided that the troops of Jamūn and Ḳanaūj were to oppose Govind Rāi of Delhi, while the Sulṭān encountered Pithor Rāi. Govind Rāi fell by the sword of Narsing Deo,

done on the previous occasion.[1] [2] Leaving behind at a distance of three *kuroh* his army, family, foot, horse, insignia of royalty and the umbrella of sovereignty, Mu'izz-ud-dīn proceeded against Pithor Rāi with his famous and valiant cavalry numbering 40,000.[3] The Sultān divided his army into four equal sections, and ordered them to attack the army of the infidels from the four different quarters.[4]

and defeats the Hindu army under Pithor Rāi.

Thus, when the elephants and the cavalry of the Hindus [5] would fall upon one of his sections, the rest would make a simultaneous assault upon them (Hindus) from the other three sides. By the help of Almighty Allah, the Hindus were pressed hard and their line gave way; when their adversaries came up and attacked them in the centre, they got perplexed and made a stampede. Govind Rāi was killed in battle: Pithor Rāi who had been riding an elephant, exchanged it for a horse and made his retreat, but he was taken prisoner in the vicinity of Sarsuti, and sent to hell.[6]

---

son of Bijoy Dev of Jamūn. Pithor Rāi was captured alive and sent to Ghaznīn, where he was deprived of his sight.

Atif gives another version of the battle. He says that the Sultān in order to separate Pithor from his own territory, made a retreat. The battle took place in mouza' Shihāb-ud-dīn, in which Pithor Rāi was defeated and taken prisoner. The Rāi was later put to death by Mu'izz-ud-dīn.

Another writer says that Pithor Rāi was killed in the battle, and Govind Rāi escaped: whilst another historian says that "both were captured and slain." See Raverty, p. 466, f.n. 1.

1 MBL بر میعاد باز هم : JNS بر معتاد اول باز هم.

2 Ferishta repeats the account given in Tāj-ul Ma'asir and relates how when the Sultān arrived at Peshawar, an old sage prostrated before him and wanted to know the Sultān's design, in reply to which Mu'izz-ud-dīn said,.. "Since the time of my defeat at Hindustan.. I have never slumbered in ease or walked but in sorrow and anxiety, I have, therefore, determined with this army to recover my lost honour from those idolators or die in the attempt. The sage then blessed him. Reaching Lahore, the Sultān despatched Kawam-ul Mulk Humzvy to Ajmir with a declaration of war should the Indians refuse to embrace the true faith. Pithor Rāi sent a haughty answer.

3 Badaoni also gives the same number.

4 The conflict took place in the former field of battle—Tarain.

5 According to Ferishta the Hindu army consisted of 300,000 horses, 3,000 elephants and a body of infantry

6 The account given in Tāj-ul Ma'asir is different: According to this work, the Rāi was taken prisoner and his life was spared. At Ajmir he was detected in an intrigue (which is only obscurely hinted) and killed at the orders of Mu'izz-ud-dīn. Tab-i-Akb. and Ferishta agree with Yahiya. Badaoni merely states that Pithor Rāi was taken prisoner.

This victory took place in the year 588 H. (1192 A.D.). *Help us oh God against the unbelievers!*

The Sulṭān conquers Sarsuti, Hansi: ravages Ajmir.

Mu'izz-ud-dīn then conquered the forts of Sarsuti and Hansi;[1] plundered and ravaged Ajmir, the capital of Pithor Rāi;[2] and imprisoning the infidels of the Sivalik regions, and placing Malik Ḳuṭub-ud-dīn Aibak, his slave in the fortress of Kuhram[3] with a strong detachment returned to Ghaznīn.

Kuṭub-ud-dīn conquers Mirat and Dehli.

The same year Malik Ḳuṭub-ud-dīn Aibak conquered the strongholds of Mirat and Dehli from the kinsmen of Pithor Rāi and Govind Rāi: the aforesaid infidels (kinsmen of Pithor and Govind) fled to Jhaban.[4]

And seizes Kol: makes Dehli his capital.

Next year, 589 H. (1193 A.D.), Ḳuṭub-ud-dīn laid siege to the fortress of Kol,[5] and taking up his residence in Dehli made it his capital. He then subjugated the country round about Dehli.

Mu'izz-ud-dīn marches against Jai Chand of Kanauj and defeats him.

In 590 H.,[6] Sulṭān Sa'iyid (Mu'izz-ud-dīn) left Ghaznīn with a strong army, and advanced against Ḳanāūj via Dehli. Rāi Jai Chand, the powerful chief of Ḳanāūj, who possessed more than 300 elephants, marched against him and gave him battle in the vicinity of Chandwār[7] and Etāwah. By the Grace of Allah, the Muslims were crowned with victory[8]. The Rāi[9] was killed and his elephants fell into the hands of the victors. *Thank Allah for this!*

---

1 Ferishta says that the forts of Sarsuti, Sāmāna, Kuhram and Hansi surrendered after the victory.

2 The country according to Ferishta, was delivered over by the conqueror to Gola, or the natural son of Pithor Rāi.

3 Badaoni writes that Kuhram was situated at a distance of 70 Kurohs from Dehli.

4 JNS reads جهاتين: MBL and MBM جهاين.

5 40 m. North of Agra.

6 Badaoni gives 589 H., Tab-i-Akb. and Ferishta also of same opinion.

7 Tab-i-Nas., Chandwāl: MBL, MBM, and JNS read Chandwār and Etāwah: Tab-i-Akb., Badaoni and Ferishta all agree with these MSS. Chandwār has not yet been identified: the only place, says Raverty, which bears a similar name is Chandpur or Chandanpur, in the district of Farrukhābād.

8 Ferishta says that Jāi Chand sustained a signal defeat from the vanguard of the Ghiznevide army led by Kuṭub-ud-dīn.

9 Ferishta writes that the number of slain on that day was so great that it was

With a rich booty the Sulṭān returned to Ghaznīn[1] leaving Malik Kuṭub-ud-dīn in Dehli. The latter took the forts of Thankir, Gwalior[2] and Badāōn,[3] and sacked most of the countries of Nahrwālah.[4]

Kuṭub-ud-dīn conquers Thankir, Gwalior and Badāōn.

As the maliks of Turkistān and the infidels of Khitā had come to the aid of (the king of) Khwārizm,[5] Mu'izz-ud-dīn advanced into Khwārizm with a large army in the year 601 H. (1204-05 A.D.), but on account of the lack of forage in the army the Sulṭān had to withdraw his forces. The same year, news came that the Khōkhars and the tribes inhabiting in Koh Jūd[6] had broken out into revolt. The Sulṭān made his way to Lahore. On his reaching the neighbourhood of Lahore, Kuṭub-ud-dīn came from Dehli with his own force and joined him. The

The Sulṭān marches against Khwārizm.

The Sulṭān to Lahore.

---

long ere the body of the Rājā could be found by his friends: till at length his corpse was recognised by his artificial teeth which were fixed in by golden wires.

[1] Ferishta writes that after the victory the Sulṭān marched to the fort of Asni, where Jāi Chand had laid up his treasure, and took gold, silver, and precious jewels. He then marched from thence to Benāras, broke 1,000 temples and consecrated them to the worship of the true God. From thence he returned to the fort of Kol, where he confirmed Kuṭub-ud-dīn in the vice-regency of India. After this he took the route to Ghaznīn. Tab-i-Akb. and Badaoni agree with Yahiya.

[2] MBM تهكير : MBL بهنكير : JNS بهيونكانون : Tab-i-Akb. Thankir : Tab-i-Naṣ. بهنكر : Ranking, Bhangar : proper reading in Thankir (the Modern Bianāh): Tab-i-Naṣ. and Badaoni give the date of the siege 591 H., Alfi 596 H. and Tāj-ul Ma'asir 592 H.

[3] MBM كاليور : MBL and JNS agree with MBM. Tab-i-Akb. Gwalior: Badaoni omits it. Acc. to Badaoni and Tab-i-Naṣ. the siege of Thankir etc. took place in 591 H.

[4] Tab-i-Naṣ. says that Nahrwālah was conquered in 593 H. Ferishta writes that in aid of Gola, the natural son of Pithor Rāi who was expelled from Ajmir by Hemraj one of his relations, Kuṭub-ud-dīn marched against Hemraj, defeated and killed him.

[5] The ruler of Khwārizm applied to Gūrkhan of Kara Khitā for assistance (Ranking, p. 71, f.n. 7): Ferishta writes that Kurra Beg, the general of Gūrkhan, king of Khitā and Othman Khān Samarkandy advanced to the relief of Khwārizm Shāh. The Sulṭān was forced to retire towards Khorasān and took refuge at the fort of Andkhoo, but on paying a large ransom to Othman Khān was suffered to return to his own dominions.

[6] MBM كوه خود : JNS كوه خود : MBL كوه جود : Koh Jūd or Jūd mountains may be identified with the Salt Range situated in part of the Shāhpur Dist. of the Rawalpindi Division.

rebels, some of whom in fear of Mu'izz-ud-din's army took refuge in the hills and some in the banks of the river, were pinioned and made food for the sword. The Sulṭān shouldered his way to Ghaznīn and bade farewell to Ḳuṭub-ud-dīn who returned to Dehli.

The murder of the Sulṭān.

When Mu'izz-ud-dīn arrived at the village of Damyak,[1] the Fida'i Mulaḥidah[2] all on a sudden appeared before the royal camp and wounded him: so that, the late Sulṭān Sa'ivid, the martyred Ghāzī, succumbed to it:[3] this incident occurred on the 3rd Sha'bān, 602 H.[4] (Wednesday, March 15, 1206 A.D.).

It is said that, the Sulṭān left after his death 1,500 *man*[5] of diamonds of most precious kind in his treasury! The quantities of cash and other jewels may be estimated from this. Never-the-less, nothing but good character could he take with him. Born empty-handed, he departed from this ephemeral world carrying nothing away.

---

[1] Situation variously given: (*a*) west of Jhilum, (*b*) on the Nilab, (*c*) a village beyond Indus on the road to Ghaznīn. (*d*) Ferishta writes Rohtak.

[2] MBL خلائی ملاحد : MBM فلائي ملاحد : JNS فلائی کهوکهر ملاحده : Alfi, and the authors of Tab-i-Akb., and Jami'-ut Tawarikh agree in saying that the Sulṭān was killed by the Khokhars, whereas, Ferishta is of opinion that the assassins of the Sulṭān were Gakkars, a race distinct from the Khokhars. Tab-i-Naṣ. writes that the Sulṭān died at the hand of the Mulāḥidah: the author of Tāj-ul Ma'asir is of similar opinion. The Hindu version, supported by Abul Fazl and others, ascribe the death of the Ghaznī ruler to the arrow thrown by Rāi Pithor. Ferishta relates in detail how 20 Gakkars, who had lost some of the relations in the late wars, entered into conspiracy against the king's life, how these assassins found their way to the sleeping Sulṭān's tent and killed him by no fewer than 20 wounds.

[3] MBL adds the following lines after this: MBM and JNS have no mention of them: the following verse are also to be found in Tab-i-Naṣ. Tab-i-Akb. and Badaoni.

To chronicle this event of the Emperor Ghāzī it has been said:

Qita'h.

"The martyrdom of the king of sea and land Mu'izz-ud-dīn,
From the beginning of the world the like of whom no monarch arose.
On the third day from the 1st of Sha'bān in the year six hundred and two.
Happened on the road to Ghaznīn at the stage of Damyak."

[4] Ferishta gives Sha'bān 2: Tab-i-Akb., Sha'bān 3: other histories Sha'bān 1.

[5] A *man* is equal to 8 pounds nearly. In Tab-i-Akb. and Badaoni the amount of diamond has been estimated at 500 *mans*.

Verse.

Those jewels and treasures which could not be counted up,
Even Sam[1] and Faridun[2] could not carry them away.

The period of Mu'izz-ud-dīn's rule lasted for 32 years and few months. *God is more aware of the real facts.*

An account of Sulṭān Ḳuṭub-ud-din Aibak Al-Mu'izzi.

His early life and career.

Sulṭān Ḳuṭub-ud-dīn, the slave of Mu'izz-ud-dīn Sâm, was unparalleled in bravery and kindness.[3] While young he was brought from Turkistan to Nishapur, where Ḳâẓī-ul Ḳuẓẓat Imâm Fakhr-ud-dīn Abdul 'Azīz Kufī, a descendant of Imâm-i-A'ẓam Abû Ḥanīfâ Kufī—*May God be pleased with him!*—bought him, and like his own son taught him the Koran and the archery. He became perfect in a short while. When he attained adolescence, he was sold by a merchant[4] to Mu'izz-ud-dīn, the ruler of Ghaznīn. Devoid of comeliness but an embodiment of all perfect qualities Ḳuṭub-ud-dīn exhibited signs of greatness. As his little finger was broken, he was called Aibak-[5] i-Shil. Owing to his having diligently and loyally rendered service to the Sulṭân, he was shown in a short while great favour and distinction, and his dignity waxed day by day. After the conquest of Hindustan, Kuhrâm was conferred upon him in fief. In 589 H. (1193 A.D.), Ḳuṭub-ud-dīn conquered the fort of Mirat.[6] Two years later he took the fortress of Thankīr.

---

1 Son of Noah. 2 King of Persia.

3 Tab-i-Naṣ. calls him "Second Hâtim."

4 Ferishta says that after the death of Fakhr-ud-dīn, Aibak was purchased by a merchant and was then presented for sale to Mu'izz-ud-dīn.

5 Tab-i-Akb. and Ferishta are also of same opinion; Badaoni writes "on the occasion of the eclipse of the moon had a broken little finger." Ranking (p. 77, f.n. ys, "whether the finger was broken at the time of the eclipse, or whether it was genital defect does not appear, but from the text before us the connection of moon is the cause of the name, not, as has been said, the broken finger." Raverty (p. 513) translates, "and the little finger (of one hand?) had a fracture, and on that account he used to be styled Ī-bak-i-Shil (the powerless fingured)." The word Shil in Persian means, "impotent, paralysed, weak powerless, soft." The author of Jâm'i-ut-Tawârikh calls him Ibak-i-lang—"lang" meaning maimed injured. JNS incorrectly writes ایبک شو instead of ایبک شل .

6 Tab-i-Naṣ. writes 587 H: Ferishta gives 588, and says that in the year 589 H.

In the year 593 H.,[1] he proceeded to Gujrat, plundered and ravaged the territory of Rāi Bhim Deo,[2] who had once opposed Mu'izz-ud-dīn, and took revenge upon the enemy for his past actions.[3]

The title of Sulṭān conferred on Ḳuṭub-ud-dīn.

After the death of Sulṭān Mu'izz-ud-dīn, Sulṭān Ghiās-ud-dīn Maḥmud, the son of the elder brother of the deceased, sent a canopy of state to Malik Ḳuṭub-ud-dīn, and conferred on him the title of Sulṭān. In 602 H. (1205 A.D.), Ḳuṭub-ud-dīn set out from Dehli, and came to the auspicious city, of Lahore.[4] On Tuesday,[5] the 18th Ẕīlka'da (June 26, 1206 A.D.) of the same year, he took his seat on the throne at Lahore, and conferred valuable gifts, largesses, and robes of honour upon his amirs and maliks. To such an extent did he extend his hand of liberality that people called him Sulṭān Ḳuṭub-ud-dīn *Lakh-baksh*.

Ḳuṭub-ud-dīn's accession at Lahore.

War between Ḳuṭub-ud-dīn and Tāj-ud-dīn, and the latter's defeat.

After some time, hostility arose[6] between him and Sulṭān Tāj-ud-dīn Yelduz, a Mu'izzi slave, who had ascended the throne of Ghaznīn after the death of Mu'izz-ud-dīn, respecting Lahore. Determining upon engagements, both drew up their own forces in battle order. God, The Holy[7] and the Most High, conferred victory upon Ḳuṭub-ud-dīn, and Tāj-ud-dīn, being worsted made his way to Karmān.

Ḳuṭub-ud-dīn occupies Ghaznīn, but has to abandon it.

The fortress of Ghaznīn fell to Sulṭān Ḳuṭub-ud-dīn, who sat on the imperial throne for four days,[8] spending the time in amusements and

---

Ḳuṭub-ud-dīn relieved Hānsi from Jeewan Ray, a general of the Rāja of Nahrwala, in Gujrat. Tab-i-Naṣ. says that in 588 H. Ḳuṭub-ud-dīn captured Dehli.

[1] Ferishta gives 591 H

[2] JNS and MBM رای بهیلم : MBL رای و بیلیم : Tab-i-Naṣ. reads Bhim Deo

[3] Ferishta writes that in the year 599 Ḳuṭub-ud-dīn took Kālinjar, Mahobā (capital of Kalpi) and Badāōn.

[4] JNS, MBL لاهور : MBM لوهور : Tab-i-Naṣ. لوهور : Correctly speaking, the reference is here to Ḳuṭub-ud-dīn's march into the Lahore *territory* (not to his going to the *city* of Lahore merely) to join his master the Sulṭān against the Khokhars.

[5] Texts read روز سه شنبه . According to "Indian Ephemeris" Vol. IV. by L. D. S. Pillai, the 18th Zilka'da is Monday and not Tuesday.

[6] JNS and MBM مخالف پیدا امد : Should be مخالفت :

[7] MBM and JNS omit تبارک و.

[8] Badaoni gives "40 days".

fun. Most of the maliks and the Mu'izzi amirs of Ghaznīn secretly co-operated with Tāj-ud-dīn and welcomed him from Karmār. When Tāj-ud-dīn reached the confines of Ghaznīn, and the vanguard of his army made its appearance, the people of the city joined hands with him, so, Sulṭān Kuṭub-ud-dīn abandoned Ghaznīn by the route of *Sang-i-Surākh* [1] and retired to Lahore. Ghaznīn then reverted to Sulṭān Tāj-ud-dīn.

While playing golf [2] at the maidān of Lahore, the Sulṭān, by the decree of Allah, had a sudden fall from his horse, and the bow of his saddle struck against his breast. The Sulṭān died, and was interred at the auspicious city of Lahore. The late Sulṭān Shams-ud-dīn Iyal-timish constructed a mausoleum for him.

Kuṭub-ud-dīn's death.

Verse.

The necks of many a valiant it broke, this old Sphere circular,
Rely thee not, as much as thou canst, on the Sun, the Moon and the Jupiter!

The death of the Sulṭān occurred in 607 H. (1210-11 A.D.). His period of authority from the conquest of Dehli till the time of his death lasted for twenty years and a few months, and his reign with the royal canopy and a *dūr-bash* and the title of sovereignty lasted for four years. *God is more aware of real facts.*

An account of Sulṭān Shams-ud-dīn Iyal-timish.[3]

Malik Iyal-timish was the slave of late Sulṭān Kuṭub-ud-dīn Aibak Al Mu'izzī. On the latter's death, the Kutbī amirs and maliks placed Arām Shāh, the son of Kuṭub-ud-din, on the throne in order that the disturbance in the country might be set at rest. Malik Nāṣir-ud-dīn Kubāchā, the son-in-law of Kuṭub-ud-dīn marched towards Sind, and took possession of the *akṭā's* of Multān, Uchch,

Arām Shāh placed on the throne.

---

1 JNS از راه سوراخ : MBL and MBM از راه سنگ سوراخ : Tab-i-Akb. and Badaoni agree with MBL and MBM.

2 All the three MSS. read گوی بازی : Tab-i-Akb and Ferishta write "chougan"

3 MBL, MBM and JNS write ایلنمش : Some writers write ایلتمیش, while others ایلتتمش and ایلتمشی : Some scholars suppose that owing to errors of transcribers of the Turkish compound word the ل has become displaced and the word should really be written اینتلمش *ay-tutulmash<eclipse of the moon.* (Ranking. 89 f.n. 1).

Bhakhar, and Siwistān.[1] Sipah Sālār 'Ali Isma'el, the *Amīr Dād*[2] (the chief justice) of hazrat Dehli, with the other nobles who befriended him sent letters of welcome to Malik Iyal-timish, who was then the amir of Badāōn. With all his forces the Malik reached hazrat Dehli in all haste, and seized it. Leaving Dehli, Arām Shāh came outside the city. But as some of the people having collected round Arām laid the foundation of enmity and approached Dehli, Malik Iyal-timish had also to come out of the city and to fight with them.[3] In the engagement which took place between the two in the plain of Jud[4] the Most High and Holy God, crowned Iyal-timish with victory; Arām Shāh and the Kutbi amirs were defeated.

Malik Iyal-timish invited by nobles from Badāōn.

Battle between Arām Shah and Iyal-timish; former's defeat.

Ascending the throne at the imperial palace in the year 607 H. (1210 A.D.), the victor assumed the title of Sultān Shams-ud-dīn and brought under his jurisdiction the outlying districts.

Iyal-timish's accession to the throne.

In the year 602 H. (1215 A.D.), he proceeded to Lahore, which after the death of Sultān Kutub-ud-dīn had passed to Sultān Tāj-ud-dīn Yelduz, who hailed from Ghaznin, and came *vis-a-vis*. In the battle[5] that followed, the Most High and Holy God, rewarded Shams-ud-dīn with victory: Tāj-ud-dīn was taken prisoner to Badāōn, where he died in captivity. The tomb of Sultān Tāj-ud-dīn, *May God shed lustre upon his demonstrations!* lies on the bank of Suthā in the confines of Badāōn. To sum up, after the victory Shams-ud-dīn retraced his way to Dehli.

Iyal-timish marches against Tāj-ud-dīn, defeats and imprisons him.

Badaoni writes, (Ranking P. 88), "the reason of the name Iyal-timish is that his birth occurred on the night of an eclipse of the moon, and the Turks call a child born under these circumstances Iyal-timish."

[1] MBL, MBM سومستان : JNS سيوهان : Ferishta, Shivuran.

[2] Ferishta here gives the name of two persons—Amir Ally Isma'el and Amir Daud Delimy.

[3] JNS is here faulty MBL and MBM quite correct.

[4] MBM حود : JNS جوسي :

[5] According to Badaoni and Tab-i-Akb. the battle took place on the confines of Tara'in which was known as Serāi Talāwari.

Iyal-timish marches against Nāṣir-ud-dīn Ḳubācha: latter's death.

Sulṭān Nāṣir-ud-dīn Ḳubācha, who had once been defeated by Shams-ud-dīn in the confines of Uchch met the latter again in Uchch and Multan in the year 615 H.[1] (1216 A.D.), and was again put to rout. Pursued by the victors, the vanquished fell back on the banks of the river Punjab,[2] and failing to swim across it, was drowned.

Advent of Jalāl-ud-dīn Khwārizm Shāh, and his return.

In the year 618 H. (1221 A.D.), Sulṭān Jalāl-ud-dīn Khwārizm Shāh who laid siege to Ghaznīn by driving out Tāj-ud-dīn, evacuated it owing to the attack made upon him by the accursed Jengīz Khān and came towards Lahore with all his family, horsemen and attendants. Being informed of this, Shams-ud-dīn rode to Lahore. Sulṭān Jalāl-ud-dīn[3] fell back towards the mountains and retired to Kashmir and Bakhli,[4] while Iyal-timish returned to his capital.

The Sulṭān's march to Lakhnauti

In the year 620 H.[5] (1223 A.D.), the Sulṭān marched with his army towards Lakhnauti, and promising safety to Ghiāṣ-ud-dīn 'Auẓ[6] Khalji brought him under subjection, had the proclamation read and coins struck in his own name. He placed in charge of his eldest son the territory of Lakhnauti, and giving him the title of Sulṭān Nāṣir-ud-dīn,[7] and granting him the royal canopy, a *dur-bāsh* and other paraphernalia of royalty, returned to his capital, Dehli.[8]

---

1 Ferishta writes 614 H., and says that the battle took place at Munsoorea, on the banks of the Chinab.

2 All the three MSS. read آب پنجاب : Tab-i-Naṣ. reads "the river Sind." Tab-i-Akb. gives no name of the river.

3 JNS writes انار اللّه after Sulṭān Jalāl-ud-dīn, but MBL and MBM omit it.

4 MBM and JNS تلنکی : Badaoni writes, "Jalāluddīn... went towards Sind and Siwistan," and from there by way of Kuch and Makran arrived at Karman and Iraḳ. The author of Tab-i-Akb. is of same opinion.

5 In Tab-i-Akb. Badaoni and Ferishta the date is 622 H.

6 MBL and MBM عوض : JNS عوغی : Ferishta reads Ghiāṣ-ud-dīn Bakhtiyār Khalji.

7 JNS reads ناصر الدین ازلن او خود خطاب کرت : MBM ناصر الدین خود خطاب کرد : correct reading would be ناصر الدین خطاب کرد :

8 Ferishta writes that authentic historians have opined that Iyal-timish in 612 H., marched against Naṣir-ud-dīn Ḳubāchā and laid siege to Oocha.

In the year 623 H. (1226 A.D.), the Sulṭān took his way to the fortress of Rantambor,[1] and coerced the rebels of the place. The year following, he advanced to Mandwar[2] and Ajmir, and brought under his subjection those two countries with their out-lying parts. The same year he returned to his capital, Dehli.

and to Rantambor.

In the year 626 H. (1229 A.D.), there came to the court of the Sulṭān ambassadors from Dār-ul Khelāfat bringing robes of honour of the Khelāfat, *May God perpetuate his Khelifate!* The Sulṭān fulfilled the conditions of reverence and homage, and put on those robes along with his sons, the chiefs, and his old officers. It beggars description how the Sulṭān felt supreme pleasure and happiness from putting on that robe. Domes were erected in the city and drums of joy beaten. After some time the Sulṭān respectfully bade farewell to the embassy and sent large presents to the Khalif.

Ambassadors from Dar-ul Khelafat comes to the court of Iyaltimish.

The same year,[4] came the news of the death of (Sulṭān Nāṣir-ud-din) the eldest son of Iyal-timish, who had been made the ruler of Lakhnauti. The mourning ceremonies being over, the Sulṭān marched against Lakhnauti.[5] and set at rest the insurrection that had there broken out. Placing Lakhnauti, under the charge of Malik 'Alā'-ud-dīn Jānī,[6] he returned to Ḥaẓrat Delhi.

Death of Sulṭān Nāṣir-ud-din; Iyaltimish to Lakhnauti.

In the year 629 H. (1231 A.D.), the Sulṭān marched against

---

[1] MBM رنتهور : JNS and MBL رنتبهور

[2] JNS مندو : Ferishta, "Mando and the country of Malwa": Tab-i-Akb. Mandwar: it was situated 5 miles north of Jodhpur.

Badaoni writes, "Arab Ambassadors came from Egypt." Tab-i-Akb. reads, "envoys came from Arabia." Ferishta agrees with Tab-i-Akb.

[3] JNS reads در حضرت دهلي : MBL and MBM در حضرت دارالخلافت : The latter reading is correct.

[4] Tab-i-Naṣ. writes that the news of the death reached the Sulṭān in Jamadi-ul auwal 627 H.

[5]. According to Badaoni the Sulṭān proceeded to Lakhnauti in 627 H.

[6] JNS ملک علاء الدين خاني : Badaoni and Tab-i-Akb. give the name as Iz-ul Mulk Malik 'Alā'-ud-dīn Khāfī.

Gwalior;[1] the accursed Bisal Mālik[2] was invested the fort; at the end of eleven months, with the help of the Most High Allah, the garrison was reduced to submission.[3] The Sulṭān left the upkeep of the fortress under a Kotwal, and returned to his capital, Dehli.

The Sulṭān to Gwalior.

In the year 631 H.[4] (1233 A.D.), the Sulṭān invaded Malwah[5] and punished its rebels by destroying their temple that had been constructed some three centuries ago. Later marching against Ujjein he took it, and had the temple of Mahākāl deo[6] destroyed from its foundations. The picture and the effigy of Bikramājit[7] with the other images that had been placed on the board, were taken out and carried away to ḥaẓrat Dehli) and placed at the gate of the Jami' Masjid[8] to be trampled upon by the people.

To Malwah and Ujjein.

In the year 633 H. (1235 A.D.), the Sulṭān led his army to Bhilsān[9] where an illness seized him: whereupon, he ordered for an immediate return, and reaching Dehli, on Monday, the 20th Sha'bān, 633 H. (April 30, 1235 A.D.), he wandered by the door of mortality to the door of permanency.

To Multān: Sulṭān's return to Dehli and his death.

---

[1] Ferishta writes that it had during the reign of Arām fallen into the hands of the Hindus.

[2] MBL میلک دیو بیل : MBM and JNS بیسل مالک : Tab-i-Naṣ. میلک دیو لعین. پسر بسیل لعین : Tab-i Akb. Milak Deo Basil: Raverty, Mangal Deva: Thomas (Chronicles of the Pathan Kings of Delhi, 66) Trailokya Deva, the son of Bisāla Dev: Ferishta, Raja Dewbul.

[3] Tab-i-Naṣ. says that the fort was taken on 26th Safar, 630 H. (1232 A.D.)

[4] Tab-i-Naṣ. gives 632 H.

[5] Badaoni and Tab-i-Akb. write that the Sulṭan took Bhilsa. It was on the Betwa, and was a place of Hindu pilgrimage.

[6] Ferishta calls it Mahakaly and says that the temple was formed upon the same plan with that of Somnath. It is said to have occupied 300 years in building, and was surrounded by a wall 100 cubits in height.

[7] Badaoni writes, "Rai Vikramajit from whom the Hindus reckon their era".

[8] Ferishta writes that the images were broken at the door of the great mosque. Badaoni says that the Ṣulṭān placed the images on the ground in front of the door of the mosque of old Dehli and ordered the people to trample them under foot.

[9] MBL بهلستان : JNS and MBM بهیلسان : Tab-i-Naṣ. بنیان : Tab-i-Akb. Multān Bhilsan is a fortress and a city in Malwah.

Verse.

Who is he, in this old world revolving,
Who beats the drum of *lemanu-l Mulk*[1] except The God?

May the Holy Creator immerse that just Sulṭān in His mercy and may He by the grace of Nabi and his pious descendants keep this heavenly exalted emperor in peace and safety till the day of Resurrection! Sulṭān Shams-ud-dīn ruled for twenty-six years and a few months. *God is more aware of real facts!*

An account of Sulṭān Rukn-ud-dīn Firoz Shāh.

Accession of Rukn-ud-dīn and distribution of presents, etc., to the Amirs.

Sulṭān Rukn-ud-dīn Firoz Shāh was the son of late pardoned Sulṭān Shams-ud-dīn Iyal-timish.[2] Three days after the mourning rites, in agreement with the maliks, imāms, the chiefs and the Shamsi slaves, he[3] ascended the throne in the royal residence at ḥazrat Dehli on 22nd Sha'bān 633 H. (May 2, 1236 A.D.). Opening the door of the treasury, (the new Sulṭān) bestowed robes of honour upon all and rewarded them with gifts. Extending his hand of prodigality, he abandoned himself to such a pleasure and enjoyment, that the affairs of the State were neglected. The conduct of all business of the state and country remained in the hands of the Sulṭān's mother, Shāh Turkān.[4]

Affairs of state conducted by Shāh Turkān.

The harem of Shams-ud-dīn was ruined owing to her old rivalry.[5] Prince Kuṭub-ud-dīn Muḥammad Shāh, the son of Sulṭān Iyal-timish by his second wife was blinded and put to death. For all this,

---

[1] The following line of the verse of the Koran, لمن الملک الیوم اللہ الواحد القہار, refer to the day of the Ressurrection, when being questioned by God, the dead will say in reply that the sovereignty belongs to Him, Who is Supreme and Alone. لمن الملک means, "for whom is the sovereignty?"

[2] MSS. read التمش:

[3] Ferishta writes that in 625 H., Iyal-timish appointed his son, Rukn-ud-dīn, governor of Badāōn, and later as his assistant in the Punjab.

[4] Badaoni calls her Shāh Khatun, a Turkish slave girl. Tab-i-Akb. is of similar opinion.

[5] Tab-i-Nas. says that she had experienced envy and jealousy from some of the other ladies of the harem: Tab-i-Akb. writes "she had been jealous of them, and as soon as she obtained an opportunity she had some of them put to death with much degradation, and treated others with ignominy."

most of the amirs, and maliks of Dehli and the neighbouring countries parted company with the Sulṭān Rukn-ud-dīn, and laid the foundation of opposition. For example, Prince Malik Ghiāṣ-ud-dīn Maḥmud Ṣhāh, brother of Sulṭān Rukn-ud-dīn and the Amir of Oudh, turned away his head from the rule of allegiance and seized the revenue that had been sent from Lakhnauti to the Sulṭān. Malik 'Izz-ud-dīn Sālārī rebelled in Badāōn. Malik 'Alā'-ud-dīn, the governor of Lahore, Malik 'Izz-ud-dīn Kanjān, the amīr of Multān, and Malik Saif-ud-dīn Kuji, the governor of Hānsi, all assembled together and broke out into open rebellion. Meanwhile, Malik Niẓām-ul Mulk Junaidi, the vizir of Sulṭān Rukn-ud-dīn, out of fear fled from Dehli and went to Badāōn to join with 'Izz-ud-dīn Sālārī. Together, they emerged out of the latter place and joined hands with the amirs, who had effected a junction at Lahore. In order to suppress the rebellion, the Sulṭān turned towards them, and when he reached the vicinity of Kuhrām, the following attendants of the aforesaid amirs, who had set out against Rukn-ud-dīn to Mansurpur, viz., Tāj-ul Mulk,[1] Muḥammad Dabir,[2] *mushrif-i-mamālik*, Bahā'-ul Mulk,[3] Karim-ud-dīn Zāhid, Ẓiā-ul Mulk, son of Niẓām-ul Mulk, the vizir, Khwājah Rashīd and Amir Fakhr-ud-dīn, having made up their minds returned to Dehli,[4] and entering all at once the royal harem swore their allegiance to Sulṭān Raẓia, the daughter of Sulṭān Shams-ud-dīn. They, then, dethroned Ṣhāh Turkān, the mother of Sulṭān Rukn-ud-dīn. When the Sulṭān was informed of this, he hastened to Dehli and with successive marches reached Kilokharī. The amirs, Maliks and the Shamsī attendants, who had always been on his side, entered Dehli and made homage to Sulṭān Raẓia. Afterwards the army came outside the city and seized Sulṭān Rukn-ud-dīn at Kilokhari, and brought him before Razia, who put him in prison where he died.

Rebellion of the Amirs.

The Amirs swore allegiance to Sulṭān Raẓia.

Imprisonment of Rukn-ud-dīn

---

[1] Ferishta writes Tāju-d-dīn Zobeidy.

[2] Ferishta writes Malik Mahomed Dabir.

[3] Tab-i-Akb. and Ferishta read Bahāu-d-dīn Ḥusen.

[4] This text differs from that of Tab-i-Nas.: according to the latter these men did not return to Dehli, but were slain by the Turkish amirs and the slaves of the imperial household. Tab-i-Akb., Ferishta and Badaoni all agree with Yahiya.

Verse.

Curse be to this hump-backed,
For, one who is better than he,[1] did it nourish and kill!

This event took place on Sunday, the 18th Rabi'-ul-auwal, 634 H. (Nov. 19, 1236 A.D.). The period of his rule was six months and eight days. *God knows the truth!*

An account of Sulṭān Razia.

Her accession.

Sulṭān Razia was the eldest daughter of Sulṭān Shams-ud-dīn, who on his return from the expedition of Gwalior made her his heir-apparent. In short, she ascended the imperial throne at Dār-ul Mulk Dehli on Sunday, the 18th Rabi'-ul-auwal, 634 H. (Nov. 19, 1236 A.D.).

Outbreak of the Kirāmitah and Mulāhidah.[2]

In the month of Rajab of the aforesaid year a body of Ḳirāmiṭah and Mulāḥidah, who having collected together from different parts of Hindustan had settled down in ḥaẓrat Dehli, instigated by Turk,[3] a learned man who in the gatherings in which he addressed used to call the 'Ulama of the orthodox people[4] *Nāsibī* (settersup), and to style them *Murjī*[5] (procrastinators), entered from the two sides of the *Jami' Masjid*, on Friday. These heretics came upon the Muslims who were engaged in Friday prayers. A good many Muslims attained martyrdom and many were trodden under foot. Malik Naṣir-ud-dīn Bālārāmi,[6] Imām Nāṣirī[7] the Poet, and other amīrs came to the rescue with a large army, and the Musalmans, who out of dread, had ascended the roof

---

[1] MBL بسیار ازین گونه ; MBM read similar: JNS بسیار از این کوز :

[2] Except Tab-i-Nas., Tab-i-Akb., Badaoni and Ferishta do not refer to this outbreak. "The fact of Ferishta's being a Shī'a may account for his eschewing the matter."

[3] JNS نوری ترک : MBL and MBM ترک : Tab-i-Nas., "Nur, the Turk; he was a Turk and his name was Nur-ud-dīn."

[4] Refer to the Sunnīs.

[5] "The name of one of the heretical sects among the Muḥammadans, who procrastinate, and consider good work unnecessary, and faith sufficient, and that all Musalmāns will be saved, as hell is only reserved for infidels." Raverty 646 f.n. 7.

[6] MBM بدارامی : Tab-i-Nas., Nasīr-ud-dīn, Ai-yitim, the Balārāmī.

[7] Tab-i-Nas., Amir Imām-i-Nāṣiri.

of the *Masjid*, poured down stones and bricks upon them, killed them and quelled that outbreak.

Revolt of the Amirs.

Subsequently, Nizām-ul-Mulk Junaidi, Izz-ud-dīn Kanjān, Muhammad Sālāri,[1] who had once rebelled against Sultān Rukn-ud-dīn, now advanced to the gates of the city and assumed a hostile attitude against Sultān Razia. Malik Nasir-ud-dīn Taysī,[2] the amīr of Oudh, reached Dehli in aid of Sultān Razia. Welcoming him and then winning him over, the hostile amīrs stopped the Malik from rendering any aid to the Sultān. At last, when the hostility continued long, Razia marched outside the city and encamped on the bank of the Jaun. Repeated engagements took place between Razia and the rebellious nobles, but with no result: at length, peace was effected at the intervention of the priests and the Sheikhs of the city. Muhammad Sālāri and Kanjān secretly went over to the side of the Sultān, and one night, they assembled in front of the royal pavilion with a view to seize Malik Jani,[3] Malik Kuji[4] and Nizām-ul-Mulk.

Flight of the Amirs.

When the aforesaid amirs were apprised of this, they dared not oppose (the Sultān) any further, and being disunited amongst themselves made a stampede. The Sultān being informed of this state of things, sent an army in pursuit of the fugitives. Malik Kuji was seized; Malik Jāni attained martyrdom near Pāyal;[5] and Malik Nizām-ul-Mulk went away towards the Bardār hills.[6] The imperialists then wheeled round. When order was restored in the country, Razia appointed

Kutub-ud-din Husen sent against Rantambor.

other officials, and sent Malik Kutub-ud-dīn Husen[7] against Rantambor[8] to put down the insurrection that had broken out on the death of Sultān Shams-ud-dīn.

---

[1] Tab-i-Nas., Malik 'Izz-ud-dīn Muhammad Sālārī.

[2] Tab-i-Akb. writes Malik 'Izz-ud-dīn Hānsi: Tab-i-Nas. reads Malik Nusrat-ud-dīn Tayasa'ī, the Mu'izzi.

[3] MBM ملک خاني :

[4] MBM كوحي : Tab-i-Nas. كرچي.

[5] MBL and MBM حد بابل : Elliot and Briggs call Bābal, Bābul and Babool. Pāyal, or Pāyil, Long. 76° 5′ Lat. 30° 40′.

[6] Tab-i-Akb. and Ferishta read Sarmur hills.

[7] MBL قطب حسن.

[8] MBM نتهور : MBL رنقبور JN8 رنتهنبور Rantambor is situated in the province of Ajmi, 75 miles S.E. of Jaipur.

Jealousy of the nobles.

Malik Jamāl-ud-dīn Yakut, the Abyssinian, was made lord of the stables, and the constant companion of the Sulṭān, for this he became the object of jealousy of the nobles and the amīrs.

The dress of the Sulṭān.

It so happened that Sulṭān Raẓia wore the high cap, the coat and the male dress; at length, she would come out with veils on. She never rode but on elephants.

Revolt of Malik 'Izz-ud-dīn.

Meanwhile, the news regarding the hostility of Malik 'Izz-ud-dīn Kanjān,[1] the amīr of Lahore, reaching her, Raẓia marched against him, and defeated and compelled him to sue for peace. On the 19th Sha'bān, 637 H. (Thursday, 15th March, 1240 A.D.), she returned to Dehli.

Revolt of Altunia.

Subsequently, Malik Altunia,[2] the feoffee of Tabarhindah revolting, the Queen despatched a force against him on the 9th Ramzan (Tuesday, 10th April, 1240 A.D.). Some of the amīrs, maliks, and the Shamsī slaves joined with him, and having rebelled, put Jamāl-ud-dīn Yakut,[3] the Abyssinian, to death.

Verse.

Away turned Fortune her reins from her (Raẓia) environs,
When she discerned a scar on the hem of her garment!

Raẓia imprisoned.

They, then, imprisoned Raẓia[4] and put her in the fort of Tabarhindah: having sent letters to the amīrs of Dehli asking them to enthrone Mu'izz-ud-dīn, the son of Sulṭān Shams-ud-dīn, they dispersed in haste.

Verse.

Every head that the Heaven has raised,
Likewise, throws a halter round their neck!

---

[1] Ferishta calls him Malik Kabir Khān.

[2] MBM التونية : JNS التوسة : Tab-i Akb. gives the name as Malik Ikhtiār-ud-dīn Altunia.

[3] MBL ملک جمال الدین : JNS omits ملک :

[4] The subsequent events up to the death of Raẓia have been narrated in detail in Tab-i-Naṣ., Tab-i Akb. and Ferishta.

The period of Sulṭān Raẕia's rule in the Dar-ul Mulk Dehli extended to three years, five months and twenty-one days. *God knows the truth !*

An account of Sulṭān Mu'izz-ud-dīn.

His accession.

Sulṭān Mu'izz-ud-dīn was the youngest son of Sulṭān Shams-ud-dīn. After the imprisonment of Sulṭān Raẕia in the citadel of Tabarhindah,[1] the prominent amīrs, and maliks placed Sulṭān Mu'izz-ud-dīn on the imperial throne in the royal palace, on Monday,[2] the 28th Ramẕān, 637 H. (Apr. 22, 1240 A.D.). The amīrs and maliks, who were the partisans of Raẕia, reached the capital on Sunday,[3] the 13th Shawwāl of the aforesaid year (May 13), and made their homage to Sulṭān Mu'izz-ud-dīn, on condition that Ikhtiār-ud-dīn Aitkin would be appointed as the *naib*. When Malik Ikhtiār-ud-dīn became the vizir, he in conjunction with Malik Muhaẕẕab-ud-dīn Nizām-ul Mulk took up the control of the entire government of the realm into his hand, and married the sister of Sulṭān Mu'izz-ud-dīn who had been married to the son of the Ḳāzi Naṣir-ud-dīn, and had been repudiated by him. He assumed the triple *naubat*, and stationed an elephant at the entrance of his own residence.[4] Such an increasing dignity and obedience to his authority produced a great dislike in the mind of the Sulṭān. On Monday, the 8th Muharram, 638 H. (30th July, 1240 A.D.), by command of the Sulṭān, two intoxicated Turks[5] martyred Malik Aitkin by the wound of a knife at the White castle. They inflicted on Nizām-ul Mulk two wounds in the side, but as his life still remained he got away from the assassins, and continued carrying on the affairs of the State as of old.[6]

Assumption of supreme authority by Ikhtiār-ud-dīn.

---

1 Ferishta writes Bitunhda.

2 It is Sunday and not Monday. Cf. An Indian Ephemeris, by L. D. S. Pillai, vol. iv, p. 82.

3 It is Monday acc. to Indian Ephemeris.

4 Tab-i-Akb. writes that at this period none but the Sulṭān could keep an elephant.

5 MSS. read ترک بچه: Tab-i-Akb. reads Fidā-i. This name was applied to the agents of the chief of the Assassins, or Sheikh-ul-Jibal. A Fidā-i was one wh was ready to sacrifice himself in order to carry out the task assigned to him.

6 Badaoni makes the mistake by killing Ait-kin and Muhazzab-ud-dīn both at

In the month of Safar (Aug.-Sep.) of the same year, Malik Altunia[1] espoused Sulṭān Raẓia in the *nikaḥ* form, and set out for Dehli. Muḥammad Sālāri and Malik Ḳarā Ḳash deserted the Sulṭān and went over to their side. Sulṭān Mu'izz-ud-dīn led a force against them, and fell in with them near the city. Sulṭān Raẓia and Malik Altunia were defeated, and later seized near Kaithal by the Hindus who despatched them in fetters to the Sulṭān.[2] Both were put to death on the 25th Rabi'-ul-auwal (Sunday, 14th Oct., 1240 A.D.).

'Altunia marries Raẓia: both defeated and put to death.

Badr-ud-dīn Sunḳar had been appointed *Amir-i-Ḥajib*; but he disobeyed the orders of Niẓām-ul-Mulk and sought to acquire superiority over him; for all these Niẓām-ul-Mulk cherished unfriendly feeling with him. When Badr-ud-dīn learnt this, out of dread, he tried to bring about a revolution. On Monday,[3] the 17th Safar, 639 H. (27th Aug., 1241 A.D.), Badr-ud-dīn Sunḳar convened some of the rich and powerful nobles at the residence of Sadr-ul Mulk,[4] the grandson of 'Ali Musi, the *mushrif-i-mamalik*, in order that they could deliberate upon bringing a change in the Government. The Ṣadr-ul-Mulk was despatched to summon Niẓām-ul-Mulk. When Niẓām-ul-Mulk heard the announcement of the Ṣadr-ul-Mulk's coming, there was at that time with him one of the Sulṭān's confidants.[5] He kept him concealed in a place where he

Badr-ud-dīn tries to bring about a revolution.

---

one time. Ferishta's version is entirely different: Tab-i-Akb. cuts this matter very short. Tab-i-Naṣ. version is similar to Yaḥīya's.

1 MBL لا تونیه : MBM الtونیه : JNS agrees with MBM.

2 Tab-i-Akb. writes that the Sulṭān twice sent Malik Tigin against Raẓia and Altunia. In both the campaigns Tīgin was successful. In the last expedition Tigin met his adversaries near Kaithal.

Tab-i-Naṣ. says that Raẓia and Altunia "attained martyrdom at the hands of the Hindus". Ferishta agrees with our author.

3 It should be Tuesday.

4 Tab-i-Akb. writes that the amirs met together at the house of Ṣadr-ul-Mulk: Ferishta says that they met at the house of Tāj-ud-dīn Kotwal. Tab-i-Naṣ. reads "at the residence of the Ṣadr-ul-Mulk, the Sayyid, Tāj-ud-din, 'Ali Mūsāwī who was the Mushri'f-i-Mamālik.

5 Ferishta relates that a faithful servant of the king, assuming the character of a mad man, was allowed to overhear the conversation that took place at the meeting.

might hear their conversation. Niẓām-ul-Mulk, then, called upon the Ṣadr-ul-Mulk to appear, in order that he might relate to him all about the (proposed) change in the empire, and win over to their side the enemies and those that had made a common cause in that movement. Niẓām-ul-Mulk made (suitable) answer and bade him (Ṣadr-ul-Mulk) farewell. He then despatched the confidential person of the Sulṭān to the Emperor asking him to represent all that he had heard from the Ṣadr-ul-Mulk and requesting the Sulṭān, on his behalf, that he should mount and come upon that party, so that, by the prosperity of the Emperor, the rebels would be defeated and driven away. When the person apprised the monarch of the state of affairs, the Sulṭān, at once, set out. Badr-ud-dīn Sunḳar, on being informed of this, went over to the Sulṭān, who conferred the *aḳṭā'* of Badāōn upon him and asked him to proceed there: the rest of the amīrs who had been on his side, out of fear, fled away.

Badr-ud-dīn and Ṣadr-ul-Mulk imprisoned.

Four months later, Badr-ud-dīn Sunḳar returned from Badāōn, and, as the Sulṭān was incensed against him he ordered him to be imprisoned along with Ṣadr-ul-Mulk Mūsā [1] and both of them died in captivity.[2] Niẓām-ul-Mulk, nursed malevolence for the wounds that he had received from the knife, attempted to create a bad blood between the amirs, maliks, and the Sulṭān. He continued to raise the Sulṭān's apprehensions against them.

Appearance of the Mughals at Lahore.

Afterwards, it so happened that the Mughal armies having reached Lahore carried on hostilities. Malik Karā-Ḳash, the feudatory of Lahore, was an experienced and a clever warrior;[3] but the inhabitants of Lahore did not act as the conditions of union demanded, and in fighting and in keeping guard, showed much neglect. When the disposition of the people became evident to Malik Ḳarā-Ḳash, he left the city at night with all his retainers and set out towards Dehli. The infidel Mughals gave him a chase, but the Most High God, took the Malik and his men out of their clutches.

The vizir, although he secretly favoured the conspiracy excused himself from attending the consultations.

[1] Tab-i-Naṣ. writes Sayyid, Tāj-ud-dīn, 'Alī Mūsāwī.

[2] Tab-i-Akb. writes that the Sulṭān ordered Badr-ud-dīn to be executed.

[3] MBL او مرد دلاور بذاته : JNS, MBM او بذاته مرد :

As no ruler remained in Lahore, on Monday,[1] the 16th Jamādī-ul Ākhir, 639 H. (22 Dec., 1241 A.D.), the infidel Mughals obtained possession of the city, martyred the Musalmans, and made captive their dependants. When this bad news reached Sultān Mu'izz-ud-dīn, he made the amīrs, maliks, and every other renowned chiefs swear allegiance to him anew, and despatched Kutub-ud-dīn Husen and Nizām-ul-Mulk with a big force to coerce the Mughals. Reaching the banks of the Bēah,[1] Nizām-ul-Mulk sent a secret representation to the Sultān to the effect that those amīrs and maliks would never become obedient, and that it was advisable that an edict should be issued by His Majesty authorizing him and Malik Kutub-ud-dīn to destroy the amīrs by such means as might be attainable. When that representation reached the Sultān, he, according to the way of inadvertence and haste issued a farmān in conformity to the object for which the petition was made and despatched it to Nizām-ul-Mulk.

Kutub-ud-dīn Husen and Nizām-ul-Mulk sent against the Mughals.

When the edict reached him, Nizām-ul-Mulk showed the very edict itself to the amīrs and maliks saying that the Sultān had issued that mandate respecting them. All of them became incensed against the Sultān, and paying Nizām-ul-Mulk homage pledged themselves to effect the expulsion and dethronement of the Sultān. When the news of this disaffection on the part of the amīrs reached the Sultān, he despatched Sa'iyid Kutub-ud-dīn, the Sheikh-ul-Islam[2] of Dehli, for the purpose of pacifying them. On his reaching the destination, much opposition under the instigation of the amīrs, was exhibited, and, (so) he returned back.[3] Nizām-ul-Mulk and Malik Kutub-ud-dīn followed after him to Dehli and laid the foundation of hostility. The Sultān was invested in the fortress, and the attempt made by several men of eminence of the

Treachery of Nizām-ul-Mulk and hostility of the Amīrs.

---

1 "Where the town of Sultānpur now stands." Ferishta.

2 Badaoni, Tab-i-Akb. and Ferishta writes that the Sultān sent Sheikh Kutub-ud-dīn Bakhtiar Ushi in order to pacify the nobles. But the venerable saint in question, after whom the Kutub Minar at Dehli is named, died six years previous to this time—(Tab-i-Akb. A.S.B., B. I)., p. 80, f.n. 2).

3 Tab-i-Akb says that the rebellious nobles could not in any way be satisfied and so the Sheikh returned to Dehli.

city to bring about a reconciliation proved a failure. The siege was carried on for four months—from the 19th Sha'bān 639 H. (Sat., 22 Feb., 1242 A.D.) until the month of Ẕil-Ḳā'da[1] (May-June). There was casualty on both sides, and all the environs of the city was desolated. This prolongation of the disturbance was caused by Fakhr-ud-dīn Mubārak Shāh, the head *Farrāsh*,[2] who wielded influence over the Sulṭān refused to assent to any accommodation. On the night of Saturday, the 8th Ẕil-Ḳā'da, 639 H.[3] (10 May, 1242 A.D.), Niẓām-ul-Mulk in company with his soldiers found access into the fortress, killed Mubārak Shāh, the root of all trouble, and threw the Sulṭān in prison, where he died.

The Sulṭān invested in the fortress.

His imprisonment and death.

Verse.

This old universe is a palace of double gates,[4]
Lay not the foundation of permanent abode on this transitory world!

The period of his reign was two years, one month and fifteen days. *God knows the truth!*

An account of Sulṭān 'Alā'-ud-dīn Mas'ūd Shāh.

Sulṭān 'Alā'-ud-dīn Mas'ūd Shāh was the son of Sulṭān Rukn-ud-dīn Firoz Shāh. When Mu'izz-ud-dīn Bahrām Shāh was imprisoned Malik 'Izz-ud-dīn Balban[5] ascended the throne at the imperial palace, and had the proclamation once read in the city by the proclaimer. The greater part of the amīrs and maliks, who did not approve of this, drove him out, and presently bringing out Nāṣir-ud-dīn, Jalāl-ud-dīn and 'Alā'-ud-dīn,[6] who were under im-

Accession of 'Izz-ud-din-Balban.

---

[1] Tab-i-Akb. and Ferishta give 8th Ẕil-Ḳā'da, (Sat., 10 May).

[2] The servant who spreads carpets, makes bed, and pitch the tents on journeys. Tab-i-Naṣ. reads فخر الدين مبارک شاه فرخي.

[3] Tab-i-Naṣ. reads Tuesday, 18th Ẕil Ḳā'da.

[4] JNS and MBM که خانه دو در است : MBL که در خانه.

[5] Balban had occupied the throne for one day.

[6] Nāṣir-ud-dīn and Jalāl-ud-dīn were the sons of Iyal-timish. 'Alā'-ud-dīn was this son of Rukn-ud-dīn, MBM adds Sulṭān before 'Alā'-ud-dīn. The texts read "Sulṭān" before Nāṣir-ud-dīn.

prisonment in the white castle, placed 'Alā'-ud-dīn on the throne in the metropolis, Dehli, on Saturday, the 8th Zil-Kā'da, 639 H. (10 May, 1242 A.D.). The people administered a pledge of fealty to the Sultān. Malik Kutub-ud-dīn Husen,[1] became the Deputy of the kingdom, and Muhazzab-ud-dīn Nizām-ul-Mulk[2] was made the vizir Malik Karā-Kash became Amir-i-Hājib (Lord Chamberlain) Muhazzab-ud-dīn Nizām-ul-Mulk took all the functions out of the hands of the Turkish Amirs and brought them under his control. So, the amīrs conspired against him, and on Wednesday,[3] the 2nd Jamādi-ul-auwal, 640 H. (Oct. 28, 1242 A.D.) they assassinated him in the plain of *Hauzr-ānī*. The office of vizir then passed to Sadr-ul-Mulk Najm-ud-dīn Abu Bakr.[4]

The Amirs dethroned 'Izz-ud-din and placed 'Alā'-ud-dīn on the throne.

The Amirs killed Muhazzab-ud-dīn.

The Mughals in Uchch and their retirement.

Some time afterwards, when the *aktā's* of the empire and the affairs of the kingdom were put in order, the news relating to the army of Mughals, whose leader was the execrable Mangutah,[5] arrived from Uchch. Having collected his forces from all quarters the Sultān marched against them. When he reached the banks of Beah, the Mughals were informed that an immense Muslim army, the like of which had never been collected by any of the previous sovereigns was advancing against them. Panic-stricken, they made their way to Khorāsān, and the Sultān returned to Dār-ul-Mulk Dehli.

Tyranny of the Sultān.

In the meantime, a number of Abyssinians and worthless persons had gained access to the presence of the Sultān, and used to influence him in the committal of unworthy acts and habits, so much so that (the practise

---

[1] Tab-i-Nas. reads Hasin in place of Husen.

[2] MBL reads ملک مهذب الملک و الدین و نظام الملک وزیر ممالک.

[3] It is "Tuesday" according to the Ephemeris by L. D. S. Pillai; iv, 87.

[4] JNS صدر الدين ابو بكر :

[5] MBM منكوبه : JNS منكوبه .

Most writers such as Nizām-ud-dīn, Badaoni, and Ferishta here make mention of the Mughal invasion of Lakhnauti. In fact, no invasion of the kind ever occurred. The author of Tab-i-Nas., who was living at the time and even staying in the Lakhnauti territory, refer to the appearance of the infidels of Jājnagar before the gate of Lakhnauti in the year 642 H.

of) killing the amīrs and seizing their chattels was gaining place in his nature, and he was steadfast in resolve (in that habit). All his good qualities turned away from the laudable path and inclined towards sensuality, pleasure and the chase, to such a degree of excess, that the affairs of the kingdom began to be neglected. The amīrs and the maliks agreed together and secretly despatched letter of invitation to Sulṭān Nāṣir-ud-dīn, the then Governor of Bahraich. When Sulṭān Nāṣir-ud-dīn reached Dehli, 'Alā'-ud-din Mās'ūd Shāh was seized and cast into prison on Sunday, the 23rd Muḥarram, 644 H. (June 10, 1246 A.D.) and during that confinement he was received into the Almighty's mercy.

The Amirs invite Nāṣir-ud-din, and imprison 'Alā'-ud-din Mās'ūd Shāh.

Verse.

This world is the bank of the river Death, that disturbs the mind,
Take heed, be afraid of the river surges, and place not thy feet on the coast!

The period of his rule was four years, one month and one day. *God is more aware of the real facts.*[1]

The account of Sulṭān Nāṣir-ud-dīn Maḥmud, son of Sulṭān Sa'iyid Shams-ud-dīn Iyal-timish.

Sulṭan Nāṣir-ud-dīn was the son of Sulṭān Sa'iyid Shams-ud-dīn Iyal-timish. Out of affection for Malik Nāṣir-ud-dīn Maḥmud, who breathed his last at Lakhnauti, (this sovereign) was distinguished by the name of Nāṣir-ud-dīn Maḥmud.

When Sulṭān 'Alā'-ud-dīn was imprisoned, Nāṣir-ud-dīn ascended the imperial throne in the White Palace at the capital, Dehli, on Sunday, the 23rd Muḥarram, 644 H. (10 June, 1246 A.D.). Three days after the event he granted public audience. The people rendered him homage on the day of his accession to the throne[2] and were rewarded with dignities.

His accession.

The post of vizīr was conferred on Malik Balban,, the Shamsī slave; he was given the title of Ulugh Khān, a canopy and a durbash two branched and

Balban made vizir.

---

[1] MBL omits this line.

[2] MBL عامۀ خلایق جلوس خاص بر سلطنت او بیعت : MBM عام داد عام جلوس سلطنت او بیعت. JNS عامه جلوس سلطنت او بیعت کردند :

ornamented baton; the whole administration of the empire was vested in him, and he brought them under his control.

The Sulṭān's march to Banian.

In the first year of his accession, the Sulṭān marched towards Banian,[1] laid waste the Jud hills[2] and Nandanah.[3] He then encamped himself for some time on the bank of Sudrāh,[4] but owing to the scarcity of fodder in his army, he made his way back to the capital Dehli.[5]

To Kanauj.

In the year 645 H.[6] (1247-48 A.D.), the Sulṭān set out for Hindustan vîa Doab;[7] reaching Ḳanauj, he conquered the district of Balsandah[8] which was situated in the heart of the country and was the stronghold of the unbelievers. The Rāis Dalki and Malki were taken prisoners.[9] The Sulṭān, then, returned to Dehli richly laden with booty.[10]

---

1 Banian is the name of a hilly tract west of the upper part of the Sind-Sāgar Doābah. Tab-i-Akb. (A.S.B., p. 86) and Tab-i-Naṣ. (A.S.B., 208) read Multān. Raverty, 67., f.n. 6.

2 Jud is the part of the Salt range. Lat. 32°, Long. 71°: JNS خود

3 Nandanah, between Jhelum and Peshawar. (Ranking 128, f.n. 3.) MBL, MBM, and JNS read نندنه : Tab-i-Akb. and Badaoni read Nandanah.

4 A name of a part of the Chinab; (Tab-i-Akb., B. De, 86, f.n. 2): cf. Raverty, 678, f.n. 1: Badāoni, "on the banks of Indus". Tab-i-Akb., "bank of the Sind". Ferishta, Sodra:

5 Tab-i-Naṣ., Tab-i-Akb. and Badaoni agree in saying that the Emperor made Ulugh Khān, the commander of the forces and sent him to the Jud hills and Nandanah, and that it was Ulugh Khān who had to return owing to the difficulty of obtaining subsistence.

6 Tab-i-Akb., 2nd Shā'bān, 645 (Mon., 2 Dec., 1247 A.D.).

7 MBL, MBM and JNS در طرف میان دو آب.

8 JNS بلندە : MBL بلسندە : Tab-i-Akb. (86, f.n. 5), Talsandah: Ferishta, Bitunda: Tab-i-Naṣ. Talsandah. Raverty identifies it with Tilsurra, 12 miles S.S.W. of Ḳanauj. (See Raverty, p. 679, f.n. 6.)

9 The text of Tab-i-Naṣ. (A.S.B. 211) and Raverty show that Dalki and Malki is a tract of country. Tab-i-Akb. (A.S.B. 86, B. De). Badaoni makes no reference: Ferishta says that the Ranas Dalki and Malki resided at Kalinjār. All that can be definitely said is that this Rānah's territory was in the vicinity of the River Jaūn or Jumna, which is between Kālanjar and Karah. See B. De, 86, f.n. 7, and Raverty, 682, f.n. 5.

10 Tab-i-Naṣ. writes, "of one description of horses alone, 1,500 head fell into the hands of the Musalman forces, and, from this, one may infer the extent of other booty".

The Imperialists' march to Mewāt.

In the year 646 H.[1] (1248-49 A.D.), the forces of Islam pushed on towards the skirts of the hills of Mewāt.[2] The place was sacked and a large booty collected. Having chastised the contumacious people of the neighbourhood, they retired to Dehli.

To Nāgor, Gwalior, Chanderi, and Mālwah.

Meanwhile, intelligence arrived that Malik 'Izz-ud-dīn Balban had raised the standard of rebellion at Nāgor. The Sulṭān proceeded to Nāgor in 649 H. (1251-52 A.D.), and when he neared the place Malik 'Izz-ud-dīn made his submission. His rebellion was put down. Thence the Sulṭān moved towards Gwalior,[3] Chanderi, and Mālwah.[4] The accursed Chāhar Deo, who was the greatest of all the infidels of that tract of country, advanced to Mālwah with 5,000 horse and 200,000 foot, and he was at length routed. After the conquest the Sulṭān returned to Dehli.

To Lahore, Multan, and Uchch.

In the year 650 H. (1252-53 A.D.), the Sulṭān marched against Lahore, Multān, and Uchch.[5] After suppressing the rebellions in those quarters he turned back (to Dehli).

The Sultān marched against Bardar and Bijnor; ravaged Katehar, and proceeded to Oudh.

Next year (651 H.[6]), the Sulṭān led his army to the skirt of the mountains of Bardar and Bijnor,[7] and plundered the rebels. Entering Santur along the foot of the hills, he proceeded by the banks of the Rahab and laid waste Katehar in revenge for the blood of Malik Mu'izz-ud-dīn Darakhshi,[8] and having imprisoned the inhabitants he moved to Badāon; thence, he took his way to Oudh, and after putting down the rebels of that country he returned to Dehli.

---

1 Ferishta gives 6 Shā'bān, 646 H. (Tues., 24th Nov., 1248 A.D.).

2 Tab-i-Naṣ. adds Rantambor also. JNS جانب کوهیان بیرات.

3 MBL کالیور : JNS کوالیر : Raverty (690) and Elliot, Gwalior.

4 Tab-i-Naṣ. and Ferishta add also Nurwul (Nurwar) which is situated 40 m. east of Bhopal, in Lat. 23°. 18′. Long. 78°

5 Tab-i-Naṣ. gives 22 Shawwāl 650 H. (26 Dec. 1252 A.D.)

6 Tab-i-Naṣ. gives 652 H.: Tab-i-Akb. and Badaoni agree with Tab-i-Naṣ.

7 MBL بردار و بعور : MBM بردار و بیعور : JNS بردار و پجور : Tab-i-Akb., Tab-i-Naṣ., and Badaoni write Bijnor.

8 Raverty writes "Durmashi", which signifies that he was a native of Darmash, or that his family, originally came from a place so called. The word "Durmashi"

The Sulṭān marched against Kutlugh Khān, and defeated him.

In 654 H. (1256-57 A.D.), the Sulṭān marched against Ḳutlugh Khān, who having deserted Malik 'Izz-ud-dīn had befriended the Hindus. In company of a group of infidels and those Amīrs, who in dread of the Sulṭān had joined him,[1] the Khān rallied to the defence. With the assistance of the Most High Allah the army of Islam came off victorious, while their opponents got perplexed and were put to rout. The Sulṭān gave them a chase so far as the Sirmor hills, and then retired to Dehli.

Ulugh Khān was sent against Kutlugh Khān and Malik 'Izz-ud-dīn.

In 655 H., news came that Ḳutlugh Khān and the other Amīrs had combined themselves with Malik 'Izz-ud-dīn Kashlu Khān, the Amīr of Multān and Uchch. Ulugh Khān was sent against them with a large army. When Ulugh Khān marched against the insurgents, a number of people of the city (Dehli), viz., Sa'iyid Ḳuṭub-ud-dīn, the Sheikh-ul-Islām and Ḳāzī Shams-ud-dīn Bahraiji, sent letters to Ḳutlugh Khān and Kashlu Khān inviting them to come to the capital and to seize it; the citizens, too, secretly promised them their homage. When the couriers from Dehli carried this piece of news to Ulugh, he represented the true state of affairs to the Sulṭān urging to him to issue mandates ordering the Amirs to return to their own *aḳṭā's*, so that the rebellion might not grow further. The Sulṭān did accordingly. But the letters of the Amīrs had already reached Ḳutlugh Khān and Kashlu Khān. Traversing a hundred *Kuroh* in two days,[2] they left Sāmāna and reached the vicinity of Dehli: but being informed of the fact that the aforesaid Amīrs having left the city (Dehli) had returned to their fiefs, they became worried and contemplative. The Sulṭān fortified the gates of the city, and sent out the Amīrs of Dehli against them. Bereft of all strength for opposition, (the rebels) were defeated. Kashlu Khān retired to his own country, and, later on, presented himself before the Sulṭān with most of his attendants.

---

was wrongly read by Niẓām-ud-dīn, the author of Tab-i-Akb. as در مستي "in a state of intoxication", and so he has committed an error in saying that Malik 'Izz-ud-dīn was murdered "while in a state of intoxication". See Raverty, p. 697, f.n. 6.

MBM reads ملک عز بافته : JNS ملک یافته.

[1] MBM and JNS read خایف شده بودند پیش آمده.

[2] Tab-i-Naṣ. reads 2 days and a half.

The rebellion was (thus) put down. This news reaching him, Ulugh Khān returned to Dehli, laden with booty, on Tuesday, the 11th Jamādi-ul-Ākhir, 655 H. (26th June, 1257 A.D.).

Appearance of the Mughals in Uchch and Multān.

Towards the end of this year, there came from Khorāsān, the accursed Mughal armies in the neighbourhood of Uchch and Multān.[1] Kashlu Khān Balban made a common cause with them and joined the invaders. The Sulṭān raised an army for their suppression; when they learnt that the Sulṭān was advancing towards them with a large army, they retired towards Khorāsān.

Embassy from Turkistān comes to the Dehli Court.

Next year, in 656 H. (1258 A.D.), embassies[2] from Turkistān reached (the court of) the Sulṭān; and, in accordance with the condition of honour and respect, the ambassadors were rewarded with rich presents and valuable gifts: they, then, took their adieu with souvenir from the Court.

Imperialists sent against the Mughals.

The same year, on Sunday, the 6th Muḥarram (13th Jan., 1258 A.D.), the Sulṭān led his army for the suppression of the infidel Mughals, and drew up his army in the vicinity of Dehli. Then, were enrolled from all sides the Amīrs and the Maliks with their armies and equipage. The Sulṭān returned to the capital.

Embassy from Lakhnauti.

In 657 H.,[3] two elephants and a large amount of cash arrived at the court of the Sulṭān from Lakhnauti. Towards the end of Shawwāl of the same year (Oct., 1259 A.D.), in conformity to the royal mandate, Malik Kazlal Khān[4] Sanjar came to the court with a large army.[5]

---

[1] Tab-i-Naṣ. writes that Hulāū (or Hulākū), the head of the Mughal infidels, fled discomfitted before the troops of the Lord of the Faithful, Musta'sim Billah, from the gate of Baghdād.

[2] There is no mention of this embassy either in Tab-i-Naṣ. or Tab-i-Akb., but Badaoni makes reference to this embassy in his work (A.S B. 93).

[3] Tab-i-Naṣ. gives Wednesday, the 4th Jamādī-ul-Ākhir, 657 H.: but it is Thursday (not Wednesday), 29th May, 1259 A.D., according to Pillai's Ephemeris, IV. 120. Ferishta places this event in 664 H.

[4] MBM كرللغان : JNS worm-eaten. Tab-i-Naṣ. (A.S.B. 227) زنمر خان سنجر : Raverty (714) Malik Tāj-ud-din Sanjar-i-Tez Khān.

[5] He came from Oudh in order to accompany Ulugh Khān in his expedition into the Koh-payah.

On the 13th Safar, 658 H. (Thursday, 29th January, 1260 A.D.), Ulugh Khān was sent out to coerce the rebels of Mewāt,[1] with 10,000 horsemen, and numerous brave and experienced footmen. When the Imperialists reached the *Koh-payah* Mewāt, a huge booty and a large number of cattle fell into their hands: after chastising the miscreants, they returned to Dār-ul-Mulk, Dehli.

Ulugh Khān was sent against Mewāt.

Meanwhile, the Sulṭān fell sick, and by the decree of the Most High Allah, he breathed his last on the 11th Jamādi-ul-auwāl, 664 H. (Thursday, 18th Feb., 1266 A.D.).

The death of the Sulṭān.

Verse.

Come, and take a lesson from the dust,
It is the place of repose of honourable kings!

His reign lasted for nineteen years, three months and sixteen days. *God knows the truth!*

An account of Sulṭān Ghiās-ud-dīn Balban.[2]

Three days after the observance of funeral rites consequent on the death of Sulṭān Nāṣir-ud-dīn, the Amīrs and Maliks placed Sulṭān Ghiās-ud-dīn Balban on the imperial throne in the White Castle, on the 13th Jamādi-ul-auwal, 664 H. (Saturday, the 20th Feb., 1266 A.D.). The pillars of State, the Vizirs, Amīrs and Maliks all paid him homage.[3] In those days when Balban held the rank of a Khān[4] and the reins of sovereignty were in his hands, there prevailed a serene atmosphere in the country. In those days he led his forces to Koeldakir,[5] and having punished the rebels of that country returned (to Dehli). Later on, he ravaged the Koh-payah Santur,[6] and made the chiefs

His accession.

---

1 Tab-i-Naṣ. میو: Mew, Mewṛā, or Mewṛah, or Mewātīs all refer to a most contumacious race. The territory they inhabited includes the British Dists. of Mathura, Gurgāon, part of Ulwar and Bharatpur.

2 Tab-i-Akb. and Badaoni call him Sulṭān Ghiaṣ-ud-dīn Balban-i-Khurd.

3 MBM دوکان نقد را اعرا و ملوک بیعت : MBL ارکان وزراء و امراء ملوک بیعت JNS omits it

4 MBM and JNS همدران ایام : MBL در ایام.

5 MBL, MBM, and JNS read کویلد کیر.

6 The Kumāon Hills.

of those places food for the sword. He laid the foundation of a fortress at *Makar-khachuri*,[1] and giving it a new name returned to the capital. Afterwards he went out to the environs of the city and built a fort there. Thence he proceeded with successive marches to the Jud hills.[2] His two sons joined the Sulṭān and were kindly received.

Some time afterwards, the Sulṭān marched against Hindustān. Reaching the banks of the Ganges, he ordered fortresses to be erected at Battiālī[3] and Bhojpur.[4] In the meantime, there came to the Sulṭān the report relating to the death of Sher Khān, the feoffee of Lakhnauti. Lakhnauti was conferred upon Amīn Khān; Tughral was appointed as the Deputy; the Sulṭān, then, took his way to Dehli.

The Sulṭān marched to Lahore : erected a fort there.

Later on, the Sulṭān led his army to Lahore, and there reconstructed the fort that had been pulled down by the accursed Mughals in the reign of late Mu'izz-ud-dīn Bahrām Shāh. Having sent out the people of the villages, judges, prelates, chiefs, citizens and merchants, the Sulṭān made them live in that city (Lahore).

Tughral assume independence.

Meanwhile, the Sulṭān laboured under a fit of sickness, and as he remained unseen by anybody for days together. the people became suspicious ; this news was spread abroad. When this information reached Lakhnauti, there had at that time sprung out an enmity between Tughral and Amīn Khān, and both were engaged in hostilities against the other. Tughral gained success, and Amīn Khān was made a prisoner in his hands. The former assumed the royal canopy and adopted the title of Mu'izz-ud-dīn.

After some time, four royal mandates were issued to Amīn Khān, Tughral, Jamāl-ud-dīn Kandazi[5] and Abtakin Musa[6] to the

---

1 MBL, MBM مکر کهجوری : JNS کل کهچوری

2 MBM, JNS کوه خود .

3 Tab-i-Akb. (B. De, 100) Patiāli. : In Aliganj tahsil, 22 miles north of Etah.

4 West of Arrah and north of Sasserām.

5 MBL قندری : JNS قندزی.

6 MBL ابتکین موسي : MBM and JNS ایتکین : Tab-i-Akb. Malik Aitakin Muedarāz.

effect that his (Sulṭān's) enemies had caused him affliction for a few days, and the Most High God had granted him a speedy cure; that the drum of joy be beaten, cupolas erected, amusements held, prisoners liberated and theologicians rewarded: that if anybody had been justly suspended by the Tribunal of Fate, he should be presented with cash from the royal treasury and provided with an asylum. When this royal mandate was issued, and it reached Tughral, he advanced with his army to Bihar, and imprisoned Abtakin, Jamāl-ud-dīn Ḳandazi, and Amīn Khān at Nārkilāh.[1]

Turmati sent against Tughral: the former's defeat.

When the news of Tughral's rebellion reached the Sulṭān, he sent out Malik Turmatī[2] to put down Tughral. The latter having made his retreat from Turmati lay in ambush. Turmati imprudently gave him a chase. Suddenly, Tughral drew up his forces in battle array and falling upon the central column of his enemy gave him an overthrow at the first onset. Turmati made good his escape to Oudh.

Shahāb-ud-dīn was sent against Tughral.

Subsequently, the Sulṭān put Malik Shahāb-ud-dīn, the Amir of Oudh, at the head of the army, and placing Kajru Tamar Khān[3] under the Malik, ordered the latter to send Turmati on the gibbet on the bank of Saryu and then despatch the body to Tughral. The order of the Sulṭān was carried into effect. When they reached the vicinity of Lakhnauti, Tughral came and met them, and in the battle which ensued, he vanquished his opponents.

The Sulṭān personally leads the army against Tughral.

On receiving this information, the Sulṭān was much annoyed, and he resolved upon leading the army himself Learning that the king was personally taking the field, Tughral retired to Nārkilāh on a boat. The Sulṭān sent out Malik Ikhtiār-ud-dīn Nēk Tars[4] with a strong force to seize Tughral. Meanwhile, Rāi Danuj[5] sent a letter informing the Sulṭān of his intending visit for the purpose of paying him respect, and requesting him that he would stand

---

[1] MBL نار کیله : MBM مار کیله : JNS بار کیله.

[2] Tab-i-Akb. (B. Do, 108) Tamar Khān Shamsī : Ferishta, Malik Tirmany Toork.

[3] MBM ملک کجرو حاتم خان ; JNS agrees with MBM.

[4] Badaoni reads Malik Ikhtiār-ud-dīn Beg Birlās. Tab-i-Akb. Malik Barbak Beg Tars: Ferishta, Malik Yar Beg Birlass.

[5] Tab-i-Akb. Bhojrai; Badaoni, Dhanuj.

up on the Rāi's arrival. The fact that a Muslim king ought not to show proper respect to an infidel made the Sulṭān pensive. Malik Nēk Tars, who was present, forbade the Sulṭān to be thoughtful and advised him that, prior to the Rāi's arrival (at the court), the Sulṭān should take his seat on the throne with a falcon on his hand: and that, with the approach of the Rāi and on his having rendered him homage, the Sulṭān should stand up and let the falcon go. At this, the people would surmise that the Sulṭān had left his seat to set the bird in motion: the petition of the Rāi would, thereby, be complied with. The Sulṭān expressed warm approbation of the Malik's advice, and acted accordingly. He rewarded the Malik with valuable presents. The Rāi promised, by every possible means, to bring Tughral before the Sulṭān. The Sulṭān, then, set out with successive marches, and on his reaching Lakhnauti, Tughral, out of dread, retired to the forest, and was followed by the Imperialists. Malik Nēk Tars fell upon Tughral and imprisoned him alive. Later, he flayed Tughral, and sent the body to the Sulṭān.[1] Bestowing Lakhnauti upon the younger prince, Bughrā Khān, who was formerly the Amīr of Sāmāna, the Sulṭān returned to Dehli.

Tughral killed: Lakhnauti was bestowed upon Bughrā Khān.

After the Sulṭān's arrival at Dehli, *Khān-i-Buzurg*, i.e., Muḥammad Sulṭān, the eldest son of Sulṭān Ghiās-ud-dīn, came to the court from Multān. The prince was in charge of a fief, situated on the west and a dependency of Multān, from Malim to Junati; it was situated mostly on the sea-coast, at a distance of 60 *kuroh* from Thatha. Amir Khusru and Amir Ḥasan, the two poets, were the attendants and the companions of the Prince, who was adorned with laudable and praiseworthy accomplishments. He remained with his father for some time and then returned (to his fief). Two years later, he entered into a conflict against the accursed Mughals[2] at the garden

Arrival of Muḥammad Sulṭān at the Court

[1] According to Tab-i-Akb., Tughral fell off from his horse by the shot of an arrow from Tughral Kush; and his head was cut off by Malik Mukaddar and sent to the Sultān. Ferishta says that Malik Mukaddar, brother of Malik Yar Beg, shot Tughral with an arrow, and later cut off his head.

[2] Badaoni says that their leader was Samar. Ziā-ud-dīn Barni calls him Samar. Ferishta writes Timur Khān: Tab-i-Akb., Temur.

of Nayyir,[1] on the bank of the river Lahore, and attained martyrdom.[2] The account of the advent of the detested Mughals, and the attainment of martyrdom by *Khān-i-Buzurg*, has been written in an elegy by Amir Ḥasan Alā' Sanjarī,[3] *May God be pleased with him!* Thus runs the elegy on *Khān-i-Shahīd*.[4]

The death of Muḥammad Sulṭān, the eldest Prince.

It is an old story[5] that the tyrannical sphere, although for a while it makes a bond of agreement and gives a promise of security, turns,[6] and inconstant[7] destiny, although for a time it proposes to show acquiescence and gives promise of faith, changes. The treacherous-eyed Heaven, the pupil of whose generosity is sullied by the defect of the mote of meanness,[8] although, at first like a drunken man without any reason for[9] liberality, it gives away a thing, yet at the end, like a child although a sense of shame[10] would forbid it, takes it back. The well-known custom of the oppressive times[11] is this, as experience and hearsay,[12] what we see, and what we hear, that equally teach, that whomsoever it finds coming to perfection like the moon, it wants to blacken his face of perfect beauty with the stain of loss; and whenever any one rises over our heads like a cloud, it scatters his gem[13] (of greatness) in little

The elegy on Khān-i-Shahid: inconsistency of destiny.

---

1 Badaoni, Bāgh-i-Subz.

2 Badaoni (Ranking, 188) writes that this event took place in Ẕil-ḥijjah, 683 H. (Mar.-Apr. 1282 A.D.). Ẕia- Barni gives 684 H.

3 Badaoni writes Mir Ḥasan of Dehli. Ẕia-ud-dīn Barni attributes this lament to Amīr Khusrū. Ferishta is of similar opinion. "It seems probable therefore that the lament should be attributed to Amīr Khusrū. The "Ḥasan" may have had its origin in a copyist's error." Tab-i-Akb., Khwaja Ḥasan:

4 Like our author, the other writers, such as, Nizam-ud-dīn, the author of Tab-i-Akb. and Badaoni have also made use of this elegy in a similar connection. I am indebted to Raverty and Mr. B. De for the translation of the elegy.

5 دير ياز است : Raverty translates it thus, "It is an old story." B. De writes (p. 113) "these words do not make sense."

6 MBL, MBM, JNS مي گردد : Tab-i-Akb. برمي گردد.

7 The three MSS. read ناسازوار : Tab-i-Akb. ناسازگار.

8 خسلست : MBL خاست. 9 MBM باعث : MBL عنه : JNS باعنه.

10 MBL جافى : MBM and JNS حالى.

11 Three MSS. read حيائى : Tab-i-Akb. خيانتي.

12 MBL بتسامع : MBM مسامع : JNS worm-eaten.

13 MBL جراهر : MBM جوهر : JNS خواهر.

particles on all sides of the horizon.[1] In this parterre of perplexity, and in this garden of regrets,[2] no flower has bloomed without a thorn and no heart has escaped the thorn of anguish. Alas! how many young plants are there, which from the effects of the autumn of calamity show a pale and withered face instead of a fresh beauty; and how many flowers lie trampled in the dust (blown down) by the rough blast of time.

Verse.

Look! how hath autumn spread cold![3]
Look! how the young cypress[4] hath it turned old!

One of the examples of this allegory[5] is the departed Emperor, Ḳaan[6]-i-Mulk G͟hāzī. *May God make manifest his demonstrations, and make His scales heavy with His Mercies!* On Friday,[7] the last day of the month[8] of Ẕīl-ḥijjah, 683 H.[9] (8 Mar., 1285 A.D.), when,

The death of the Prince is one of the examples of vicissitudes of Fortune.

Verse.

The moon like kindness in the hearts of infidels,
Nowhere in the world[10] could be seen!

and the Sun with the company of the army of Islam came forth with uplifted sword: the great prince who was the Sun in the sky of the state, with the light of holy war[11] shining on his noble brow,

---

1 MBL and JNS اطراف آفاق پراگنده : MBM omits آفاق

2 MBL and MBM باغ حیرت و بستان حسرت : JNS omits حیرت.

3 In Tab-i-Akb. (A.S.B. 98), this line is somewhat different: it reads در باغ خزان به بین که چه حد سروری کرد (See! how hath autumn shown its power in the garden): but the three MSS. of Tārīkh-i-Mubāraks͟hāhi reads در باد خزان ببین که چه حد سردی کرد : MBL writes سردار instead of در باد : Badaoni's text agrees with Yaḥiya.

4 MBM and JNS read سرو. MBL سر.

5 MBM and JNS تمثیل واقعهٔ MBL adds حور after واقعهٔ.

6 JNS خان MBL, MBM قآن.

7 Acc. to Indian Ephemeris, vol. IV, 172, it is *Thursday.*

8 Tab-i-Akb. reads سوم ماه. Badaoni agrees with Yaḥiya.

9 Tab-i-Akb. gives 693 H.: Badaoni has 683 H.

10 MBL, JNS, MBM omit در جهان.

11 MBL نورانیت عذو : MBM نوایت عدو : JNS نور ثبت عذ.

and whose excessive zeal in the splendid heart for holy warfare was firm,[1] put his auspicious foot in the stirrup.

Arrival of Tamar Mughal.

They explained to his intellect which solved all difficulties,[2] that the accursed Tamar[3] had arrived with all his forces within three[4] *farsangs.* When morning broke, he started from the camp on his march, and halted at a distance of one *farsang* from the accursed ones.

Battle at Bāgh-i-Nayyir.

He chose as his battle-field a place within the boundaries of Bāgh-i-Nayyir on the bank of the river Lahore,[5] so that he had in his neighbourhood the water of the Dehandhi.[6] He fortified the place strongly, and made such dispositions that when the infidels came against him, both rivers[7] should be in the rear[8] of his army, so that no part of his troops would be able to take to flight, nor would any danger befall any part of his army from the infidels.

The disposition reflects the Prince's prudence.

In very truth, these precautionary measures showed how great the prudence[9] and how wonderful the strategy of that world-conquering Khān[10] was. But when evil destiny overtakes one, the strings of all plans get entangled,[11] and no skill is of any avail.[12]

---

1 MBL ثابت وّ راسخ : MBM and JNS omit راسخ .

2 MBM and JNS بد رای مشکل کشای : MBL, etc., سب آن بد رای .

3 MBL تمر ملعون : MBM تمر خاقان : JNS تمر بادشاه .

4 MBM بسه : MBL بفرسنگي : JNS agrees with MBM.

5 MBL لاهور : MBM لهاورا : JNS هاورا .

6 The three MSS. read دهندهي : Tab-i-Akb. و منڈي : Badaoni دبهي : Dihandah, the name of a river near Ajodhan, S.W. of Dipalpur.

7 The Ravi and Satlaj. The battle was fought close to Multan. (Raverty, 190, f.n. 2).

8 The MSS. and Badaoni read در عقب لشکر : Tab-i-Akb. در عون لشکر .

9 MBM در غایت حذم : MBL غایط جذم : JNS غایت جرم .

10 MBM and JNS ان خان جهان ستان بوده است : MBL خان جهانست آن بوده است .

11 JNS مصالح از تاب برود : MBL and MBM مصالح ارباب برود .

12 JNS, MBM ملک همه تدبیرها انتظام نشود : MBL adds از before انتظام

Verse.

Him whom doth evil fortune meet,
His affairs to his enemy's wishes fall;
When fortune like a mad man goes astray,
Wisdom like a night-blind into a well doth fall.

By chance that day[1] the Moon and the Sun who are connected[2] with kings,[3] were suspended in the sign of the Fish; and Mars, the redness of whose face is caused by the blood of the nobles of the State, drew out the arrows of destruction[4] and the bolts of ruin from the quiver of that sign against that Orion girdled K͟hān, who was like Leo coming forth[5] from a watery sign; the house of fear and calamity and the proofs of sedition and signs of harm thus became evidently manifest, while the hint and indication[6] of the proverb "*In Face of Fate wide becomes straight*" became written on the consecutive pages. In short, at midday, when the horseman of the sky was in the region of the noon, the life of the world-illuminating Emperor drew near the hour of destruction. Suddenly dust appeared from the direction of those infidels; and the K͟hān-i-G͟hāzī mounted his horse that same hour, and ordered that all his soldiers, adherents, officers and men should act according to the text, "*kill the infidels all of them,*"[7] drew them up in a line hundred times stronger than the wall of Alexander,[8] and after arranging the right and left wings, stationed his own highly accomplished person in the centre, like the moon among all the stars for a holy war.[9] The heathen Tātārs, *on whom be loss and ruin*, crossed the

---

1 MBL آب روز : JNS and MBM آن روز.

2 MBL سنت : MBM and JNS نسبت.

3 MBL بملک : JNS and MBM ملک.

4 JNS خذلانه : MBL and MBM خذلان.

5 MBL آن برج : JNS and MBM از برج.

6 MBL امن و اشارت : JNS اما من و اشارت : MBM رمز و اشارت

7 Ḳorān, IX. 5.

8 It is commonly known as the wall of Gog and Magog: It had been built by Alexandar to restrain the wild natives of Northern Asia.

9 MBL قلب گاه چون صف دو شاه و در جمیع کواکب ماه بانفعال کفار تبار علیهم اللعنة الخ MBM ......, چون صف بادشاه و در جمیع کواکب ماه با میعاد کفار تتار etc. JNS agrees with MBM.

river of Lahore,[1] and confronted the ranks of the Muslims. These barbarians, born in deserts, and friends of desolation, placed owl's[2] feathers on their accursed heads. The Ghāzis of Islam, consisting of Turk and Khalji Maliks, and the notables of Hindustan, and the entire body of soldiers, lifted up their hands in the prayer-ground of battle, crying "*God is Great*"; for the reason that the Holy Prophet, *may the blessings and peace of God be upon him*, has identified holy war with prayer, saying "*we betake ourselves to holy war against the greatest from holy war against the smallest.*"[3] In their first onset they put to the sword some of the strongest men of the Mughal cavalry; and the lances of the Maliks in attendance on the prince so struck in the bodies of the foes that the blood spurted out from every one of them like the spears, and the arrows of the sixty Turks, who were in attendance on the prince, so struck the persons of the Tātārs that the garments worn by them were torn to shreds.

Verse.

At the first onset, the Prince's arrow sprung ;
The Tātārs, all at once, inert became !

The great lord, the lion-hearted prince struck with his sword, which like his faith was stainless, and rushed out each time from the line of battle, the sword as it were trembled, in the battle-field, at the excellencies of the monarch, and becoming all tongue addressed to him, "For this day leave the work of destruction of these accursed ones to the slaves of thy greatness, and do not move out in thy own gracious person; for the sword hath two faces, and the scimitar of Fate is pitiless in its wounding—no one can say what will happen to whom, through the decree of the Almighty. I blink my eyes at the fatal eye![4]

---

1 MBL از آب لاهور : MBM لب آب لهاوُر : JNS agrees with MBM.

2 The Arabs look upon the owl as a bird of ill omen :

3 There are two *Jihāds*. The greater warfare (*Al-Jihādu-l Akbar*) which is against one's own lust: and "the lesser warfare" (*Al-Jihādu-l Asghar*) against infidels.

4 JNS من از عین الکمال چشم می زنم : MBM چشم می زنم : Tab-i-Akb. می ترسم.

Verse.

Go not! for I place thy dust on my eyes,
Act not, for I am afraid of the evil eyes,
The sky hath not such a bright face seen!
I throw myself on that fire as a sacrifice.

As long as he strenuously performed the duties of fighting and warfare, each of the weapons spoke as follows with a tongue suited to its condition. Said the lance, "Withdraw, Oh Prince! thy hand from me, for the tongue of my blade has become blunt with much smiting and slaying; and I have no power left now to strike thy enemy in the face. God forbid that when I strike I make a futile stroke." Said the arrow, "oh! thou! whose true aim has untied the knot of the nodes, do not go to attack these wicked men: for I myself in my flight may throw dust on my head. God forbid that the narrow-eyed Turk of the sky, who is in the fifth mansion, should shoot an arrow of destruction at you, in the way of tyranny and ruin, from the bow of hostility and malevolence, from his place of ambush at the door of the eighth mansion." The lasso said, "you should not allow the string of deliberation to escape from the hand of thought to-day, for I am contorted with anxiety at this hasty conflict and ill-considered battle; wait a while! in the place of deliberation, for Islâm and the Muslims are like the tent ropes connected with the tent of your favours. Oh God! in dealing with this people, do not so long delay putting the halter round their necks.

Verse.

I have with gladness put my head in a noose before thee,
Thou art my lassoer, who takest me with the noose of thy locks!

In short, that Prince, the defender of the faith, the destroyer of infidelity, carried on the battle with great energy and vigour against that band of heathens,[1] with the whole main body of his troops, from noon till sunset. The shouts of the victorious and the cries of those eager for the fray, deafened the ears of the earth, and the hearing of the sky, and the fiery tongues which flew up from the

---

[1] MBM بهم قلب و سپاه با این گروه JNS: سهم قلب سپاه کفر گاه بهم قلب و سپاه
MBL: گمراه بهمه قلب سپاه باین گروه گمراه.

heads of the lances, and the tongues of the swords, which did not err by a single letter in delivering the messages of death, all uttered this text, "*that it was the day on which men fled from their brethren.*"[1] The surface of the earth, like the eyes of old men, who had lost their sons, overflowed with blood; and the face of the sky, like the heads of sons, who had lost their fathers, was covered with dust.

Verse.

Why does the steel of the sword glow like fire, oh father!
That it may place the mark of orphanage on my heart.

In the very midst of this trouble, the very heart of this danger and confusion, an arrow from the aim of fate suddenly reached the wing of that falcon of that field of foray, and the bird of his life took its flight from the cage of the body to the gardens of the compassionate and the meadows of Riẕwān.[2]

Verily we belong to God, and verily to Him do we return![3]

At the same moment, the backbone of the religion of Muḥammad—*may the peace and blessing of God be upon him*—broke like the hearts of sorrowful orphans, and the structure of the faith of Aḥmad fell down like the tombs of the poor. Strength passed away from the arm of the State, and radiance from the Sun of Islam! Exactly at the hour of sunset, the moon of the life of the prince, whose fortune had become pale, set in the west of death. The sky like a mourner, put on a blue robe, and black tears began to flow over its cheeks. Saturn, like the faithful mourner, put on a black robe, and shouted lamentations for the Prince's death to the people of Hindustan. Jupiter, grieving for that corpse, covered with dust, threw down his blood-stained robe and his torn garments and turban in the dust.

And Mars, may the hand of his power become narrow like the eyes of the Turks, and (may) the face of his life become tight and black like the curls of Negroes; and owing to this grief, a thorn pierced the heart of blood; and was trembling like the Fish before the Sun, and like the ram in the hands of the butcher. The Sun

---

1 Ḳorān, LXXX. 34.

2 Riẕwān is the name of the door-keeper of the garden of Paradise.

3 Ḳorān II. 150, 151.

did not rise for shame, as it had not prevented such a catastrophe, and sank in the earth. When Venus saw what misery had been caused to all existences by this war, she changed the tone of her tambourine,[1] and began singing in a different tone. Instead of playing on her instruments, she wept over the death of that magnanimous Prince, who had ever been so generous to all his servants. Mercury,[2] who like a secretary used to write the records of his victories in his wars and excursions, blackened his face, after this calamity, with the ink of his ink-stand, and made a robe of paper for himself with the leaves of his own records. The bright moon in the shape of a very thin crescent on the horizon, on that day of world-upheaval, was striking its head on the wall and performing all the customary mourning duties.

Verse.

Thou placest thy face in the dust, alas! I do not wish thee thus
Oh moon of my life! I do not wish thee to be under the ground;
If thou goest a-hunting thy dust is my life:
Thy companionship is pleasant for me. I do not wish thee thus.

May the Great and Holy God, raise the pure and saintly soul of that victorious Prince to a higher position, and a more elevated place, and make him taste the full cup of his own beauty, greatness and glory! May every grace, kindness and favour, which he evinced towards this broken down worthless one, be the cause of his attaining a higher rank and the obliteration of errors. Amen, Oh Lord of the worlds!

The eldest son of the deceased prince received Multān in fief; and appointed heir-designate.

In short, when this intelligence reached the ears of the Sulṭān, he observed funeral ceremonies for three days and having conferred the designation of K͟husru K͟hān, and the *akṭā*· of Multān upon the eldest son of the martyred prince, appointed Malik Kajr,[3] his *locum-tenens.* Some time after, malady overcoming the Sulṭān's constitution, he appointed K͟husru K͟hān his heir-designate, made the nobles offer their homage to him,

---

1 Ṭanbūr is a kind of mandolin with chords of brass wire.

2 Mercury is called *Dabīr-i-Falak*, the scribe of the sky.

3 MBL كجر : MBM and JNS كجر .

and also ordered for the despatch of Kaiḳubād, the son of Bug͟hra K͟hān near his father to Lak͟hnauti.

The Death of the Sultān: Kaiḳubād raised to the throne.

After the Sulṭān had passed to his rest, Kajr, the deputy, addressed to the Maliks and Amīrs, "The disposition of K͟husru K͟hān is violent, if he sits on the throne he would keep alive none." Malik-ul Umra Malik,[1] the Kotwāl of Dehli, sided with him; the other Amīrs, too, co-operated with them: Malik Beg Sāoḳ,[2] Ḥasan Baṣra[3] and 'Alā' Dabir, who had been hostile to them, were removed from the country.[4] The *aḳṭā'* of Multān was conferred upon K͟husru K͟hān, and he started towards his fief with his attendants and equipage. Kaiḳubād, the son of Bug͟hra K͟hān, was raised to the throne in the year 686 H. (1287 A.D.).

Verse.

Oh heart! this worldly mansion has no permanency and stability,
Keep your hands off from the world, that has no consistency!

The period of Sulṭān G͟hiāṣ-ud-dīn's rule extended to twenty-two years, and a few months. *God knows more the real facts!*

Account of Sulṭān Mu'izz-ud-dīn Kaiḳubād.

His Accession.

Sulṭān Mu'izz-ud-dīn Kaiḳubād was the son of Bug͟hra K͟hān and the grandson of Sulṭān G͟hiāṣ-ud-dīn Balban. The observance of funeral rites having been come to a close, Mu'izz-ud-dīn ascended the imperial throne in the royal palace, in conformity to the wishes of the Amīrs, Maliks, Imāms, and Ḳāẓis in 686 H. (1287 A.D.). Every section of the people of the city made fealty to him. The new Sulṭān permitted the old officers of the State to continue in their offices, and he also appointed some new hands.

Conferment of posts on the Amirs.

Thus Malik Turki[5] became the royal chamberlain; Malik Niẓām-ud-dīn was appointed the chief justice: Malik Jāorji[6]

---

[1] MBM كوتواليک حضرت: Tab-i-Akb., Malik-ul Umra Fak͟hr-ud-dīn Kotwal.

[2] MBM سادق. [3] Barni writes (121) حضرت خواجه حسین بصري.

[4] JNS makes no mention of this event.

[5] Ẓīa Barni calls him Malik Ik͟htiar-ud-dīn Turki: Tab-i-Akb., Malik Barbak Beg Tars: Badaoni, Malik S͟hahak.

[6] MBM جاورحي: Tab-i-Akb., K͟hāroji.

received the post of the chief sword-bearer; Khwāja Khaṭīr-ud-dīn obtained the designation of Khwājā-i-Jahān.

After the expiry of six months, Sulṭān Mu'izz-ud-dīn granted public audience at Kilokhari, on a Friday.

With the object of imprisoning some of the Amīrs of the Neo-Muslims, a stratagem was devised.[1] The Amīr of Multān was ordered to send a representation stating that, owing to the advent of the accursed (Mughals) with a large army to the vicinity of Multān, he had drawn up the royal forces, and having attacked the enemies had, by the prosperity of the Emperor, driven them away. In short, after the tidings of victory was read to the people, the royal farmān emanated summoning every Amīr and Malik for offering their congratulations. With all his *entourage* ready for action, Malik Niẓām-ul Mulk posted himself on the top of the Kiosk. When the Maliks and Amīrs came (before the Sulṭān) for offering their felicitations (the following notables, such as), Malik Beg Sarak,[2] the *Amir-i-Ḥajib* (Lord Chamberlain), Malik Ghāzī, the *Vakildar*,[3] Malik Karīm-ud-dīn, the *Naib-i-Barbak*, Malik Bahrām, the *Akhur-beg*, Malik Jāorji, the chief sword-bearer, Malik Mughlati, the *Muṣallā-dār*[4] were taken prisoners. Mughlati and Jāorji were forced to leave the country; the other Amīrs were martyred.

Subsequently, Malik Shāhik was appointed *Amīr-i-Ḥājib*, and bestowed with the title of Ajbar Khān.[5] Amir 'Ali became the chief sword-bearer; Aḥmad Fakhr[6] was made the Vakildar; Malik Tamāchi received the office of the Deputy Chamberlain; Malik Turki

---

1 MBL بجهت دست اوردن بعضی امرای نو مسلمانان حیله کرد ; MBM ... نو مسلمانان حیل کرده JNS ; ...... نو مسلمانان خیل کرده

Niẓām-ud-dīn Ahmad (Tab-i-Akb. 120) states that the Chief Justice, in pursuance of the foolish thought of acquiring power and empire, devised means for the extirpation of the Balban dynasty. he deceived the young Sulṭān and obtained permission for the massacre of the Mughal Amīrs, who were all seized and slaughtered for their staunch adherence to the cause of the Sulṭān.

2 MBL ملک بیگ سارق : MBM ملک بیل سارق : JNS agrees with MBM.

Tab-i-Akb., (121), Malik Shāhbak, the feudatory of Multān.

3 The Vakildar was the officer who superintended the ceremonies of presentation.

4 Muṣallā means a pulpit or a carpet for praying upon. Muṣallā-dār, then, was the keeper of the royal carpet.

5 Badaoni Wazīr Khān.

6 Badaoni قیام الملک.

became the *'Ariẓ*. 'Ali Shāh Koh Judī and Khuram, his brother, obtained situations at the court and kindred dignity. Malik Jhaju [1] obtained Samānā in fief, and his daughter entered the royal harem. Malik Kabki became the head sword-bearer, and Malik Sha'-bān Sablik, the *Shaḥnah-i-Bārgāh*.

Advent of the infidel Tatārs under Tamar.

When order was restored in the country, the Sulṭān bent upon marching against Hindustan, halted his forces at the vicinity of Dehli on Sunday, the last day [2] of Ẓil-ḥijjah, of the aforesaid year (Feb., 1288 A.D.). Meanwhile, there came the report of the advent of a large army of the infidel Tatār [3] under their leader Tamar, [4] and of their having ravaged Lahore and Multān and imprisoning a large number of inhabitants. The Sulṭān appointed Khān-i-Jahān Shāhik Bārbak [5] at the head of three thousand cavalry to coerce the accursed insurgents. When the army of Islam (*i.e.*, the Imperialists) reached near Lahore, the accursed tribe took to their heels without any contest, and were hotly pursued so far as the hill-skirts of Jamun.[6] A great many was made food for the sword, and a large number was taken captive and despatched to the Sulṭān.

Meeting between Bughra Khān and Mu'izz-ud-dīn.

In the meantime, there came the report that, Bughrā Khān, the father of the Sulṭān, who had ascended the throne of Bengal under the title of Nāṣir-ud-dīn, was advancing against Dehli with a huge force. Sulṭān Mu'izz-ud-dīn too, having mobilized his forces from all sides of the country, made for Oudh, with the object of encountering him. As the river Saryu intervened between them, the father and the son remained encamped on either banks and none could ford the river. The Ghiāṣi Amīrs and Maliks came between the father and the son, and brought about a reconciliation between the two. Sulṭān Nāṣir-ud-dīn crossed the Saryu with his attendants and came to Oudh. Both the father and the son sat side by side, very near each other, on the same throne at

---

[1] Tab-i-Akb., Malik Jhaju: Badaoni, Malik Chhajū.

[2] The 30th of Ẓil-ḥijjah fell on Thursday and not on Sunday. See Ind. Ephemeris, IV, 178.

[3] MBL كفار تتار : MBM كفار تبار : JNS agrees with MBL. [4] Badāoni, Itīmar.

[5] According to Tab-i-Akb. and Ferishta Shāhik Barbak and Khān-i-Jahān were two different personages: but Badaoni agrees with Yaḥiya.

[6] Badaoni, Jud hills.

Chabutra Tābsi.[1] Afterwards, Sulṭān Nāṣir-ud-dīn bade farewell to his son and returned to his camp. At length, Sulṭān Mu'izz-ud-dīn made a presentation of Arabian horses, and valuable gifts to his father, and Sulṭān Nāṣir-ud-dīn, on his part, having sent in return huge elephants with litters and delicacies to his son, turned his way towards Lakhnauti. Amir Khusru, *upon him be mercy and forgiveness*, gives a complete account of the (above) incident (meeting between the father and the son) in his *Kirān-us-Sa'dain*. Sulṭān Mu'izz-ud-dīn returned and took up his residence at Kilokhari.[2]

Ajbar Khān and Malik Turki punished: Fīroz Bagrash Khilji becomes Shaist Khān.

In the year 687 H.[3] (1288–1289 A.D.), Ajbar Khān finding that he had lost the favour of the Sulṭān took his way to the Kohpayah, out of fear, and was joined by Malik Ṣalāḥ-ud-dīn, Malik Daulat Shāh, and Malik Hoshang. Malik Aitmar[4] Kujhan received the post of *Barbak* (master of ceremonies). Some time after, Ajbar Khān joined the Sulṭān at *maidān-i-Sair-gāh*,[5] where Mu'izz-ud-dīn had granted public audience. In conformity to the royal order, (when the Khān approached the royal presence) he was not greeted with "*Bismillah*", at which he was upset. A farmān was issued to Malik Kotwal ordering him to address Ajbar Khān with the following words, that he had broken the sanctity of contract and had failed to work according to the stipulation, and as such what was the proper punishment for him. The Khān remained silent. Malik Kotwal put Ajbar Khān, his sons and brothers into confinement in his (Kotwal's) house. They breathed their last in the prison. Then Malik Turki was put in chains and done away with. Fīroz Baghrash Khilji[6] became the '*Ariz-i-Mamalik* and obtained the title of Shāist Khān.

Dissipation of the Sulṭān and his illness.

The Sulṭān indulged mostly in amusements and pleasures. From extreme dissipation, extreme lasciviousness, and constant drinking he was attacked with illness.

---

1 MBL چبوترهٔ تابسی : MBM حوتره تابسی : JNS چوتره تابسي : Amir Khusrū, in his Kirān-us-Sa'dain fixes the meeting between father and son as having taken place at Ajūdhya on the banks of the Ghāgra.

2 MBL قصبهٔ كيلو كهري : JNS and MBM قصد كيلو كهري.

3 Badaoni, 689 H.

4 MBL ايتم : JNS agrees with MBL.

5 JNS ميدان سير :

6 Badaoni, Fīroz Khān bin Yaghrash Khilji.

Malik Āitmar Kujhan[1] with the other Amīrs and Maliks, resolved upon imprisoning Shaist Khān, who was a man of experience and incapable of performing any wrong action.[2] Malik Aḥmad Chap, the *Amir-i-Ḥājib* of Malik Āitmar Kujhan, and a former attendant of Shaist Khān's son, revealed the conspiracy of Āitmar Kujhan to Shaist Khān forbidding him to go to the house of the Amīrs when called for it. The Khān sent out, as his courier, his paternal uncle named Ḥajā Ḥussain to Baran; and set on foot a story to the effect that the Mughal army had found their way to Samānā, in view of which it was imperative that the Khiljis should set out with their cash, effects and necessary things at night and crossing the Jaun opposite Ghiāspur should pitch their camp there. It was his intention to secede from Dehli with all his entourage and to proceed elsewhere. He called for the presence of Malik Khamush and Malik 'Izz-ud-dīn, his brother and nephew respectively, and told them that as he was unwell they should remain with him that night. They agreed to what he said. At daybreak, Shaist Khān struck his camp at Firoz-koh, also called Bhukal-pāhāri,[3] and began to muster the army of Ḳanauj. Malik Darpi, the grantee of Ḳanauj, had also encamped near Shāist Khān: at this time, the aforesaid Āitmar deputed a messenger near them, so that they might be induced to come on the pretext that they had been invited by the king; but Shāist Khān drove him off. A second individual was despatched; in a like manner Āitmar would send persons near Shāist Khān, and the latter would refuse him admittance. Finding that Shāist Khān was not coming, and with a view to dispel his apprehension, Aitmar mounted on a horse and rode towards the Khān. The latter, too, was mounted: both made obeisance to the other. Malik Āitmar, then, enquired, "You have been summoned so many times! Why didn't you turn up?" Replied the Khān, "Some of the mounted attendants of the army

The Mughal Amirs conspire against the Khiljis.

[1] Badaoni, Malik Ḥimār Kachhan:

[2] The Mughal Omrahs headed by Aitmar Kujhan and Aitam Surkha, jealous of the power of the Khiljis, issued a proclamation proscribing the name of all the principal Khiljian officers. They conspired together to remove out of the way those nobles who were not Turks.

[3] Ferishta, Bahadoorpoor; Badaoni, Bahāpur.

of Kanauj are worn out: Malik Sa'ati intends presenting himself to the Sulṭān and accompanying his stirrups to Dehli." Down camé Āitmar from his horse, when Shāist Khān caught hold of his hands and said, "Thou art a person of such a nature that thou dost want to kill men as thou would a sheep, and throw him into the river. Thou mayest do with me whatever pleaseth you".[1] Then, he decapitated Āitmar, and placing his severed head on a spear, put it in front of the palace at Kilokhari. Malik Darpi, the chief of Kanauj, joined Shāist Khān. Meanwhile, there came Fakhr-ud-dīn, the Kotwal, and his sons for offering felicitations to the Sulṭān, on the advent of the new month. Catching sight of him, Shāist Khān had the Kotwal called and retained near him, and sent the sons to the cutcherry. Then, all the Amīrs and Maliks befriended Shāist Khān. The day following, he drew up his kindred and prepared them for action: he made Ḥisām-ud-dīn, his second son,[2] the vanguard of the forces, and drew up his men at Kilokhari in expectation of an engagement. The Ghiāṣi and Mu'izzi Amīrs and Maliks, on their part, made themselves ready for action[3] with elephants and a big army. Malik Naṣīr-ud-dīn, the keeper of the elephants, took the beasts out, and drove them towards Kilokhari. Sulṭān Mu'izz-ud-dīn, whose illness was due to drinking, could not ride on a horse: seated under the royal canopy, he was carried[4] to the top of the palace at Kilokhari by some of the attendants, such as, Kāẓī 'Alam, Amir 'Ali, and two eunuch slaves of the palace. Arjini Paik[5], one of the royal servants, with his men had taken his stand among the elephants, when Malik Jhaju advancing towards him, yelled out, "We wish to place him (Sulṭān Mu'izz-ud-dīn) upon a boat, and take him to Sulṭān Nāṣir-ud-dīn at Lakhnauti, and to place Prince Kaikā'ūs on the imperial throne."

As the Ghiāṣi line had come to an end, and the government and family of Balban had become extinct, Malik Nāṣir-ud-dīn, Arjini

---

[1] MBM omits و در آب مي اندازيد اين چنين بر من مي خواهيد بكنيد :

[2] MBM پسر ما يكى : MBL, JNS پسر ميانگي :

[3] MBM جنگ بيرون امدند : MBL مستعد جنگ آمدند : JNS مستعد جنگ برون آمدند.

[4] MBM برداشت : JNS agrees with MBM : MBL برداشته :

[5] MBL بايک :

Paik and the other Amīrs withdrew the elephants and the forces from the court. Finding an opportunity, S̱hāist Ḵẖān put his son Ḥisām-ud-dīn at the head of five hundred horsemen and despatched him to the palace. He (S̱hāist Ḵẖān) placed Prince Kaikā'ūs, the son of Sulṭān Mu'izz-ud-dīn, on his lap and brought him outside (the palace); he then took this Prince to Chabutra Sijāni [1] and placed him on the throne. Further, he appointed Malik Ḥasīn, his own cousin, to keep a watch over the (new) Sulṭān in the palace at Kilokhari. S̱hāist Ḵẖān, then, turned towards Malik Jhaju, and addressed him thus, "This Prince is like a son to you; he has become the Sulṭān, be you his representative: let me have the districts from Multān and Tabarhindah to Dibalpur,[2] so that I may depart this very moment." Jhaju answered thus, "The vizirate and the vice-regency will suit you best; let me have the fief of Karah so that I may go there".

Prince Kaikā'ūs placed on the throne.

Fakẖr-ud-dīn, the Kotwal, turned himself to S̱hāist Ḵẖān and said, "The Just and Great God has created you for abundant wealth. Do what Malik Jhaju says". Afterwards [3] S̱hāist Ḵẖān presented Jhaju with a robe of honour and sent him to Karah.[4] The royal court was, by the Ḵẖān's order, established at Siri.[5] The Prince was seated in the court, while S̱hāist Ḵẖān took his position at the parties. The imperial army was encamped there. Next day, Sulṭān Mu'izz-ud-dīn, who had taken his seat in the court, was made a prisoner.[6] Dying out of thirst and hunger, Sulṭān Mu'izz-ud-dīn wrote the following lines on the occasion:

Verse.

The horse of my excellence [7] is standing on the plain.
The hand of my generosity is under an anvil,

---

1 MBL سیجاني : MBM, JNS سبحاني : Tab-i-Akb., "Nasiri Chabutra".

2 MBL سیالپور : MBM and JNS دیبالپور :

3 MBM omits بعده.

4 MBL کوه : JNS, MBM کره.

5 MBM در سیر : JNS سری : MBL سیري.

6 Nizām-ud-dīn Aḥmad, Badaoni and Ferishta opine that the Sulṭān was done to death by the hired assassins.

7 MBM اسپ هژبر : MBL and JNS اسپ هنرم.

My eyes that never beheld less than gold mines and jewels,[1]
Come, and see, how much is it perplexed to-day![2]

This event took place on the 19th Muḥarram, 689 H.[3] (Wednesday, 1st Feb., 1290 A.D.). Sulṭān Mu'izz-ud-dīn's rule lasted for three years and a few months!

God knows more the real facts!

An account of Sulṭān Shams-ud-dīn Kaikā'ūs.

Sulṭān Shams-ud-dīn Kaikā'ūs was the son of Sulṭān Mu'izz-ud-dīn Kaikubād. When Sulṭān Mu'izz-ud-dīn attained martyrdom in the palace at Kilokhari, Sulṭān Shams-ud-dīn, his son, was raised to the throne in the year 689 H. (1290 A.D.) at the Chabutra Sijāni.[4]

Kaikā'ūs raised to the throne.

Shāist Khān became his deputy, and it was during the period of deputyship that the country acquired stability[5] in course of three months.

Shāist Khān, his vice-regent.

On the expiry of three months, Malik Āitam Surkha and some of the Ghiāsi slaves made an attempt to liberate Sulṭān Shams-ud-dīn from the control of Shāist Khān, and also to assassinate the latter. With this object in view, they sent a manifesto to Malik Baktab,[6] the Deputy Amīr-i-Ḥajib; the latter held out insincere hopes,[7] and asked them to wait till he was ready. In the *interim* he mounted a horse, and going near Shāist Khān, informed him of their treacherous plots;[8] immediately, the Khān sent out his son Ḥisām-ud-dīn with a few horse, in all haste, to the court of the Sulṭān in order to carry him over. When the Sulṭān was brought near Shāist Khān, Aitam Surkha and the other attend-

The Ghiāsi slaves attempt to kill Shāist Khān.

---

1 MBL کان گهر کم کردیدی : JNS and MBM کان گهر کم دیدی.

2 JNS امروز بیابان چه حیران مانده است . MBM امروز بتانان : MBL امروز بیابیین : Badaoni, امروز برای نان.

3 Ferishta gives 687 H. Badaoni agrees with Yaḥiya: MBL omits Muḥarram:

4 MBM صبجاني : MBL سیجاني : JNS agrees with MBL.

5 MBL ملک بد تدار خیش بماند : MBM reads نماند instead of بماند : JNS agrees with MBL.

6 JNS بکتره.

7 MBM ایشان را زبان فریب داد : MBL بزبان فریب : JNS agrees with MBL.

8 MBL omits و از مکر ایشان اعلام داد : JNS and MBM retain it.

ants, getting scent of this, set out in pursuit of the Sulṭān with their arms concealed. Approaching Shāist Khān, they drew out their weapons and entered into a conflict; they did not allow Shāist Khān and the Khiljis to take to their horses. Malik Ikhtiār-ud-dīn, the eldest son of Shāist Khān, fell from his horse, when Malik Aitam Surkha dealt upon him two or three blows of the sword, none of which was effective. Malik Ikhtiār-ud-dīn drew out his bow and discharged a fatal shot at Aitam. The deceased's head was placed on a spear. The following lines have been written in this connection :

Verse.

The prince who set the country in order by his wisdom,
Discharged an arrow, and put an end to the enemy :
In the dynasty of Malik Shāh there was danger [1] that day,
That very house did he save that day with a single arrow!

When Aitam Surkha was killed there appeared disunanimity in the rank. Meanwhile, Shāist Khān placed Sulṭān Shams-ud-dīn on a horse, and having taken him to the palace at Kilokhari, confined him there. He, then, ascended the throne; Sulṭān Shams-ud-dīn died while a prisoner.

Verse.

The drink of the heaven is tasteless,
The work of the world is jugglery!

Sulṭān Shams-ud-dīn Kaikā'ūs' rule extended for three months and a few days. *God knows more the real facts!*

THE HOUSE OF KHILJI.

The account of Sulṭān Jalāl-ud-dīn Firoz Shāh.

Sulṭān Jalāl-ud-dīn Firoz Shāh was the son of Baghrash Khilji.[2]

Accession of Jalāl-ud-dīn.

When the rebellion of Aitam Surkha was put down, and Sulṭān Shams-ud-dīn was confined

---

[1] JNS در خانه ملک شاه خلف بود آن روز : MBL, MBM خلل بود instead of خلف بود.

[2] Nizām-ud-dīn Aḥmad following other authoritative histories, such as, *Tabakaṭ-i-Maḥmud shāhi* of Ḥakim Kirmānī Jaunpuri, is of opinion that the tribe of Khalj were the descendants of Kālij Khān, son-in-law of Chingiz Khān. Kālij became Khālij by a change of letter, and by frequency of use became Khalj. But Badaoni

in prison, Sulṯān Jalāl-ud-dīn seated himself[1] on the throne in the palace at Kilokhari with the acquiescence of the Amīrs and Maliks, in the month of Rabiʿ-ul-Āḵẖīr, of the same year (689 H., April-May, 1290 A.D.).[2]

Conferment of titles and posts on the Nobles.

He entrusted to his own relatives most of the affairs and business of the State. His eldest son received the title of *Ḵẖān-i-Ḵẖānān*, and the districts near about (Dehli) in fief: his second and third sons were designated Arkalī Ḵẖān[3] and Ḳadr Ḵẖān respectively. Malik Hasīn, the Sulṯān's uncle, received the title of Tāj-ul-Mulk: Malik Ḵẖamaush obtained the post of *ʿAriẕ-i-Mamalik*; Malik Naṣīr-ud-dīn Baḳbaḳ became *Amir-i-Ḥajib*; Malik Ḵẖuram, the *Vakildar*: Malik Baktat,[4] the *Deputy*[5] *Amir-i-Ḥajib*; Malik Ikẖtiār-ud-dīn Hindu Ḵẖān Gẖiāṣi, the *Deputy Vakildar*; Malik Naṣīr-ud-dīn Kohrāmi, the *Ḵẖās Ḥājib*; Malik ʿAz-ud-dīn, the (Sulṯān's) nephew (brother's son), the *Ḳurbeg*[6]*-i-Maimna*; Malik ʿAuẕ *Ḳurbeg-i-Maisrā*; Malik Aḥmad Chap,[7] the *Sar-i-Jāndār-i-Maimnā*; Malik Hurnamār, the *Sar-i-jāndār-i-Maisrā*: Malik ʿAlā'-ud-dīn, the son of Sulṯān's brother, the *Aḵẖurbeg-i-Maimnā*; Malik Ataji,[8] the *Aḵẖurbeg-i-Maisrā*; Ḵẖwāja Ḵẖaṯīr-ud-dīn became Ḵẖwāja-i-Jahān; Kamāl-ud-dīn Kāfuri, the *Naib-i-ʿāriẕ*; Fakẖr-ud-dīn Kuji received the office of *Dad-begī*: Asad-ud-dīn[9] Waḳim,[10] became the *Sahm-ul-Ḥasẖm* and *Shamlah' Ḥasẖm*.[11]

---

says that "this ancestry has no real authority" and as a matter of fact there is no connection whatever between Kālīj and Ḵẖalj. "In some histories it is said that Ḵẖalj is the name of one of the sons of Yāfiṣ (Japhet), the son of Noah, and that Ḵẖiljis descended from him."

1 Ferishta writes that he was 70 years old when he came to the throne. He changed the colour of the royal umbrella from red to white: built a new town opposite to the Muʿizzi palace, and called it "the Rocky citadel," and Sẖahr-i-naū (new town).

2 Acc. to Tab-i-Akb. Firoz ascended the throne in 688 H. Ferishta, 687 H.; Badaoni, 689 H. Ẓia Barni, 689 H. Amir Khusru, 689 H.

3 MBM ازكلي خان: MBL and JNS Arkali Ḵẖān.

4 MBM بكنت: JNS بكنت.

5 MBM omits *Naib*: JNS omits "Deputy".

6 JNS قربيک

7 JNS احمد جب.

8 MBM اماجي: JNS ملک اجاجي.

9 MBL Asẖad.

10 MBM و قسم: JNS agrees with MBM.

11 MBM omits و شملة حشم.

in the month of Sha'bān of the above year (689 H. Aug. Sep. 1290 A.D.), Malik Jhaju[1] raised the standard of insurrection at Karah.[2] Amir 'Ali, the *Sar-i-Jāndār* and the grantee of Oudh, and the Amīrs of Hindustan sided with him. Some of the Jalāli Amirs, who held fiefs towards the Hindustan, such as, Malik Tāj-ud-dīn Kujī, Malik Muḥammad Kutlugh Khān, Malik Naṣrat,[3] the *Saḥnah-i-Bārgāh*, Malik 'Ali Beg and Malik Ḳibrān, all assembled at Kark.[4] When the aforesaid Amīrs marched against Dehli, Malik Alb Ghāzī[5] the feoffee of Kark, and Malik Bahadur remained at Kark. The above Amīrs deputed Malik Siliḳ[6] near those two nobles for enquiring of them the reason of their delay in co-operating with the rebels. Malik Alb Ghāzī and Bahadur caught hold of Siliḳ and struck off his head. They, then, addressed the (recalcitrant) Amīrs in the following terms, "Being Ghiāṣī slaves, we intend marching against Jhaju." They left Karḳ for Badāōn, and from thence having forded the Ganges, they reached Bijlānā where they drew up their forces, and awaited in hourly expectation of Jhaju's arrival.

The rebellion of Malik Jhaju.

When this intelligence reached the Sulṭān, he left Dehli in charge of Khān-i-Khānān, and dividing his forces into two halves, he placed the one under his son Arkali Khān, whom he sent towards Amroha,[7] while the other, he personally led to Kol and Badāōn. Malik Jhaju came from Kābar; and Arkali Khān marched towards Jobād.[8]

The Imperialists marched against Jhaju.

The two forces faced each other on the bank of Rahab,[9] and the fight commenced. After the fight had continued for some days,[10] there appeared before Jhaju a certain individual, Piram Deo Kotla[11] by name, who having related to him (Jhaju

Imperialists meet Jhaju: the latter's flight.

---

1 Ẓia Barni-Malik Chhaju.

2 MBM در کوه.

3 MBM قتلغخان نصرة.

4 MBM and JNS کیرک.

5 MBM البغاری : JNS agrees with MBM.

6 MBM سلبق : JNS agrees with MBM.

7 MBM امروة : JNS, MBL امروهه.

8 MBL در جو باد رفت : MBM در حواله رفت : JNS agrees with MBM.

9 MBL آب وهب : MBM, JNS رهپ : Badaoni, Rahab.

10 JNS, MBM چند مبا روز جنگ قایم ماند : MBL چنانکه قایم ماندند.

11 JNS بیوم دیو و ملک : MBM بیوم دیو کویله و ملک : MBL بیرم دیو کوتله بر ملک جهجو آمدة.

how the Sulṭān Jalāl-ud-dīn Fīroz was advancing in the rear, advised him to take recourse to flight; (whereupon), Malik Jhajū lost all powers of resisting the enemy, and made a precipitate retreat during the night. At day break, Arkali Khān having crossed the river, ran after him and sent Bhim Deo[1] to hell: Alab Ghāzi, was slain; and Malik Mas'ud Akhurbeg and Malik Muḥammad[2] Balban were put in chains. Arkali Khān received in fief the vicinity of Anhari Kithor,[3] and Malik 'Alā'-ud-dīn obtained Karah. Almās Beg became Akhurbeg: The Sulṭān turned his way to the capital.

The Sulṭān marched to Sannām.

Subsequently, the Sulṭān directed his forces towards Sannām, against 'Abdullāh Bachcha, the prince of Khorāsān,[4] who had, with a large army made his appearance there. In the conflict that took place between the two forces, there was a heavy death roll on both sides, but the fight continued without any cessation. At length, peace was effected, and both sent enormous presents to the other. 'Abdullāh made his way towards Khorāsān, and the Sulṭān to the capital.

Death of Khān-i-Khānān. Sulṭān marched to Mandwar.

Meanwhile, Khān-i-Khānān fell victim to a disease and breathed his last. Arkali Khān came to Dehli from Multān, and the Sulṭān having left the Khān at the capital,[5] proceeded to Mandwar. It was the evening prayer-time when His Majesty reached his destination.

Malik Fakhr-ud-dīn Kujī informed the Sulṭān that Malik Mughlati, his (Fakhr-ud-dīn's) brother Tāj-ud-dīn Kujī, Harnumar, Malik Mubarak, the *Shikār-beg-i-Ghiāsi*, had thought of rebellion. The Sulṭān was vigilant that night: at day-break, he granted public audience, when every Amīr and Malik came to pay their respects to him. Turning towards Mughlati, the Sulṭān addressed him thus, "The Great and Holy God has not conferred upon me

---

1 JNS. MBM بهليم ديو : MBL بهيم ديو .

2 MBM omits Muḥammad: JNS, MBL retain it.

3 MBM ابهري كسينهور , JNS ابهري : Badaoni, Kasamkūr (or Shamsābād).

4 MBM omits خراسان : JNS and MBL retain it.

5 MBM در دهلي : MBL بدهلي : JNS agrees with MBM.

the territory through your help: however dost thou try, it would not go away from me. What wrong have I done to thee that thou hast rebelled in this way?" Then, the Sulṭān bestowed upon him Badāōn in fief, and rewarding him with a robe of honour, bade him farewell. Malik Mubārak received Tabarhindâh; the office of *Sar-i-jāndār* was taken away from Harnumar and given over to Malik Bughra Kandāli.[1] Afterwards, the fortress of Mandwar was conquered: and the Sulṭān, with successive marches, reached the capital. Reaching the palace at Kilokhari, he arranged for merry-making for a day, and having taken his seat among some of his slaves he caused the following two quatrains to be composed:—

Conquest of Mandwar.

Verse.

I wish not thy afflicted ringlets to be entangled,
I like not that pomegranate-face[2] of thine be dried up:[3]
For a night I like to have thee bereft of skirts on my lap,
Yea, I utter this in voice loud, and wish it not be concealed![4]

Some time after, on another occasion, Malik Algho made a slanderous report (to the Sulṭān) against Sidi Moulah[5] stating that every Amir and Malik had joined with him (the Moulah), and advising His Majesty to put in

Sidi Moulah.

---

[1] MBM كنداني : JNS كندابي.

[2] MBM گلنارين : JNS كلناران : MBL گلنارت.

[3] JNS پرمرده : MBM تبسيده : MBL تفشيده.

[4] MBM بوميده : MBL, JNS پوشيده.

[5] Nizām-ud-dīn, Badaoni and Ferishta give the following introductory account of the Moulah: Sidi Moulah, a darwesh, appeared in Dehli and settled down there. He opened the doors of charity and alms-giving to the poor. His lavish doles and unrestrained expenses caused no small wonder among the people, who attributed their source to the Darwesh's familiarity with alchemy and natural magic. Most of the Amirs and Maliks became his disciples and close friends. People began to apprehend that he wanted to seize the country by the help and assistance of these people.

Ferishta relates how one Ḳāẓī Jalāl-ud-dīn Kāshānī, who was in confidence of the Moulah, began to inspire the latter with views of ambition. The Darwesh, to his misfortune, assumed a tone and manner indicative of his design on the throne. The Moulah engaged Mir Mohsun Kotwal and Nutty Pyhlwan two of his persons to join the king's retinue on Friday, as he went to the public mosque, and to assassinate him.

chains, Sidi Moulah, Ḳāẓī Sheikh Jalāl-ud-dīn Kāshāni,[1] his sons, Malik Tatār, Malik Lanki,[2] Malik Hindu, the son of Tari'y,[3] Malik Az-ud-dīn Bughān Khān and Hāthia Babak.[4] They were captured and placed in confinement.

Subsequently, on the third day, during the Friday prayers, the prominent people of Dehli were summoned before the Sulṭān. A sitting accommodation was provided in the palace, and the Emperor was seated on a raised platform.[5] Sidi Moulah, and the other Amīrs appeared before the Sulṭān, when the latter turned towards the Moulah and accosted him thus, "Why should a darwesh make himself busy[6] with the affairs of the empire, or the business of the realm?" The Sheikh replied that the charge had been maliciously attributed to him.

The Sulṭān, then, turned towards Ḳāẓī Jalāl-ud-dīn,[7] and said, "One who is intelligent and a man of eminence is raised to the rank of a Ḳāẓī; how could you think of rising to a greater dignity than this?"[8] Replied the Ḳāẓī, "This is a false accusation; by God! this is a false indictment that is being made against me by Malik Yaûm-ud-dīn: I am innocent!"

The Sulṭān flew into rage and commanded Sahm-ul-Ḥashm to make an end of Hāthia Babak with a mace. The son of Tari'y was thrown at the feet of an elephant. Then, Amīr Hindu was called upon to appear before the Sulṭān, who interrogated him thus, "I had once excused thee for thy insurrection. What dost thou say now?" Thus answered Amīr, "What your Majesty observeth is quite true: when I once thought of rebellion your Highness was pleased to pardon me."

---

1 MBM كليساني : JNS agrees with MBM.

2 MBM كنكي : JNS كنكر.

3 MBM پسر نوعي : JNS ترغي : Barni طرغي.

4 JNS بابک.

5 MBL در سرای محضر ساختند سلطان در منظر نشسته بود · MBM ساختند...... در منتظر... : JNS agrees with MBM.

6 MBL چه سرد : MBM and JNS چه گرز.

7 MBM Ḳāẓī Jalāl.

8 JNS چون دانشمندي بزرک شود قضا باید تو ازین بزرک چه خواستی شدن : MBM دانشمندی : MBL دانشمند : MBM بزرک چه خو حواستي شدن : MBL خواهي شدن.

Verse.[1]

"So that, kings who bestow gold and silver in charity might learn,
It's the custom of Firoz Shāh, the refuge of the Sulṭāns, to bestow life!"

"In the name of the Most High Allah, now, for no sin, I am going to be sentenced to death. If your Majesty condescends, I might defend my cause."

The Sulṭān, then, turned to the Darweshes[2] and exclaimed, "Why dost thou not avenge me on Sidi Moulah!" Two Kalandar slaves and one Ḥaidari jumped forward and whipped out their razors; then, having shaved off the pure-souled Siddi's whiskers up to the chin, stabbed him in the side with the sack-maker's needles. When Sidi Moulah fell down, they struck his head with stony beads that lay scattered. Then, Arkali Khān signed to his elephant-driver to drive the elephant over the Moulah. The elephant ran over him and tore him to pieces.[3] Tradition goes, that a month prior to this incident, that pure-souled and generous dispositioned Sheikh, *on whom be mercy and forgiveness*, used to hum the following verses, day and night:—

Verse.

None but the excellent are slaughtered in the kitchen of love;
The lean, the old and the ugly they kill not.
Flee not, Oh! sincere lover! from slaughter,
He whom they slay not is no better than a corpse!

The others, by the royal order, were removed.

Three days after the occurrence narrated above, a pit,—in length about 10 *gaz* and in width 3—was dug out: in it a great fire was kindled for throwing into it the remaining adherents of the Moulah. Placing the turban round his neck, Arkali Khān interposed on their behalf, and caught hold of the Sulṭān's legs. His Majesty showed compassion on them.

---

[1] Excepting MBL, MBM, and JNS have no mention of this verse.

[2] Tab-i-Akb. writes, "The Sulṭān then turned to Sheikh Abu Bakr Tusi Ḥaidari, the chief of the Ḥaidari Kalandars". Badaoni supports Tab-i-Akb.

[3] MBL adds after this, و سیدی استغفار می کرد : JNS and MBM omit it.

[4] MBL مرد مردان : JNS مردار بود : MBM مرد مردار مرد .

The Sulṭān marched to Rantambor.

Subsequently, the Sulṭān marched his troops towards Rantambor.[1] Arkali Khān[2] left for Multān without taking leave of the king. For the reason that Malik 'Alā'-ud-dīn, the feoffee of Karah, had gone to his abode[3] the Sulṭān became excessively discomposed and uneasy. He encamped himself at Kālpur[4] and built a platform and a lofty cupola with the following verse, a composition of his own,[5] inscribed on it :—

---

1 Tab-i-Akb. writes 689 H., Ferishta, 690 H., Tab-i-Akb. relates, in detail, the incidents of the expedition: The Sulṭān seized Jhain (Ujjein), destroyed the temples and carried away much booty. Being unwilling to entail the curse of widows and the orphans upon him, he gave up the seige.

Tab-i-Akb., Badaoni, and Ferishta make reference to the following incidents :—

(a) In the year 691 H. (1292 A.D.) the Mughals invaded Hindustan with a large army. The Sulṭān set out to repel them. After several skirmishes, the Mughals commenced negotiations. Gifts and presents were exchanged between the parties. Alghu, the grandson of Chengiz Khān, with some Mughal noblemen, became Musalmans. Ghiāṣpur (later changed to Mughalpur) was assigned to them for their residence. The Mughals got the name of the Neo-Muslims: Alghu was honoured with the hand of one of the Sulṭān's daughters.

(b) At the end of the year 691 H. (Acc. to Ferishta, 692 H.) the Sulṭān marched against Mandu (Badaoni, Mandwar), and having devastated the country returned to Dehli.

(c) About the same time, Malik 'Alā'-ud-dīn, the nephew of the Sulṭān, having obtained leave, marched against Bhilsah, pillaged the country and returned with much spoil. Two brass idols brought from those parts, were cast down in front of the Badāōn gate to be trampled upon by the people. For this glorious achievement the Sulṭān raised 'Alā'-ud-dīn to a higher rank, and gave him Oudh as an additional fief. 'Alā'-ud-dīn then submitted a representation asking for permission to enlist fresh troops, so that he might invade Chanderi, a land full of riches. The object of 'Alā'-ud-dīn had been to establish an independent power. Accordingly, after taking leave of the Sulṭān at Dehli, 'Alā'-ud-dīn went to Karah, where leaving Malik 'Alā'-ul-Mulk as his deputy in Karah and Oudh he marched towards Deogīr on pretence of going to Chanderi. He marched through Elichpur. Ramdeo, the ruler of Deogīr, with a large force opposed 'Alā'-ud-dīn, who routed him and conquered Deogīr.

2 He had been left at Kilokhari to manage the affairs of the kingdom in the Sulṭān's absence.

3 MBM جائي بود رفته : JNS, MBL جائي رفته بود.

4 MBL كالبور : JNS كالبور : MBM كالپور.

5 JNS and MBM از انشای خود : MBL adds خاص before خود.

Verse.

I whose foot-steps rub[1] the head of heaven,
How can a heap of stone and earth augment my dignity ?[2]
Those broken stones with water I have thus arranged,[3]
Some broken heart may find repose there.

The Sulṭān summoned Malik Sa'iyid Muntaḳi and Rājā 'Ali and enquired, "Is there any defect in the quatrain ?" With one voice they replied in the negative adding that it was quite agreeable. Answered His Majesty, "You say all this in order to humour me; but, I shall show you its defect by the following two couplets;" then, he composed the following *Rubai'ay*[4]:—

Perchance some traveller may pass by this spot[5]
Whose tattered garment is the satin mantle[6] of the sky ;
Perchance from the felicity of his breath or auspicious footsteps
One atom may fall to my lot: this will suffice me.

'Alā'-ud-dīn marched against Deogir and sacked it.

Subsequently, intelligence arrived that Malik 'Alā'-ud-dīn had gone to Deogīr, and having sacked the place and securing a rich booty, numerous elephants and horses had marched back to Karah. The Sulṭān found his way back to Dehli,[7] and deputed Malik 'Imād-ul-Mulk and Ẕiā-ud-dīn, the Mushrif, to Malik 'Alā'-ud-dīn. Malik 'Alā'-ud-dīn confined them, and spread a false

---

[1] MBL سايد : MBM and JNS شايد.

[2] JNS, MBL چه قدر افزايد : MBM چه دور افزايد.

[3] MBM and JNS نهاديم درست : MBL بنهادم دست.

[4] A verse of four hemistiches.

[5] MBL درين جا گذر كس باشد : MBM and JNS درين خاكدرس شد كس.

[6] چرخ اطليس : The highest of all the heavens is called اطليس because it has no stars. The literal meaning of اطلس is "worn out". Its secondary meaning is "satin".

[7] Tab i-Akb., Badaoni, and Ferishta relate that the king having one day assembled his council requested their advice what would be prudent for him to do under the circumstances. Malik Aḥmad Chap advised the king to advance with his army towards Chanderi, and encamp on the road along which lay 'Alā'-ud-dīn's route to Karah. Fakhr-ud-dīn Kūjī, perceiving that the Sulṭān was opposed to this advice, advised him to wait till 'Alā'-ud-dīn should arrive at Karah, and if it should then appear that he cherished treasonable views one assault of the king's forces would put an end to his ambition. The king adopted the advice of Kūjī, and marched back to Dehli.

report to the effect that he was fleeing away from the Sulṭān, and making his way towards Lakhnauti. Malik Rīhān sent a memorial to the Sulṭān stating that Malik 'Alā'-ud-dīn was panic-stricken, and that he had implored help from him. Muḥammad Khiṭāb, who having fled from Malik 'Alā'-ud-dīn had joined with Ḳadr Khān, should be imprisoned and be handed over to 'Alā'-ud-dīn, unless[1] he (Khitāb) solicits help from the latter.

The Sulṭān marched to Karah.

When this representation reached the Sulṭān, he proceeded by river and ordered his army to proceed along the banks. When the Sulṭān reached Karah, Malik 'Alā'-ud-dīn sent Almās Beg to attend on His Majesty with a large amount of jewels that had been secured during the sack of Deogīr. Thus enquired the Sulṭān, "Why is it that Malik 'Alā'-ud-dīn is not coming?" Almās represented, "He is afraid and intends proceeding to Lakhnauti. If your Majesty wills that the Malik should have no apprehension you should personally proceed and bring him."[2] The Amīrs and Malik withheld their consent to this proposal. Paying no heed to their advice, His Majesty accompanied by some of his select attendants, such as Khuram, the Vakildar, Malik Fakhr-ud-dīn Kujī, Malik 'Auẓ Kurbek, Malik Jamāl-ud-dīn Abu-l M'ālī, Naṣir-ud-dīn Kuhramī, Ikhtiār-ud-dīn, the Deputy Vakildar and Turmati, the *ṭasht-dār*, crossed the Ganges during the afternoon prayers. It was here, on the bank of the river, that arrangements had been made for the Sulṭān's halt; and the Sulṭān took up his quarters there. Malik 'Alā'-ud-dīn went near him with a large following, and fell at the feet of the Sulṭān, of pure morals. Out of excessive affection, the Sulṭān placed his hands on the beards of 'Alā'-ud-dīn and kissing him addressed, "I am like a father to thee; have I reared thee up for so many years in order that thou should'st flee away from me in fear." Malik 'Alā'-ud-dīn held the hands of the Sulṭān.

Maḥmud Sālim, the silāḥdār,[3] whipped out his dagger and

---

[1] MBL تا مکر : JNS agrees with MBL.

[2] Niẓām-ud-dīn, and Badaoni relate how Almās had strict orders to use all the means he could devise and all the craft he could command to separate the Sulṭān from his army and bring him to 'Alā'-ud-dīn.

[3] MBL سالم بلید صردار : JNS, MBM سالم سلاحدار :

stabbed the Sulṭān, who died[1] after a few strokes.[2] They placed the head of the murdered king on a lance;[3] the other Amīrs having received wounds, ran towards the boats. Malik 'Alā'-ud-dīn hastened forward and got hold of the bow strings; most (of the royal attendants) threw themselves into the river and got themselves drowned. Malik Fakhr-ud-dīn Kūjī was taken prisoner. Malik 'Alā'-ud-dīn proclaimed himself Emperor. Malik Aḥmad Chap led the imperial forces to Dehli near Ḳadr Khān. As Arkali Khān, the second son of the deceased Sulṭān, who was worthy of the sovereignty, committed delay in setting out from Multān, (the Amīrs) placed Rukn-ud-dīn Ḳadr Khān on the throne with the title of Sulṭān Rukn-ud-dīn Ibrāhim Shāh. Most of the Amīrs and Maliks of Dehli paid him their homage.

Jalāl-ud-dīn murdered.

'Alā'-ud-dīn proclaimed himself Emperor.

Accession of Sulṭān Ibrahim Shāh on the throne at Dehli.

Subsequently, Malik 'Alā'-ud-dīn advanced towards Dehli with successive marches. At every stage of his journey he scattered gold over the soldiery:[4] accordingly, the people joined him from all sides. Reaching the banks of the Jaūn, he placed a ballista and a sling there and hurled gold out of it. The Amīrs of Dehli sent him their promise (of co-operation) and made fealty, and almost every day two or more Maliks deserted their side for 'Alā'-ud-dīn.

'Alā'-ud-dīn marches towards Dehli and scatters gold.

Being informed of this, Sulṭān Rukn-ud-dīn lost all power of opposition and took the road to Multān near Arkali Khān, in company with Malik Ḳuṭub-ud-dīn, Malik Aḥmad Chap and Bughrā Gilānī.

Rukn-ud-dīn's flight to Multān.

---

1 Acc. to Badaoni the massacre of the Sulṭān took place on the 17th Ramẓān, 694 H. (Sunday, 31st July, 1295 A.D.).

2 Badaoni writes that on receiving the wound from Salīm, the Sulṭān made for the boat, but Ikhtiār-ud-dīn inflicted a second wound which killed the Sulṭān.

3 The head of the Sulṭān was carried round Karah and Manickpur, and taken to Oudh.

4 MBM اجھوما زد: JNS, and MBL اجھوما زر لشکر را میداد: Ẓia Barni relates that at every stage that they marched, five *mans* of gold stars were discharged among the spectators from the front of the royal tent.

Next day, Malik 'Alā'-ud-dīn went across the Jāūn, and took up his quarters at Siri, ascending the throne, three days later, on the 19th Ẓil-ḥijjāh, 695 H. (Thursday, the 18th Oct. 1296 A.D.).[1]

Accession of 'Alā'-ud-dīn to the throne.

Verse.

Hast thou seen the acts of the tyrant-heaven and its star,
Mention it not: what is the heaven, its revolution, or its arched vaults.
How has it cast the sun of the kingdom into the dust!
Let dust be on the head of its sun of glory!

The deceased Sulṭān Jalāl-ud-dīn ruled for seven years and a few months. *God knows more the real facts!*[2]

An account of Sulṭān 'Alā'-ud-dīn[3] Muḥammad Shāh.

Sulṭān 'Alā'-ud-dīn Muḥammad Shāh was the son of Malik Shahāb-ud-dīn Khilji.[4] When Sulṭān Rukn-ud-dīn had left for Multān, ('Alā'-ud-dīn) ascended the throne at the imperial palace, with the consent of the Amīrs and Maliks, on the 22nd Ẓil-ḥijjah, of the aforesaid year (695 H.).[5]

Accession of 'Alā'-ud-dīn, Sunday, the 21st Oct. 1296 A.D.

The Sulṭān went to the Ruby Kiosk, and bestowed suitable titles and posts upon every one, e.g., Almās Beg, the Sulṭān's brother, was raised to the dignity of *Amīr-i-Ḥajib-i-Barbak*, and he received the designation of Ulugh Khān; Malik Harnumār became the *vakildar*; Amīn Khān and Malik Suneḥ became Nakṣh Khān; and Malik Amāji became Arslān Khān. The *akṭā'* of Sāmāna was conferred upon Arslān Khān; Yusuf, the sister's son (of the Sulṭān) became

Bestowal of titles and posts on Amirs.

---

[1] MBL adds ابن رباعي مي گفت : JNS and MBL omit it.

[2] MBL and JNS الله علم با الصواب : MBM بالصواب و اليه المرجع و المآب.

[3] JNS علاء الدين علاء الدولة.

[4] JNS omits this line. It simply writes—علاء الدين علاء الدولة كه برادر زادهٔ سلطان جلال الدين خلجي بود.

[5] Ferishta says "in the latter end of the year 696 H.". Badaoni gives 29th Ẓil-ḥijjah 695 H. Amir Khusru, in his Tārikḥ-i-'Alāī, states that the accession took place on 16th Ramẓān 695 H. Ẓia Barni gives no date, but mentions the year only (695 H.).

Z̲afar K̲h̲ān; Sanjar Ḥarbun received the title of Alab K̲h̲ān;[1] Sulaimān S̲h̲āh, the brother's son (of the Sulṭān) became Alab K̲h̲ān; the Sulṭān's second nephew (brother's son) was honoured with the title of Kutlug̲h̲ K̲h̲ān: Malik K̲h̲amaush became Bag̲h̲ras̲h̲ K̲h̲ān;[2] Malik Naṣrat became Naṣrat K̲h̲ān:[3] Malik Tāj-ud-dīn Kuji received the title of Tamg̲h̲āj K̲h̲ān; Fak̲h̲r-ud-dīn Kuji was honoured with the honorific, Bug̲h̲rā K̲h̲ān; Moulānā Tāj-ud-dīn obtained the office of *Sar-i-pardāh-dar.*[4]

The eyes of Arkali K̲h̲ān and Sulṭān Rukn-ud-dīn put out.

In the month of Muḥarram, 696 H. (Oct.-Nov. 1296 A.D.), Sulṭān 'Alā'-ud-dīn sent out Ulug̲h̲ K̲h̲ān and Alb K̲h̲ān to Multān[5] against Arkali K̲h̲ān and Sulṭān Rukn-ud-dīn. When they reached Multān, Arkali K̲h̲ān and Rukn-ud-dīn dared not oppose them, but shut themselves up in the citadel. The people and the inhabitants of Multān begged for protection and made overtures for peace. They caught hold of Arkali K̲h̲ān and Sulṭān Rukn-ud-dīn and brought them over to Ulug̲h̲ K̲h̲ān, who took them with him to the Sulṭān. When the party arrived at Abhuhar[6] there reached a farmān asking to draw the pencil over the eyes of the two captives, and to consign them to the Kotwāl of Hānsi. The order was obeyed. Likewise, pencils were drawn over the eyes of Aḥmad C̲h̲ap and Alg̲h̲o, and despatched to Gwalior.[7] Malik Harnumār received the *aktā'* of Multān. Ulug̲h̲ K̲h̲ān joined with His Majesty. The others who had befriended Arkali K̲h̲ān were sent to Kuhrām having their eyes put out. Arkali K̲h̲ān[8] and Arslān K̲h̲ān were removed under fetters from Sāmāna to Bahraich, where they were hanged with a bow-string round their neck. Harnumār was summoned from Multān, blinded and then sent to Uchch. The fief of Multān was bestowed upon Alb K̲h̲ān.

---

1 JNS and MBM صنجد خسر پورهٔ البطان.

2 JNS and MBL بغر شغان : MBM بغر صیغان :

3 JNS and MBM omit نصرت خان.

4 JNS میر پر دادار.

5 JNS and MBM omit در ملتان.

6 Badaoni writes "Bhuhar, a place in the vicinity of Hānsi."

7 MBM جدا کردند : MBL and JNS در گوالیر فرستادند.

8 MBM and JNS omit Arkali K̲h̲ān.

The same year[1] the accursed armies ravaged the vicinity of Manjahur.[2] The Sulṭān detached Ulugh Khān and Malik Tughluk, the Amīr of Dibalpur, with a big force to march against them. Reaching the destination, they learnt that the Mughals having sacked the place were advancing with a large booty. Ulugh Khān lay in ambush, and then attacked them. Accordingly, the accursed were defeated at the first onslaught; a large number of them took recourse to flight, and a great many taken prisoners.[3]

Appearance of the Mughals: their defeat.

On another occasion, Kutlugh Khwajāh the king of Turkistan,[4] led his forces against Hindustan. As the Mughals approached Kili, the Sulṭān deputed Ulugh Khān and Zafar Khān with a large army against them. In the conflict that took place at Kili, Zafar Khān received martyrdom; the Mughals were put to the worst. Kutlugh Khwājah retired with his men to Turkistān, and went to hell.[5]

Re-appearance of the Mughals: their second defeat.

---

1 Ẓia Barni, Tab-i Akb., and Ferishta makes reference to this invasion. Ẓia Barni places it in 696 H. and says that Ulugh Khān and Zafar Khān were sent against the Mughals. Tab-i-Akb., and Ferishta place it "in the second year of 'Alā'-ud-din's reign". Tab-i-Akb. says that Ulugh Khān and Zafar Khān were sent. Ferishta writes Aluf Khān was sent by 'Alā'-ud-dīn against Amīr Dāūd, the king of Mawar-ul-Nahr, and the leader of the Mughals.

2 Ferishta writes Siwistan: Ẓīa Barni (Bib. Ind. 250) Jālandhar: Tab-i-Akb., Jāran-mahur; Badaoni, Jārin Manjhur.

3 Ẓia Barni (*ibid.*, 251) writes that in the third year of his accession the Sulṭān sent Ulugh Khān and Nasrat Khān to invade Gujrat. Tab-i-Akb., and Ferishta are of similar opinion. But there is no mention of it in this work and Badaoni

4 MBM, JNS خراسان.

5 Our author has omitted to mention another Mughal invasion that took place prior to the Khwājah's. Ẓia Barni, Badaoni, Tab-i-Akb., and Ferishta refer to this invasion: we may look upon this invasion as the second, and the Khwājah's as the third, that took place in 'Alā'-ud-din's reign. The leader of the second invasion, acc. to the authors, was Saldi, which Briggs translates as Choldy. Badaoni places the 2nd invasion in 698 H.: Ferishta in 697 H. Tab-i-Akb. in "third year of 'Alā'-ud-dīn's reign: Badaoni makes a confusion between the first and the 2nd invasions of the Mughals, and says that Saldi was defeated at Jarin Manjhūr.

According to Ẓīa Barni, Kutlugh was the son of Naud (Ferishta, Amīr Dāūd).

Zafar Khān commanded the right wing and Ulugh Khān the left wing of the imperial army.

Mughal invasion under Targhi.

On the third occasion, Targhi,[1] one of the *Margans*[2] of that country, with about one lakh foot and 20,000 horse, brave and warlike, proceeded to Baran along the skirts of the hills.[3] Malik Fakhr-ud-dīn, the *Amīr-dād*, and the holder of Baran, shut himself up in the fortress.[4] The Sulṭān ordered off Malik Tughluk with a big detachment to Baran. On the arrival of the imperial army Malik Fakhr-ud-dīn, the *Amīr-dād*,[5] having emerged out of the citadel and joining hands with Malik Tughluk made a night-attack on the accursed (Mughals). By the help of Allah, the ill-fated army (Mughals) was put to rout and driven back. Targhi was made captive and taken to Dehli by Malik Tughluk.[6]

Mughal invasion[9] under Tartak and 'Ali Beg.

On the fourth occasion, Muhammad Tartak[7] and 'Ali Beg,[8] the princes of Khorāsān, beat up innumerable brave and intrepid recruits and divided their forces into two halves: one of these proceeded along the foot of the Sirmor hills to the bank of the Beah, and ravaged (the places); the other harried Nāgor. The Sulṭān nominated Malik Nāib,[10] his personal slave, and Malik

---

1 MBM and JNS نوعي.

2 MBL مركنان: MBM and JNS مركنان: Badaoni, "*Margans*": he explains the word as "an expert archer". It is a Turki word. See Ranking, 250, f.n. 5.

3 JNS, MBM دامن کوه کرده: MBL دامن کوه گرفته.

4 JNS مردم برن حصاري شد: MBL, MBM ملک فخر الدين امير داد مقطع برن حصاري شد.

5 JNS ملک فخر الدين امير زاده.

6 Tab-i-Akb., and Ferishta give a different version. According to them, Targhi made his return to his native country for no appreciable cause. Tab-i-Akb., suggests the two following reasons for Targhi's return: (1) the intervention of Sheikh Nizām-ud-dīn, and (2) Targhi was seized with panic. Ferishta, following Tab-i-Akb., suggests the intervention of the Sheikh to be the cause of Targhi's return. Badaoni, on the other hand, supports Yahiya and says that Targhi was taken prisoner.

Tab-i-Akb. further adds that, at the time when Targhi came to India, 'Alā'-ud-dīn was engaged in the siege of Chitor.

7 MBM تدنق: Ferishta, Khwāja Tash: Ẓīa Barni, Taryāk and Ziyāk: Tab-i-Akb., Tartak: Badaoni, Turtak.

8 Tab-i-Akb. writes 'Ali Beg was the grandson of Chengiz Khān.

9 Ferishta gives 704 H. (1304 A.D.).

10 MBL ملک نايب خود: MBM ملک نابک. JNS ملک نانک بندہ خود: Badaoni, Malik Mānick, Nāib Kāfur Hazārdināri. Ẓīa Barni and Tab-i-Akb., Malik Nāyak Akhurbeg.

Tughlak, the Amīr of Dibalpur, and ordered them off to Amrohā.[1] It so transpiring that the Mughals having secured a rich spoil[2] were advancing along the Rahab, Malik Nāib hastened forward.[3] The opposing forces met each other, when the army of Islam came off victorious. Both the princes were taken prisoners;[4] the chains and fetters that had a longing for the necks of the accursed embraced them in accordance with the (phrase), "*catch them and put them under chains*". The army of Islam put fetters round their necks and carried them off to Dehli: the booty and the beasts of burden which the Mughals had seized fell in the hands of the victors. A great many of the execrable army was made food for the remorseless[5] sword, while a large number took to their heels, defeated and perplexed.

Mughal invasion under Ikbālmandāh and Kik.

On the fifth occasion, Ikbālmandāh[6] and Kik[7] raised an army in order to revenge the death of Muhammad Tartak and 'Ali Beg, and ravaged the frontiers of Multān. On this occasion, the Mughal army was innumerable: but, as they had witnessed the victories of Sultān 'Alā'-ud-dīn[8] and had on previous occasions been defeated and worsted, they dared not advance any further. The Sultān sent Malik Nāib and Malik Tughluk against them with a large army, and before they reached their destination, the Mughals

---

[1] JNS انمروهه. [2] MBM بسدار غنایم بی شمار.

[3] ملک مانک از عقب رسید Badaoni writes : استعداد جنگ پیش اهنگ در امد.

[4] MBL - غل و زنجیر که مشتاق گردن آن ملعون بود معانقه کرد - خذوه - فغلوه
لشکر اسلام ایشان را غل در گردن کرده در حضرت آوردند

JNS and MBM omit these lines.

[5] JNS and MBM omit بی دریغ.

[6] Ẓia Barni, Badaoni, and Tab-i-Akb. agree with our author. Ferishta calls him Eibuk Khān, an officer of Amīr Dāūd Khān, ruler of Mawar-ul-Nahr; and places the invasion in 705 H

[7] Ẓīa Barni, Kank: Badaoni, Kapak: Tab-i-Akb., Kabek: Ẓīa Barni and Badaoni do not say that Ikbālmandāh was the joint leader of this expedition. According to them the leader of this invasion was Kank (Ẓia Barni) or Kabek (Tab-i-Akb.). These two writers refer to a separate invasion of the Mughals under the sole leadership of Ikbālmandāh. This invasion (Ikbālmandāh's) was the last or the eighth invasion, that took place in 'Alā'-ud-dīn's reign.

[8] JNS چون از روزی MBM : چون از لشکر فیروزی سلطان علاء الدین معاینه کرد
سلطان : MBL فیروزی سلطان.

retired after harrying the country and laying their hands on a rich booty. The two Maliks ran in their pursuit and fell upon them, taking the accursed Kīk prisoner and seizing the plunder acquired by the Mughals. Triumphant and laden with spoils of war, the army of Islam pursued its way to the capital. Ultimately, the Mughals conceived such a dread of the army of Islam that they dared not turn their faces towards Hindustan again.[1]

An incident in the convivial party of the Sulṭān.

It is said that the Sulṭān quaffed copious draughts[2] of wine, and that he would drink in company of his intimate friends. (Once) some of the assembled guests perceiving that it was getting late, made signs to each other that it was time to break up. The Sulṭān happened to perceive it, and he cried out, "Mutiny! Mutiny!!"[3] Ḳāẓī Bahā was done to death, and the rest fled away. Next morning, when the Sulṭān sent for the Ḳāẓī, he was informed that the latter had been assassinated the previous night.

Wine-drinking banned.

On that instant, the Sulṭān ordered that all the wine-vessels should be broken (to pieces) before his presence. He vowed never again to drink wine, and ordered it to be proclaimed that the sale of liquor was banned, and those who would drink wine would be incarcerated.[4]

Massacre of the Neo-Muslims.

In the year 697 H. (1297-98 A.D.), the Sulṭan became anxious to root out the newly converted Mughals.[5] At that time,[6] it so happened that some of these[7] Neo-Muslims, who were living in the city, betrayed trust, as the Sulṭān had been suspicious of them, and were

---

[1] Ẓia Barni and Nizām-ud-dīn (Tab-i-Akb.) refer to another advent of the Mughals, thirty to forty thousand strong, in the Sivalik hills. They were all imprisoned at Narainah (Barni) or Tarainah (Tab-i-Akb.). This invasion may be looked upon as the seventh of its kind.

[2] MBL شربتی : JNS شربی.

[3] MBM گفت غدر قاضي : JNS and MBL کفت غدر غدر.

[4] JNS and MBM در زندان کنند : MBL در زندان ابر کنند.

[5] JNS and MBM مغل و نو مسلمانان : MBL مغل نو مسلمانان.

[6] JNS, MBM در اثناء آن : MBL اثنای آن.

[7] JNS, MBL نو مسلمانان تني چند : MBL نو مسلمانانی چند.

kept in close confinement.[1] Their manners gave signs of malevolence, and it was so arranged by them that when His Majesty would proceed un-armed to *Sair-gâh* for hawking, and his attendants would be engaged in the sport, the Neo-Muslims would come upon the party and kill the Sultân and his followers. The spies carried this piece of news to the Auspicious King,[2] who secretly directed the feoffees of the cities and the provinces[3] and exacted from them a sincere promise to make an end of the Neo-Muslims living in the empire, so that not a single individual speaking the Mughal language[4] was left alive.

The Sultân marched against Deogir.

Afterwards, the Sultân having marched out against Hindustan, and fitted out an expedition, for the second time, against Deogir:[5] in those days, when he enjoyed the rank of an Amīr, he had conquered it and secured from the place rich booty and heavy spoils of war. He (now) established his authority in that part of the country.

Ulugh Khân sent against Gujrat 1298 A.D.

When the Holy and Great God restored order in the empire, and granted respite to the Sultân after the defeat of the ill-fated army (Mughals), the Emperor nominated Ulugh Khân[6] with a large army against Gujrat, with instructions for its annihilation,[7] in the year 698 H.[8] (1298-99 A.D.). In those days Karan Râi Gujrâtī possessed 30,000 horse, 80,000 foot and 30 elephants.[9] At the ap-

Badaoni writes that these Neo-Muslims were goaded by the extortion of the revenue collectors. Ferishta says that although no particular cause is assigned for it, the Sultân suddenly took into his head to discharge all Neo-Muslim soldiers. Some daring fellows entered into a conspiracy to murder him. The plot being discovered, some 15,000 of these unhappy wretches were killed in the streets of Dehli.

2 JNS, MBM خبر بسمع سلطان : MBL این خبر شنیع بسلطان.

3 JNS بر مقطعان بلاد ممالک MBM بر مقطعان بداد ممالک : MBL بر متعلقان بلاد ممالک.

4 MBL مغل گویان : JNS, MBM مغلی گویان.

5 Tab-i-Akb. says that Malik Nâib Kâfur Hâzâr-dinâri, along with the other Amīrs and Maliks was sent against Deogir: Ram-deo, the Deogir Raja, and his sons, who were taken prisoners to Dehli were treated with generosity and the title of *Rây-i-Râyân* was conferred upon the Râi.

6 Tab-i-Akb. says that Nasrat Khân was also sent with Ulugh.

7 JNS, MBL تا دمار از آن دیار بر ارد : MBM تا ده از ازان دبار بر ارد.

8 Ferishta gives 697 H.: Badaoni 698 H.

9 JNS and MBM سي هزار سوار و هشتاد هزار پیادهٔ و سي زنجیر پیل MBL

proach of Ulugh Khān, the Rāi, who failed to take courage in both hands, was defeated and the country sacked: the Khān captured twenty elephants,[1] and ran in pursuit of the Rāi so far as Somnāth: "owing to his ill-omened advent the temple of Somnāth was put to destruction This temple which had been the chief centre of worship of the Hindus and the Rāi-Rāyāns"[2] was levelled to dust and a Masjid was constructed in its place.

The Mughal soldiery attempt at rebellion Their failure.

Thence Ulugh Khān made his way to Dehli: reaching the vicinity of Jalwar,[3] he occupied himself with verifying the amount of property,[4] which had fallen into the hands of his people during the sack of Gujrat and of the temple. He put his soldiers under the bellows[5] and made them drink saline water. Some of the Mughals, who had accompanied Alb Khān[6] and Ulugh Khān, e.g., Yaljak,[7] Kasri, Begi,[8] Tamghān, Muhammad Shāh, Tamarbagha,[9] Shādi Bagha, Kutlugh Bagha,[10] had neither the power of opposing him, nor were they willing to give up the treasure: they receded[11] from the Khān and attempted to put him to death. Having failed in their attempt, some of them fled over to Rāi Hamir Deo of Jhāban,[12] while others fled perplexed hither and thither. Ulugh Khān then set out with successive marches to Dehli.

سي هزار سوار جرّار و هشتاد هزار پيادهٔ نامدار و سي زنجير پيل مهيب سرخ رو و كوه پيكر و عفريت هيكل داشت.

[1] Badaoni and Ferishta write that among the ladies of Rāi Karan's harem that fell into the hands of the Muslims, was one Dewal Rānī, of whom Khizr Khān, the son of Sultān 'Alā'-ud-dīn became enamoured. Mir Khusru wrote in verse—'Ashīqa—a book on Khizr Khān and Dewal Rāni.

[2] The portion within the inverted commas is to be found in MBL, and not in JNS or MBM.

[3] JNS الور : MBL, MBM جالور : Badaoni, Alwar.

[4] JNS لالي ها : MBL, MBM اموالی.

[5] JNS, MBM ذمه : MBL دمه.

[6] JNS, MBM omit Alb Khān.

[7] JNS يلعق : MBL ملعق.

[8] JNS تيكه : MBM تبكه : MBL بيگى.

[9] JNS تمر تغه : MBM agrees with JNS, MBL تمر بغه.

[10] JNS قتلعيعه : MBM قتلعبعه : MBL قتلع بغه.

[11] MBL بر گشتند : JNS, MBM باز گشتند.

[12] JNS جهائين : MBL, MBM جهابن

Ulugh Khān proceeds against Rantambor and Jhāban, 699 H.

In the year 699 H. (1299-1300 A.D.), Ulugh Khân proceeded with a large army against Rantambor[1] and Jhâban. There lived a Râi, Hamir Deo[2] by name, who took shelter in the fortress. "This citadel with entrenchments all round, was situated on the summit of the hills where even the eagles could not fly".[3] The Rāi had under him 12,000 cavalry,[4] innumerable foot and famous elephants. Reaching his destination, Ulugh drew up his forces in battle array. Both the forces made their return from those places and encamped themselves. The couriers were despatched from the place to the Sulṭān in order to inform him about the invulnerability of the fortress and the skill and capacity of its occupants, and to invite the august stirrups on the scene of action for laying waste that territory. When the couriers conveyed the news of the actual state of affairs, the Sulṭān drew up his forces, and with forced marches set out for Rantambor, which he conquered; he sent the accursed Hamir Deo to hell. Further, he laid his hands on the elephants, baggage and the treasures (of the vanquished Rāi): he established a police-outpost at the fortress, and put the *aḳṭā'* of Jhâban under the supervision of Ulugh Khān.[5]

The Sulṭān marched to Chitor

From thence (the Sulṭān) marched towards Chitor,[6] and conquered it also. Here Khizr Khān received a ruby-canopy. Chitor was designated Khizr-ābād and conferred upon Khizr Khān. The Sulṭān, then, marched back to Dehli.[7]

---

[1] MBM رنتنبور. [2] MBM همیرهٔ دیو : JNS, MBL همیر دیو.

[3] The portion under the inverted commas is not to be found in JNS or in MBM, but in MBL.

[4] MBM ده هزار : JNS, MBL هشتاد هزار.

[5] Nizām-ud-din, Badaoni and Ferishta refer to the following incidents that took place while the siege of Rantambor was going on:

(a) rebellion of Akat Khān, the nephew of the Sulṭān and his failure,

(b) revolts of Umar Khān and Mangu Khān, the two other nephews of the Sulṭān,

(c) the foundation of disturbance by Haji Moula.

[6] Badaoni places this expedition in 699 H., Ferishta in 703 H.

[7] MBL reads رایات اعلی بفیروزی و پیروزی بجانب : MBM and JNS omit بفیروزي و پیروزي Nizām-ud-din and Ferishta relate how when the Sulṭān was engaged the siege of Chitor, Targhi, the Mughal, invaded Hindustan.

In the year 700 H. (1300-1301 A.D.), the Sulṭān[1] appointed Malik 'Ain-ul-Mulk Shahāb Multāni with a big force against Malwah for the extirpation and destruction of the rebels of that country,[2] and putting an end to their wickedness: the Malik had also orders from the Sulṭān to confer the robes of safety and the presents of protection on those who would agree to put on the collars of obedience.

Shahāb Multānī sent against Malwah.

There lived in those days at Malwah, a chief, Koka by name,[3] who had under him 40,000 horse and one lakh foot. When the Imperialists reached Malwah, Koka, not being able to stand against them, made good his retreat, and his territory was put to spoliation.

Spoliation of Malwah.

There was a rebel at Siwanah[4] named Satal Deo,[5] who fortified himself in the fortress with a big force. The imperial army in spite of their best efforts failed to take it.

The Sulṭān left the capital by way of hunting and marched towards Siwanah: on the very day that he arrived, His Majesty conquered the fortress:[6] How wonderful! Allah, the Great and the Glorious had conferred prosperity and victory on that just Emperor, the cherisher of his subjects and attendants!"[7] The Sulṭān sent the accursed Satal Deo to hell.

The Sulṭān marched to Siwanah.

The same year,[8] the fortress of Jalor capitulated to Kamāl-uddin Kark, and the rebel Kastmar Deo[9] was sent to hell. The Sulṭān, then, made his way to the capital.

The capitulation of Jalor.

---

[1] MBM omits سلطان.

[2] MBM مفسدان ان دیار قلع و قمع کند : MBL مفسدان دیار را قلع کند : JNS مفسدان آن دیار را قلع در بر کند.

[3] Badaoni writes کوکا نام رائی : Ferishta says "Koka, the Raja of Malwah," and he places this expedition in 704 H.

[4] Ranking (264), "Sorath."

[5] JNS سلدیو

[6] MBM قلعهٔ مذکور فتح کرد : MBL قلعهٔ مذکور زیر و زبر گردانید : JNS agrees with MBM.

[7] The portion under the inverted commas is omitted in JNS, but not in MBL and MBM.

[8] Badaoni gives 701 H.

[9] JNS کستهه دیو : MBM agrees with JNS. MBL کستهه دید : Badaoni, Kanhar Deo.

The royal forces proceed against Tilang.

In the year 702 H. (1302-1303 A.D.), the Imperial army marched against Tilang.[1] When they reached their destination, the Rāī of Tilang, who had under him innumerable elephants, horse and foot ared not oppose the Imperialists, and took shelter in the fort he royal forces besieged the fort and laid waste and plundered the surrounding country.[2] The Rāī of Tilang sought for quarters, and having sent elephants and treasure as a present, made his homage. The imperial army then returned to Dehli.

Malik Nāib Barbak sent against Ma'bar.

Subsequently, Malik Nāib Barbak.[3] was sent against Ma'bar with a large army. Reaching Ma'bar, the Royalists ravaged and plundered the country and secured much treasure along with other things. They took possession of hundred elephants, and despatched to hell thousands of valiant infidels. The country of Ma'bar came under the control of the imperialists. Laden with victory, Malik Nāib wheeled round towards Dehli.

The marriage of the Prince.

When Sulṭān 'Alā'-ud-dīn obtained some leisure from the work of conquering kingdoms, he set himself to celebrate the marriage of his son.[4] He ordered that those who were in charge of (preparing) the almanac and those who calculated the events by the aspect of the stars should specify an auspicious date for the marriage celebration of the Prince. The astrologers, in conformity to the royal mandate,[5] ascertained a day of good omen in accordance with the computation of the calendar and the aspect of the stars. In con-

---

1 Telinga or Telingana was one of the principal kingdoms of Southern India. Badaoni writes Tilang and Marhat.

JNS is here erroneous: there seems to be a big gap here: MBL and MBM seem to be correct: JNS reads

سنه اثنی و سبعمائه کشکوها بغایت متردد شد و از هتهناپور در آمروه رفت نیز
فرمانی دیگر رسید که خبر دور باش و انچه علامت بادشاهي باشد در حضرت فرستد ـ
خضر خان اطاعت کرد هرچه علامت بادشاهي بود بحضرت فرستاد *

2 MBL ولایت بتمام نهب و تاراج کرد : MBM ولایت نهب

3 MBM omits باربک :

4 MBL, کار خیر شاهزاده بنیاد نهاد : MBM شاهزادگان :

5 MBM منجّمان بر حکم فرمان اعلی : MBL نیک ترین حکم :

junction with an auspicious day big[1] domes were raised, and they were decorated with folds. The Muslim and Hindu musicians played on the musical instruments: the heaven was made[2] to revolve in an orbit. A few days after the Sulṭān fell victim to hectic fever[3] Khizr Khān, the eldest son of the Sulṭān, made a vow that on the restoration of the Sulṭān's health by the grace of the Most High God, he would set out on foot to Hathnāpur upon a pilgrimage to the holy men. God the Most High[4] restored the Sulṭān's health after a few days. In fulfilment of the vow he had made, Khizr Khān set out upon a pilgrimage to Hathnāpur.[5]

Malik Nāib poisons the Sulṭān.

Malik Nāib informed the Sulṭān that Alb Khān (the maternal uncle of Khizr Khān), wanted to instal Khizr Khān on the throne and to become Nāib himself, and he had even this in his mind to do away with the Prince[6] afterwards. He had a desire of making himself all-in-all in the State.

The Sultān, whose health was upset, lacked in discrimination; he regarded this assertion as the truth and instantly gave orders the execution of Alb Khān.

Execution of Alb Khān.

When Alb Khān entered the royal palace, Malik Kamāl-ud-din Kark and Malik Nāib seized him and put him to death. Malik Nāib informed the Sultān of the murder of Alb Khān[7] and induced him, on the ground that Khizr Khān had taken alarm, to issue instructions to the effect that the Prince should proceed to Amrohā, which would be conferred upon him in fief; and that he might engage in hunting in the skirts of the hills, and that, until a command was issued summoning him to the presence he was not to return to the court[8] The imperial

---

1 MBL فلک سای : MBM فلک سایه :

2 MBL فلک را چرخ اوردند ; MBM در چرخ اوردند.

3 MBL زحمت تپ : MBM omits تپ :

4 MBM حق نعالی : MBL حق سبحانه تعالی.

5 MBL بربارت پیران : MBM omits پیران .

6 MBL او را نیز تمام کند : MBM کار او را نیز تمام کند .

7 MBL کار البغان پرداخت : MBM البغان را پرداخت .

8 MBL تا فرمان طلب صادر نگردد اصلا در حضرت اعلی نیاید : MBM نگردد در حضرت نیاید .

order reaching him, Khizr Khān became sad and distracted.[1] He left Hathnāpur for Amrohā. At Amrohā, a second firmān reached him asking him to return to the court[2] his canopy and staff of office, and all the other insignia of royalty. Khizr Khān obeyed the order, and returned whatever insignia of royalty he possessed. A few days after this incident, (Khizr Khān) thought within himself that he had never committed any breach of trust for which he could apprehend chastisement and reprehension, that if he had gone to His Majesty without his firmān, out of paternal affection he could not be wroth with him, and would forgive[3] him even if he had committed any wrong. Mounted on a horse, he left Amrohā and reached near the Sulṭān on the second day. He made an obeisance to his father, who out of filial affection embraced him and kissed the head and the face of the Prince,[4] in qualities Yusuf-like,[5] and in disposition angelic: he then bade the Prince see his mother. When Khizr Khān went to meet his mother, the treacherous Malik Nāib[6] entered into the private apartment of the Sulṭān and represented that the Prince had come to the palace with evil intentions without orders. The Sulṭān, who had been bereft of all perception and understanding,[7] gave orders to arrest Khizr Khān and Shādi Khān and to send them to the fortress of Gwalior.[8] The two innocent brothers were put in chains and sent to Gwalior on the third day.

Khizr Khān and Shādi Khān sent to Gwalior.

A few days after, the Sulṭān's disease underwent an increase and he finally succumbed to it.[9]

The Sulṭān's death.

---

[1] MBM متردد و متامل : MBL omits متامل .

[2] MBL بحضرت اعلی فرستد : MBM در حضرت فرستد .

[3] MBM بگذارد : MBL بگذرد

[4] MBL بوسه بر سر و روئی آن شاهزادهٔ یوسف صفت فرسته منش داد : MBM بوسه بر روی او داد فرمود.

[5] Joseph, the patriarch.

[6] MBL ملک نایب حرامخوار قواشي بردار پس دریده پیش بریده محل خلوت یافت : MBM and JNS حرام خوار محل خلوت .

[7] MBM نمانده بود و خوف MBL : سلطان را چندان ضبط و هوش نمانده بود فرمود گشته فرمود : JNS agrees with MBM.

[8] JNS and MBM کالیور : MBL گوالیر .

[9] Badaoni gives 715 H. (1316 A.D.). Ferishta writes, 6 Shawwāl, 716 H.

Shihāb-ud-dīn, the son of 'Alā'-ud-dīn placed on the throne.

On the 7th Shawwāl, 715 H. (Sunday, 9th Jany. 1316 A.D.), Malik Nāib placed the Sulṭān's son, surnamed Shihāb-ud-dīn, on the throne and bestowed on him the designation of Sulṭān Shihāb-ud-dīn; he himself acted as the regent. He sent Malik 'Ikhtiār-ud-dīn Sambal[1] to Gwalior to put out the eyes of Khiẓr Khān and Shādi Khān. On being informed of this, Khiẓr Khān wept bitter tears, and awaited death.[2] Sambal, the traitor, carried out the commission and returned.

Eyes of Khiẓr Khān and Shādi Khān put out.

Malik Nāib murdered.

Malik Nāib, then, deliberated upon seizing the 'Alā'i Amīrs and Maliks and putting them to death. While Malik Nāib was devising means for carrying out his nefarious plans, Mubashshir and Bashīr, the attendants of Sulṭān 'Alā'-ud-dīn's bed-chamber, became anxious and they wanted to kill that wicked fellow. One night an opportunity awaited them; with drawn poniards and their countenances concealed from one ear to the other,[3] they secretly crept out, and dealt blows upon that traitor with their sharp[4] daggers. He slipped out into the harem, but was brought out of it by force and had his head severed from the body.[5] Subsequently, Mubārak Khān, who had taken refuge in the sacred harem came outside[6] and made homage to Sulṭān Shihāb-ud-dīn; he became Nāib to Sulṭān Shihāb-ud-dīn, and served in this capacity for four months. As Sulṭān Shihāb-ud-dīn was a minor and inexperienced, the Amīrs and Maliks placed Mubārak Khān under their observation[7] and did not allow him to stir out (of the palace).

Mubārak Khān became Naib to Sulṭān Shihāb-ud-dīn.

---

[1] Ẓīa Barni says that the Nāib sent his barber to blind the princes.

[2] MBL دل بر قضای مرگ نهاد : MBM دل زبر قضاد : JNS دل بر قضا نهاد.

[3] MBL بر کشیدند تیغ بر کشیدند و سپرها در بنا گوش بسته بمکر بالا رفتند : MBM و سرها در بناگوش بسته یکسر بالا : JNS agrees with MBM.

[4] JNS and MBM omit بران :

[5] Niẓām-ud-d'n (Tab-i-Akb.) states that this event took place exactly 35 days after Sulṭān 'Alā'-ud-dīn's death.

[6] MBL مبارک خان که درون پنهان بود از حرم معترم بیرون امد : MBM and JNS مبارک خان از حرم مانده بود بیرند :

[7] MBL بر مبارک خان نظر داشتند : MBM بر مبارک خان ان نظر : JNS agrees with MBM.

Later on, Mubārak Khān sent Shihāb-ud-dīn to an exile,[1] and seated himself upon the throne with the title of Sultān.[2] This event took place in the year 716 H.[3] (1316-17 A.D.).

Mubārak Khān ascends the throne.

Verse.

Till the world exists, such things happen and will happen again,
Such things will happen to everyone at the end!

Sultān 'Alā'-ud-dīn's reign lasted for twenty years and one month.[4] *Allah knows the truth!*

An account of Sultān Kutub-ud-dīn Mubārak Shāh.

Sultān Kutub-ud-dīn Mubārak Shāh was the son of 'Alā'-ud-dīn. Having sent Sultān Shihāb-ud-dīn into exile, he ascended the throne in the palace at Dehli, on Sunday,[5] the 20th Muharram of the aforesaid year (716 H.[6], 14th Apr.. 1316 A.D.). He distributed titles and apportioned appointments among his men: *e.g.*. Khusru. the Sultān's body-guard. became Khusru Khān. Mahmud Muhammad Moulā became Mir Khān,[7] Malik Dinār became Zafar Khān, Malik Fakhr-ud-din Junā. the son of Ghāzi Malik, became *Amir-i-Ākhur*:[8] Malik Kisar became *Khās-Hajib*: Asbah. *Kurbeg-i-Maisra*; Malik Lakhi Maho. *Kurbeg-i-Maimna*;[9] Bashir Mua'zi,[10] *Nāib-i-Khās Hājib*: Beg Rozmani. *Sar-i-Jāndar-i-Maimnā*; Hasan Beg. *Sar-i-Jāndār-i-Maisra*; Khwājah Hāji Shab Nawis, *Nāib-i-'Ariz-i-mamālik*.

His succession.

Conferment of titles and posts.

---

1 JNS and MBL جلا کرد : MBM جدا کردند :

Zia Barni and Nizām-ud-dīn state that Sultān Shihāb-ud-dīn was sent to Gwalior. Acc. to Badaoni, he ruled for three months and a few days.

2 MBL و خود را سلطان خطاب کرد و بر تخت سلطنت جلوس فرمود : MBM خود ,
بر تخت : JNS agrees with MBL.

3 Zia Barni. Nizām-ud-dīn. Badaoni. and Ferishta give 717 H.: Amir Khusru, 716 H.

4 Ferishta writes 20 years and some months.

5 Acc. to Indian Ephemeris, p. 234, it is Wednesday.

6 Zia Barni, Badaoni. Nizām-ud-din, and Ferishta (7 Muharram) give 717 H.

7 JNS شبر خان :

8 Master of the Horse. Ākhur. a Turki word. means stable.

9 JNS کل کلمی نعویه :

10 MBM معقدی :

The Sulṭān's expedition to Deogir not supported by the Amīrs.

In the year of his accession to the throne, the Sulṭān made up his mind to proceed against Deogir; but the Amīrs and the Maliks disapproved of the idea. It was not advisable that the Emperor who had recently ascended the throne and had lately taken possession of the country, should go far away from it in quest of expedition.

Verse.

Not commendable is it, from either prudence or wisdom,
That the world's king should move from his place;
Who knows what are the evil designs of evil wishers.
What black treachery lies inside sincerity?
That shrub [1] is best that takes hold of a wide space. first,
And extends, then, its roots and branches [2] in every direction.

Afterwards, the Sulṭān addressed them thus, "Is there any one among you who can fancy, how in spite of my many brothers living the country devolved upon me?" All replying in the negative, the Emperor continued, "When the Righteous and the Most High God conferred the country on me not with the intervention or favour of any one else no power can snatch it away; [3] but when the time for its confiscation arrives none can, likewise, put it off. It has been said [4]:—

Verse.

With sword and wisdom God has bestowed on me,[5]
None but God will seize it back."

The Sulṭān marched to Deogir.

Then, the Sulṭān marched against Deogir,[6] and having taken up his residence there for some time, left Yak Lakhī at the place and returned to Dehli.

---

1 JNS شده آن به : MBM تنه آن که جا : MBL بنه به که.

2 JNS, MBM بیغ شاخ : MBL بیغ و شاخ.

3 MBM مقدور که باشد که از من بستاند : MBL مقدور باشد که : JNS مقدور که از من.

4 JNS and MBM omit و این بیت می گفت.

5 JNS and MBM خدا دادما را : MBL خدا داد ما را.

6 This expedition took place in 718 H. (1318 A.D.). Acc. to Ẓia Barni, "upon the death of Malik Nāib Kafur, Deogir threw off his subjection, and was taken possession of by Harpāl Deo and Rām Deo. Acc. to Nizām-ud-dīn, Harpāl Deo was the son-in-law of Rām Deo"

Rebellion of Asad-ud-din.

When the Sulṭān reached Khī Sākunah,[1] Asad-ud-dīn, the son of Malik Khamūsh, entered into a conspiracy against the Sulṭān, and a few of the royal attendants joined hands with him. Ārām Shāh, the son of Khuram Khajuri, the *Vakildar-i-Jalālī*, gave this information to the Sulṭān at midnight. At day-break Asad-ud-dīn and Malik Maṣri[2] were arrested and put to death. From thence, the Sulṭān with forced marches proceeded to Dehli.[3]

Rebellion of Yak Lakhi.

Later on, Yak Lakhī raised the standard of hostility at Deogir, and assumed the paraphernalia of royalty. The Sulṭān ordered off Khusru Khān with a big army to quell the insurrection[4] of Yak Lakhī.

Khusru Khān sent against Yak Lakhi.

On the arrival of the Khān, the soldiery of Deogir, who had assembled at the place, brought Yak Lakhī a prisoner with fetters round his neck (like the saying), "*catch hold of him and put him under chains*"; Khusru Khān despatched him off to His Majesty.

Khusru Khān marched against Tilang and Ma'bar.

Khusru Khān marched from Deogir, and having ravaged the country of the Rākho,[5] took possession of a rich booty.[6] Later on, he took his way to Tilang, whose Rai instead of meeting the invader shut himself up in the fort. Khusru Khān laid siege to the fort,[7] and a few days after, the besieged, in a state of helplessness, offered a hundred and odd elephants, cash and valuables, as a token of servitude, and made a promise of alle-

---

1 JNS and MBM بالا کهنی ساکونه : MBL بالا کهی ساکونه : Ẓīa Barni, Ghāt-i-Sākūn: Badaoni, Badra i-Sākūn.

2 No mention of his name in Ẓia Barni and Niẓām-ud-dīn.

3 Ẓīa Barni, Niẓām-ud-dīn and other historians relate how the Sulṭān, on his arrival in Dehli began to do things, which were calculated to cause the destruction of his power, and to bring about the downfall of his empire. He put to death Khiẓr Khān, Shādi Khān, and Malik Shihāb-ud-dīn; his violent and vindictive spirit which possessed him led him to kill Ẓafar Khān, the Governor of Gujrat.

4 MBL بجهت دفع : MBM, JNS سبب دفع.

5 JNS راتهور : MBM راکیهر : MBL راکهو.

6 MBL غنایم فراوان از زر سامت و ناطق : JNS and MBM omit از زر سامت و ناطق.

7 MBM حصار را مهر کرد : JNS, MBL حصار را محصر کرد

giance to the Emperor receiving in return a khila'at from K͟husru K͟hān.

From thence, K͟husru K͟hān marched against Malki,[1] and having laid his hands on twenty elephants, and a diamond weighing six *dirm* proceeded to Ma'bar. Here, too, he seized elephants and valuables.

K͟husru K͟hān attempts at rebellion.

With innumerable treasure and unnumbered elephants under his possession, K͟husru K͟hān wanted to hoist the insignia of rebellion, so that he might remain there. The following Amīrs and Maliks of the court, who bore him company during the expedition, such as, Talabg͟ha Bag͟hda, Malik Talabg͟ha Nāgori, Malik Ḥājī, the *Nāib-i-'ariẓ*, Malik Tamar, Malik Tigīn, Malik Mal, and others, being in concert with one another, took him by force to Dehli and made a report on the state of affairs to the Sulṭān. The latter did not believe the accusers, rather, he awarded Khusru with rich and valuable presents, and killed the Amīrs.

The Sulṭān murdered by K͟husru K͟hān: the latter's accession to the throne.

Some time afterwards, that traitor K͟husru K͟hān, the offspring of rebellion, took resort to treachery and co-operating himself with a few Barāo[2] slaves, his own kinsmen, lay in wait for the Sulṭān in the palace. It was the time for *Nemāz-i-K͟huftan* when that traitor of evil-destiny, and his brothers and relations went in hiding. The Sulṭān was intoxicated that night, when he was seized and wounded:[3] by the force of his physical strength, due to his youth and intoxication, the Sulṭān freed himself from that traitor and fled towards the palace that was under guard: but the traitor pursued him and caught hold of his ringlet; he then felled the Sulṭān on the ground and stabbed him on the breast with his dagger, so that the martyred Sulṭān came out of the transitory abode and marched towards the everlasting dwelling-place.

---

[1] JNS ميتلي : MBM متلي : MBL ملکی .

[2] MBL, MBM چند نفر برادر و اقرباء خویش : JNS چند نفر بر او اقربای خویش .
Barāo is the name of a caste of the menial class, who are found in large number in Gujrat. Ẓia Barni, Badaoni and Niẓām-ud-dīn read *Parwāri*.

[3] The portion under the asterisk has been omitted in JNS.

Having done to death that emperor of pure faith, the traitor ascended the throne and assumed the title of Sulṭān Nāṣir-ud-dīn. He brought the widow of the late Sulṭān in his own harem.[1] This event took place on the 5th Rabi'-ul-auwal,[2] 720 H. (Tuesday, the 15th April, 1320 A.D.).

Accession of Khusru Khān

Verse.

The bed of the delicate one became thorny,
There appeared trouble from his bed of brocade.[3]

The rule of Sulṭān Ḳuṭub-ud-dīn lasted for four years and a few months.[4] *God knows the real facts!*

An account of Sulṭān Nāṣir-ud-dīn Khusru Khān.

Nāṣir-ud-dīn Khusru Khān was one of the slaves of 'Alā-ud-dīn.[5] In their younger days, Khusru Khān and his brother fell into the hands of the Muslim army[6] and became incorporated with the body of Sulṭān's personal slaves. During the rule of the late Sulṭān Ḳuṭub-ud-dīn they remained near his Majesty's person and were included in his retinue:[7] Khusru Khān was appointed as the *Nāib*: of faulty origin and improper judgment, he thought it reasonable for his own interest to adopt unwholesome means[8] and took recourse to ungratefulness in return for the benefits done to him.[9]

His early career.

---

1 MBM and JNS omit this line.

2 JNS and MBL omit 5th Rabi'-ul-auwal.

3 MBL زدیبا و ششترین : MBM ششترس : JNS زدنیا و شش درش : We have adopted Badaoni who writes,—زدیبای بسترش :

4 MBM چهار سال و دو ماه و یازده روز بوده : JNS and MBL چهار سال و چند روز :

5 Badaoni says that at first his name was Hasan Barwabacha.

6 JNS, MBM لشکر اسلام : MBL omits لشکر :

7 MBL احتشام و اختصاص گرفت : MBM احتشام گرفت ان مملکت : JNS احتشام گرفت.

8 MBL صواب کار خویش درین کار نا صواب دید : JNS and MBM کار خویش درین دید.

9 MBL کمال کفران نعمت : JNS and MBM بکمال.

Verse.

It is its nature that a tree is bitter;[1]
Either thou dost plant[2] it in the Garden of Eden,
Or, dost water it from the River of Paradise,
Or sprinkle honey or pure milk in its root,[3]
The species that it brings forth at the end,
Or the fruits—are all bitter!

Cruelties of Khusru Khān, and the predominance of the Hindus.

To sum up, after the assassination of the late Kuṭub-ud-dīn and the princes, Khusru Khān engaged himself in uprooting the 'Alā'ī family. Some of the princes, the sons of the late Sulṭān 'Alā'-ud-dīn, those who, owing to the misfortunes of Time, the cruel mother, were left, in the course of past events, in the laps of their mother in the harem, such as, Farid Khān, Abu Bakr Khān, 'Alī Khān and Bahādur Khan, were dragged out and had their eyes blinded in 721 H. (1321-22 A.D.). Those 'Alā'i Amīrs and Maliks who were hostile to him he executed;[4] while others, viz., 'Ain-ul-Mulk Shihāb Tāj Multānī, and sundry others,[5] he set at variance. Most of the Hindus became prosperous[6] and they gained the upper hand. The Hindus, confident of their position as the relations of Nāsir-ud-dīn Khusru Khān, subjected the Muslims to cruelty and outrage, carried away the ladies of the harem, and put to plunder the treasure that had been accumulated in the days of 'Alā' ud-dīn.

Verse.

All those hidden treasures of times past,[7]
Whose number none could fancy;
To Hindus he entrusted with the keys of their doors,[8]
So that, each carried away the required quantity![9]

---

1 MBL تلخ اشت : JNS and MBM تلخ امد.

2 MBL در نشانی : JNS, MBM بر نشاني.

3 MBL به بیخ : JNS, MBM همه انگبین.

4 MBL دست اورده بعجواری و زاري تمام نابود و نیست گردانید : JNS and MBM بدست آورده بکشت.

5 MBL چند نفر دیگر : JNS and MBM چند ندوی.

6 JNS هنوز روز مانده : MBL, MBM هنود فرمانده :

7 MBL and MBM همه گنج و انباء دیرینه سال : JNS, نفان زاسمانهاء دیرینه سال.

8 MBL and MBM کلید درش : JNS خذاین درش.

9 MBL and MBM بمقدار بایست : JNS بمقدار بایسته.

Perplexity of the Amirs and Maliks.

And some of those Amīrs and Maliks, who enjoyed freedom from restraint, were bewildered and perplexed.

Khusru Khān confers titles, etc., upon his attendants.

Nāṣir-ud-dīn Khusru Khān sent firmāns in every direction demanding supplication from the people. On each of his attendants he conferred titles and surnames; Ḥisām-ud-dīn, his own brother, became Khān-i-Khānān; Yusuf Sufī became Sufī Khān: 'Ain-ul-Mulk Multānī was styled 'Alm Khān: Ikhtiār-ud-dīn Sambal was bestowed with the title of Ḥātim Khān: Kamāl-ud-dīn Sufī became the Vakildar: Malik Fakhr-ud-dīn Junā, the son of Ghāzī Malik, the *Akhur-beg-i-kuṭbi*, became the *Akhurbeg*.

Flight of Fakhr-ud-dīn Junā to Dibalpur.

Now, Khusru Khān demanded that the Amīrs and Maliks in the surrounding countries should come to Dehli. Some came, while others revolted. One day, he asked Malik Fakhr-ud-dīn Akhurbeg, to come to the court with some Arabian horses.[1] The latter, who had been sorrow-stricken at the disorder in the house of Sulṭān 'Alā'-ud-dīn, made excuses, and secretly wrote epistles to Ghāzi Malik[2] warning him against any reliance he might make on the traitor[3] or against coming to the court,[4] and assuring him that, God willing, he would join with him. A few days after, finding an opportunity, he mounted on a horse and rode off towards Dibalpur; he took along with him the son of Bahrām Āynah.[5]

Verse.

Seated on the Arab horse, fast as lightning[6]
Together they rode in one direction!

---

[1] MBL گفت تا چند از سر اسپ تازي برق کند : JNS and MBM گفت که چند سر اسپ تازي برق کنند.

[2] MBM ملک غازي.

[3] JNS سخن این کافر نعمت استوار نداری : MBM سخن کافر نعمت استوار نداری MBL زینهار این کافر نعمت را استوار نداری.

[4] MBL اتفاق باین بد عهد نکني : JNS اتفاق با او نکني : MBM اتفاق امون نکني.

[5] JNS بهرام ابیر : MBM بهرام امیر : MBL بهرام آینه.

[6] براق (Burāk) meaning swift as a lightning: it is thus described in *Mish-*

Ghāzī Malik seeks help from the Amirs.

Being informed of the flight of Fakhr-ud-dīn, Nāṣir-ud-dīn sent a battalion of horse in pursuit of the fugitives, who though being chased for three nights and days could not be overtaken. Malik Fakhr-ud-dīn, in company with the son of Malik Bahrām set off with great precipitancy near Ghāzī Malik, and related to him, how a sedition had broken out, and how the people had shown their contempt for Islam. Ghāzī Malik sent epistles seeking aid from the 'Alā'ī Amīrs and Maliks, such as, Malik Bahrām Aynah, Malik Mughlaṭī, the Amīr of Multān, Malik 'Ain-ul-Mulk Shihāb Multānī, Muhammad Shāh, the son of the Amīr of Siwistān, Malik Yaklakhī, the 'Alā'i slave and the Amīr of Sāmāna, exhorting them to take revenge upon Khusru for the murder of Sulṭān Kuṭub-ud-dīn.[1] As soon as the letter reached him, Malik Bahrām Aynah[2] went near Ghāzī Malik. Mughlatī,[3] the Amīr of Multān, wrote in reply, "I am only an Amīr of Multān; I dare not rebel against Dehli with my few cavalry and infantry".

Correspondence between Ghāzi Malik and the other Amīrs.

'Alī Al-Khaṣuṣ, the Amīr of Dibalpur, abandoned his vicious thought of rebelling, and rendered his submission. When the Amīr of Multān wrote Ghāzī Malik to the above effect, the latter secretly addressed the inhabitants and the Maktā'āns of Multān. Bahrām Sirāj, one of the chiefs of Multān, came with a big following, and Mughlatī being informed of this, ran away and moved towards the canal which Ghāzī Malik had dug out. The people of Multān sent horse and foot in his pursuit, and he was taken out and killed. Previous to this, Muhammad Shāh, the Amīr of Siwistān, had been confined by the people of that place, and when the letter of Ghāzī Malik reached them, they addressed Muhammad Shāh thus, "If you render your assistance to Ghāzī Malik we shall let you free." Muhammad complying with their command was set

---

kātū-l Maṣābih (Mathews II, 651): "after this a white animal is brought for me to ride upon. Its size was between that of a mule and an ass, and it stretched as far as the eye could see. The name of the animal was Burāk". Raverty, 292, f

[1] MBL استدملی خون ملطان : MBM استدای چون : JNS agrees with MBM.

[2] MBM ایبه.

[3] MBL مغلتی : JNS agrees with MBL, MBM مغلطی.

free. He thus wrote to Ghāzī Malik "Following this letter, I shall be going on a pilgrimage [1] to you, and shall (then) relate everything concerning my captivity and the lack of assistance from my soldiers." But Yeklakhī, the Amīr of Sāmāna, sent the very letter of Ghāzī Malik to Nāṣir-ud-dīn Khusru Khān, and explained to him the reason of Ghāzī Malik's animosity: then drawing up his forces he led them towards Dibalpur.[2] When he reached its vicinity, Ghāzī Malik, too, became ready for action: at the first onset, Yeklakhī met with reverses, and he retired to Sāmāna, whence he wanted to proceed to Dehli near Nāsir-ud-dīn. In the meantime, the people of Sāmāna assembled together and had him murdered. Malik 'Ain-ul-Mulk Multānī wrote from Dehli the following answer in reply to the letter of Ghāzī Malik, "I cannot come, but I shall return to my own country. I shall not help any side: the one among you who would siege Dehli, to him I shall make my submission."

When all the replies to the letters reached Ghāzī Malik he flew

Ghāzī Malik called Bahrām Aynah.

into rage, and having called near him Malik Bahrām Aynah, he told him that the Hindus had seized the countries of the Muslims, and the family of 'Alā'-ud-dīn had been extinct: and that he intended assassinating them in retaliation: as he (Bahrām) had for years rendered him his obedience he should likewise do at that moment: so that with his help he could wield his scimitar like a trusty servant. They entered into covenant with each other and came out.

Meanwhile it was reported that the imperial revenue from Mul-

Ghāzī Malik plunders royal treasury.

tān and Siwistān and innumerable horses were being taken to Dehli. Ghāzī Malik, the second Haidar, ordered his forces to plunder he treasure and horses, and pay out the soldiery their salaries for wo years in advance.

With all such prosperity in his favour, Ghāzī Malik set out from

Defeat of Nāṣir-ud-dīn's army.

Dibalpur by forced marches and reached Sarsuti. Nāsir-ud-dīn Khān had also despatched Khān-i-Khānān, his own brother and Sufī Khān [illegible] a big force against Ghāzī Malik. The two forces met each

---

1 حرام .

2 MBM مستعد کرده از شهر دیبالپور.

other at *Ḥauẓ-i-Bhâti,*[1] when the Almighty God conferred victory upon Ghāzī Malik, and the army of Nâṣir-ud-dīn met with defeat.

Ghāzī Malik meet Nāṣir-ud-dīn.

Losing their elephants and attendants, Khān-i-Khānān and Sufī Khân fled to Dehli. From thence, Ghāzī Malik led his troops towards Dehli by forced marches. Nâṣir-ud-dīn Khusru Khân, too, having come out, collected his men from all sides and arranged his forces near Belkush,[2] so that the one wing of his army remained at *Ḥauẓ-i-Khāṣ,* and the other at Andbantha.[3] Having seized the treasure of Sulṭân 'Alā'-ud-dīn, he (Nâṣir-ud-dīn) bestowed salaries and rewards of three and four years' pay on his men. He then brought out of the harem the 'Alā'i princes, whose eyes had been already put out, and killed them. Ghāzī Malik, too, encamped himself in at the compound of Raẓia's tomb and drew out his forces. On Friday, Nâṣir-ud-dīn Khusru-Khān mounted on a horse, arranged his army and prepared himself for action. On the other side, Ghâzī Malik marshalled his forces; in the conflict which took place between the belligerents, Nâṣir-ud-din enjoyed a triumph at first, and worsted the Malik's men. Ultimately, Ghāzī Malik led his own band of three hundred cavalry, men as firm as mountain, against his opponents who numbered thousands, so that at the first onset there was a breach in the line of Nâṣir-ud-dīn, who fled to Matark[4] with some of his Amīrs; here he was put to plunder.

At first Ghāzi Malik was defeated: his success in the second battle.

Triumphant and victorious, Ghâzī Malik returned to his camp, and passing the night there, he rode to Dehli in the morning and ascended the imperial throne under the title of Sulṭân Ghiāṣ-ud-dīn.

Accession of Ghāzi Malik.

On the second day, when it was so reported that Khān-i-Khânān, the brother of Khusru Khân, had concealed himself in the garden,[5] a farmân was issued to Malik Fakhr-ud-dīn to seize the rebel and to

Execution of Khān-i-Khānān, brother of Khusru Khān.

---

[1] Badaoni reads Hauẓ-i-Thaneshwar: Tab-i-Akb. Indarpath.

[2] Ẓia Barni, *Ḥauẓ-i-'Alā'i*: Badaoni, *Ḥauẓ-i-Khāṣ.*

[3] MBL اندبتنهه : MBM اندبهنهه : JNS آمد ستهيه.

[4] MBL, MBM خود در مترکه رفت : JNS خود سر در کم رفته.

[5] Ẓia Barni and Tab-i-Akb. read the garden of Shādī Khān: Badaoni reads "tomb of Malik Shādī".

carry him to the bazar of Dehli. He was executed there on 721 H. (1321-22 A.D.).[1]

Verse.

Whatever thou doest leaves a mark,
Whatever thou givest, receiveth back!

The sovereignty of Nāṣir-ud-dīn Khusru Khān lasted for four months and a few days. *God knows more the real facts and He is the place of refuge and the repository.*[2]

THE HOUSE OF TUGHLUK.

Account of Sulṭān Ghiāṣ-ud-dīn Tughluk Shāh,[3] Ghāzī Mulk.[4]

His character.

Sulṭān Ghiāṣ-ud-dīn Tughluk Shāh was a kind and just Emperor; chaste and pure, the Sulṭan had in him an innate[5] attachment to accumulation[6] (of everything), to the construction of edifices, to making places habitable, and to the protection (of the country). In ingenuity, thrift, knowledge, and adroitness he was unparalleled. He would always read the divine precepts for five times[7] and would never enter into his harem without saying his *nemāz-ī-khuftan.*[8]

---

1 Badaoni gives 720 H.

2 MBL adds after this و الیهٔ المرجع و المآب : JNS and MBM omit this.

3 Ferishta, in giving the origin of the Tughluk dynasty states that Tughluk was the father of Ghiāṣ-ud-dīn and that he was a Turki slave of Balban. Ibn Batuta writes that Tughluk was the stock of Karauna Turks, who live between Sind and Turkistan. Speaking of Karaunas, Marco Polo says that they are the sons of Indian mothers and Tartar father. Wassaf calls the Karaunas "the most fearless of the Mongols". Their name has been connected with Karaun Jidun, by which the Mongols knew the mountains separating the Gobi desert from China and Manchuria. H. H. Howorth (Hist. of the Mongols, III) identifies them with Kara Tartars of Khorasan. Mr. Ishwari Prasad (Med. Ind., p. 229, f.n. 1) writes that Karaunas were of the tribe of the Mongols of Central Asia.

Ghiāṣ-ud-dīn Tughluk was the issue of the union between Tughluk and a woman of the Jat tribe, who were formerly the cultivators of Lahore.

Another historian opines that Tughluk is but a vulgarism of Kutlugh.

4 MBL and MBM read سلطان غیاث الدین تغلق شاه etc. نادر شاه کریم و عادل بود و در طبیعت او همه فراهمی و عمارت : JNS begins with و در طبیعت او.

5 JNS معبول is a error for مجبول.

6 همه فراهمي.

7 خمس اوقات فرایض.

8 Of the "five hours of praying" *punj uakt-i-nemaz*, prescribed by Muham-

His accession, 1st Sha'bān, 721 H., 24th Oct., 1321 A.D.

Upon the whole, after the defeat of Nāṣir-ud-dīn, Sulṭān Ghiāṣ-ud-dīn ascended the throne in Dehli, on Saturday, the 1st Shā'bān, of the above-mentioned year (721 H.),[1] with the consent of the *amirs*, *maliks*, prelates, chiefs, *ḳāẓīs* and the people.[2] He honoured the 'Alā'i *amirs* and *maliks* by conferring upon them dignities, mansions, and *aḳtā's*.[3] The old families which had come down he promoted: to some of his own relatives he gave surnames and titles, *e.g.*, Malik Fakhr-ud-dīn, his eldest son, became Ulugh Khān, and was made his heir-apparent:[4] to his other sons, he gave the titles of Bahrām Khān, Zafar Khān, Nuṣrat Khān[5] and Maḥmud Khān: Malik Asad-ud-dīn, his brother's son, he made *Naib-i-Barbak*,[6] and Malik Bahā'-ud-dīn, his sister's son, he made *'Ariẓ-i-mamālik* (muster-master) and confirmed the *aḳṭā'* of Samānā and the title of Gurshāsab Malik[7] on him. Malik Shadi (another nephew) was made the Vizir, and the king's son-in-law.[8] The old officers and assistants of the state were favoured with[9] suitable employments.

Conferment of titles, dignities, etc., upon Amirs.

Ulugh Khān's march against Tilang, 721 H., 1321 A.D.

When the business of the state was brought into order, His Majesty sent out Ulugh Khān with a vast force against Tilang,[10] and Ma'bar in the same year. Attended by the royal train[11] Ulugh Khān set out, and was co-operated with the forces of

---

madan law, the *nemāz-i-khuftan* is said before going to bed, two hours or more after sunset.

1 Ẓia Barni (Elliot III, 229), Tabaḳat-i-Akbari (Bib. Ind., 208) and Al Badāoni (Bid. Ind., 221) give 720 H.

2 MBM omits سايد الانام .

3 Assignments of lands on feudal or copyhold tenure.

4 JNS والي an error for ولى .

5 In Ẓīa Barni (ibid) this name comes last.

6 The Deputy Grand-Usher.

7 MBL كر شباشب ملك : JNS كرشاست .

8 JNS ديوان وزارت بعدة شادي داد و دماد كرد : MBL ديوان وزارت بعهدهٔ شادي داد و داماد خود كرد .

9 MBL مناسب حال ارزاني داشت : MBM مناسب ارزاني : JNS agrees with MBM.

10 Ẓīā Barni writes Arangal and Tilang. JNS and MBM omit معبر .

11 MBL با كوكبهٔ و دبدبهٔ بادشاهي : JNS and MBM omit و دبدبهٔ .

Chanderi, Badāōn, Oudh, Karah, Dalmu, Bangarmu[1] and the other *aḳṭā's*. On his way, he entered Deogir and took its forces along with him and having arrived at Tilang[2] invested Arangal, which for the last 700 years, since the days of his ancestors, had been the capital of Rai Ladar Mahādeo.[3] With his entourage and his chiefs, the Rāi shut himself up. At Arangal there were two forts, one constructed of stone and the other of clay, both being noted for excessive impregnability. Laying siege to the mud[4] fort, Ulugh ordered (his men) to spoil it,[5] to collect booty and bring in forage for the army. The soldiery secured an ample supply of provisions, and they pushed on the siege whole-heartedly. The conflict was vehement, and there was casualty on both sides.

Investment and sack of Arangal.

A few days after, no intelligence (of the Sulṭān) having been received at Dehli, 'Ubaid, the poet, spread a (false) report that the Emperor was dead:[6] he employed the *amīrs* and *maliks*[7] such as Malik Takīn[8] and others for assassinating Ulugh Khān. Being informed of this, the latter came out with fifty horse, and the contumacious *amīrs* left the place for their respective *aḳṭā's*. When Ulugh Khān reached near the Sulṭān by forced marches and narrated to him the whole incident, His Majesty issued *farmāns* ordering (his own officers) to put the (rebellious) *amīrs* to death, wherever they were found out. Thus, ere the revolters could reach their destinations, they were put to destruction. Malik Ḥisām-ud-dīn Abū-Reja, *mustaufī-i-mamālik*, was ordered by the Emperor to proceed to

Rebellion of 'Ubaid, his failure and execution.

---

[1] MBM سكرموٴ.

[2] MBM ملتان.

[3] Ferishta (Briggs I, 403) and Ẓia Barni (Elliot III, 231) have Laddar Deo: T.A. (213) reads Rāi Rudar Deo; Al Badāoni (222) has Rāi Ladar Mahadeo. The personage referred to is Pratap Rudra Deva II, the Kakatiya Rājā of Telingānā.

[4] MBL گلی : MBM گلین : JNS كلي.

[5] MBL نهب و تاراج : MBM omits تاراج : JNS omits نهب.

[6] MBL سلطان غياث الدين نماند و برحمت حق پيوست : MBM omits برحمت etc. JNS agrees with MBM.

[7] T.A. 212. A secret meeting was held with Sheikh Zāda-i-Damaski, Malik Tamar, Malik Tigin, Malik Mal Afgan, and Malik Kafur (the keeper of the sea).

[8] MBM ملک تکین : MBL ملک تكني : JNS agrees with MBM.

Oudh[1] and bring on the followers of Malik Tigīn.[2] He went out to his destination and got hold of the men. Malik Tāj-ud-dīn Talkānī, the son-in-law of Malik Tigīn, who had made good his escape from the prison, was seized on the banks of the Saryu and decapitated. The son of Malik Tigīn, and his retinue, were taken to the Emperor, who ordered that every one, women and men, young and old, should be thrown under the feet of elephants in front of the *dākhul* and that 'Ubaid the poet, should be placed in an inverted position on the gibbet.[3]

'Abu Reja sent to Oudh against Tigin: Latter was imprisoned and killed with his family.

The chroniclers narrate that 'Ubaid, the poet, was one of the attendants and servants of the Sheikh-ul-Islām, Sheikh Nizām-ul-Huk-wa-ul-Shara'-wa-ud-dīn: 'Ubaid nursed a spite against Amir Khusru, for which the generous-minded Sheikh ever remained anxious.

Meanwhile, a certain Hindu adopted the Muslim faith; Sheikh Nizām-ud-dīn used to train him up; once the Sheikh gave him two dentifrices; the newly converted Hindu enquired of the Muslim 'Ubaid how would he use those dentifrices, on which the latter told him that he would put the one in his mouth, and the other in his buttocks. Every day he did the same, till his buttocks became swollen. One day, sorrow-stricken, he came near the Sheīkh-ul-Mushāekh and reported, "Oh, Sheikh! of the two dentifrices that you had been pleased to give me, that one that I put into my mouth was quite good, while the other, that I put into my buttocks was quite bad"! The Sheikh-ul-Mushāekh became thoughtful and enquired, who had taught him to do that. The man told him that it was 'Ubaid, the poet. Immediately, the Sheikh exclaimed by his pearl-scattering mouth, "Oh, 'Ubaid! thou makest sport with sticks"! From this utterance, those present knew that 'Ubaid would be impaled, for the words of the Sheikh cannot be false.[4]

---

1 JNS فرمان شد نابه دراور برود : MBL and MBM تا در اودهه برود : Badaoni (223) has ملتان و جلمیر .

2 MBL طقاني : He was the Governor of Oudh. (T.A. 212.)

3 MBL بردار کردند : MBM and JNS بردار : T.A. *ibid.*, "impaled alive". Ferishta writes, "they were buried alive".

4 JNS and MBM omit, "The chroniclers ....false".

In the year 724 H., Ulugh Khān was again sent against Tilang. Rāi Ladar Mahādeo[1] shut himself in the fort for the second time. After playing it for a few days with arrows, *naweks*,[2] stones and *maghrebi* (?),[3] the Khān captured the interior and the exterior of the citadel, and conquered Arangal. The aforesaid Rāi and all the other Rāis with their wives, children, elephants, and treasures were imprisoned. A despatch of victory was sent to the Emperor; domes were constructed at Dehli, and the people made rejoicings. The whole of Tilang was brought under control, and *muktia'as* and managers were appointed.[4] The prince then wended his way to Jājnagar, and laid his hands on forty big elephants. Triumphant and victorious, he returned by the way he came, and some time after, retraced his steps to Dehli.[5]

Second expedition to Tilang under Ulugh Khān: 724 H., 1323 A.D.

Conquest of Arangal.

Ulugh's march to Jājnagar: his return to Dehli.

Again, in 724 H., the Sultān having resolved upon the invasion of Lakhnauti,[6] made Ulugh Khān his vice-regent at Tughlukābād, which had been made his capital for the last three years and a few months, and placed all the affairs of the kingdom under his management during his own absence. The Sultān

The Sultān's expedition against Lakhnauti. 724 H., 1323 A.D.

---

[1] MBL, MBM رای لدر مهادیو : JNS رای کرن مهادیو .

[2] ناوک : An arrow made of reed with a notch on the side.

[3] Text has—بزخم تیر و ناوک و سنگ و مغربی : Zia Barni (Ell. III, 233) writes, "after plying it for a few days with arrows from the *nāwaks* and stones from the *maghribs*".

[4] Zia Barni and T.A. relate that the Rāi was sent to Dehli under the escort of Malik Bidār, and that Arangal was re-christened Sultānpur.

[5] Zia Barni states (p. 234) that when Arangal was taken and the elephants arrived from Jājnagar, several Mughal armies attacked the frontiers but were repulsed.

[6] The cause of this invasion has been given by Zia Barni. He says that certain nobleman came from Lakhnauti complaining to the Sultān of the oppressive laws, tyranny and distress under which they and the other Muhammadans laboured.

According to Nizām-ud-dīn, "some of his (Sultān's) well-wishers made representations to him of the tyranny, etc., of the rulers Bangalah"

Some say that Shihāb-ud-dīn, and Nasir-ud-dīn the princes of Lakhnauti, having been expelled by their usurping brother Bahadur went to Dehli and sought the intervention of Tughluk Shāh. (Jahwari Prasad, Mediaeval India, p. 232, f.n. 1).

personally led his army by forced marches to Lakhnauti and conquered it.[1] Meanwhile, a despatch came announcing that Bahādur S͟hāh alias Nudah,[2] the king of Lakhnauti,[3] had been imprisoned by Haibat-ul-lāh of Kasur.[4] His Majesty made his way to the capital, carrying with him Bahādur S͟hāh.[5] Reaching in all haste

The Sulṭān's return to the capital.

Afg͟hānpur,[6] where a pavilion had been hastily raised[7] for the royal audience,[8] the Emperor granted an interview (to the nobles of the court) and ordered, "Bring up those elephants that have been captured during the sack of Lakhnauti, and make them run together". The construction was newly made: the earth under the erection

Death of the Sulṭān.

trembled, and by divine pre-ordination it gave way.[9] The late Sulṭān G͟hiās̱-ud-dīn Tug͟hluḳ S͟hāh attended by one servant[10] fell under it and was martyred in Rabiʻ-ul-auwal, 725 H. (Feb.-Mar., 1325 A.D.).[11]

---

[1] Ẓīa Barni and T.A. have: when the Sulṭān reached Tirhut, Naṣir-ud-dīn, the ruler of Lakhnauti, and the other *rāis* and *rānās* swore allegiance to him.

[2] JNS reads نوده : Badaoni has توده.

[3] JNS بهادر شاه عرف نوده بادشاه لکهنوتي : MBL عرف بوده.

[4] MBL, JNS and MBM have هيبت الله قصوري : Ẓīa Barni (p. 234) states that Tatar K͟hān *pisar-i-khanda* (foster son) of the Sulṭān, put a chord round the neck of the Sulṭān of Lakhnauti and conducted him to the Emperor. T.A. (213), Badaoni (224), Ferishta (406) are of the same opinion.

[5] Sunār-gānw was absorbed into the empire: a canopy and a *durbash* were conferred on Sulṭān Naṣir-ud-dīn, the ruler of Lakhnauti.

[6] It was situated at a distance of 3 *curoh* (6 miles) from Tug͟hluḳābād. T.A. (214) and Badaoni (224).

[7] The building was built in course of three days. T.A. and Badaoni.

[8] بار جاى an error for بار شاهى.

[9] Niẓām-ud-dīn writes (T.A. 214) that when the Sulṭān entered the pavilion, a table was spread: after the food had been taken away, the nobles came out, leaving the Sulṭān to wash his hands. At this moment the roof fell in. Badaoni supports Niẓām-ud-dīn and adds that after the arrival of the Sulṭān at Afg͟hānpur, Ulug͟h K͟hān accompanied by the nobles went forward to meet him and spread the table. The Sulṭān ordered that the elephants which had been brought along with him from Bengal should be made to run. As the structure was fresh and weak, the elephants made the earth tremble and down came the edifice.

[10] Ẓia Barni (235), "Five or six other persons". Ferishta (407), "Five of his attendants".

[11] It is apparent how Yaḥiya, who must have laid under contribution Ẓia Barni, attributes the collapse of the structure to divine pre-ordination and exonerates Muḥammad Tug͟hluḳ from the charge of patricide. Ẓia Barni, in his *Tārīk͟h-i-Firoz*-

The story runs that it was at this place where lay the earthly remains of Sheikh-ul-Ḳiṭāb, Sheikh Muḥi-ud-dīn, Niẓām-ul-Huḳ-wa-ul-Shara'-wa-ud-dīn. At the time when the Sulṭān had set out on his expedition, the Sheikh had exclaimed through his pearl-scattering mouth, "Dehli is distant from thee"! When the Sulṭān, triumphant and victorious, reached Afghānpur he said, "Having placed my foot on the breast of the enemy I have returned". But, this news reaching the ears of Hazrat Sheikh-ul-Ḳiṭāb, he persisted. "Dehli is distant from thee"! This incident took place in the aforesaid month.[1]

Couplet.

If thou dost place the world under thy feet,
Eventually thou hast to lie in your place (grave)!

Malik Sulṭān Ghiāṣ-ud-dīn Tughluḳ Shāh, the deceased, reigned for four years and a few months.[2]

---

shāhī, has clouded the issue and suppressed the truth by cleverly taking recourse to equivocal statements and metaphorical expressions. And there are sufficient reasons for it. Ẓia Barni, says Niẓām-ud-dīn Aḥmad in his *Tabaḳat-i-Akbari*, wrote his work in the reign of Sulṭān Firoz, who had a very great regard for Muḥammad Tughluḳ, and in deference to the reigning monarch he was reticent about the matter. Ibn Batuta, the Moorish traveller, who visited India in the third decade of the 14th century, suspects that the crown prince encompassed his father's death by ordering the building to be erected so that it might fall down at a particular moment. Besides, the act of raising to dignity and honour of Aḥmad Ayaz, the chief architect of the empire, by Muḥammad Tughluḳ, confirms the suspicion against the latter. Niẓām-ud-dīn, like Batuta, suspected treachery on the part of Muḥammad Tughluḳ. But Ferishta does believe the accusation to be true, and is inclined to believe the statement of Haji Muḥammad Ḳandhāri that the pavilion was struck by lightning. Al Badaoni is in company with Batuta and Niẓām-ud-dīn and is not free from suspicion, for says he, the construction of the edifice was unnecessary and superfluous, and is an evidence of unlawful desire on the part of the prince, who made it concave or hollow on purpose.

1 Badaoni writes that the Sulṭān, on account of the ill-will he bore to Sheikh-ul-Mashāekh, sent a message to the Sheikh while on the way to Lakhnauti to this effect, "After my arrival at Dehli, either the Sheikh will be there or I". The Sheikh replied, "Dehli is still some way off".

This well-known Persian proverb "Dehli is still some way off", like the parallel passage—"It's a far cry to Loch Awe"—express the futility of an incompetent person attempting any task.

2 MBL reads اللّٰه أعلم بالصّواب و إليه المرجع و المآب : MBM omits إليه, etc., JNS omits the whole sentence.

Account of Sulṭān Muḥammad Shāh, the eldest son of Sulṭān Ghiās-ud-dīn Tughluḳ Shāh.[1]

His accession, Rabī'-ul-auwal, 725 H. (Feb.-Mar., 1325 A.D.).

Sulṭān Muḥammad Shāh was the eldest son of Sulṭān Tughluḳ Shāh.[2] When Tughluḳ Shāh received martyrdom, and his funeral obsequies were performed in course of three days, he ascended the throne in the imperial palace in the month of Rabi'-ul-auwal of the aforesaid year (725 H.). Some forty days later[3] he left Tughluḳābād for Dehli.

Later on, domes were erected in the city, and the markets and the lanes were decorated with coloured and embroidered cloth. From the time that the Sulṭān set his foot in the city till he entered the imperial palace, gold and silver coins were rained from the back of the elephants among the populace, and gold was scattered in every street lane, and house.[4]

Conferment of titles, etc., on Amirs.

Some time after, in the first year of his accession, when order was restored in the country, the Amīrs and the Maliks, the chiefs and the grandees, who were friendly with the Sulṭān received suitable titles and surnames. For example, Malik Firoz,[5] the Sulṭān's cousin, was appointed *Nāib-i-Barbak*; Malik Aḥmad Ayaz,[6] the officer-in-charge of the palace, received the title of Khwāja-i-Jahān; Malik Ḳabul became Malik Kabīr; Malik Sar-tez became 'Imād-ul-Mulk; Malik Maḳbul became Ḳawām-ul-Mulk; Malik Khuram Munīr obtained the title of Zahir-ul-jiush; Ḥamid Komlī[7] received eminence and became Razi-ul-Mulk; Malik Pindār Khiljī became Ḳadr Khān and he obtained the *aḳtā'* of Lakhnauti; Malik Ḥisām-ud-dīn Abu-Rejā

---

1 JNS ذکر سلطان محمد شاه خونی بن سلطان غیاث الدین تغلق شاه غازي ملک. Badaoni calls him Sulṭān Muḥammad 'Ādil.

2 This line is omitted in JNS.

3 The period here mentioned of, *i.e*, forty days is the same as that enjoined to the Israelities. The period of three days is enjoined on the Muslims, except in the case of widows, who must perform the special ceremony of mourning called Iḥdād for four months and 10 days.

4 JNS کوچها : MBL, MBM خانها.

5 MBM ملک فیروز.

6 MBM ملک زاده احمد عیاض.

7 JNS and MBM حمیر لوبکی.

became Niẕām-ud-dīn and the vizir of Lakhnauti; Malik 'Az-ud-dīn Yāḥiyā became 'Aẕam-i-Mulk and was rewarded with the *aḳṭā'* of Sātgaon; Moulānā Ḳawām-ud-dīn became Ḳutlugh Khān and he received the office of *Vakildar*; Muḥammad, Ḳawām-ud-dīn's eldest son, became Alb Khān and he obtained the *aḳṭā'* of Gujrat; Moulānā Kamāl-ud-dīn, the brother of Ḳutlugh Khān, became *Ṣadr-i-Jahān*; Moulānā Niẕām-ud-dīn, Ḳutlugh's second brother, became 'Alim-ul-Mulk; Niẕām-ud-dīn Kamāl-Surkh[1] became Mukhliṣ-ul-Mulk Shihāb Sulṭānī became Tāj-ul-Mulk; Moulāna Yusuf became Dāwar-ul-Mulk;[2] a royal princess was given in marriage to Moulānā Yusuf; Malik Ḳirān became Safdar-ul-Mulk; Malik Begī became Sar-i-dawāt-dār;[3] Moulana Shahāb-ud-dīn Abu Rejā became Malik-ul-Tajār and he received the estate of Nowsary.

Sulṭān's expedition to Deogir, 727 H. (1326-27 A.D.).

In the year 727 H.,[4] the Sulṭān marched against Deogir, and he populated every Kuroh from Dehli to Deogir by *Dhāwāh*[5]. To them lands were granted, so that their revenue might go towards the payment of their salaries. When any courier arrived at any post he was received and taken to the next Dhāwāh.

The road from Dehli to Deogir populated: trees planted: rest-houses constructed.

At every post, rest-houses and monasteries were set up with a venerable prelate (over those establishments), and proper arrangements are made for the supply of victuals, so that whenever any guest appeared there, he was ministered with food, water, betel-leaf,[6] and lodging. On either sides

---

[1] MBL صرح: [2] MBM دوار الملک.

[3] MBM سرود انداز: The term (*Sar-i-dawāt-dar*) means, chief of the King's writing table.

[4] Badaoni gives 729 H., Ferishta, 739 H.

The fact that gold coins containing in the margin the inscription, "struck in the metropolis of the tribes of Islām" were struck in the name of the Sulṭān in 727 H., falsify the date of Ferishta.

Ibn Baṭuta's statement that the Sulṭān having taken offence at the inhabitants of Dehli because they threw into his audience hall abusive papers criticising his policy, decided to destroy their city, is based upon hearsay evidence and is not supported by Muḥammadan writers.

[5] Dhāwāh means "paiks" or "runners".

[6] The distribution of betel forms an important part on all ceremonial occasions, generally as a final act of hospitality before the guests depart. Here the text is not clear: it reads thus و هر الاغی که بیاید در کهت برنشانده برسو کرانه دهاوه برسانند MBM read در گهنت in place of در کهت.

of the road, continuous rows of trees were planted, the traces of which remained for many years. Deogir was called Daulatābād and made the imperial seat.

The crown-mother, princes and others evacuate Dehli for Deogir.

Makhdūma-i-Jahān, the crown-mother, along with the entire family, the Amīrs and Maliks, notable and renowned persons, attendants, slaves, elephants, horses, the treasury, and the hidden wealth of the emperor were carried over to Daulatābād. After Makhdūma-i-Jahān had reached Daulatābād, the princes, the prelates, and the chiefs of Dehli were ordered to proceed to the new capital. They carried out the royal fiat, and obtained the eminence of the Sulṭān's interview. His Majesty doubled the quantity of the gifts and stipends paid to them; and made, in addition, a present of gold for defraying expenses in connection with the construction of their dwelling houses. Every one became contented.[1]

Revolt of Bahādur Gurshasab.

Towards the end of the same year (727 H.) Malik Bahādur Gurshasab,[2] the *'Ariẓ-i-lashkar* (Inspector General of Forces) raised the standard of hostility. Khwāja-i-Jahān was sent against him with a big force, and on his arrival at the destination, the aforesaid Bahādur, opposed him with his few attendants,[3] but meeting with defeat at the end, was made a prisoner by the Hindus who despatched him to the court where he was executed.

Khwāja-i-Jahān was sent against him.

'Alī Khaṭaṭī sent to Multān against Iba.

Subsequently, 'Ali Khaṭaṭī was deputed towards Multān with a view to bring the followers of Bahrām[4] Aynah. Arriving at the place 'Ali Khaṭaṭi exercised severity in the despatch of Bahram's household: he made Bahrām sit in the court of justice and held out reproaches and strong expressions at him, so that the people became afraid.

---

[1] Badaoni writes that the desolation of Dehli and its desertion was a source of great discomfort to the inhabitants, large number of the feeble and widows, the helpless and indigent perished by the way, while even those who arrived in safety, could not settle there.

JNS مدفه العال : MBL مروح العال : MBM مفروح العال.

[2] MBL کرشناسب : JNS که شباشب.

[3] MBL با مقدار جمعت : MBM مقدار از جمعیت.

[4] JNS, MBM and Ẓia Barni, بهرام ایبه.

One day, out came Luli, the son-in-law of Bahrâm from his house, when he was thus addressed to by 'Ali Khaṭaṭī, "Why dost thou not despatch your dependants? Thou desireth that they should not go! Thou art acting villainously"! Luli enquired, "Whom dost thou call villain?" 'Alī informed, "To him who is sitting within the house". Luli questioned, "How dare you form such a hypothesis?" Alī Khaṭaṭī ran after Luli and got hold of his ringlets, but the latter threw him down, and asked his sword-bearer to sever off his head from the trunk. 'Alī was killed and his head was placed on a spear.

The following day Bahrām Aynah broke out into rebellion.

The Sulṭān proceeded to Multān. Defeat and death of Bahrām.

When the Sulṭān was put abreast of the position of affairs, he left Deogir for Dehli, whence having collected a heavy contingent, he formed the design of proceeding to Multān. On his arrival, Bahrām Aynah came upon him, and in the battle that took place between the forces, the latter, subsequently, met with reverses and was done to death. He was decapitated, and his head was brought before the Emperor, and most of his followers were made food for the sword.

The Sulṭān pardoned the Multānis.

The Sulṭān made up his mind to set the blood of the inhabitants of Multān flowing like rivers. Sheikh-ul-Islām, Kuṭub-ul-'Alam Sheikh Rukn-ul-Huk-wa-Shara'-wa-ud-dīn made an intercession on behalf of the people of Multān; having bared his venerable head, he presented himself at the court of the Sulṭān: the Sulṭān accepted the intercession of the holy Sheikh, and granted clemency to the Multânis who had sided with Bahrām.

Multān bestowed upon Kawām-ul-Mulk.

The *aktā'* of Multān was situated on the frontiers of Sindh; it was bestowed upon Malik Kawām-ul-Mulk[1] in fief.

The Sulṭān proceeded to Multān: flight of Shāhu Lodi.

A few years later, His Majesty sent out Bihzād (to Multān), and after the latter had been assassinated by Shahu Lodi,[2] the Sulṭān pursued his march against Dibâlpur, when Shâhu fled towards the hills.

---

[1] Badaoni, Malik Kawām-ul-Mulk Maķbūl.

[2] Tab-i-Akb. Shahu Afghan: Badaoni, Shahu Lodi Afghan.

Multān placed under 'Imād-ul-Mulk.

At this time Sheikh Kuṭub-ul-'Alam paid the debt of nature, and His Majesty conferred the *akṭā'* upon 'Imād-ul-Mulk Multānī.[1] Some of the renowned Amīrs and Maliks, attended with 50,000 horse entered the country of 'Imād-ul-Mulk, and the Emperor took his way to the metropolis, Dehli.

Advance of Tarma Shīrīn, the Mughal, against Dehli.

In the year 729 H.[2] (1328-29 A.D.), Tarma Shīrīn Mughal, the brother of Kutlugh Khwāja, the king of Khorāsān, marched against Dehli with a vast army, conquered most of the citadels, and put under confinement the people of Lahore, Sāmāna and Indari to the borders of Badāōn: when his army reached the banks of the Jaun, he retraced his way back.

The Sulṭān to Kalāpur: the latter bestowed on Majīr-ud-dīn.

Having collected his forces between Dehli and Ḥauẓ-i-Khāṣ, the Sulṭān encamped there, and when the defeated Tarma Shīrīn crossed the river Sindh, His Majesty ran after the fugitives with a heavy battalion to the borders of Kalāpur.[3] The Emperor bestowed the ruined fortress of Kalāpur upon Malik Majīr-ud-dīn Abu Rejā[4] so that he might repair it. Having despatched some notable and brave chiefs against Tarmā, the Sulṭān paced his way to the capital, Dehli.

Taxation of the country doubled: other laws,

Subsequently, His Majesty was pleased to increase the taxes of the country twenty-fold.[5] *Khahri* was produced and pasturage laid out.[6] Cattle was branded, the houses of the people were computed, and the

---

1 JNS and MBM دران وقت وفات شیخ قطب العالم شده بود شیخ عود سلطان ملک عماد الملک سلطاني را مفوض.

2 Ferishta (Briggs I, 413) places this invasion in 727 H., and gives the name of the Mughal leader as Toormooshreen Khān, the chief of the tribe of Chogtay. The writer continues, "unable to cope with the enemy in the field, the Sulṭān sued for peace and sent valuable presents to soften the invader, who at last consented to withdraw to his own country retreating through Gujrat and Sindh. Ẓia Barni does not, in his work, refer to this eventful irruption, and that is owing to, as Ferishta conceives, the fear of giving offence to Firuz Tughluk". Tab-i-Akb., like Ẓīa Barni, is also silent on this point. Badaoni refers to this invasion and places it in 729 H.

3 JNS, MBM and Badaoni read Kalānor.

4 MBM محي الدين ابورجا :

5 MBL خراج ولايت يکی به بيست کنند : JNS and MBM يکی بده و يکی به بيست.

6 JNS and MBL کهري وجدائي : MBM کهري وحرائي.

sown-fields were measured.[1] The royal order promulgated the business laws,[2] and fixed the price-current of grain.[3] For these reasons, the people left off their cattle and betook themselves to the forests, and the malefactors gained in strength.[4]

The people of Dehli ordered off to Daulatābād.

Later on, a royal mandate[5] was issued enjoining upon the people[6] of Dehli and its neighbourhood, to move off *en masse* to Daulatābād. The houses of the city people were purchased, and the owners were paid in cash from the treasury. In accordance with the royal fiat, all the inhabitants of the city and its suburbs, were despatched towards Daulatābād. The city was so evacuated, that the city-doors remained shut for days together: the dogs and cats made no noise in the city. The riff-raffs and the ruffians that remained in the city, carried off chattels from the houses and put those things to plunder.

Dehli re-populated.

At length, the royal order emanated to the effect that the theologians and the prelates, the chiefs of the cities and the leaders of villages should come up and settle down in the city.[7] The Sulṭān rewarded them with presents and gifts: the whole of Daulatābād was populated by the inhabitants of Dehli.

Introduction of copper tokens.

Owing to the bestowal of abundant presents and rewards upon the people, the Exchequer was bereft of money. All the sources of income and the means of import[8] were closed.[9] The copper *tankas* were

---

[1] MBL كشتها مي پيمودند : JNS and MBM كشتها مي نمودند.

[2] JNS and MBL وفاها فرماني مي گرفتند : MBM مي بستند.

[3] MBM omits نرخ فرمانى مي بستند.

[4] Ẓia Barni, who hailed from Baran, a district which was distressed from the effects of this enhancement, is vehement in his denunciations against the Sulṭān. This fiscal measure of the Sulṭān, he says, led to the impoverishment of the ryot, the ruination of the land, arrest of cultivation and all sorts of other evils.

[5] MBL فرمان قضا مضا : JNS and MBM omit قضا مضا.

[6] JNS and MBL ساكنان : MBM سكان.

[7] Ẓia Barni narrates that the importation of the people did not populate the city: the Sulṭān's attempt did not reconcile the people and the old prosperity of Dehli did not return. The abandonment of the city, excessive misfortune, difficulty in travelling and the desolation of the city proved an impediment to the people. Those who returned were way-laid, and those who reached the city found no peace.

[8] MBL ابواب داخل و خارج بكلي : MBM داخل بكلي : JNS agrees with MBM.

[9] MBL مسدود و مندرس شد : MBM and JNS مسدود شد.

issued as tokens, and their value was enhanced to twenty-five times; they became current on a equal footing with the *Tankā-i-lāl*:[1] any one who showed reluctance to receive it used to be punished severely. In collusion with one another,[2] the Hindus and the evil seekers established a mint in every village, struck copper coins, sent them to the city, and received in exchange gold, silver, horses, arms, and precious articles. It was for this reason that the contumacious gained in strength.[3] Some time after, the people of the far off countries refused to accept the copper tokens, and one gold coin rose to the value of fifty or sixty copper coins. Owing to the cheapness of the copper tokens, His Majesty, perforce, called in those currency and proclaimed that whoever possessed copper coins should bring them to the treasury, and receive gold coins in exchange. The people profited greatly by this arrangement and they became wealthy.[4] Gold was drained out of the treasury, and the copper tokens were rejected.[5] For a long time they (copper coins) remained lying in heaps in the palace of Tughlukābād.

onquest of Ḳarājal.

The Sulṭān issued orders for the conquest of Koh-i-Karājal,[6] which lay between the countries of India and China. He sent out 80,000 horse under leaders

---

[1] MBL مهری بمقدار بیست کانی و ان را به یک تنکهٔ حال نرخ نهاد : MBM بمقدار بیست پنجکانی و ان را یک تنکهٔ حال نهال هرکه در ستودن : JNS agrees with MBM.

[2] MBL مفسدان مواسات و موالات : MBM omits موالات : JNS agrees with MBL.

[3] MBL and JNS قوت گرفتند : MBM قوت کردند.

[4] MBL مبلغی مال خلق بردند - و بدین سبب غنی گشتند : JNS and MBM مبلغی خلق بدین سبب غني گشت.

[5] MBL, MBM مهرمس مردود شد : JNS مهرمس نا مردود شد.

[6] Badaoni and Ferishta give 738 H. Badaoni, Tab-i-Akb., and Ferishta read Himachal. Briggs identifies Himachal with Nepal and the countries on both sides of the Himalayas. According to Ferishta the leader of this expedition was Khusru Malik, the sister's son of the Emperor. In the opinion of Ẓia Barni, the Sulṭān's conception was, that as he had undertaken the conquest of Khorasān, he would first bring under the dominion of Islam this mountain, so that the passage for horses and soldiers and the march of the army might be rendered easy.

Ferishta writes that having heard of the great wealth of China, the Emperor conceived the idea of subduing that Empire; but in order to accomplish his design it was found necessary first to conquer Himachal. The nobles and councillors of the king tried to convince him of the futility of the scheme, but failed to do so. MBM قراحل:

and ordered them that on their arrival at the Ghati, they should establish garrisons, so that their return-journey might not be arduous. Reaching the aforesaid place, the imperialists established posts, and when they entered the mountains of Ḳarājal, the scarcity of provisions and the narrowness of the passes began to be severely felt. The hill-men took possession of the posts, and assassinated those who were placed in charge of the garrisons. The army that entered into those places were slain to a man, some of the commandars were taken prisoners and kept for some time near the Rāi. Such a force was never collected afterwards. This event took place in 738 H. (1337-38 A.D.).

Fakhr-ud-dīn assumes royalty at Sonārgāon.

Later on, Bahrām Khān breathed his last at Sonārgāon, and on 739 H.[1] (1338-39 A.D.), Malik Fakhr-ud-dīn, the sword-bearer of the deceased, became rebellious and assumed the insignia of royalty under the designation of Sulṭān Fakhr-ud-dīn. Malik Pīndār Khilji Ḳadr Khān, the ruler of Lakhnauti, Malik Hisām-ud-dīn Abu Rejā, the *Mustaufi-i-mamālik*, 'Aẓam-i-Mulk[2] 'Az-ud-dīn Yaḥiya, the feoffee of Satgāon and Firoz Khān, the son of Naṣrat Khān and the Amīr of Karah, marched to Sonārgāon against the rebel. The latter, also, came out with his men to meet them, and in the contest which followed, Fakhr-ud-dīn being worsted took to his heels. The elephants and horses of the fugitive were taken possession of; Ḳadr Khān remained at that place, while the other Amīrs retired to their respective fiefs.

When the rainy season drew in, most of the horses in the army of Ḳadr Khān died. He had collected a vast amount of silver species, and had, after two or three months, stored it up in heaps[3] in his own house saying that, in like manner would he stock the silver before the presence of His Majesty, so that the more the silver was stocked the more would it be serviceable to the Sulṭān. Malik

---

1 MBL نسع و سبعمائة : JNS and MBM تسع و ثلاثين و سبعمائة : Badaoni reads 739 H. : Ferishta, 741 H.

Ẓīa Barni and Ferishta place Fakhr-ud-dīn's rebellion after that of Bahrām Aynah.

2 MBL omit ملک : JNS and MBM retain it.

3 MBL بکجا تودة میرد : JNS and MBM بکجا بردة میرن.

Hisām-ud-dīn [1] advised him thus, "It is detrimental to amass a huge wealth in the remote *akṭā's*, for the people would covet it and would be suspicious as to why the money is not being sent to the Emperor. Whatever wealth and cash have been collected should be despatched to the treasury: nothing could be better than this." Kadr Khān paid little attention to him, and neither did he give to the soldiery their due, nor did he send the wealth to the treasury.[2] The soldiers coveted the wealth, and no sooner than Fakhr-ud-dīn arrived. Kadr's men sided with him (Fakhr-ud-din) and assassinated the latter (Kadr).

'Ali Mubārak took possession of Lakhnauti.

Fakhr-ud-dīn took his seat at Sonargāon, and left his slave, Mukhliṣ at Lakhnauti.[3] 'Alī Mubārak, the Inspector of Troops under Kadr Khān, put Mukhliṣ to death and possessed himself of Lakhnauti. But he showed no sign of sovereignty, and sent a petition to His Majesty to the effect that he had occupied Lakhnauti, and if His Honour would condescend to despatch one of his slaves there and instal him on the throne, he (Fakhr-ud-din) would pay his respects to the Emperor. The Sulṭān issued orders that Yusuf, the Governor of the city (Dehli) should be conferred with the rank of a Khān, and deputed (to Lakhnauti). In the meantime, Malik Yusuf dying His Majesty gave no attention to it, and none did he despatch to Lakhnauti. 'Alī Mubārak, owing to his opposition to Fakhr-ud-dīn, perforce, assumed the insignia of royalty, and called himself Sulṭān 'Alā'-ud-dīn.

Iliyās Hāji ascends the throne of Lakhnauti.

Some time after, Malik Iliyās Hāji, who had a big following, having joined with the Amirs, Maliks and the people of Lakhnauti, put 'Alā'-ud-dīn to death, and ascended the throne under the designation of Sulṭān Shams-ud-dīn.

Iliyās imprisons Fakhr-ud-dīn and kills him.

In the year 741 H. (1340-41 A.D.), Iliyās marched against Sonārgāōn, and having put fetters round Fakhr-ud-dīn turned on his

---

[1] MBM حسام مي گفت.

[2] MBL او نمي شنيد . نه حق لشكر به لسكرى داد : JNS زر نمي شنيد نه حق لشكر بلشكر مي داد : MBM او نمي شنيدند حق لشكر بلشكر مي داد.

[3] MBL در لكهنوتي گذاشت : JNS and MBM برداشت.

heels: subsequently, he assassinated the latter at Lakhnauti. Thenceforth, Lakhnauti passed under the control of Sultān Shams-ud-dīn and his sons, and never afterwards came under the authority of the Emperors of Dehli.

Rebellion of Malik Ibrāhim.

In the year 742 H.[1] (1341-42 A.D.), Sa'iyid Hasan Kithili, the father[2] of Malik Ibrāhim, the purse bearer, fermented a revolt at Ma'bar,[3] and having killed some of the Imperial officers that had been appointed to that district, and gaining over the others to his own party, put himself in possession of the entire country of Ma'bar.[4]

The Sultān marched to Deogir.

The Sultān proceeded to Deogir[5] for the purpose of quelling that disturbance, and on his arrival at Tilang was taken ill, and was forced to return. It was rumoured that the corpse of the Sultān was being conveyed in a palanquin. Malik Hoshang who had withdrawn himself from the rebellion,[6] having learnt that the Sultān was still living, joined His Majesty. The Sultān returned by uninterrupted marches to Dehli, and left Daulatābād in the custody of Kutlugh Khān. Thus the rebellion in Ma'bar remained unchecked. Meanwhile, famine had broken out in Dehli.

Rebellion of Gulchunder and Halājaun.

In the year 743 H. (1342-43 A.D.), Gulchunder and Malik Halājaun[7] put to death by treachery Malik Tatār Khurd, the Governor of Lahore,[8] and raised the standard of hostility. Khwāja-i-Jahān was sent out to suppress the rebellion, and when he reached Lahore he was opposed by Malik Halājaun and Gulchunder Khokhar, who

---

[1] JNS and MBM اثنين و اربعين و سبعمائه : JNS احدى و اربعين و سبعمائه.

[2] JNS بندۀ ملک ابراهيم.

[3] The western coast of the peninsula.

[4] Badāoni writes, Hasan revolted on the grounds of the severity of the Sultān's Governors, and the innovations introduced in the laws and the number of executions.

[5] MBL در ديوگير رفت : JNS از طرف لکهنوتي ديوگير : MBM لکهنوتي ديوگير.

[6] MBL از فتنه متواری شد : ملک هوسنگ بديدهن MBM بديدهيرا رفته متواري : JNS ملک هوسنگ بر موهيرا متواري شده.

[7] JNS کلغندۀ ملک هلاچون : MBM گلچندر و ملک هلاچون : MBL کلچند روز و ملک هلاجون : Badaoni, Kul Chander Khākhar and Malik Halājaun.

[8] Badaoni writes, "they put to death by treachery Malik Halājaun and Kul Chunder Khākhar and Malik Tatār Khurd, the Governor of Lahore"

were at last defeated. Khwāja-i-Jahān, having put down the rebellion, returned from the expedition.

The Sultān started to Multān against Bihzād.

In the year 744 H.[1] (1343-44 A.D.), the army of Fakhr-ud-dīn Bihzād being in straits[2] became rebellious. Shāhu Lodi Afghān rebelled in Multān and killed Bihzād. Malik Nuā[3] who had accompanied the deceased fled from Multān to Dehli. The Sultān personally started on an expedition to Multān. Meanwhile famine was raging in the city with such a fury that man was devouring man.

Verse.[4]

To such an extent the famine that men from extreme want of victuals, like the candle,
Burnt their own bodies on the fire and killed themselves.

"It is customary among the apostles to abandon those things that are beyond the power."

Flight of Shāhu Lodi.

On the Sultān's approach to Dibālpur, Shāhu Lodi dared not put forth opposition[5] and made good his escape towards the mountains. Having made his return from Dibalpur, His Majesty conferred Multān upon 'Imād-ul Mulk Sartez, and passing through Sannam,[6] and Sāmāna massacred[7] the Sa'iyids of Kaithal and the other Muslims. He conveyed the chief men of those districts to the suburbs of the city, conferred upon them villages and districts, and bestowing on each

Massacre of the Sa'iyids of Kaithal.

---

1 Ferishta places this event in 742 H.

2 MBL تنگ آوردن لشکر فخر الدین بهذاد : JNS and MBM لشکر از فخر الدین :

3 Tab-i-Akb. ملک بهورا :

4 This verse is omitted in JNS and MBM.

5 MBL طاقت مقاومت : JNS and MBM طاقت استقامت.

6 60 miles to the west of Sirhind.

7 Zia Barni writes, the Sultān put down the rebels (of Sannām and Sāmāna) who had formed strongholds, withheld tribute and created disturbances and plundered on the road. Many of them became Muslims and some placed in the service of noblemen.

Ferishta says, "the tribes of Mundulla, Chowhan, Meeana, Bhurteea and others who inhabited the country about Sannām and Sāmāna, unable to discharge their rents, fled to the woods. The King massacred several thousands of them"

Tab-i-Akb. writes, bands of Mundāhvis, Chauhāns, Bahtians, and Minahs.

gold belts and head dresses gave them a place of abode there. The Sulṭān entered the city and ordered the people to proceed to Hindustan and to stay there for some time in order that they might be freed from the famine.[1]

Advent of the people of Khorāsan.

In the meantime, the people of Khorāsān,[2] in the hope of receiving the bounty of the Sulṭān, who was extremely lavish in making gifts to those people, came to India. Each of them received in proportion (to their rank) silver, gold, precious stones, horses, clothes, robes (of honour), gold belts, wrappers, caps, presents and gifts of other things, such that they never beheld before. All the big mansions in the prosperous city were owned by them. They used to purchase all articles, such as, slaves, gold and silver, paper and books, and sent those articles to Khorāsān.[3]

The rebellion of the Governor of Karah put down.

In the year 745 H. (1344-45 A.D.), Malik Niẓām,[4] the Governor of Karah, who prided himself upon the few slaves which he had collected round him, raised the banner of insurrection. Shahr-ul-lah, the brother of 'Ain-ul-Mulk, having collected his forces from Oudh, attacked and defeated his army and seized him, and thereby put down the rebellion.

Disturbance at Bidar created by Shihāb-Sulṭāni.

Later on, in the same year, Shihāb-Sulṭānī[5] created disturbance in Bidar and won over the people of Bidar to his side. Kutlugh Khān marched against him to quell the insurrection.[6] The youngest son[7] of Shihāb-Sulṭāni came out to

---

[1] Ẓīa Barni and Tab-i-Akb. write, "At this time Kanya Paik (Naik) the Hindu leader at Warrangal broke out in rebellion and took possession of the country. There was also a second rebellion at Kampilah (in the Doab)".

Ferishta says, "that Krishna Naig, the son of Ludder Deo united to his forces the troops of Bilal Dew, Raja of Carnatic, and of the Rajas of Ma'bar and Diwar Sumoodra and reduced Arrangal".

[2] Badaoni writes, "the people of Khorāsān, Irak and Samarkand".

[3] Badaoni writes, "in this year (744 H.) Hājī Sa'īd Ṣarṣari arrived from Egypt bearing the diploma of the Khelafat of Egypt with a banner and a robe of honour, conferring upon the Sulṭān the title of Nāṣir-i-Amir-ud-Mū'minin".

[4] JNS نظام الملك : Ẓīa Barni, Niẓām Māin: Tab-i-Akb. Niẓām Mābin: Badaoni, Niẓām-ul-Mulk: Ferishta, Niẓām Bein, the Governor of Sambhal.

[5] Ẓīa Barni and Tab-i-Akb., "who bore the title of Naṣrat Khān".

[6] MBL دفع شراو : MBM and JNS ننقة شراو.

[7] JNS and MBL پسر خرد : MBM پسر خرد.

meet him with his forces, but failing to offer any resistance he was put to the worst. He took shelter in the fort of Bidar. The father and the son together shut themselves up in the fort. Ḳutlugh Khān offered them safety[1] and despatched them to Dehli.

Rebellion of 'Alī Shāh.

In the year 746 H. (1345-46 A.D.), 'Alī Shāh,[2] the sister's son to Ẓafar Khān 'Alā'ī and the Amīr Ṣadah of Ḳutlugh Khān, set out (from) Deogir (to Gulburgah) for the collection of revenue; as that part of the country was denuded of soldiers, zagirdārs and the chiefs, he gained over his brothers to his side, and treacherously slew Bahran,[3] the Governor of Gulburgah; taking much spoil went to Bidar, and having slain the deputy of that place, put to plunder vast properties, and took possession of Bidar.

Ḳutlugh Khān marched against the rebel and defeated him.

Being informed of this (rebellion). the Sulṭān sent Ḳutlugh Khān, with some Amīrs, Maliks, and equipage from Dhār to suppress the outbreak. When Ḳutlugh Khān reached the place, 'Alī Shāh advanced to meet him and giving battle was routed. 'Alī Shāh took shelter in the citadel (of Bidar). Ḳutlugh Khān invested the fortress, and a few days after, 'Alī Shāh was made prisoner along with his brothers and sent near the Sulṭān at Sargdāori.[4] The Sulṭān sent them to Ghaznīn in exile,[5] but afterwards recalled them thence and put them all to death before his presence.

Revolt of 'Ain-ul-Mulk.

In the year 747 H.[6] (1346-47 A.D.), the Sulṭān led his forces towards Hindustān: approaching Sargdāori, he was joined by 'Ain-ul-Mulk,[7] who made a

---

1 MBL بلمان دست آورد : JNS and MBM بامان در آوردة.

2 JNS and MBL علي شه : MBM and Ẓia Barni عليشاه : Badaoni, 'Alī Sher; Ferishta, Amir 'Alī.

3 Ẓia Barni, Bahīran.

4 MBL سر گداوری : JNS سرک دواري : MBM سرک داوري : Ranking, Sarkdawārī: Tab-i-Akb., Sargdwārī: This place is situated in the Farrukhabad District.

5 MBM جدا کرد : JNS and MBL جلا کرد.

6 JNS اربع و اربعين.

7 He held the territory of Oudh and Zafarābād.

present of goods and precious things, by way of servitude, to him. His Majesty having decided upon the despatch of ‘Ain-ul-Mulk to Daulatābād with his cavalry, retainers and brothers, summoned Ḳutlugh Khān near him. This specific news[1] reaching ‘Ain-ul-Mulk, he became suspicious, and considered the Imperial order to be the pretext of the Sulṭān who was sending him out of Hindustān in order to bring him to ruin.[2] For this reason, he took alarm, and fled by night from Sargdāori with forced marches, forded the Ganges and went over to oudh. Prior to the revolt of ‘Ain-ul-Mulk,[3] the Sulṭān had, under his (‘Ain-ul-Mulk) command sent most of the elephants, horses, arm-bearers and other troops to the other bank of the Ganges for (securing) abundant provisions (for the army); and had kept near him only a few foot at the request of Malik Firoz Mulk, the *Nāib-i-Barbak*, who petitioned that most of the horses and foot soldiers were marching to the ford, and that, as some (attcndants) should necessarily be preserved for the hunts, it was not judicious to send them all away. At that time some of the horses were left at the stables. Shahr-ul-lah, the brother of ‘Ain-ul-Mulk, carried off the horses and the elephants from the ford, and tempting the aforesaid soldiery carried them with him.[4] ‘Ain-ul-Mulk and he, with elephants, horse, and equipage proceeded with successive marches to Ḳanauj, and thence crossing the Ganges descended. The Sulṭān summoned some of the Amīrs and Maliks who had, previous to this, been given leave to return to their fiefs,[5] such as, Khwāja-i-Jahān to Dhār, and Malik ‘Imād-ul-Mulk to Multān; they had only proceeded to Bianāh when they were recalled. The other Amīrs, also, came from other sides. From thence, His Majesty moved onwards and encamped near the fortress of Ḳanauj.

---

1 JNS and MBL این صغن نوعي : MBM این نوعي .

2 Tab-i-Akb. writes, “Before this a number of writers who had been accused of embezzlement in Dehli....had left Dehli....and had gone to Audh, and thrown themselves in the protection of ‘Ain-ul-Mulk. This excited the anger of the Sulṭān, but he considered it inexpedient to show it”.

3 JNS and MBM مختلف شد : MBL متخلف .

4 MBL طوایف مذکور را نیز ترغیب کرده برابر خود روانه کرد : JNS and MBM مذکور را بترغیب برابر خود روان کرد .

5 JNS and MBL بجانب اقطاعات خویش : MBM بجانب او اقطاعات .

During the afternoon prayers, 'Ain-ul-Mulk crossed the river at the ford of Lidbah [1]. When the Sulṭān was informed of this, he exclaimed, "For them Lidbah is an evil augury: let us be prepared!" Towards the close of the night, he reached the place where the army was quartered, and proceeding on foot commenced hostilities in the manner of the people of Hindustān.[2] The Sulṭān, on his side, had divided the elephants and the forces in different sections. At the first attack, the enemy was defeated: receiving a wound, Shahr-ul-lāh fell back towards the Ganges, and was carried away by the stream. Likewise did the whole of his army, horse and foot, fall into the river—some of whom were drowned, while some who safely crossed the river fell into the hands of the Hindus who plundered them.

Battle between the Sulṭān and 'Ain-ul-Mulk.

'Ain-ul-Mulk was taken prisoner. Bereft of head dress, he was placed on an ass by Ibrāhim Bangi, and taken to the Sulṭān, who put him to detention before the *dākhul* for some time; but, subsequently, he was let off, and was received with much kindness by the Emperor. From that place the Sulṭān took his way to Dehli.

'Ain-ul-Mulk imprisoned and later set free.

His Majesty ordered Kutlugh Khān to appear before him from Daulatābād, with his attendants and equipage. The latter, in compliance with the mandate, left his brother 'Alam-i-Mulk at that place, and made his way to Dehli [3].

Kutlugh Khān proceeds to Dehli.

---

[1] JNS and MBM بوقت نماز دیگر در گذر لیدبه گذارا شد : MBL دیگر در گدارا به گدارا شد : Tab-i-Akb. read Bangar Mau.

[2] MBL بر طریقی که در جنگهای هندوستان جنگ میکردند بعرب پیوستند . JNS : بر طریقی که در جنگلهای MBM : بر طریقی که در جنگلها جنگ میکردند بعرت etc. Badaoni writes, "....like the thieves and *Gawārs* (of India) took to the wood and fought on foot."

[3] Our author fails to mention two other events of the reign during this period:—

(1) The Sulṭān's march to Bahraich to pay his devotion at the tomb of Salar Mas'ud Shahid.

(2) His rendering of homage to the Sulṭān of Egypt, and the arrival of an embassy from the latter.

Vide Tab-i-Akb. (Tr. B. De., A.S.B., pp. 227-29) and Ẓia Barni (Bib. Indica. 2191

In the year 748 H.[1] (1347-48 A.D.) the *Amirs Ṣadah*[2] of Dihu'i[3] and Barodā[4] put to death Mukbil, the slave Khwājā-i-Jahān who was the Nāib-vizir of Gujrat, and was proceeding to the court, and stirred up rebellion[5]; furniture, revenue, horses and arms were carried off by them. Malik 'Aziz[6], the ruler of Dhār[7] marched against the aforesaid Amīrs Ṣadah, but he was also killed.

The rebellion of Amirs Ṣadah.

The Sultān led an army against the Amirs.

The Sultān marched out with the object of quelling this rebellion, and reaching Gujrat he deputed sundry Amīrs, such as, Malik 'Alī Sher[8], the head of the sword bearers, Malik Aḥmad Lājīn[9] and some other nobles to Daulatābād near 'Alam-i-Mulk, with a view to bringing the Amīrs Ṣadah of Daulatābād near the Sultān. In compliance with the farmān, 'Alam-i-Mulk despatched the Amīrs Ṣadah. When the Amīrs Ṣadah of Daulatābād, in company with the aforesaid Amīrs reached Manickgunj,[10] they took alarm suspecting that they had been asked to come near the

---

1 Ẓīa Barni gives 745 H. Badaoni, 748 H.

2 Tab-i-Akb. says, "At that time the Yuzbāshis were called the Amīrs Ṣadah." Fenshta calls them *Amīr judeeda* and explains, that "this term meaning '*New officers*' was given to the newly converted Mughals and their descendants who had embraced Muḥammedan religion, and the service of the Kings of Dehli at the same time."

Elliot gives "Foreign Amīrs", Ranking, "Captains of hundreds".

3 Tab-i-Akb., Deoli: Ranking, Dabho'ī; JNS دمهوئی: MBM دسهوئي.

4 JNS بروادہ: MBL برودرہ.

5 Ẓīa Barni and Niẓām-ud-dīn give the following cause of the rebellion: the slaughter of about 800 Amīrs Ṣadah by the base-born 'Aziz Himār, (who had been appointed to Dhar and Malwah) on the ground of their being foreigners, caused those of Deogir and Gujrat and every other place to write and to break out into insurrection.

6 MBL ملک عزیز: Ẓīa Barni reads 'Azīz Ḥimār: Tab-i-Akb. and Badaoni, 'Aziz Khamār.

7 JNS and MBM omit ضابط دهار.

8 JNS and MBM ملک علي سر جاندار: Badaoni is of same opinion: but Tab-i-Akb. writes, "The Sultān deputed Zin Bandah who bore the title of Maj-ud-dīn, and the son of Rukn Tānessari." Ẓīa Barni reads Maj-ul-Mulk instead of Maj-ud-dīn.

9 MBM ملک احمد احمد لاجین.

10 MBL درگهی مانک گنج: JNS در کهنتی بایک کنج: MBM در کهتي بانکه ؟. Ranking, "at the pass of Manickgunj".

Sulṭān for being slain. At night, they came to a common understanding and rebelled; and during the course of their progress they assassinated the aforesaid Amīrs. Malik Aḥmad Lājin was put to death, and other Amīrs took to their heels. The above-mentioned Amīrs Ṣadah made for Daulatābād[1]. 'Alam-i-Mulk[2] shut himself up in the palace of Daulatābād. In return for 'Alam-i-Mulk's kind treatment with the Amīrs Ṣadah, the latter granted him safety and sent him near the city. They raised to the throne one Isma'īl Makh[3] and gave him the title of Sulṭān Nāṣir-ud-dīn. The Sulṭān, on receipt of this information, moved onwards, and sent out an army for the suppression of the Amīrs Ṣadah of Dihu'ī and Barodā. The latter opposed the Sulṭān's army, but being defeated at length, retired to Daulatābād, and joined hands with the Amīrs Ṣadah of that place. From thence, the Sulṭān, also proceeded to Daulatābād and met Isma'īl Makh, who lost his power of opposition and meeting with failure betook himself to the fortress of Dhārā-gir[4]. A good many people were put to the sword, and of the Muslims of Daulatābād some were either imprisoned or plundered, and some bore company with Isma'īl.

Insurrection of Malik Taghi in Gujrat.

While the Sulṭān was at Daulatābād, tidings arrived of the rebellion in Gujrat of Malik Ṭaghi, who having put to death Malik Muzaffar[5] had obtained possession of all his treasure and chattels. The Sulṭān left Malik Jouhar, Khudawand Ẓādah Kawām-ud-dīn, Sheīkh Burhān-ud-dīn Balārāmi, and some other Amīrs at Dhārā-gir[6]; directed Malik 'Imād-ul-Mulk Sartez[7] with a big force to hunt up the forces of Daulatābād, that had after the defeat fled towards Bidar: and personally departed towards Gujrat in pursuit of Ṭaghi. The army of Daulatābād, whose leader was Ḥasan Kānku, lay in ambush and fell upon 'Imād-ul-Mulk, killing the

---

[1] MBL دولت آباد حصاري شده.

[2] MBL ملک عالم: Badaoni, Ma..k 'Alam.

[3] Tab-i-Akb., Malik Makh, brother of Malik Mal Afghān: Ẓīa Barni, Malik Yak Afghān: Badaoni, Isma'īl Fatḥ.

[4] MBM دهار کر: JNS دهارا کر: Badaoni, "fortress of Dhārānagar by which is meant the citadel of Daulatābād". Tab-i-Akb., Dhārāgarh.

[5] He was the deputy of Sheīkh Mu'iz-ud-dīn, the Governor of Nahrwāla.

[6] MBM دهارا گیر.

[7] MBL عماد الدین شیرم: Ẓīa Barni, Sartez-i-Sulṭānī.

latter. Meeting with defeat, the army of 'Imād-ul-Mulk fled to Daulatābād. Malik Jauhar and the other Amīrs, who were at Daulatābād, could not sustain the opposition and gave up the siege. Hasan Kānku pursued them and came to Daulatābād, and having driven out Isma'il Makh ascended the throne under the title of 'Alā'-ud-din. Since then, some of the districts of Daulatābād passed under the control of Hasan Kānku and his descendants.

Hasan Kānku ascends the throne of Daulatābād.

In pursuit of the rebel in Gujrat, the Sultān moved about from place to place.[1] Twice did Taghi confront him, and twice was the rebel defeated. In this expedition was Malik Firoz Mulk summoned from Dehli, and he joined the Sultān.

The Sultān in Gujrat against Taghi.

After some time, Malik Kabir[2], the son of Kabul Khalifatī breathed his last. Khwājā-i-Jahān and Malik Makbul Kawām-ul-Mulk remained at Dehli.

Death of Malik Kabir.

The utmost endeavour and effort, diligence and labour of the late Sultāns—*May God illuminate their demonstrations!*—and of Sultān 'Alā'-ud-dīn Khilji particularly—*May the light of God be on his tomb!*—were towards the progress of Islām, showing compassion to the Faith, securing of benefits, safety of the roads, repose of the people, tranquillity of the empire, habitation of the country and the conquest of kingdoms. But now, in their stead, are manifest, the weakness of Islām and the languor of the Religion, the crimes of the irreligious and the disturbance of the rebels, the terror of the traveller and the affliction of the people, the insurrection in the country and other regions, oppression in place of justice, and infidelity in place of Islām have taken a firm root. These are due to various reasons:—

The causes that led to the disorder in the empire.

---

[1] A fuller account of the Sultān's campaigns in Gujrat is to be found in Zīa Barni. (Bib. Indica, 260 *et seq.*)

[2] Badaoni, Gir. Badaoni writes that the Sultān had delegated the control of all important affairs to Malik Kabir.

Of Malik Kabir, Tab-i-Akb. writes, "After the arrival of an ambassador from Egypt to Dehli, bringing to the Sultān a farmān sanctioning his rule, the Sultān sent along with the precious jewels and other gifts, Malik Kabir, the chief of his guards and made him part and parcel of the Khalif's property. He got a memorial executed by Kabir, containing a stipulation that he would serve the Khalif.

Firstly, Tarmā Shirin Mughal[1] sacked and plundered the people of the towns, villages and the neighbouring places, and these places never again recovered their prosperity.

Rapine of Tarmā Shirin.

Secondly, the tribute to be paid by the inhabitants of the country were increased to ten or twenty times and the live-stock were numbered: consequently, the people deserted their houses and cattles, and took recourse to evil company: the contumacious gained in strength: subsequently, the country was put to plunder and it was totally ruined.

Increase of tribute: numbering of live-stock.

Thirdly, there was a general absence of rain, and a severe famine broke out in all parts of the country. For example, there was not even a drop of rain for seven years, and even a vestige of cloud was not to be seen in the skies.

Absence of rain: outbreak of famine.

Fourthly, the inhabitants of Dehli were removed wholesale to Daulatabād, and the people were taken to the city from the rotten parishes, but on the next occasion were compelled to evacuate their places. The goods which they had received from their forefathers, they left behind them and came outside the city. Afterwards, neither those chattels reached them, nor could they procure any other. Neither was the city re-populated nor the towns.

People of Dehli removed to Daulatābād.

Fifthly, a contingent of about 80,000 cavalry with their slaves and attendants that was sent against Ḳarājal suddenly entered the orifice of death[2] were killed to a man, so that not even a couple returned: such a force had never been collected since then.

Contingent sent against Ḳarājal put to death.

Sixthly, of those who in fear of their life had raised the standard of insurrection in the country, some were killed and some became funky. In short, those places were devastated and the rebels gained in strength. "They began committing blood-shed, and there was no one who could oppose them, because, the Sulṭān had ruined his whole army and attendants

Devastation of places.

---

[1] JNS and MBM ترمه شیرین.

[2] JNS and MBL سوراخ اجل در رفت : MBM سوراخ در رفت.

to such an extent that they had no provision for sustenance left [1]."

The people of the city oppressed.

Seventhly, the people of the city and the vicinity, the Amīrs, the Maliks [2], the prelates, the chiefs, the religious heads, the poor, the beggars, the fakirs, the artisans, the money-lenders, the cultivators, and the workmen were all alike smitten with the sword of violence and oppression, high-handedness and tyranny. The corpses of the dead formed a heap in front of the Sulṭān's platform, so much so that the executioners even became weary of dragging the bodies of the victims. The affairs of the State rapidly declined, and the concerns of the Government became defective. From those quarters that formerly arrested the growth of insurrection, there now appeared outbreak of sedition. While one portion of the country was enjoying rest, there befell a terrible calamity on its other portion. The foundation of sovereignty that had been made stable under the previous Sulṭāns, now became totally rotten [3]. For all these reasons, the Sulṭān became bewildered and perplexed. Though he knew that the disorder in the country, the injury to Religion, the internal confusion and the external sore were chiefly the consequences of his own action, yet he could ill-afford to stem the tide of all those ills. No trace was left of the necessaries for Government, or of the power for the maintenance of sovereignty. By God! the Sulṭān had thrown away every ball before him from his earthly mansion and, himself remained alone in it, so that when his turn came he would follow suit!

Tradition respecting punishment of offenders.

A tradition runs that elaborate arrangements had been made for the purpose of punishing and putting to death the victims. The Sulṭān caused four *Muftis* (expounders of Muhammadan law) live in the Kiosk, and whenever any accused was brought in, prior to his being punished, the Sulṭān opened discussion with the aforesaid judges. Thus had he told them, "If any of the accused is unjustly killed, and if thou dost fail to speak the truth on his behalf, you shall be held responsible for his blood."

---

1 Portion under the inverted commas is omitted in JNS and MBM.

2 MBL adds after this معارف و مشاهید; JNS and MBM omit them.

3 This sentence has been omitted in JNS and MBM.

The judges, accordingly, left no stone unturned in adducing proper proof of the innocence of the accused. In case they were defeated in argument, the accused, no matter even if it was midnight, was immediately put to death. On the other hand, if the Sulṭān was worsted, he ordered for a second sitting of the *Muftis*, so that he might come across something in refutation of their statements. Failure on the part of the judges to point out an error in the King's argument led to an immediate punishment of the culprit, and contrariwise, on the Sulṭān's failure, the prisoner was let off the same moment. Whether such a procedure, one knows not, was adopted to give relief to the people, or, it had any other objective!

A story of Sulṭān's high-handedness.

It is related that once the Sulṭān wearing his shoes made his way to the court of justice of Ḳāẓī Kamāl-ud-dīn, *Ṣadr-i-Jahān, the Diwān-i-Ḳāẓī-i-Shahr* and made a complaint, how he had been unjustly called a tyrant by Sheikh-Zādāh Jāmi. "Let him be called forth," concluded the Sulṭān, "and substantiate my high-handedness, but if he fails, let a penalty, according to the laws, be inflicted on him." When the Sheikh-Zādāh was summoned by Ḳāẓī Kamāl-ud-dīn, he confessed (to having said it) and the Sulṭān asked him to enumerate his oppressive acts. The Sheikh-Zādāh, in reply, said, that everyone whom the Sulṭān had punished, legally or otherwise, it was his prerogative[1]: but how could his action of imprisoning and entrusting the wife and children (of the victims) to the executioners be justified in any religion? The Sulṭān took recourse to silence and made no answer. Coming out of the court of justice, the Sulṭān ordered that Sheikh Zādāh be manacled and put in an iron cage. During the course of the Sulṭān's progress to Daulātābad, the cage was placed on an elephant and carried along with him[2]. On the Emperor's return to Dehli, the Sheikh was taken out of his place of confinement before the court of justice and beheaded[3].

This design of narrating the causes that led to the disorder in the empire, and the oppressive measures of the Sulṭān in this work, is improper and an evidence of mistake.

---

1 MBL العهدة علیک الهدة : JNS and MBM الهدة علیک.

2 MBM simply writes مقید کرده درمیان قفص او را بالای پیل داشته برده بود.

3 MBL گردن زد : MBM دو نیم زد : JNS agrees with MBM.

Hemistich.

It is criminal to narrate the errors of the Great[1]!

Nevertheless, this account has been put to writing on purpose that the possessors of wealth and strength may take lesson from it, and be careful! *Take lesson, Oh men! having insight!!*

As a matter of fact, when the affairs of the kingdom was at their lowest ebb owing to the excessive tyranny and oppression of the Sulṭān, in anxiety he fell a prey to disease[2]. But notwithstanding his ill-health, he set out against Thatha with the object of running down Ṭaghi, who had joined the tribe[3] of the place. A few days after there was a relapse of his illness.

The Sulṭān marched against Ṭaghi and his illness.

Amīr Ḳazghan[4], the deputy of the Emperor of Khorāsān, sent Altun Bahādur Mughal with 5,000 horse, plenty of presents and valuable gifts near the Sulṭān. "This army remained with the Sulṭān during the expedition." When the Sulṭān neared Thatha, his disease

The Sulṭān's death.

increased[5] till on the 21st Muharram 752 H. (Sunday, 20th March, 1351 A.D.) he died on the bank of the river[6].

Couplet.

In pride he who puts not his feet on the dust,[7]
Dust he becometh at length, and is tread upon[8] by people.

The Sulṭān ruled for seven and twenty years. *God knows the truth.*

---

[1] JNS and MBM خطاى بذرگان : MBL خطا.بر بذرگان.

[2] Badaoni writes, "the disease of Phthisis". See Ranking, 319.

[3] Tab-i-Akb. calls them "Somra": Ẓia Barni, "Sumra": f.n. 4.

[4] Ẓia Barni, Amīr of Farghan.

[5] Badaoni, Tab-i-Akb. and Ferishta quote Ẓia Barni in saying that the Sulṭān kept the fast on the *Ashura* (the 10th day of Muḥarram) and when it was over he ate some fish. The fish did not agree with him, his illness returned and his fever increased.

Ashura is the only day of the Muḥarram observed by the Sunni Muslims, being the day on which it was said God created Adam and Eve, Heaven and Hell, the Tablet of Decree, etc., etc.

[6] Ẓia Barni reads, "on the banks of the Indus at 14 cos. from Thatha".

[7] JNS and MBL ننهادي بر خاک : MBM ننهند بر سر خاک.

[8] MBL خاک شده خلق بر او مي گذرند : MBM خاک شود برسر او بر گذرند :
JNS agrees with MBM.

Account of Sulṯān-ul A'ẕam Abu-l-Muẕaffar[1] Fīroz Shāh, May God bless his sepulchre !

Parentage and character of Fīroz Shāh.

He was the son of *Aspdār*[2] Rajab, the younger brother of Sulṯān Ghāzī Ghiāṣ-ud-dīn Tughluk Shāh. When the Holy and the Great God, munificent in gifts and the bestower of sovereignty, upon him whom He pleases, conferred kingship upon this Emperor (Fīroz Shāh), of habits angelic and qualities Muhammad-like, gentle, kind and just, every act of oppression, tyranny, high-handedness, violence, and every instance of ruination of the country, and rebellion of the people that had been manifest in the reign of the deceased Sulṯān Muhammad Tughluk, was substituted for justice and equity, the adornment and exaltation of the country, and the safety of the roads. There was an abundance of learning (in the country), and a great many theologians and holy persons appeared (in his reign).

His accession.

On the 23rd Muharram[3] of the above year (752 H., Tuesday, 22nd March, 1351 A.D.) he (Fīroz Shāh) ascended the throne on the bank of the Sindh.[4] People flocked to his court from all sides ; the chiefs and the nobles, fully and whole-heartedly, acknowledged his authority and approved of his actions[5].

The Imperialists were harassed by the Mughals.

The Sulṯān drew up his forces as usual[6], and having made up his mind to proceed to Dehli on the following day arranged his troops. On that day the Mughals, who had come in (Sulṯān's) aid, having joined themselves with Nauroz Karkaj fell upon the royalists[7]. A firman was issued ordering that the baggage-

---

[1] MBL ابو المظفر فیروز شاه السلطان : JNS ابو المظفر سلطان فیروز شاه.

[2] MBL اسپلار : MBM اسپدار : JNS illegible.

[3] Afif, Ẕia Barni and Niẕām-ud-dīn write 24th Muharram.

[4] On the demise of Muhammad Tughluk the army that had been led by him to Thatha fell into utmost disorder, and was assailed by the Mughals in front and the rebels of Thatha in the rear. As there was no one possessing the ability to redeem the soldiers from the hands of the Mughals, the chief men of the army entreated Firoz to ascend the throne.

[5] بیعت عام کردند و موافقت نمودند.

[6] برسم طویل فرود آورد.

[7] JNS reads—همان روز مغلان که برای مدد آمده بودند باشتغال نوروز کده کر—

train should be carried forward along the river Sindh with forces on both its sides. The Mughals appeared and put to distress the attendants of the baggage-train: the imperial army made a further advance. Being defeated the Mughals retired to their countries. The Sulṭān by continuous marches arrived at Siwistān and recited the *Khuṭbāh*[1] in his name on Friday.

Defeat of the Mughals.

It was during this expedition that Malik Ibrāhim obtained the office of *Naib-i-bārbak*, Malik Bashira[2] was invested with the post of 'Ariz-i-Mulk and he received the title of 'Imād-ul-Mulk. Ḳamr-ud-dīn, the Secretary of late *Malik-ul-Sharḳ* Malik Kabir in Gujrat, Bahrām Ghaznin, Malik Noor[3], the *Sar-i-dawat-dar*[4], Malik Nua, Sheikh Ḥasan Sarbarhanah and other Maliks who remained there were rewarded with special robe of honour and excessive favours. Sa'iyid 'Alā'-ud-dīn Rasuldār, Saif-ud-dīn and Malik Saif-ud-dīn[5], the Superintendent of the elephants, were sent against Khwāja-i-Jehān at Dehli. Moulānā Muḥammad 'Imād[6] and Malik 'Alī Ghori were deputed against Ṭaghi, the chief of Sindh and Thatha. Other officers marched against Khudawand Zādāh Ḳawām-ud-dīn[7] and 'Ain-ul-Mulk at Multān; and some against Malik Maḥmud Bak at Sannām, and some to other districts and towns.

Conferment of presents on the members of the court at Siwistān.

صفها كشيد اتفاق جنگ كردند : MBL and MBM read كركر : Zia Barni كرگى : Tab-i-Akb. كركين : Nizām-ud-dīn gives a more detailed account in his Tabaḳat-i-Akbari. He relates that after the death of Muḥammad Tughluḳ when confusion overtook the army, Malik Firoz considered it advisable that he should * * separate the 3,000 Mughal horsemen, whom Amir Kazghan had sent to assist Sulṭān Muḥammad, from the main army, so that it might be saved from their depredations. * * * Two days after Sulṭān Muḥammad's death Nauroz Gurgin, the son-in-law of Barmah Shirin, who had been brought up by Sulṭān Muḥammad, ungratefully joined the Mughals, and incited the latter to stretch their hands to ravage * * *.

[1] *Khuṭbah* or *Khuṭbet* the two synonymous terms refer to the oration delivered every Friday after the afternoon service, in the principal Muhammadan mosques in praise of God, the Prophet and his descendants. This was pronounced in former times by the reigning Khalif, or the heir-apparent.

[2] Afif reads شيرابدو حشم (Bib. Ind., p. 48). Elliot (III, 277) has Shīrābrū chasm.

[3] MS. illegible.

[4] Keeper of the seals.

[5] MBL رسولوار والدين ملك بسيف.

[6] MBM مولانا عماد مذكور.

[7] MBM بر خداوند زاده بر قوام.

A general firmān was issued to the various parts of the kingdom granting compassion, favour and education to the subjects. The coffin of Sulṭān Muḥammad was placed on an elephant with the royal umbrella over it, and taken to Dehli with successive marches.

Khwāja-i-Jahān sets up the son of the late Sulṭān Muḥammad Shah, 3 Safar, 752 H., Friday, 1st April, 1351 A.D.

In order to convey the news relating to the demise of Sulṭān Muḥammad, Malih, a slave of Khwāja-i-Jahān, set out (from Thatha ?) on the third day, and reaching the city (Dehli) carried the intelligence to his master[1]. Struck with wonder, and without careful investigation or consideration,[2] Khwāja-i-Jahān brought out a youth of obscure origin,[3] describing him as a son of Sulṭān Muhammad. With the consent of *amirs* and *maliks* of Dehli, he placed him on the throne,[4] on the 3rd Safar (1st April) of the aforesaid year, under the designation of Sulṭān Ghiāṣ-ud-dīn Maḥmud, and himself managed the affairs of the kingdom. Sa'iyid Rasuldār and Malik Saif-ud-dīn reached Dehli and showed the auspicious firmān of the Emperor (Firoz Shāh) to them (Khwāja-i-Jahān and his associates). As Khwāja-i-Jahān had undertaken the work without any proper thought, he perforce, persevered in his actions. Some of the *amirs* and *maliks*, such as, Malik Natho,[5] the chamberlain, A'ẓam-i-mulk Hisām-ud-dīn Sheikh-Zādāh Busṭāmī,[6] Mālik Ḥasan Multāni, and Malik Hisām-ud-dīn Adhak co-operated with him; while others, *e.g.*, Sharf-ul-Mulk, Malik Dilān,[7] Amir Kaṭalbaghah,[8] Malik Khaljiū, Malik Ḥasan *Amir-i-Mirān*, Kāẓī Misr,

---

1 Afif narrates that a slave named Malik Tūntun (Ẓiā Barni, Altun) had been sent from Dehli by Khawāja-i-Jahān to Sulṭān Muḥammad (at Thatha ?) and just on the Sulṭān's death, he started on his return journey to Dehli.

2 MBL بی تفحص و تامل, MBM بی تامل.

3 Sir Wolsey Haig is of opinion that there is much to justify the belief that the child was Muḥammad's son and that the allegation that he was not was an attempt by panegyrists to improve their patron's feeble hereditary title. *Cambridge History of India*, III. 174 : *Journal Royal Asiatic Society*, July, 1922.

4 MBL بر تخت مملک و سریر سلطنت : MBM omit سریر سلطنت : JNS agrees with MBM.

5 MBM نتهو صاحب حاجب.

6 MBL ملک حسام الدین متوادهک : MBL omits Malik Ḥasan Multāni, and Malik Ḥisām-ud-dīn.

7 MBL ملک دیدان : Tab-i-Akb. دهیلان.

MBM قتبغه : MBL قتلبغه و ملک نوالجی و ملک حسن.

Khwāja-Bahā'ud-dīn Thikrah, Malik Muntajab Balkhi, Malik Badr-ud-dīn Buthāri secretly sent petitions expressing terms of sincerity to the Emperor,[1] *May God exalt him!* Khwāja-i-Jahān invited Mahmud Bak from Sannām, but the latter showed his negligence, and sent a petition guaranteeing help to the King (Firoz Shāh). Letters had also been despatched to Khudawand-zādāh Tarmud and 'Ain-ul-Mulk at Multān, but they transmitted this letter of Khwāja-i-Jahān to the Emperor, who (thus) became apprised of Khwāja-i-Jahān's enmity. Khudāwand-zādāh and 'Ain-ul-Mulk were honoured with compassion and special presents from the King for their having joined the imperialist cause.

Learning that the King was approaching against him with continuous marches, and that a large number of men had flocked to his standard, Khwāja-i-Jahān sent as messengers, Sa'iyid Jalāl-ud-dīn Karmati,[2] Malik Dilān,[3] Moulānā Najm-ud-dīn Rāzi, and Da'ud, his own Moulānā Zādāh[4] (for the purpose of explaining to Firoz Shāh) that the empire was still in possession of Sulṭān Muhammad's family; that Firoz Shāh should either accept the office of deputy and the heirship and devote himself with energy to the performance of the affairs of the empire or he (Firoz) might choose some of the *aktā's* of Hindustān, and any noble whom he might select could join him.

On the arrival of the aforesaid embassy, Firoz placed it under guard, and summoning together the chief of the Sheikhs, Kuṭub-ul Aulia' Naṣir-ul-Huk-ul-Shara'-ud-dīn,[5] *May God have mercy on him,* Moulānā Kamāl-ud-dīn Sāmāna and Moulānā Shams-ud-dīn Bākharzī[6] explained to them thus, "Thou dost all know, how I was the favourite of the late Sulṭān, and further, thou must have heard, how Khwāja-i-Jahān has placed on the throne a young lad as the *soi-disant* son of Sulṭān Muhammad; if the late Sulṭān had any issue

---

[1] MBL reads Sheikh Zādāh Nizāmi, Malik Masn Multāni and Malik Ḥisām-ud-dīn expressed terms of sincerity to the Emperor.

[2] T.A. (for Tabakat-i-Akbari), (Bib. Ind.), 42, Sayyad Jalāl.

[3] JNS reads زيلان : T.A. (*ibid.*), 242, Malik Dhilan.

[4] T.A. (*ibid.*) has "His own Moulānā Zādāh."

[5] T.A. reads Sheikh Naṣir-ud-din Muhammad Aubdi.

[6] JNS reads اخرزي : T.A. reads Bākharzī. MBM باخرزي : MBL خرزي.

left[1] I might have been in the know, and if he had any son he must have had placed him under my guardianship, for, none was a better patron or a friend of his than I. Him (the false heir) has the Khwāja placed on the throne and the people of Dehli have accepted him as their ruler." In conclusion the Sulṭān enquired, "What in your opinion is the exigency of the hour, what do you advise me to do, and what is the proper step to be taken (now)?" Thus replied Moulānā Kamāl-ud-dīn, "Whoever has undertaken the duties of the empire ever since the beginning has the priority of claim, and he is the sovereign."

The emissaries who had arrived, such as Sa'iyid Jalāl-ud-dīn Karmati, Moulānā Najm-ud-dīn Rāzi and Malik Dilān remained near Firoz Shāh, while (Sheikh) Da'ud, the Moulānā Zādah of Khwāja-i-Jahān returned. A firmān was issued stating that if Khwāja remembers his obligations to the Sulṭān for the latter's having conferred upon him the favours and his past services, he would do well to give up his opposition caused by his foolishness and aberration and to betake himself to the path of obedience, as in that case, more favour would be shown to him and his faults and sins condoned. Returning to Dehli, (Sheikh) Da'ud brought the (above) firmān to Khwāja-i-Jahān who (notwithstanding the Emperor's attempt to bring about a reconciliation) increased his vigour, magnificence, strength and opulence[2]; the people joined him from all sides.

Meanwhile, Malik Abu Muslim, Malik Shahīn Bak, sons of Malik Mahmud Bak came to the Sulṭān with their petitions and presents, and were favoured with (royal) compassion. When the Emperor arrived at Sarsuti,[3] Malik Kawam-ud-dīn[4] arming himself came out of Dehli at the time for the meridian prayers, on Thursday, the last day of Jamādi-ul-ākhir of the same year (752 H., Aug. 1351 A.D.), with his equipage, attendants and harem, and sought

---

[1] MBL پسرکي بودی : MBM بسری بودی.

[2] MBL او بدید که شوکت وقوت خدایگاني تضاعف مي شد او بزور و شوکت: MBM.

[3] "It is 90 *Kos* from Dehli," Afif. In the course of his progress from Thatha to Dehli, Sulṭān Firoz Shāh took the route by Dibalpur, Multān, Ajodhan and Sarsuti.

[4] Kawam-ul-Mulk, Afif (Ell. III, 283); he was also called Malik Makbul. He was the ablest noble in the kingdom, and was a Brahman of Telingana who had accepted Islam. MBM قوام الملک.

refuge from the Emperor. Amir Mu'azm Kutbgha, too, joined Kawām-ud-dīn, and his couriers came to the Sulṭān at Fateḥābād[1] on the same day. It was here (Sarsuti) that tidings arrived of the birth of Shāhzādah Fateḥ Khān, and the news of the death of Taghi (also) reached him (the Sulṭān) there from Gujrat. On the day following, as Kawām-ul-Mulk had come out, Khwāja-i-Jahān, of necessity, went near the Sulṭān, and alighting himself at *Hauẓ-i-Khāṣ*[2] appeared with the adherents before the Sulṭān at Hānsi,[3] and stood concealed before the assembly with turbans round his neck.[4] The Emperor ordered that Ahmad Ayaz (Khwāja-i-Jahān) should be made over the *Kotwāl* of Hānsī,[5] and Malik (Ghiāṣ-ud-dīn) Khiṭāb should be conveyed to Tabarhindah:[6] Manthu, the chamberlain, was exiled to Sannām, and Sheikh-Zādah Bustāmī was ordered to leave the country. Ḥisām-ud-dīn Adhak and Masan[7] were kept detained by the general of the army.

Firoz's arrival at Dehli and his accession.

In the month of Rajab of the aforesaid year (752 H., August-September, 1351 A.D.) the Sulṭān entered Dehli. The people welcomed him, and received royal favour (in return). At the fortunate aspect of the stars,[8] the Emperor alighted at the imperial palace[9] on the 2nd Rajab (Thursday, the 25th August, 1351 A.D.), and engaged himself in carrying on the administration of the State and looking after its welfare.[10]

---

1 Fathābād was the name given to the newly constructed city at the site of Ikdār where the Crown-Prince Fath Khān was born. Elliot III, 283.

2 Afif, *Hauz-i-Khāṣ-i-'Alā*.

3 MBM منزلها هانسي.

4 Afif writes, "Khwāja went into his presence with a chain around his neck, his turban off, a *talika* on his head, and a naked sword fastened to his throat, and took his standing low down among the attendants." JNS and MBM read حجاب ایستادند MBL reads حجابات ایستادند.

5 Tabaķat-i-Akbari (Bib. Ind., 243). Badaoni (*ibid.*, 243), and Ferishta (Briggs I, 448) agree in saying that Khwāja-i-Jahān should be made over to the Kotwāl of Hānsī, whereas, Afif describes how the Emperor wished to reinstate Khwāja as *Vizir*. At length, Sāmāna was assigned to him in *in'ām*, and when he had set out for that place was beheaded by Sher Khān.

6 The boy whom Khwāja-i-Jahān had proclaimed as Sulṭān.

7 JNS unintelligible.

8 MBL بطالع سعد و به پیروزی : JNS and MBM omit و به پیروزی.

9 MBL قصر همایون : MBM قصر حانون : JNS قصر خاتون.

10 Afif writes, "The Sulṭān conciliated his subjects by remitting all debts due to

In the month of Safar, 753 H. (March-April 1352 A.D.),[1] Firoz Shāh marched towards the Sirmor[2] (hills), and after a lapse of four months he came back to Dehli.

Birth of second prince, Muhammad, 3rd Jamādi-ul-auwal. June 17, 1352 A.D.

On Monday,[3] the 3rd Jamādi-ul-auwal,[4] of the year, Prince Muhammad Khān[5] was born. This joyful and happy tidings and auspicious news was conveyed to His Majesty; the advent of the blessed Prince was looked upon as auspicious:

Verse.

Be it auspicious, fortunate, happy and prosperous,
The advent of this star in the sign of the Zodiac (where) the Sun (is)[6]

The Emperor signalised the birth of the prince with feasts and rejoicings. This prince was born during the period of the Sulṭān's sovereignty, and from the day of his birth, the prosperity and splendour of the empire were on the increase.

The Sulṭān proceeds to Kalānor.

Upon the whole, a few months later, of the year, His Majesty marched towards Kalānor, and hunting in Manjahur[7] retraced his way to Dehlī.

Construction of edifices and conferment of titles, etc., on Amirs.

The same year, the Sulṭān laid the foundation of the Jami'a mosque near the palace, and a madrassa on the *hauz-i-khāṣ*![8] He conferred the title of Sheikh-ul-Islām on Sheikh-Zādah Ṣadr-ud-dīn,[9] grandson of Sheikh Kabir Kutub-ul-Aulia-Bahā'-ul-

---

the State; reduced the demand on account of land revenue; abolished levying of benevolences and the vexatious cesses; appeased with gifts the heirs of those who had been executed in the late reign, etc., etc.

[1] Badaoni gives 753 H., T.A. gives 5th Safar, 753 H., Ferishta writes 5th Safar, 754 H. The Sulṭān went there for excursion and sports.

[2] In the Punjab, bet. 30′ 20′ and 31° 5′ N. and 77° 5′ and 77° 55′ E. on the west bank of the Jamuna and south of Simla.

[3] Acc. to Ind. Ephemeris, Pillai IV, 306, it is Sunday.

[4] Badaoni gives the date, Rajab 753 H.

[5] Later known as Nasir-ud-dīn Muhammad Shāh.

[6] JNS and MBM omit the couplet.

[7] MBL منجهور MBM مجهور JNS agrees with MBL.

[8] Nizām-ud-din, Ferishta, and Badaoni simply write, "the Sulṭān laid the foundation of lofty edifices on the bank of the Sarsuti."

[9] Badaoni calls him Sheikh Ṣadr-ud-dīn Multāni, and says that the lofty building built on the bank of Sarsuti was given to Ṣadr-ud-dīn.

Ḥuḳ-wa-Shar'a-wa-ud-dīn Zakaria, *May God have mercy on him*; Ḳawām-ul-Mulk Malik Maḳbul,[1] the Nāib Vizir, was made the Vizīr, and was honoured with the designation of Khān-i-Jahān; he, further, received a large cushion and gold embroidered pillows. Khudāwand Zādah Ḳawām-ud-dīn received the title of Khudāwand Khān and became the *Vakildar*; Malik Tātār became Tātār Khān; each *amir* obtained different kinds of umbrellas; *Malik-ul-Sharḳ* Sharaf-ul Mulk was made *Naib Vakildar*; Khudāwand Saif-ul-Mulk,[2] the Shikārbeg; Khudāwand-zādah 'Imād-ul-Mulk, the chief Silaḥdar: 'Ain-ul-Mulk received the post of Mushrrif of the countries.[3] Malik Ḥasin, Amir-i-Mirān, became the *Mustaufi* of the empire.[4]

Sulṭān's first expedition to Lakhnauti.

In the month of Shawwāl, in the year 754 H. (November, 1353 A.D.), the Sulṭan started with a large army on an expedition to Lakhnauti.[5] Leaving Khān-i-Jahān in charge of the State, great and small, the Sulṭān with continuous marches reached his destination.[6] On the King's arrival in the neighbourhood of Gorakhpur, Udaya Singh waited upon him and having presented twenty *lacs* of tankas, and two elephants became the recipient of imperial favour.[7]

Udaya Singh of Gorakhpur submits.

On the 27th Rabi'-ul-Auwal[8] (755 H., Monday, 21st April, 1354 A.D.), the Sulṭān arrived at the fort of Ikdālah,[9] and there was

---

[1] MBL omits "Malik": JNS and MBM retain it.

[2] MBL omits Khudawand.

[3] Niẓām-ud-din says that 'Ain-ul-Mulk received the post of *Mustaufi* and *Mushrif of the Diwān*.

[4] This line has been omitted in JNS.

[5] In 1345 Iliyās Ḥājī, styling himself Shams-ud-dīn Iliyās Shāh had made himself master of W. Bengal, and after having overthrown Ikhtiār-ud-dīn Ghāzi Shāh, the ruler of E. Bengal in 1352, established his dominion over the whole of Bengal. The proclamation that was issued by Firoz Shah in 1353 A.D. explained the cause of the invasion to be the wrongs and oppressions of Iliyās Ḥaji. See *J.A.S.B.*, XIX, 1923, No. 7, pp. 253-290.

[6] Afif writes, "the Sulṭān followed by way of Champaran and Rachap": Barni says, "the march was through Gorakhpur, Kharosa, and Tirhut".

[7] Niẓām-ud-din writes, "Rāi Kapur, also, paid the tribute of several years, and both of them (Kapur and Udaya Singh) joined the army".

[8] JNS and MBM read 28th Rabi'-ul-Auwal. Ferishta (Brigg. I, 449) and Niẓām-ud-din (Bib. Ind., p. 245) write 7th Rabi'-ul-Auwal. We have adopted the latter version.

[9] Iliyās who had rashly invaded Tirhut with the object of annexing the s.-

a great battle. The Bengalis were defeated, and their casualty was very great. Shahdeo,[1] their chief, with several others was killed on that day. On the 29th of the month, the Sulṭān left the place, and encamped on the bank of the Ganges. Iliyās Ḥājī took refuge in the fort of Ikdāla, and on the 5th Rabi'ul Ākhir (Tuesday, the 29th April, 1354 A.D.), he marched out at the time for the meridian prayers with his equipage, attendants, and countless Bengalis.

Flight of Iliyās Ḥāji.

The Sulṭān drew up in order of battle, and immediately as Ḥājī perceived it, he was alarmed and fled.[2] The imperialists made a hot pursuit and laid their hands upon the canopy and forty elephants:[3] and a large number of Iliyās' horse and foot was made food for the sword. The Sulṭān halted there for two days,[4] and on the third day, he made his way to Dehli.[5] Some months afterwards, His Majesty laid the foundation of the city of Firozābād,[6] *May Allah protect it from all evils!*

Foundation of Firozābād.

---

eastern dists. of the Kingdom of Dehli, retired, at the approach of Firoz, to his own capital Pandua, and thence to Ikdāla.

Westmacott, in *Calcutta Review* (July, 1874) places Ekdalah (Akdalah) some 42 m. on the Maldah side of the river Tangan and North of Gaur and Lakhnauti. Major Raverty (Tabaḳat Naṣiri, Bib. Ind., p. 591, f.n.) identifies Akdalah with Damduma, a corruption of Damdamah, in the pergh. of Debekote, between Lakhnauti and Dinajpur. Wolsey Haig places Ikdāla on the island in the Brahmaputra (*Cambridge Hist. of Ind.* III, p. 176).

1 MBL متیدانو مقدم نایکان MBM سهدیو مقدم پایکان JNS سهدیو مقدم پایکان. There is no mention of Shahdeo in Niẓām-ud-din, Badaoni, Ferishta, and Afif.

2 A detailed account of the battle has been given by Afif.

3 MBL چهل زنجیر پیل MBM omits زنجیر; JNS چل پیل.

4 Afif says that the new names which the Sulṭān gave to Ikdāla and Pandwah were Azādpur and Firozabad respectively.

5 "The rains having commenced, Firoz Shāh had to abandon the investment, came to terms with Iliyās and retired towards his own dominions by the Manickpur ferry." Afif.

6 The Sulṭān returned to Dehli on the 12th Sha'bān (756 H., July 12, 1355 A.D.).

This Firozābād was different from its name-sake which arose from the change of name of Pandūah. This new town situated on the banks of the Jumna, occupied the sites of the old town of Indarpat and 11 other villages or hamlets, and contained no fewer than 8 large mosques.

Construction of Canals.

In the year 756 H. (1355 A.D.) the Emperor went[1] in the direction of Dibalpur, and excavating a canal from the Sataldar[2] took it to Jhajjar,[3] a distance of 48 Kurohs. The next year, he excavated the Firozâbad canal from the vicinity of Mandati[4] and Sirmor hills;[5] and uniting seven other canals with it, took it as far as Hansi.[6] From that place he extended it to Arâsan,[7] and there laying the foundation of a strong fort, gave it the name of Ḥisar Firozâ.[8] Below the Kiosk, an extensive reservoir was constructed, which was filled up with water from that channel. Another canal was excavated from the Khakhar (Ghaggar), and conducting it past the fort of Sarsutī was taken to Harni-Khirah.[9]

---

1 "Went to hunt," T.A. (*ibid.*, 245).

2 MBL ستلدر: JNS ستلج: T.A. "Satlad"; Ferishta, "Sutloog".

3 MBL جهجر Badaoni, "Jahjar"; Ferishta, "Kugur". Jhajjar, a town within 40 m. of Dehli, in the Rohtak dist., Punjab. JNS جهجر.

4 MBL, JNS مندني: Ferishta, "Mundvy"; Badaoni, Mandūi or Mandilī; T.A. "Mandal"; Elliot, "Mandati". Mandawi, a village in Karnal dist., Punjab, on the route from Hansi to Ludhiyana, and 51 m. north of the former town. It is situated on the left bank of the Gaggar. Distance N.W. from Cal. 1027 m. Lat. 29° 48′, Long. 76° 3′.

5 Badaoni, "Sarūr,": Ferishta, "Surmore"; T.A. "Sarmur".

6 Hisar dist., Punjab, Lat. 29° 6′ 19″. Long. 76° 0′ 19″.

7 JNS اراسني; MBL اراسن: Elliot, "Araman"; T.A., "Alisin". Badaoni, Rās; Ferishta, "Raiseen"; Afif, "Laras".

8 The foundation of Hisar was laid on the sites of two villages, Larâs-i-Buzurg and Larâs-i-Khurd.

The city and the fortress stood in the midst of a sandy desert, and was ill-supplied with water. It was to remedy this defect in the city which Firoz proposed to build here, that he caused canals to be drawn to it.

The western Jamuna canal, an important perennial irrigation work in the Punjab, taking off from the west bank of the Jamuna and irrigating Ambâla, Karnal, Hisar, Rohtak, Dehli Dists., and parts of Patiala and Jind was originated by Firoz Sh̲āh who utilized the torrent bed known as the *Chautang* to conduct water to the royal gardens at Hisar and Hansi. But after 100 years its water ceased to flow farther than the lands of Kaithal, and Akbar re-excavated the work of Firoz in 1568. In the reign of Shah Jehan, his engineer, Ali Mardan Khan undertook a more ambitious scheme, and took the water through Panipat and Sonepat to Dehli.

9 Elliot, "Harbi Khira" or Hari Khirâ: T.A. (245) "Karah": Badaoni "Harnī Khirâ"; Ferishta (Brigg: 449) "Pery Kehra": Iswari Pd. Mediæval India, "Hari Khirâ" or "Bherni-khera". Renell says (p. 73) after the meeting of the Setledge and the Beyah, the name of Setledge is no more heard of (above Multân at least), that of *Korah* being the name of the confluent waters.

In between these canals he (the Emperor) erected a fort, and called it Firozābād. Another aqueduct was drawn from Budh'ī[1] and conveyed to Jaun, thence to the fort of Firozā, and into a reservoir, and further to a point beyond it.[2]

Arrival of a robe and diploma from the Khalif of Egypt.

In the month of Ẓil-ḥijjah (December) of the same year (756 H., 1355 A.D.), on the day of 'Id-uẓ-ḥīa,[3] a robe of honour and a diploma[4] arrived from the Khalīfa Al-Ḥākim bi amrillāhi Abū Fatḥ Abū Bakr ibn Abī ul Rabī' Suleimān, the Khalīf of Egypt,[5] confirming the committal of the countries of Hind.[6]

Arrival of an embassy from Lakhnauti.

[7] * * The same year, there also came the plenipotentiaries from Iliyās Ḥājī of Lakhnauti with valuable presents. They became the recipient of excessive favours and endless affections, after which they returned. On another occasion, there (again) came presents from Iliyās Ḥājī, and (the envoys) kissed the royal feet at Hisar Firozā. Thus the Sulṭān addressed them, "My humble servants possess better effects than those that you have brought here: henceforth, you should bring such picked elephants which a King should present to a brother King".

In the year 758 H. (1357 A.D.) Ẕafar Khān Fārsi[8] came

---

1 MBL بدهي : JNS بد منى : MBM بدمني T.A. (*ibid.*, 245). "Budhi" (river): no reference of this either in Ferishta or Badaoni.

2 Afif is very concise in his statement of Firoz's canals, and refers only to the two canals, the one from the Jamuna to the city (Hisar Firoza ?) and the other from the Sutlej to the above place, the former called *Rajiwah* and the latter *Alagh-Khāni*, and both passing through Karnal. Being an inhabitant of Sirhind, and probably possessing more geographical knowledge of the Canals, Yaḥiya has given an account of the canals with greater detail. The later historians, such as, Niẓām-ud-dīn, Ferishta, and Badaoni have followed Yaḥiya.

3 JNS عيد صعيه an error for عيد الضحى.

4 دشور an error for منشور.

5 JNS دار الخلافة و مصر. و should be deleted.

6 Afif is reticent on this incident, whereas Niẓām-ud-din (*ibid.*, 245). Badaoni (*ibid.*, 245), and Ferishta (*ibid.*, 450) all agree with Yaḥiya.

7 Portion within the asterisk has been omitted in Elliot.

8 JNS and MBM read ظفر خان محمد كز فارسي. MBL كز فارسي : We have followed Niẓām-ud-din (*ibid.*, 246). Ferishta (*ibid.*, 450) writes Zafar Khan Farsy.

from Sonārgāon[1] ** by river[2] with two elephants and attached himself to the court. He was received with favour and received the office of Naib Vizir.[3]

Arrival of Ẓafar Khān from Sonargāon.

In Ẓil-ḥijjah of the year 759 H. (November, 1358 A.D.) the Sulṭān started towards Sāmāna, and there engaged himself in hunting.[4] Meanwhile, there came advices that an army of Mughals had arrived on the frontier of Dibalpur. Malik Ḳabūl *Sarpardadār*[5] (lord of the bed-chamber) was ordered to proceed with an army against them, but the enemy, before his arrival, retreated towards their own country. The Sulṭān returned to Dehli. About the end of the year, Malik Tāj-ud-dīn Betāh[6] came from Lakhnauti with some other Amirs as ambassadors, bringing with them articles as tribute, and were honoured with the royal favour.[7] In return, the Sulṭān also sent Turkish and Arabian horses, fruits from Khorāsān, and every kind of other presents under the charge of Malik Saif-ud-dīn, the keeper of the (royal) elephants, who accompanied Malik Taj-ud-dīn to Sulṭān

The Emperor marches to Sāmāna for hunting.

Retreat of the Mughals from Dibalpur.

Exchange of presents with Lakhnauti.

---

[1] Here begins the most grievous error of the copyist of the JNS. The transcription has been most wrongly done, *e.g.*, Ẓafar's arrival from Sonārgāon is to be found in p. 146 of the MS. and the subsequent events have been narrated in the following order, pp. 156, 157, 158, 151, 152, 153, 154, 155, 148 (line 7), 149, 150, 145 (line 15), 146, 147, 148, 158 (line 2).

[2] MBM ز راه دریا در تو سائین MBL دریا تو سائین.

[3] T.A. *ibid.*, 246. Badaoni makes no reference to this event: Afif, Yaḥiya, Niẓām-ud-din, and Ferishta are almost unanimous, and of these Afif is more elaborate. The latter gives, in detail, the circumstances that led to the arrival of Ẓafar Khan to seek the protection of Firoz Shāh (see Bib. Ind., p. 137 *et seq.*: Elliot III, 303). After the murder of Sulṭān Fakhr-ud-dīn, King of Sonārgāon, at the hands of Shams-ud-din, Ẓafar Khān, the son-in-law of the deceased sovereign, was sore distressed, and fled to Thatha and Dehli *en route* Hisar Firozā, to seek the protection of the Emperor

[4] Afif has passed over this incident. But Niẓām-ud-dīn (T.A. *ibid.*, 246), Badaoni (Bib. Ind. 246: Ranking I, 328), Ferishta (Briggs. I, 451) all agree with Yaḥiya.

[5] Afif, Torabānd.

[6] MBL ملک تاج الدین نتبه; JNS and MBM بیته: T.A. simply Tāj-ud-dīn; Badaoni and Ferishta give no name.

[7] There is no reference of Tāj-ud-dīn's embassy in Afif. But Niẓām-ud-dīn, Badaoni, and Ferishta all agree with Yaḥiya.

Shams-ud-dīn at Lakhnauti. Arriving at Bihar, (the party) learnt that Shams-ud-dīn had expired, and that his son had become king under the title of Sulṭān Sikandar.[1] The envoys from Lakhnauti were detained at Bihar, and the event was notified to the Emperor. The Sulṭān ordered that the presents which had been sent to Sulṭān Shams-ud-dīn should be brought back; the horses should be made over to the army at Bihār and the ambassadors (from Lakhnauti) should be conducted to Karah. The firman was carried out to the letter.[2]

Death of Shams-ud-dīn of Lakhnauti and the accession of his son Sikandar.

In the year 760 H. (1358-59 A.D.) the Sulṭān marched with a big force towards Lakhnauti,[3] leaving Khān-i-Jahān at Dehli, and after deputing Tātār Khān, who was appointed Shikdār of the country from Ghaznīn to Multān,[4] to his place of office. When the Sulṭān reached Zafrābād, the rainy season set in, so he made a halt. At this place, A'ẓam Malik Sheikh-zādāh-Bi-usṭāmī, who had been banished by the Sulṭān,[5] brought a robe of honour from the Khalif (of Egypt), and the Emperor being graciously disposed towards him, dubbed him, A'ẓam Khān.[6] Sa'iyid *Rusuldār* was sent with the messengers of Lakhnauti to the Sulṭān Sikandar, and the latter despatched five elephants and other costly presents to the court with the Sa'iyid. Before the arrival of Sa'iyid *Rusuldār*, 'Alam Khān had come from Lakhnauti as an ambassador, and to him a

Firoz Shāh's second expedition to Lakhnauti.

Arrival of a dress from the Egyptian Khalif.

---

1 Ferishta, "Sulṭān Shāh Poorbea".

2 Afif (Bib. Ind. 100-105; Elliot III, 290-92) narrates another event of importance which took place in 1358. Yaḥiya, Niẓām-ud-dīn, and Badaoni are all reticent. In 1358 Khudawand Zādah, the Emperor's cousin and her husband formed a plot against the life of Firoz Shāh, but it was frustrated by her son. The cousin was imprisoned and her husband banished.

3 The Sulṭān, by his action, broke the sanctity of the treaty made with Sikandar's father, and invaded the dominions of his son on the frivolous ground of vindicating the rights of Zafar Khān.

4 The text in the JNS تاتار خان را از حد ولایت غذنین تا ملتان شقدار کرده آنجا داشت : Elliot (IV, 9) writes, ".... and Tatar Khān as *Shikhdar* at Multān (to guard) the Ghāzni frontier". Badaoni (Raverty I, 328) writes, "Tatār Khān was sent from Ghaznin to Multān".

5 The fault being that he had become intimate with Aḥmad Ayāz.

6 Ferishta, "Azim-i-Moolk".

firmân had been issued to the effect that the Sulṭân Sikandar was foolish and inexperienced and had strayed from the path of rectitude. The Emperor had, at first, no desire to draw the sword against him (Sikandar), but as the latter had not discharged the duties of obedience, he must now understand that His Majesty was marching against him. Firoz Shâh, when the rains were over, shaped his course for Lakhnauti, and, while on the way, conferred the ensigns of royalty, such as elephants and a red pavilion, on Prince Fateḥ Khân, and directed coins to be struck in his (Prince) name and officers[1] to be appointed under him. When the Emperor arrived at Panduah,[2] Sulṭân Sikandar shut himself up in the fort of Ikdāla, whither Shams-ud-dīn, his father, had been in the habit of going for refuge. On the 16th Jamâdi-ul-Auwal, 761 H. (Saturday, 4th April, 1360), the Emperor encamped at Ikdâla. When the siege had been continued for some time, the garrison, perceiving the futility of their opposition to the assailants, capitulated in lieu of despatching elephants,[3] treasures and goods as tribute. On the 20th Jamādi-ul-Auwal (Wednesday, 8th April) of the year, Firoz Shāh marched out from Ikdâla on his return journey, and on his reaching Panduah, Sikandar made him a present of thirty-seven elephants and other valuable articles.

Sikandar takes shelter in Ikdāla.

With continuous marches[4] His Majesty arrived at Jaunpur,[5] when the rains having commenced, he quartered his army there. After the expiry of that season, in the month of Ẓil-ḥijjah of the same year (761 H., Oct.-Nov., 1360 A.D.), the Em-

The Emperor returns, via Jaunpur, Bihar, and Jājnagar.

1 Ferishta writes, "tutors". 2 Ferishta, "Bundwa".

3 "Ferishta says that Sikandar sent 48 elephants. Badaoni writes, "thirty-seven elephants". Niẓām-ud-din states, "the Sulṭān agreed to send a yearly tribute of elephants". Afif writes that on the conclusion of peace between Sikandar and Firoz Shāh on condition that Ẓafar Khān should be placed on the throne of Sonārgāon, the Emperor sent into the fort of Ikdāla a crown, worth 80,000 tankas, and 500 valuable Arab and Turki horses with an expression of wish that henceforth they might never again draw the sword. Sulṭān Sikandar, in his turn, sent 40 elephants and other valuable presents.

4 Afif says by way of "Ḳanauj and Oudh".

5 Muslim historians derive the name *Jaunpur* or *Junānpur* from Jauna or Jaunān, the title by which Muḥammad Tughluḳ had been known before his accession, but the City of Firoz was not the first site, and Hindus derive the name from Jamadagni, a famous *rishi*.

peror moved by way of Bihar to Jājnagar.[1] A firmān was issued that the baggage-animals, the women, the disabled horses, and the old men should not proceed. He left Malik Kuṭub-ud-dīn, the brother of Ẕafar Khān, the vizir, at Karah[2] with elephants and baggage. and hastened forward; on reaching Sikra,[3] he plundered it, and its ruler[4] fled. Shakr Khātūn,[5] daughter of Rāi Sādhan, and her nurse, fell into the Emperor's hands who brought her up with his own daughters.[6] The Emperor proceeded further, and left 'Imād-ul-Mulk one stage behind with some attendants and baggage. Ahmad Khān, who had fled from Lakhnauti, and had taken shelter in the hills of Rantambor,[7] joined the Sulṭān, and was honoured with great favours. The King thence proceeded to the city of Banārasi,[8] the residence of the Rāi (of Jājnagar) and crossed

Flight of the Rāi of Satgarh.

---

1 Dr. Blochman in his "*Contributions to the Geography and History of Bengal*", identifies Jājnagar with Jājpur of the present day. Raverty (Tabaḳat-i-Naṣiri, Tr. Bib. Ind., 588 f.n.) gives the following boundary of Jājnagar: on the *east*, a range of hills forming the present W. boundary of *Udisah-Jagnath*, Katāsin (on N. or left bank of the Mahānadi, some 30 miles east of Boada, in about Lat. 20° 32′ Long, 84° 50′ being the nearest frontier town or post towards Lakhan or portion of the Lakhnauti territory: further *north*, it was bounded towards the east by the river called *Braminy* running to the W. of Gangpur. Its *northern* boundary included Ratanpur and Sambalpur: on the *west* the river Wana-Ganga and its feeder Kahan: on the *south* Gudawari: S. W. Talinganah.

2 T A.. "Karah Kantakh": Afif and Badaoni, Ḳarra.

3 T.A., "Sankrah": Ferishta, "Songhur": Badaoni, "Satgarh": Elliot. "Sikra": Raverty (*ibid.*) identifies the place with the present Sirgoojah. MBM سیکره MBL سیکهره.

4 T.A., "Rāi Sārbīn": Ferishta, "Rāi Sidhun": Raverty, "Rāi Sāras": Afif, "Adāya".

5 MBL and JNS شکر خان: Ferishta also styles her *Shakr Khātūn*, signifying "the Sweet Lady". According to Raverty and Briggs "it is an impossible name for a Hindu unless she became a convert to Islam, and was afterwards so named".

6 JNS reads—شکر خان دختر رای سادهن بادایه بدست آمد: Niẓām-ud-dīn writes, "The Emperor called her (*Shakr Khātūn*) "daughter" and protected her: Raverty writes, "He called her daughter and adopted her". Ferishta is of same opinion. No reference in Afif.

7 MBL رنتهبور MBM رنتهور: Elliot, "Ranthor": Raverty (*ibid.*, 591, f.n.) "Ratanpur, in Jhar-Kundah".

8 Afif. "Barānasi": Badaoni (Bib. Ind.) Barūni: Ranking (*ibid.*, 329) Barūnasi: Niẓām-ud-dīn, Banāras: Afif states that there were two forts in Barūnasi, each populated with a large number of people: the country was prosperous and was full of inhabitants, spacious houses and fine gardens.

the Mahāndari.[1] The Rāi made his retreat towards Tilang.[2] The Sulṭān made a day's journey in his pursuit,[3] but when it appeared that the Rāi had gone far in advance, he gave up the pursuit and commenced to hunt in the neighbourhood.[4] Rāi Bīr Bhān Deo[5] sent some persons to sue for peace, (and begged) that his subjects were not killed. The Emperor, as his wont, turned aside, and (the Rāi) sent thirty-three elephants and other valuable articles as tribute. From thence the Sulṭān fell back and hunted in Badmawati and Baram Talāoli,[6] the grazing grounds of elephants. He killed two of them, and caught thirty-three alive.[7] Ẓīā-ul-Mulk composed the following quatrain[8] on the occasion:—

Flight of the Rāi of Jājnagar towards Tilang.

Rāi Bīr Bhān Deo sues for peace.

The Sulṭān's elephant hunt.

The Shāh, who with justice, to permanent power did attain,
Like the shining Sun, the environs of the world he held!
To Jājnagar he came, the elephants to hunt;
Two he killed, and three and thirty captured he.[9]

From that place the Emperor came to Karah by successive marches, and continuing his progress reached Dehli, laden with victory, in Rajab, 762 H.[10] (May-June, 1361 A.D.).

After some time, His Majesty learnt that in the vicinity of

---

1 MBL مهاندری : MBM مهاندي ; Badaoni, "Mahandūri": Afif, "مهاندری" : T.A., "Mahanadi".

2 Talinganah: T.A. and Badaoni read Tilang: Afif writes, "Rāi fled to an island in the river". Ferishta, "Tulingana".

3 Afif and Niẓām-ud-dīn write that the Sulṭān did not pursue the Rāi. Badaoni agrees with Yahiya: Ferishta is also of the same opinion.

4 During the expedition against Jājnagar the Sulṭān caused the idol of Jagannath to be rooted up and treated with every mark of indignity and then carried over to Dehli. Afif and Sirat-i-Firozshāhi.

5 Ferishta (Briggs, I, 452) Raja of Birbhoom: Badaoni, Rāi Parīhān Deo: Elliot, Rāi Bīr Bhandeo.

6 MBM برمتلاوكي.

7 MBL وسيوم و دم و دندان ايشان بياورد : MBM سير صرو دندان : JNS وصي و سه زنده گرفت.

8 Niẓām-ud-dīn and Badaoni both quote the quatrain.

9 The copyist has made a mistake in transcribing this quatrain.

10 Badaoni and Ferishta give 762 H: Niẓām-ud-dīn, 772 H. In course of their progress, the Imperialists lost their way and wandered for six months; numbers perished from hardship and privation.

Barwār [1] there was a hill of earth, out of which ran a stream that emptied into Sataldar (Satlaz [2]): it bore the name of Sarsuti. On the other side of the mound, there was another stream called the Salima.[3] If the earthen dike were cut through, the waters of the Sarsuti would fall into that stream (Salima) and (both) would flow through Sirhind and Mansurpur, to Sannām, and will have a perennial supply of water. The two streams were connected with each other, and it took some time in cutting through the hill.[4] Sirhind and for ten *kurohs* beyond was separated from Sāmāna, and put under the control of Malik Ẕīā-ul-Mulk Shams-ud-dīn Aburja. A fort was built there and it was named Firozpur.

Sirhind entrusted on Shams-ud-dīn Aburja.

[5] Finding that it was not easy to cut through the aforesaid mound, the Sultān from thence went to Nagarkot,[6] and after conquering it proceeded towards Thatha.[7] At the time when the

The Sultān marched against Nagarkot and Thatha.

---

[1] JNS and MBM بروار : MBL بردار. Ferishta, "Perwar". [2] Badaoni.

[3] Niẕām-ud-dīn, "Aslima": Badaoni and Ferishta, "Salima": "Salima has received the modern name of *Khanpoor Kee Nālā*" (Khanpur stream), Briggs (*ibid.*): "Salima" has been identified with Markanda, which rises near Nāhan and flows past Shāhābād, to the south of Ambala. Cambridge Hist. of Ind., III, 179. Badaoni writes "*The Salima is also called the Sarsuti* and this river consists of two large streams which are always flowing, and situated between these two streams there is a high mound or dyke...." Niẕām-ud-din's description is similar.

[4] Niẕām-ud-dīn, Badaoni, and Ferishta write that 50,000 spade-men were engaged for the purpose, and that inside the dike very large bones of men and elephants were found out: the bone of a man's arm was 3 yds. in length.

[5] Afif writes that "after the return from Lakhnauti, the Sultān went to Daulatābād upon a hunting expedition, and resting for a while at Bianah marched towards Nagarkot".

Here the text in the JNS is not clear: چون سلطان کافتن کوه مذکور. قابل ندید.

[6] Its Raja submitted and met with royal treatment. The name Nagarkot was changed into Muhammadābād after the deceased Sultān Muḥammad.

Afif contradicts the false statement made by the infidels that the Sultān went to see the idol *Jwālā Mukhi*, and held a golden umbrella over it. Ferishta, on the authority of some historians, says that the Sultān broke the idols of Nagarkot and mixing the pieces of cow's flesh, filled bags with them, and caused them to be tied round the necks of Brahmins. Further, that, the Sultān ordered one of the books which treated of astronomy and found in the library at Jwalamukhy consisting of 1,300 vols. to be translated in Persian by 'Izz-ud-dīn Khāni under the title of *Dalāil-i-Firozshāhi*: other books, translated in the name of Firoz, were the science of *Pingal* (Music), *Pātur Bāzi* (dealing with *A'khāra* or an entertainment held at night and consists of singing and dancing by females).

[7] The enforced retreat from Sind and the insolence of the Sindhis had rankled

king reached Thatha, Jam Bābiniya,[1] the ruler of Thatha, took refuge in a place surrounded by water[2] and fought for some time; but provisions and forage becoming scarce, men died of hunger, so that of necessity and after a struggle, the Sulṭān was obliged to retire into Gujrat.[3] The rainy season drew in: after the rains the Sulṭān marched against Thatha. The fief of Gujrat

Gujrat was conferred upon Ẕafar Khān.

was conferred on Ẕafar Khān and Niẓām-ul-Mulk, who having been dismissed[4] (from Gujrat) proceeded with a body of men to Dehli where after some time he was appointed Nāib Vizīr of the State. When the Sulṭān reappeared before Thatha, Jam Bābiniya sought

The Sulṭān's reappearance at Thatha, and the submission of Jam Bābiniya.

for quarter and waited upon His Majesty. He was taken into favour and with all the chiefs of the country he accompanied the king to Dehli. On his having shown obedience, Jam was sent in state to resume his government.[5]

---

in the memory of Firoz ever since his accession. He set out for the country with 90,000 horse and 480 elephants, and collected on the Indus a large fleet of boats which accompanied the army downstream to Thatha.

[1] MBL and MBM جام با بنهنيه: JNS جام مانهيه: Ferishta, "Jam Bany, the son of Jam Afra". Badaoni, simply "Jam". Afif, "Jām, brother of Kāi Unar, and Bābiniya, his brother's son": Mir Masum (Tairkh-i-Masum, Ell. I, 226) calls him Jam Bābiniya: The author of Tuhfatu-l Kiram (Ell. I, 342) who says that, Jam Khair-ud-din was the chief of Thatha, is not to be preferred to Mir Masum. The ruler was Jam Māli, son of Jam Unnar, and he was assisted in the government by his brother's son, Bābiniya. Cambridge Hist. of Ind., III, 180.

[2] MBM بقوت انكير معقر شده: JNS بقوت انكير: MBL بقوت انكير.

[3] "Where his troops might recruit their strength and replace their horses." C.H. I. III, 180.

Afif here describes how the Imperialists fell into the Kachi-ran (the Ran of Kach), how there were lamentations of the soldiery, and the anxiety of the Sulṭān, and finally how the supplies were sent by Khān-i-Jahān to the Sulṭān.

[4] As Niẓām-ul-Mulk had failed to send either guides or supplies to the Imperialists when they suffered during their course of progress in the Ran of Kach he was dismissed from his post,—the commandant at Gujrat.

[5] Afif states that the son of Jam, and Tamachi, brother of Bābiniya, were placed over Thatha and titles were conferred on them. The Sulṭān then marched for Dehli, taking Jam and Bābiniya with all their establishment in his train. But Mir Masum, agreeing with Yahiya writes that Jam Bābiniya after remaining in the Sulṭān's retinue for some time was restored to government of Sind. The author of *Chachnamah* is also of similar opinion.

In the year 772 H. (1370-71 A.D.)[1] Khān-i-Jahān (the Vizir) died, and his eldest son, Jūnān Shāh, succeeded to his titles. The following year, Zafar Khān breathed his last in Gujrat and was succeeded by his eldest son[2] in the fief. Then in the year 776 H. (1374-75 A.D.), on the 12 Safar (Sunday, 23rd July, 1374 A.D.), Prince Fath Khān died at Kanthur,[3] for which, the Sultān was plunged into affliction, and his constitution received a manifest shock.

Insurrection of Dāmaghāni.

In the year 778 H. (1376-77 A.D.), Shams Dāmaghāni offered annually 40 lacs of tanks, 100 elephants, 200 Arab horses, and 400 slaves, children of Hindu chiefs[4] and Abyssinians, over and above the present payment for Gujrat. The Sultān ordered that, if the present deputy-viceroy of Gujrat, Ziāu-l-Mulk Malik Shams-ud-dīn Aburja,[5] consented to these enhanced terms, he should be continued in office. Knowing that he could not pay them, and that Shams-ud-dīn Dāmaghāni had put forward an extravagant offer, Aburja did not agree to the proposal; Dāmaghāni then received a golden girdle and a silver palanquin and was appointed governor of Gujrat.

Reaching Gujrat, wild dreams and perverse thoughts entered his brain, and he raised the banner of insurrection, for he found that he was unable to fulfil his promise. At length, the *Amirs Sadah* of Gujrat,[6] such as Malik Sheikh-ul-Mulk Fakhr-ud-dīn sallied forth in a hostile manner against Dāmaghāni in the year 778 H. (1376-77 A.D.) and having slain him, severed off the head and

---

[1] Ferishta (*ibid.*, 455) gives 774 H.: Badaoni (Bib. Ind. 250: Ranking I, 333) agrees with Yahiya.

[2] Ferishta (*ibid.*) calls him Darya Khan. Acc to Ferishta Zafar's death took place in 775 H.

[3] Tab-i-Akb. كنتبوار.

[4] MSS. read مقدم بچگان ; Badaoni, "Mukuddam Zādas

[5] We have seen that Shams-ud-dīn Aburja was entrusted with Sirhind, and that in 773 H., on the death of Zafar Khān, Governor of Gujrat, he was succeeded by his eldest son. We find in C. H. I. III "Firuz was loth to disturb Zafar Khān (? Zafar Khān was already dead in 773 H.), but demanded of his deputy, Aburja, the additional contributions suggested by Dāmaghāni. On Aburjā's refusal Firoz dismissed him and his master Zafar Khān, and appointed Dāmaghāni, Governor of Gujrat."

[6] MSS. read اميران صدة گجرات ; Elliot (IV, 13) *New Amirs*: Ranking (I, 334) Amirs of Hundreds of Gujrat. Ferishta (*ibid.*, 456) "Amīr-i-Sadeeda".

sent it to the court.[1] This revolt was (thereby) put down. During the prosperous sovereignty of that good and gracious Emperor, his greatness and beneficence[2] had such an effect over every quarter of his territories,[3] that nowhere any rebellion reared up its head, nor anybody dared to be rebellious in any part, nor could anyone turn his feet from the path of obedience,[4] until this revolt of Dāmaghāni, and he quickly received the punishment for his perfidy.

Frontiers of the Empire placed under great amirs.

Frontier of Bengal placed under Mardān Daulat: Oudh, etc., upon Ḥisam-ul-Mulk.

Jaunpur to Bahruz Sulṭanī: Bihār to Bir Afghān.

Nasir-ud-din placed in charge of Multān against Mughal inroads.

The frontiers of the empire were secured by placing them under great *amirs* and the well-wishers of the Emperor. Thus, towards Hindustan, on the frontier of Bengal, the fiefs of Karah and Mahoba and the district of Dalamau[5] were conferred on Malik-ul-Shark Mardān Daulat, who received the title of Naṣir-ul-Mulk. The *aktā's* of Oudh and Sandilah[6], and the district of Kol were placed under Ḥisam-ul-Mulk Ḥisam-ud-dīn Nawā. The fief of Jaunpur and Ẓafrābād was given to Malik Bahruz Sulṭānī. The fief of Bihār to Malik Bir Afghān[7]. These *amirs* showed no laxity in coercing the insurgents of those parts and confisçating the territories on the frontiers. Thus, the Sulṭān had no anxiety for the control and safety of these parts of his dominion. But, towards Khorāsān there was no *amir* capable of withstanding the attacks of the Mughals. He (the Sulṭān) was therefore compelled to summon Malik-ul-Shark Naṣir-ul-Mulk from the fief of Karah and Mahoba, and to send him to Multān, in order to put down the disturbance created by accursed (Mughals), and punish them for their assaults. The *aktā's* of this quarter and its dependencies were placed under him, and the fief of

---

1 "Thereafter Gujrat was put under the control of **Farhat-ul-Mulk**, otherwise known as Malik Mufarrih Sulṭāni." Ranking I, 334: Badaoni (Bib. Ind., 251): Ferishta, 456.

2 JNS reads فرط و احسپان (؟ احشان).

3 JNS reads بیکار (؟ بیکر) مملکت : MBL کار مملکت.

4 دایرة : دایرهٔ اطاعت : properly circle, orbit.

5 MBL دموه : JNS and MBM دلموه.

6 JNS reads مندرد : MBM سدمد : MBL سندیله. 7 MBL ملک مر افغان.

Hindustan, such as, Karah and Mahoba were bestowed upon Malik-ul-Shark Malik Shams-ud-dīn Sulaimān, son of Malik Mardān Daulat.[1] After the assassination of Dāmaghāni, Gujrat was given over to Malik Mufarrih Sultānī, who received the title of Farhat-ul-Mulk.

Karah and Mahoba placed under Sulaimān, son of Mardān Daulat.

[2]* * In the year 779 H. (1377-78 A.D.) the Sultān rode towards Etāwah and Akhal[3]. Rāi Sabir[4] and Adharan, the *mukuddams* of Etāwah, who (formerly) having rebelled against the Sultān had been worsted, were (now) placed in safety,[5] and were taken to Dehli with their wives, children, horse, and attendants. The foundation of fortresses were laid at Akhal and Patlāhi.[6] At these places,[7] Malik Zādāh Firoz, son of Malik Tāj-ud-dīn Turk, was left with a large following and renowned[8] amirs. Having conferred the *aktā's* of Firozpur and Patlāhī[9] on Tāj-ud-dīn and the *aktā'* of Akhal on Malik Bali Afghan, the Sultān found his way to Dehli. In this year also, Malik Nizām-ud-dīn Nau,[10] amir of Oudh, who was in attendance on the Sultān, passed away, and Oudh was given over to Malik Saif-ud-dīn, his eldest son.* *

Sultān to Etāwah and Akhal.

In the year 781 H. (1379-80 A.D.) the Emperor marched towards Sāmāna: on his reaching the destination, Malik Kabūl Kurān Khuān, *amir* of the Privy Council and the Chief of Sāmāna, presented offerings, and the Sultān showed him great favours. Then, marching through Ambālā, and Shāhābād, he entered the hills of Sāntur[11] and levied tribute from the Rāi of

Governorship of Oudh devolved upon Saif-ud-din. The Sultān to Sāmāna, Ambālā Shāhābād and Sahāranpur.

---

[1] Badaoni reads "Malik Marwan".

[2] * * Portion under asterisks is omitted in Elliot.

[3] MBL اکچک; Badaoni, "Akchak": The reason of this expedition was rebellion of the Zemindars of Etawah. Forishta.

[4] MBM رای سیر.

[5] MS. reads بترغیب و استظهار در آورده.

[6] Badaoni "Batlāhi": Forishta, "Tilāi".

[7] Badaoni, "Firozpur and Batlāhī."

[8] JNS illegible. MBL امرای کبیر نامزی آنجا گذاشت : MBM omit کبیر.

[9] MBL فیروز پور بتلاهي. MBM فیروز پور و پتلاهي.

[10] MBM حسام الدین : Badaoni, "Malik Nizām-ud-dīn".

[11] MSS. read کوه پایه سانتور : Ranking, 334, "Sintur hills": Forishta, "foot of the mts. of Saharanpur": Elliot, Sahāranpur.

Sirmor and the Rāis of the hills, and then took his way back to the capital.

Rebellion of Kharku, the Katehar chief.

Just at this time,[1] there came a report of the insurrection of Kharku,[2] the Katehar chief. This Kharku had invited Sa'iyid Muhammad, who held Badāōn, and his brother Sa'iyid 'Alā'-ud-dīn, to a feast at his house, and had them basely murdered. In 782 H. (1380-81 A.D.), the Sultān proceeded against Katehar to take vengeance, and ravaged the country. The rebels of those parts were imprisoned and brought to punishment. "*Surely the Kings, when they enter a town, ruin it and make the noblest of its people to below.*"[3] Kharku (acted according to the saying:) "*the Prophets abandon those things that are beyond their power,*" and made his escape towards the country of the Mahtars.[4] The Sultān also attacked them. [5] * * When the expedition came to a conclusion, the Emperor placed Badāōn under Malik Kabūl Karan, the lord of Bed chamber: he (also) appointed Malik *Khitāb* Afghan at Sambhal for the chastisement (of the rebels) and holding firm Katehar. * *[6] The King, under the pretence of hunting, went annually to Katehar, and that country became so devastated that nothing but game lived there.

Construction of a fortress at Babuli.

And in the year 787 H. (1385 A.D.), the Sultān built a fortress at Beoli[7] which is seven *Kurohs* from Badāōn, and gave it the name of Firōzpūr, but the people called it *Pur-i-ākhhirin.*[8] Afterwards the Sultān grew weak and feeble, for his age was ninety years.

---

1 Badaoni gives 782 H.

2 MSS. read کهر کر : Elliot, Khargu : Ranking, "Khūkar" : Ferishta "Kharku or Khargoo" : Badaoni, کهر کهر.

3 Korān, Chap. XXVII, verse 34.

4 JNS reads مهتكانون : MBL مهترگان : MBM مهنکان.

5 سر پردۀ دار خاص.

6 * * Portion under asterisks omitted in Elliot.

7 JNS reads, پبولي : MBL and MBM بیولی Badaoni, "Babuli," "possibly from the abundance there of the *Acacia Arabica* known as Babul—Ranking Ferishta, "Basuli" : Elliot, "Beoli".

8 MBL بر احدین.

The nonagenarian Sulṭān becomes a puppet in the hands of Khān-i-Jahān.

Khān-i-Jahān,[1] his Vizir, held the reins[2] (of the State) and brought under his sway the affairs of the State. The Firoz-Shāhī amīrs and maliks were entirely subservient[3] to him, and those who opposed him (Vizir) were removed from the presence of the Sulṭān[4] by all possible means ; some were killed and others confined.[5] At length, matters came to such a pass, that whatever did Khān-i-Jahān say, the Sulṭān used to do. For this, the affairs of the State became slow-moving, and some loss occurred daily.

High-handedness of Khān-i-Jahān. His dismissal.

Once, Khān-i-Jahān represented to the Sulṭān how Prince Muḥammad Khān having allied himself with some amīrs and maliks, such as, Dariyā Khān, son of Ẓafar Khān, Amīr of Gujrat, Malik Ya'ḳub Muḥammad Ḥājī, the master of the horse, Malik Rāju, Malik Samā'-ud-dīn, and Malik Kamāl-ud-dīn, the son[6] of Malik 'Amr Ariz. the personal attendants of the Emperor, was after raising an insurrection. The Sulṭān had entrusted the affairs of the State upon Khān-i-Jahān, he, without thought and consideration issued the firmān that they should be taken into custody. When the prince heard this he omitted to pay his respects to the Sulṭān for some time, and although the Vizir called for his presence the latter made excuses. Then, the Vizir, under the pretence of a balance of accounts, kept Dariyā Khān, son of Ẓafar Khān, Amir of Mahoba, confined in his house. This alarmed the prince still more,[7] and he made a statement of his position to his father.[8] The Sulṭān gave order for the removal of the Vizir, and for the release of Dariyā Khān. The prince having done this,[9]

---

1 Jūnān Shāh : Briggs says Ẓafar Khān Farsy.

2 JNS مطلق الفنان, an error for مطلق العنان.

3 JNS مسنحرا او گشتند, an error for مسخر etc.

4 MBL پیش سلطان مرحوم گذرانیده MBM reads گردانیده in place of گذرانیده.

5 JNS دستکر, an error for دستگ.

6 JNS and MBM read پسران JNS simply reads Malik 'Ariẓ.

7 Ferishta relates that the prince entered into a close palanquin, and was carried to the seraglio of the Emperor.

8 JNS reads, پیش سلطان نیز او را قبول کرده بودند حاصل کردن نتوانستند.

9 MSS. read, شاهزاده محمد حل ساخته.

Malik Ya'kub, master of the horse, (brought out) [1] all the horses and foot, and Malik Kuṭub-ud-dīn Farāmarz,[2] keeper of the elephants, (made ready) the elephants with their litters and armour,[3] and took them to the prince. The Firozi slaves and amīrs, and the people of the city also joined the prince.

March of Prince Muḥammad against Khān-i-Jahān and the latter's flight.

In the month of Rajab, 789 H. (July-Aug., 1387 A.D.), with full preparations, the prince set out late one night, with a large following, to the house of Khān-i-Jahān. When the latter heard of the approach, he took Dariyā Khān out of prison and put him to death,[4] and collecting a few chosen followers entered into conflict with the prince.

At length, losing the power (of opposition) he fell back to his house, and got a wound while entering it. Unable to make further resistance, he came out (of the house) by another mountainous route with few adherents and escaped towards Mewāt, and sought shelter from Kokā Chohān, at Maḥāri.

The Vizir's followers put to death and his effects plundered.

The prince plundered the Vizir's house of all its gold and wealth, and arms, horses, and effects; he then returned to the court. (Next) he caused Malik Bihzād Fateḥ Khān, Malik 'Imad-ul-daulat, Malik Shams-ud-dīn Bazabān[5] and Malik Muṣaliḥ Muksarān[6] who had sided with Khān-i-Jahān, to be brought to the Court and executed.

Reins of Government passes to Muḥammad Khān who takes the title of Nāṣir-ud-dīn Muḥammad Shāh.

When these transactions were reported to the Emperor, he resigned the reins of government into the hands of the prince, and the amīrs and maliks and the slaves of Sulṭān Firoz and the people in general rallied round the prince. The Sulṭān grew old and feeble, so of necessity he, at length, made over to the prince the paraphernalia of sovereignty, with all the horses, elephants, effects, and equipage. He

1 The predicate is missing in JNS.

2 JNS فرامر. MBL قطب الدین شیخ فراموز Elliot "Faramuz".

3 کستوان, *Kustuwān*, *Gustuwān*, properly, horse armour.

4 Ferishta, "having first put to death Ẕafar Khān".

5 JNS and MBM read, ملک شمس الدین بزبان. MBL reads بریان.

6 JNS and MBM read ملک مصالح مکسران MBL ملک مصلح etc.

gave him the title of Nāṣir-ud-dīn Muḥammād Shāh, and betook himself to the service of God. In every Jami' mosque throughout the dominions, the *Khuṭbah* was read in the names of the two sovereigns, and in the month of Sha'ban, 789 H. (Aug.-Sept., 1387 A.D.), Muḥammad Khān ascended the throne in the palace of *Jahān numāh.*[1]

Conferment of titles, etc., on Amirs.

The titles and offices, the fiefs and allowances, pensions and gifts, and whatever had been enjoyed by any one during the previous reign were confirmed. Malik Ya'kub, master of the horse, was made Sikandar Khān[2] and was nominated to the charge of the Government of Gujrat. [3] * * Malik Rāju became Mubāriz Khān; Kamāl 'Amr'[4] became Dastur Khān; Samā' 'Amr became Mu'in-ul-Mulk; Malik Samā'-ud-dīn and Kamāl-ud-dīn obtained places near the person of the King and became the recipient of his favour[5]: the duties of the Diwan were conferred on them.* * Malik Ya'kub Sikandar

Khān-i-Jahān was seized and put to death.

Khān was sent with an army to Majāri[6] against Khān-i-Jahān. When this force reached Majāri, the accursed Kokā bound Khān-i-Jahān, and delivered him up to Sikandar Khān, who put him to death, and having sent his head to the court, went his way to Gujrat The prince then engaged himself to the duties of government.[7]

In the month of Ẓil-ḥijjah,[8] of the year,[9] 789 H. (Dec. Jany.,

---

1 JNS and MBM read جهان نما : MBL جهانبای.

2 JNS reads اسكندر خان : Badaoni and Elliot, "Sikandar". MBL : امیر اخور را سکندر خان شد MBM : ملک یعقوب امیر اخور بک را سکندر خان خطاب شد JNS agrees with MBL.

3 * * Portion under asterisks omitted in Elliot.

4 كمال عمر.

5 JNS and MBL read قرب و اختصاص : MBM قرب اختصاص.

6 MBM معاري. MBL در مجاري : JNS بدر مجاري : MBM بدر معاري.

7 JNS شاهزاده در پرداخت ملكي مشغول شد : MBM agrees with JNS : MBL reads - خود در پرداخت امور و كارهای ملكي مشغول شد.

8 Elliot, Ẓil-ḳa'da.

9 Ferishta and Badaoni give 790 H.

1387-88 A.D.), Muḥammad Khān marched towards the Sirmor hills, and there spent two months, hunting rhinoceros and elk.[1] While thus engaged, advices were received relating to the perfidious assassination of Sikandar Khān at the hands of Malik Mufarriḥ, Amīr of Khambayat and the *Amirs-ṣadah* of Gujrat. The army that had set out with the deceased, some of them wounded and some despoiled, returned to Dehli with Sa'iyid Sālār.[2] On this information, Prince Muḥammad Khān became thoughtful and anxious, and hastened to the capital. But as he was inexperienced, the prince gave himself up to enjoyment and luxury, and took no thought for avenging Sikandar Khān.[3] For five months the (old) rules and arrangements kept the affairs of the state agoing, but at length the kingdom fell into great disorder. The Firoz Shāhī slaves, numbering about one *lakh*, who had taken up their habitations in Dehli and Firozābād,[4] stirred up by the opposition shown by Malik Samā'-ud-dīn and Malik Kamāl-ud-dīn,[5] set themselves up in opposition to the prince, and joined themselves to Firoz Shāh. When the prince came to know of these facts, he sent out Malik Zahir-ud-dīn Lohri to parley with the slaves, who had assembled in the *Maidān-i-nuzul*. They, however, pelted him with stones and bricks, and thereby wounding Zahir-ud-dīn made a display of their force and rejected all overtures for peace.[6] The

Muḥammad Shāh on hunting expedition at Sirmor hills.

Assassination of Sikandar Khān.

Incompetence of Muḥammad and the Kingdom in disorder.

---

1 JNS and MBM گرگ و گوزن : MBL گرگون و گوزن.

2 Badaoni writes "Sipah-Salar".

3 Texts read, و کشته شدن سکندر خان سهل پنداشت : Badaoni (*ibid.*, 254) writes, فکر انتقام سکندر خان نکرده.

4 JNS بندگان فیروز شاهي که دهلي و فیروز اباد ساکن بودند : MBL در تنه دهلي و فیروز اباد : MBM بندگان فیروز شاهي که موازنهٔ یک لاک در بنهٔ دهلي Elliot agrees with MBL.

5 Ferishta (460) writes Baha'-ud-dīn and Kāmal-ud-dīn, cousins of Prince Muḥammad. Thus, he says, the nobles seeing the affairs in them united themselves with Princes Baha'-ud-dīn, etc., for the purpose of subverting his authority. Badaoni's version is different. He writes thus "the Sulṭān's" (Muh. Shāh) soldiery by reason of their enmity and jealousy against Sam'a-ud-dīn and Kamāl-ud-din, who were the *protégés* of Muhammad Shāh, set themselves in opposition to them, etc.

6 JNS and MBM read با صلاح : MBL بر اصلاح.

Malik, thus wounded, was obliged to retire near the prince, who was prepared for action. The prince advanced with his horse, foot, and elephants to the ***Maidān*** against the rebels; and when he fell upon them, they fled to the palace and sought refuge with the old Sulṭān. For a couple of days fighting went on, but on the third day when the prince was prepared to renew the contest, the insurgents brought out the old Sulṭān from the palace. When soldiers and elephant-drivers set eyes upon their former master they deserted the prince and came over to the Sulṭān.[1] Finding that he was unable to continue the struggle further, the prince with a small following fled towards the Sirmor hills. The camp of the prince and those of his followers were put to plunder. The city now presented a scene of great violence.

Muḥammad march against insurgents, his success.

Flight of Muḥammad Shāh to Sirmor.

Tranquillity being restored, the old Sulṭān appointed Prince Tughluk Shāh,[2] the son of his (elder) son Fateh Khān, his heir-apparent, and consigned to him the affairs of government. In the meantime, Amīr Ḥusen Aḥmad Ikbāl,[3] son-in-law of the Sulṭān,[4] who had separated from the party of the prince, was made prisoner by the Hindu amirs,[5] and taken to Tughluk Shāh who had him executed before the *dākhūl*; orders were issued to Amīr-Sadah of Samānā, directing them to seize 'Ali Khān[6] the Amīr, and bring him to the court. Malik Sulṭān Shāh Khus-dil brought Moula Zādah Malik Makbul Faraz Khān 'Ali Khān, under his own custody to Dehli. When he was brought in, the prince sent him away a prisoner to Bihār, and conferred Samānā upon Malik Sulṭān Shāh. On the

Prince Tughluk Shāh appointed heir.

---

[1] Text runs—چون لشکر و پیل بانان همه پرودهٔ سلطان بودند بیکبارگی از جانب شاهزاده روی تافته بر سلطان مرحوم پیوستند.

[2] MBL شاهزاده تغلق شاه : JNS شاهزاده تغلق MBM : تغلق شاه پسر فتح خان فتح خان.

[3] Badaoni, Mir Ḥasan : Ferishta, 'Amir Sa'iyid Ḥusen'.

[4] MBL داماد سلطان مرحوم : JNS and MBM retain it.

[5] JNS امیر هندوان گشت گرفته : MBM امیر هندوان گشت گرفته : MBL امیر هندوان گرفته.

[6] Elliot, 'Ali Khān : Badaoni, Ghalib Khān. Tab-i-Akb. agrees with Badaoni.

18th Ramẕān,[1] 790 H. (Sunday, 20th Sept., 1388 A.D.), Sulṭān Firoz, *May his tomb be sanctified*, died, worn out with weakness. It has been recorded by veracious historians and truthful chroniclers of venerable age that, since the time of Nāṣir-ud-dīn, son of late Sulṭān Shams-ud-dīn Iyal-timish, who was a second Naushirwan,[2] there has been no king (in Dehli) so just, and kind, so courteous and God-fearing, or such a builder, like the late Firoz Shāh, *May his tomb be blessed and may he dwell in paradise!* His bravery and justice won for him the hearts of his subjects. If any indigent traveller, by the decree of God, died on the way, the feudal chiefs, the holders of offices, and the chiefs of the vicinity, having called together the Imāms, the Ḳāẕis, and all Musalmans, examined the corpse, and drew up a report under the Ḳāẕi's seal, certifying that no trace of any wound was discernible on the body, and after that they buried it. Thus, by enquiries of the Ḳāẕis, all the injunctions of the Shar'a (law) were carried to the letter, and on all sides it was in no way possible that during the reign of this sovereign, any strong man could tyrannise over the weak.[3]

Death of Sulṭān Firoz. His appreciation.

Couplet.

After many a revolution of the trying sphere
Stories about his (Sulṭān's) justice remain, though he be himself dead![4]

Almighty God immersed this gentle, beneficent and just king in the divine compassion, and gave him a place in the propinquity of His mercy! The rule of the late Sulṭān Firoz Shāh, *May his tomb be sanctified*, lasted for 38 years,[5] and nine months. God knows the truth![6] The two words, "*Wafat-i-Firoz*" comprise the numerical letters of the date of his demise.[7]

---

[1] Badaoni, 16th Ramẕān, 790 H.: Ferishta, 3rd Ramẕān.

[2] The name of a King of Persia, called also Khosrou Naushirwān, in whose reign Māhomet was born in 578 A.D.

[3] The text in Elliot here terminates.

[4] JNS او شده آواره و عدلش بجای : MBL and MBM read او شده آوازهٔ عدلش بجای.

[5] Elliot 37 years and 9 months. Badaoni, "38 years and some months". Ferishta of latter opinion.

[6] JNS and MBM omit this line

[7] JNS ۷۹۰ سنه تاریخ وفات سلطان بهمین در لفظ یافته فیروز.
MBL and MBM omit this line.

An Account of Sulṭān Tug͟hluḳ S͟hāh, son of Fateḥ K͟hān, entitled G͟hiās-ud-dīn.[1]

His accession 18th Ramẓān, 790 H., Sunday, 20th Sept., 1388 A.D.

Tug͟hluḳ S͟hāh, the son of Fateḥ K͟hān bin Fīroz S͟hāh,[2] was the adopted son and the grandson of the late Sulṭān Fīroz: after the demise of the late Sulṭān, on the very day of his death in the aforesaid year (18th Ramẓān, 790 H.) he ascended the throne of sovereignty in the palace at Firozābād by the consent of the Amīrs, Maliks, and the Firoz S͟hāhi slaves, and assumed the title of Sulṭān G͟hiās-ud-dīn.

Conferment of posts and titles upon Amīrs.

The Sulṭān conferred the portfolio of the vizirate on Malik zādāh Fīroz,[3] the son of Malik Tāj-ud-dīn, and honoured him with the title of K͟hān-i-Jahān: K͟hudāwand zādāh G͟hiās-ud-dīn Turmudi[4] received the charge over the armoury: Malik Fīroz 'Alī was taken out of the prison and was conferred with the office of *Sar-i-jāndār*, the post that was held by his father. The *akṭa'* of Gujrat was entrusted upon Malik Mufarrih Sulṭānī,[5] who held it under the late reign. The *akṭa's* and other offices held by other Amīrs were not interfered with.

Fīroz 'Alī and Bahadur Nāhir sent against Muḥammad K͟hān.

Malik Fīroz 'Alī and Bahadur Nāhir[6] were despatched against Prince Muḥammad K͟hān with a large army. The Amīrs of the *akṭa's*, such as, Sulṭān S͟hāh, the Amīr of Sāmāna, Rāi Kamāl-ud-daulat-wa-ud-dīn Matīn,[7] and other Amīrs were appointed under them (Fīroz 'Ali and Bahadur Nāhir).

---

[1] MBL and MBM ذکر سلطان تغلق شاه پسر فتح خان مقلب بغیاث الدین: JNS simply reads ذکر سلطان تغلق شاه.

[2] MBL فیروز خان پسر سلطان مرحوم بن فیروز بود : MBM فیروز شاه پسر سلطان مرحوم فیروز بود : JNS تغلق شاه پسر فتح خان بن فیروز شاه.

[3] JNS and MBM فیروز شاه.

[4] MBL ترددی : JNS and MBM ترمدي : Tab-i-Akb. ترمذي.

[5] Ferishta states that he received the title of Farhat-ul-Mulk

[6] Ferishta, Muḥammad Tahir.

[7] JNS and MBM کمال الدین مین.

In the month of Shawwāl of the aforesaid year (790 H., Sept.-Oct., 1388 A.D.) the army entered the hills of Sirmor: Prince Muhammad Khān having retreated from that place retired to the top of the mountains by hostile roads and reached the fortress, Koh-i-Baknāri. The royal forces proceeded along the skirts of the hills, and when it reached the valley of Baknāri some little engagements followed, but the place (of refuge) being strong, no distress could reach the prince. From thence, he ascended the mountains and betook himself towards Sakhet.[1] The imperial army marched from Baknāri and reached the village of Arubar,[2] and encamped in the valley of Arubar near the *Chabutra-i-Kimār*.[3] The prince, then, left Sakhet and went to the fort of Nagarkot. The royalists chased him till the confines of Gwalior, but they met with much opposition in the way, so Malik Firoz 'Alī and the other Amīrs gave up the pursuit and returned. The prince secured himself at Nagarkot.

Prince Muhammad Khān pursued by the imperial army.

But Tughluk Shāh was young in age and inexperienced. Of State affairs he was ignorant and he had no experience of the wiles of fickle fortune. He gave himself up in wine and pleasure. The entire business of the government was neglected, and the Firoz Shāhi slaves asserted their power so fearlessly that the Sultān lost all control over the State.

Disorder in the country due to Sultān's youth and inexperience.

In the meantime, Sultān Tughluk imprisoned his own brother Aspdār Shāh,[4] for no reason whatsoever. Abu Bakr Shāh,[5] the son of Zafar Khān fled for refuge: Malik Rukn-ud-dīn Zanda, the deputy vizir, and several other Amīrs and slaves of Firoz Shāh made common cause with him (Abu Bakr Shāh) and raised a revolt. They despatched with their sword Malik Mubarak Kabir in the palace of Firozābād as he was retiring through the door. A great outcry, thereupon, arose

Revolt of the Amīrs.

---

[1] MBM سکهیت : MBL سکهت : JNS سکیتهه.

[2] MBM از و بر : Elliot, Aru.

[3] JNS, MBM چوترۂ قمار : MBL چبوترۂ قیمار.

[4] JNS and MBM اسپدار شه : MBL اسبلار شه : Tab-i-Akb. سلار شه.

[5] MBL omits شه : JNS and MBM retain it.

in the palace, and Sulṭān Tughluk Shāh hearing it, escaped through the door towards the Jaun. Malik Firoz, the vizir, was with him, but the traitor Rukn Zanda being apprised of his escape followed him with his own adherents and with a party of Firoz Shāhī slaves. Reaching the ford of Jaun, they put to death Sulṭān Tughluk Shāh and Malik Zādāh Firoz. Their heads were severed off the body and thrown down in front of the court. This event happened on 21st Safar, 791 H. (Friday, the 19th February, 1389 A.D.).

Flight of Tughluk Shāh.

Sulṭān Tughluk Shāh killed.

Verse.

In dust was laid low that rose of fortune, which the garden of the country
With hundred thousand blandishments reared it on its lap.

[1] How wonderful the power of God! He brings out of that door with magnificence an emperor with crown and throne, and in the twinkling of an eye, having severed off his head throws it out of that door. "Thou exaltest whom Thou pleaseth and abasest whom Thou pleasest; in Thine hand is the good: surely, Thou hast power over all things."[2]

Verse.

Thou hast seen how magnificently the crown of Alp Arslān[3] had reached the heavens.
Thou hast observed how his body ultimately came under the earth on his death:
When there were neither the stars on his belt nor were the moon-faced (slaves) with double chins,
Neither a horse under his thigh nor the reins in his hands!

---

1 JNS and MBM omit. "How wonderful........hands".

2 Korān, Chap. III, *verse* 25.

The whole of the *verse* runs thus:

"Say: Oh Allah, Master of the Kingdom! Thou givest the kingdom to whomsoever Thou pleaseth and takest away the kingdom from whomsoever Thou pleasest, and Thou exaltest whom Thou pleaseth and abasest whom Thou pleasest; in Thine hand is the good: surely, Thou hast power over all things.

3 Arslān is a surname that has been adopted by several Kings of Persia.

Account of Sulṭān Abu Bakr Shāh.

His accession to the throne.

After this, they (*i.e.*, the Amīrs) brought Abu Bakr Shāh[1] out from his dwelling, and seating him upon an elephant with a canopy over his head, proclaimed him (Emperor) under the title of Sulṭān Abu Bakr Shāh. The office of vizirate was given over to Rukn Janda.[2] At length, after a few days, Rukn Janda conspired with some of the Firoz Shāhi slaves with the intention of slaying Abu Bakr Shāh and of making himself a king.

Conspiracy of Rukn Janda and his assassination.

Abu Bakr Shāh was apprised of the intention. Some of the slaves,[3] who were unfriendly to him (Rukn Janda), anticipating his action killed him and placed him over a gibbet. The Prophet, *on whom be peace*, said, "He who dug a well for his brother himself dropped into it"

Verse.

The man who tyrannised over Dara,
Till now, the artists paint his body placed on the gibbet!

Undoubtedly, he who murders his own benefactor is thus repaid. To sum up, those slaves[4] who had sided with that unfortunate and dirty traitor (Rukn Janda) were made food for the relentless sword.[5] Abu Bakr Shāh obtained complete hold over Dehli, taking possession of the royal elephants and treasure; he increased in power daily.

Abu Bakr Shāh takes possession of Dehli.

In the meantime, the Amīrs Ṣadah of Sāmāna treacherously cut to pieces Malik Sulṭān Shāh Khush-dil with their swords and daggers at the head of the tank of Sannām[6] on

[1] Tab-i-Akb. and Badaoni write, Abu Bakr Shāh bin Zafar Khān bin Firoz Shāh.

[2] Badaoni, Rukn-ud-dīn Chanda. MBL writes رکن جندہ پلد مردار کشتہ خداوند شد : MBM and JNS omit پلید etc.

[3] Badaoni and Ferishta write that Abu Bakr Shāh got rid of Rukn Janda together with his following.

[4] JNS and MBM omit the text beginning rom "and placed him over a gibbet" and ending with "To sum up, those slaves".

[5] JNS reads ایشان نیز با او علف تیغ کشتند : MBM ایشان تیز علف تیغ کشتند.

[6] Badaoni writes, "Sāmāna".

the 24th Safar of the aforesaid year (791 H., Monday, 22nd February, 1389 A.D.). Then, taking possession of Sāmāna on that very day, they plundered the houses of Malik Sulṭān Shāh and his attendants. They cut off the head of Malik Sulṭān Shāh and despatched it to Nagarkot near Prince Muḥammad Khān with offers of assistance. The reign of Malik Sulṭān Tughluk Shāh lasted for five months and a few days.[1] *God knows the rest!*

The Amīrs Ṣadah of Sāmāna kills Malik Sulṭān Shāh.

Account of Sulṭān Muḥammad Shāh, the youngest son of Sulṭān Firoz Shāh.

Sulṭān Muḥammad Shāh was the younger son of late Sulṭān Firoz Shāh. When the intelligence of the assassination of Malik Sulṭān Shāh reached him, the Sulṭān left Nagarkot, and came to Sāmāna by way of Jalandhar by continuous marches. On the 6th Rabī'-ul-Ākhir[2] of the year above mentioned (Sunday, the 4th April, 1389 A.D.), Muhammad Shāh for the second time mounted the throne of the empire[3] at Sāmāna. The Amīrs Ṣadah of Sāmāna and the chiefs of the mountainous tracts, joined with him and renewed their vows of allegiance. Several *amīrs* and *maliks* of Dehli deserted Abu Bakr Shāh and joined Muḥammad Shāh. So that, there assembled round him in Sāmāna about thirty thousand horse, and an innumerable host of foot. From Sāmāna he marched to Dehli by successive marches, and by the time he reached its neighbourhood, the horse had increased to[4] about fifty thousand. To sum up, Abu Bakr Shāh was informed of his approach, and the slaves of Sulṭān Firoz, having before opposed the new Sulṭān, now allied themselves with Abu Bakr.

His parentage.

His accession.

---

[1] MBM reads شش ماه و هرده روز: Elliot is of same opinion. JNS and MBL read "five months and a few days

[2] Tab-i-Akb. and Badaoni write Rabī'-ul-auwal: Elliot gives 21st Rabi'ul ākhir.

[3] MBL بر تخت مملکت و سریر سلطنت: JNS and MBM omit سریر سلطنت.

[4] MBL جمع آمد MBM جمع شد JNS جمع آمده.

Battle between the Sulṭān and Abu Bakr Shāh: the former's defeat and flight.

On the 25th Rabī'-ul-Ākhir, 791 H. (Friday, 23rd April, 1389 A.D.), Sulṭān Muḥammad took up his position at the palace of Jahān-numāh, and Abu Bakr Shāh also, with his adherents and forces, was at Firozābād. On the 2nd Jamādi-ul-Auwal of the aforesaid year (Thursday, 29th April), he adherents of Abu Bakr, having taken the streets and walls of Firozābād, gave battle to the forces of the Sulṭān (Muḥammad Shāh). On that very day Bahādur Nāhir[1] came into the city with a party of his followers; and Abu Bakr Shāh, being emboldened by his approach,[2] marched on the following day into Firozābād with his innumerable horse and foot and famous elephants.[3] Between the two a severe struggle and fighting ensued, and at length, by the decree of God, the Most High, the Sulṭān's army being worsted, retreated towards their own territories. With a party of about 2,000 horse, the Sulṭān forded the river Jaun, and penetrated into the Doāb. From thence he sent his second son[4] Humāyūn Khān to Sāmāna to rally the forces; and he sent with him Malik Ẓia'-ul-Mulk Abu Rejā,[5] Rāi Kamāl-ud-dīn Main[6] and Rāi Juljain[7] Bhatti whose fiefs lay in that quarter. The Sulṭān took up his position at the village of Jatesar,[8] on the bank of the Ganges. The Amīrs of Hindustān, such as, Malik Sarwar, the Governor of the city, Malik-ul-Sharķ Naṣir-ul Mulk, the holder of Multān, Khawāṣ-ul-Mulk, the feoffee of Bihar, Malik Saif-ud-dīn and Malik Kadu, the sons of Malik Hisām-ud-dīn Nua,[9] the amīr of Oudh, the sons of Malik

The Amīrs of Hindustān join the Sulṭān.

---

1 Badaoni writes Bāhadur Nāhir Khān Zādah of Mīwāt.

2 JNS and MBM read ابوبکر شه را به امدن او تقویتي حاصل شد : MBL ابوبکر شه باحشم را بآمدن.

3 JNS and MBM write باحشم سوار و پیاده در فیروز آباد آمد.

4 Texts read پسر میانگي : Ranking writes, "younger son".

5 JNS ملک ضیاء الدین ابو رجا : MBL and MBM ضیاء الملک : Elliot agrees with JNS.

6 MBL متین : JNS میا مین : MBM مین : Elliot agrees with MBM.

7 MBL رای نو الجي : JNS and MBM جلجین and خلجین respectively. Elliot, Khul Chanw (Kul Chand).

8 MBL جیهر : JNS جیتر : MBM جیسر : Elliot Jālesar: Badaoni چیتر : Ferishta Jālesar.

9 MBL حسام الدین نوا : MBM حسام نوا : JNS ملک نوا.

Daulatyar Kambal,[1] the amīr of Ḳanauj, Rāi Sabir[2] and the other Rāis and Rānās joined the Sulṭān with about 50,000 horse and innumerable foot. Malik Sarwar[3] received the title of Khwājā-i-Jahān and the vizirate. Malik Naṣir-ul-Mulk became Khizr Khān, Khawāṣ-ul-Mulk was made Khawāṣ Khān, and Saif-ud-dīn became Saif Khān.

The Sulṭān again defeated by Abu Bakr Shāh.

In the month of Sha'bān (July-August) of the same year (791 H., 1389 A.D.), (Sulṭān Muḥammad) again marched towards Dehli. Abu Bakr Shāh came forth to meet him and reached the village of Kandli.[4] A battle took place between the two, and there was a heavy death-roll on both sides. By the decree of Allah, the Most High, the forces of the Sulṭān (Muḥammad) were defeated and Abu Bakr was victorious. The camp equipage and baggage fell into the hands of the victors, who kept up the pursuit for three *Kuroh*. The Sulṭān returned, and took up his abode at Jatesar.[5] Abu Bakr Shāh returned to Dehli.

The slaves of Firoz Shāh murdered. The Hindus become powerful.

On the 19th Ramzān (Saturday, the 11th September) of the same year (791 H., 1389 A.D.), the slaves of Firoz Shāh who were living in the districts and cities, such as, at Multān, Lāhore, Sāmāna, Hiṣār-Firozāh[6] and Hānsī[7] were unjustly put to death in one day[8] by the chiefs and people of the city under the orders of Sulṭān Muḥammad. In consequence of the contention among the Musulmāns for the throne, the infidels of Hindustān gathered strength, withheld paying the poll-tax and tribute and put to plunder the villages of the Musulmāns.

In the month of Muḥarram, 792 H. (Dec.-Jany., 1389-90 A.D.),

---

1 MBL كنبد : JNS and MBM كنبل.

2 Elliot, Rāi Sarwar.

3 JNS ملک بدور : MBL and MBM ملک سرور.

4 JNS كندلي : MBL and MBM كندلی : Elliot, Kundali.

5 MBL جتيسر : JNS and MBM جتير.

6 MBL حصار فيروزة : JNS and MBM حصار. Elliot agrees with MBM and JNS.

7 JNS مانسي.

8 JNS and MBM بحکم دومان محمد یک روز : MBL یکدیگر در یک روز.

Prince Humāyūn Khān defeated by Abu Bakr.

Prince Humāyūn Khān, having collected the Amīrs and Maliks who had been appointed to act under him, such as, Ghālib Khān, Amīr of Sāmāna, Malik Ẓia'-ul-Mulk Aburja, Mubārak Khān Halājaun and Shams Khān, Amīr of Hiṣār-Firozāh, pitched his camp at Panipath, and plundered the environs of Dehli.[1] When Abu Bakr Shāh was informed of this, he despatched Malik Shāhīn 'Imād-ul-Mulk, with four thousand horse, and innumerable foot and attendants[2] towards Panipath; and the two forces drew up in battle array at the village of Nasmina[3] near Panipath. The Almighty God conferred victory[4] upon the army of Abu Bakr Shāh, and the army of the prince being defeated fled back towards Sāmāna. His camp, baggage and equipments all became the spoil of the victors. As a matter of fact, when the forces of Dehli, under the grace of God, won repeated victories, Sulṭān Muḥammad and his army could no longer resist the enemy, and he consequently became very much depressed in spirit. Still, the Amīrs and Maliks, and the people of the country were entirely[5] on the side of the Sulṭān, and Abu Bakr Shāh dared not leave the city (Dehli) in pursuit of his defeated enemy.

Entry of Sulṭān Muḥammad into Dehli.

In the month of Jamādi-ul-Auwal (April-May) of the same year (792 H., 1390 A.D.), Abu Bakr Shāh collected his army and marched towards Jatesar.[6] He encamped about 20 *Kuroh* from Dehli, and Sulṭān Muḥammad being informed of this, left all his army and baggage at Jatesar, and started off with 4,000 light horse for Dehli. Some of the slave guards who had been left in charge of the city, shut themselves up at the Badāōn gate, and made some show of resistance; but the assailants set fire to the gate, and the defenders fled. Sulṭān Muḥammad entered the city through this gate, and

---

[1] MBL حوالی دهلي را خراب میکرد : MBM دهلي که خراب : JNS agrees with MBM.

[2] MBL سوار و پیادگان و بندگان بی شمار : MBM سوار و بندگان پیادهٔ بی شمار : JNS agrees with MBM.

[3] MBL نسمینه : MBM بسینه : JNS بسیه : Elliot, Basina.

[4] JNS and MBM فتح بخشید : MBL فتحیاب بخشید.

[5] JNS کلا و جملا : MBL کلا و جملا : MBM کلا و جملة.

[6] JNS جتسره : MBM جتیرا : MBL جتیسر

took up his quarters at the auspicious palace. All the people of the city, high and low, joined him. When intelligence of this reached Abu Bakr, he set off early on the same day with a party of his followers, and entered the city by the same gate. Malik Bahā'-ud-dīn Jangi[1] who had been left to guard the gates by Sulṭān Muḥammad, was killed on the spot. When Abu Bakr Shāh reached the auspicious palace, the Sulṭān was unaware of what had happened. Being apprised of the fact, he escaped with a small party of followers through a back door of the palace, and making his way out of the city by the gate of *Ḥauz-i-Khāṣ* he returned to Jatesar, to his army and baggage. Of the Amīrs, Maliks and the soldiers who were unable to escape out of the city, some were taken prisoner and some killed; for instance, Khalil Khān, *Naib-i-Barbak*[2] and Malik Ādam[3] Ismā'il, the sister's son of the late Sulṭān (Firoz Shāh), were taken alive, and were put to death.

The Sulṭān leaves Dehli and goes to Jatesar: his Amirs and Maliks imprisoned and killed.

In the month of Ramẓān in the aforesaid year (Aug.-Sept., 1390 A.D.), Mubashir Jab Sulṭāni,[4] who bore the title of Islām Khān, with several slaves of Firoz Shāh, without any reason turned against Abu Bakr Shāh, and opened a secret correspondence with the Sulṭān. At length, when this fact became known, Abu Bakr Shāh was utterly dumbfounded, so he left Dehli, accompanied by a small cavalry and some of his devoted followers, such as, Malik Shāhīn 'Imād-ul-Mulk,[5] Malik Baḥri and Ṣafdar Khān Sulṭāni, proceeded to the *Kotlah*[6] of Bahādur Nāhir.

Abu Bakr Shāh leaves Dehli.

---

1 MBL جكي : MBM جنكي : JNS agrees with MBM : Badaoni writes Jangi.

2 MBL omits "*Naib*": JNS and MBM retain it: Elliot agrees with JNS and MBM.

3 MBM omits Adam: MBM and JNS retain it: Elliot agrees with MBM.

4 MBL and MBM read مشبرجب : JNS مبشرجب : Badaoni, Mubashir Chap: Elliot, Mubashir Hājib.

5 MBL ملك شاهين دهلي : JNS, MBM and Elliot omit دهلي.

6 Kotlah is a Hindi word meaning a small fortress. Bahādur Nāhir was the ruler of Miwat. Here the text refers to the Kotlah of Mīwat. Firoz Shāh used to designate some of his hunting places as Kotlah. Ranking identifies "the Kotlah of Bahādur Nāhir" with Hardwar or a town in its vicinity. See Ranking, p. 344,

On the 16th Ramẓān (Sunday, the 28th August) of the same year, Mubashir Jab and the Firoz Shāhi slaves sent letters to the Sulṭān informing him of the flight of Abu Bakr Shāh. They placed Khān-i-Khānān, the youngest son of the Sulṭān, on an elephant, and raised a canopy over his head.[1]

Canopy raised over Khān-i-Khānān, the youngest prince.

On the third day, the 19th Ramẓan (Wednesday, the 31st August), the Sulṭān reached the city from Jatesar, and ascended the throne of royalty in the palace of Firozābād. Mubashir Jab received the vizirate, and the title of Islām Khān was confirmed to him. The slaves of Firoz Shāh and the people of the city joined the Sulṭān. After a few days, (the Sulṭān) left Firozābād, and went to the auspicious palace in the fort of Jahān-panāh.[2] He took the elephants from the charge of the Firoz Shāhi slaves, and placed them under old elephant keepers.[3]

The Sulṭān ascends the throne of royalty.

On account of this, the aforesaid slaves broke out into rebellion,[4] but as the Sulṭān was strong, and the elephants had all been taken into the charge of his servants, they could not withstand him.

The slaves of Firoz Shāh rebel and join Abu Bakr Shāh.

Verse.[5]

Him whom the Sun serves as the tray at night how can it ever be emptied!
(He who) contends with his own benefactor, his fortune is sure to be ruined!

---

[1] Elliot adds after this, "they conducted him to Jalesar", but there is no such reference in the three MSS.

[2] Ranking, Jahān Numa.

[3] MBL تسليم به پيل بانان قديم كردند : JNS and MBM read, به تسليم پيل بانان قديم كرده.

[4] Badaoni (Ranking, p. 345) writes that the slaves of the Firoz Shāhi party who had been a source of disturbance in the days of tumult and riot were put to death without distinction, and many of the freemen also, who came from the eastern quarters of Hindustān were taken for slaves by reason of the imperfection of the pronunciation, and were put to the sword.

Ferishta explains the fact more fully. He says that many of these slaves claimed to be natives of the country and not foreigners, whereupon Muḥammad Shāh imposed upon them the pronunciation of certain words, and those who failed in their pronunciation were treated as foreigners and put to death.

[5] The verse is to be found in MBL; JNS and MBM omit it.

So, they fled in the night, with their wives and children, and joined Abu Bakr S̲h̲āh at the *Kotlah* of Bahādur Nāhir. Such as these aforesaid slaves as remained in the city received imperial orders that they must quit it within three days, so the city was cleared of those impure rebels.[1] The story runs that, when most of those contemptible slaves had been imprisoned by the Sulṭān for three days, the latter addressed each of them, "We are the natives of the country: whoever among you instead of *Kharā* says *Khari Karjanā*, is a native of the country". For that reason most of the Hindusthānies were put to death, and the slaves of Firoz S̲h̲āh were put to the sword. This tradition is well-known in the whole of Hind and Sindh.[2] The Amīrs and Maliks of the various parts of the kingdom now came to the court, and the Sulṭān's power and dignity increased. Prince Humāyūn K̲h̲ān with Islām K̲h̲ān, G̲h̲alib K̲h̲ān, Rāi Kamāl-ud-dīn, and Rāi Juljain,[3] was sent with a powerful army to suppress Abu Bakr S̲h̲āh and the Firoz S̲h̲āhi slaves. The aforesaid Amīrs had reached the village of Mahindwārī, when, in the month of Muḥarram, 793 H. (Dec.-Jany., 1790-91 A.D.) Abu Bakr S̲h̲āh, Bahādur Nāhīr and the Firoz S̲h̲āhi slaves having assembled together fell upon the royal forces in the morning, and killed several men. But Islām K̲h̲ān drew up his division and fell upon the assailants; with his followers the prince mounted his horse, and defeated the enemy at the first charge. The royalists made a hot pursuit of the fugitives many of whom took refuge in the *Kotlah*; but, some of them were killed and some taken prisoners. This intelligence reaching him, the Sulṭān started off for the scene of the conflict, and arriving at the *Kotlah*, he encamped on the banks of Dahand. Abu Bakr S̲h̲āh and Bahādur Nāhīr sought for quarter, and came to meet the Sulṭān. Bahādur

A tradition relating to the assassination of the Firoz S̲h̲āhi slaves.

The Amirs and Maliks join the Sulṭān.

Abu Bakr S̲h̲āh and Bahādur Nāhir seek pardon.

Conferment of robes of honour upon Bahādur Nāhir: Abu Bakr sent a prisoner to Mirath.

---

[1] MBL شهر از سر آن ناپاکان پاک شد : JNS and MBM read, شهر از شر ایشان خالي شد.

[2] The reference to this story is found in MBL and MBM. JNS omits it.

[3] MBL نرالهي : JNS and MBM جلجين : Elliot, Juljain.

Nâhīr received a robe of honour and was sent back; Abu Bakr Shāh was carried away by the Sulṭān to Khandī,[1] from whence he was sent to be kept a prisoner at Mirath,[2] and there he died.

Death of Abu Bakr Shāh.

Verse.[3]

If thou dost beat the tail of the snake, thou shouldst bruise its head,
The work of wounding the snake's tail is not safe!

The duration of his reign was a year and a half.[4] The Sulṭān proceeded to Etāwah, and there he was waited upon by Rāi Bar Singh,[5] whom he gave a robe of honour and sent back. From thence, proceeding along the banks of the Jaun, the Sulṭān arrived at Dehli.

Robe of honour conferred upon Rāi Bar Singh of Etāwah.

In the year 794 H. (1391-92 A.D.), there came a report that Bar Singh, Sabīr, Adharan[6] and Bir Bahān[7] were up in arms. The Sulṭān sent Islām Khān against Bar Singh, and he personally marched to Etāwah against Sabir, Adharan and the other infidels. The accursed Bar Singh encountered the forces of Islām Khān, and by the grace of God, the Muslims came off victorious; the accursed Bar Singh was defeated and put to flight. The victors pursued (the fugitives), sending many infidels to hell and laying waste their country. *"Surely the kings, when they enter a town, ruin it and make the noblest of its people to be low."*[8] At length, Bar Singh sued for mercy, and came to wait on Islām Khān, who carried him to Dehli. The accursed Sabir and Adharan attacked the town of Balārām, but when the Sulṭān

Rebellion of Bar Singh, Sabir and others.

Defeat of Bar Singh. He sues for peace.

---

1 JNS and MBM read کهندی مردی• بون : MBL در منزل کهندي برد.

2 JNS and MBM read میرتبه : Badaoni and Elliot write Mirath: MBL اه ده.

3 This verse is to be found in MBL: JNS and MBM omit it.

4 This line is omitted in MBL and MBM, but it occurs in JNS.

5 Elliot, Narsingh: Badaoni, Harsingrāi.

6 MBL omits سبیر و ادهرن.

7 JNS read پربهان : Bar Singh and others were the Zamindars of the Doāb.

8 Korān, Chap. XXVII, 34.

reached the banks of Beāh, they fled and shut themselves up at Etāwah. The Sultān continued his marches and encamped before Etāwah. On the first day, some little fighting took place. In the night, the Rāis abandoned the fort of Etāwah and fled, and next day the Sultān destroyed it. From thence, he marched towards Kanauj, and crossing the Ganges, he punished the unbelievers of Kanauj and Dalmu, and then returning, went to Jatesar, where he built a fortress, which he called Muhammadābād.

Sabir and Adharan take shelter at Etāwah. The fortress demolished.

Construction of a fortress by the Sultān.

In the month of Rajab of this year (May-June, 1392 A.D.), a letter arrived from Khwājā-i-Jahān, who was the Sultān's *locum-tenens* in Dehli, bringing the information that Islām Khān was about to depart for Multān and Lāhore, with the object of stirring up a rebellion. The Sultān immediately left Jatesar and proceeded to Dehli, where he held a court, and questioned Islām Khān about the intentions imputed to him. The latter denied them. But an infidel named Jājar,[1] the brother's son of Islām Khān, a bad fellow who had a spite against him, gave false evidence, and Islām Khān was unjustly put to death before the court. Khwājā-i-Jahān was made *vizir*, and Malik Mukarrab-ul-Mulk[2] was sent to Muhammadābād in Jatesar,[3] with an army.

Islām Khān put to death: Khwāja-i-Jahān was made the vizir.

In the year 795 H. (1392-93 A.D.), intelligence arrived that, Sabir, Adharan,[4] Jit Singh Rāthor, and Bir Bahān, the chief of Bhanuganw, and Abhai Chand, the chief of Chandwār, had rebelled.[5] The Sultān sent out Malik Mukarrab-ul-Mulk to Kanauj against the chief of Chandwār. The aforesaid unbelievers, too, opposed

Rebellion of Sabir, Adharan and others.

---

[1] MBL جاجر : JNS and MBM جاجن.

[2] JNS مقرب العضرت.

[3] MBL reads در محمد اباد در جتيسر : JNS reads likewise, with this difference that it reads جتير in place of جتيسر.

[4] Elliot, Sarvādharan.

[5] The MS. at the disposal of late H. Elliot being faulty—a leaf having been lost or passed over—what follows in Elliot is quoted from the Tabakat-i-Akbari, which is generally in close accord with Yahiya. MBM, like Elliot's MS., has lost some pages beginning from this place: and both—MBM and Elliot's MS. begin after the accession of Sultān Mahmud Nāsir-ud-dīn Shāh "to the throne at the auspicious palace".

him with their own following. Mukarrab-ul-Mulk adopted a conciliatory attitude, and by promises and engagements induced the chiefs to submit. The Rāis paid a visit to the Malik, and the latter carried them with him to Kanauj where on the pretext of deliberating (with them) took them within the fortress. Every one went there excepting Sabir who remained behind. At last they were put to death. Sabir made his escape to Etāwah. Laden with victory and success, Mukarrab-ul-Mulk returned to Muhammadābād. In the month of Shawwāl (Aug.-Sept., 1393 A.D.), the Sultān marched against Mewāt, and putting it to plunder, he proceeded to Muhammadābād Jatesar,[1] when he fell sick. It went on increasing day by day. Just then intelligence was sent to him that Bahādūr Nāhīr had plundered the vicinity of Dehli. Notwithstanding his weakness, the Sultān proceeded on a palanquin. Bahādūr Nāhīr emerged out of the *Kotlah* and opposed him. At length, being defeated at the first onset he took refuge in the *Kotlah*. The royal forces marched in his pursuit and imprisoned many people of the *Kotlah*, and put to plunder their horses, arms and baggage. Bahādūr Nāhīr fled from the *Kotlah* and hid in the mountains of Jahar. From thence the Sultān returned to Muhammadābād, and engaged himself in the constructions of buildings and in populating Jatesar. But the Sultān's sickness grew worse every day.

The Sultān marches to Mewāt and Muhammadābād, and falls sick.

Bahādur Nāhīr plunders Dehli. Sultān marches against him.

Flight of Bahādūr Nāhir.

In the month of Rabī'-ul-Auwal, 796 H. (Jany.-Feb., 1394 A.D.), the Sultān appointed Prince Humāyūn to march against Shaikhā Khōkhar, who had rebelled and had gained possession of Lāhore. Just as the prince was about to march, he received intelligence of the death of the Sultān on the 17th Rabī'-ul-Auwal (Tuesday, the 20th January), of the same year (796 H., 1394 A.D.).

Prince Humāyūn appointed against Shaikhā Khōkhar.

The death of the Sultān.

Verse.

Oh Sādi! although the heavens nourish thee with sugár;
Wherein lies its excellence, if it kills thee with poison?

---

[1] MBL and JNS read محمد اباد جتیسر.

The remains of the Sulṭān was taken out of Muḥammadābād and carried to Dehli where it was interred at *Ḥauẓ-i-Khāṣ*. The duration of the Sulṭān's reign was six years and seven months. *God knows the truth*

Account of Sulṭān 'Alā'-ud-dīn Sikandar Shāh.

His accession.

Sulṭān 'Alā'-ud-dīn Sikandar Shāh was the second son of Sulṭān Muḥammad Shāh, and he bore the name of Humāyūn Khān. On the death of Sulṭān Muḥammad Shāh, he remained engaged in the duties of mourning for three days, and on the 19th Rabī'-ul-Auwal (Thursday, the 22nd January), of the same year (796 H., 1394 A.D.), he ascended the throne at the auspicious palace, with the consent of the Amīrs and Maliks, the Imams and Ḳāẓis of the city. The vizirate was conferred upon Khwāja-i-Jahān, and the various offices and posts were suffered to remain in the old hands. In the meantime, Malik Muḳarrab-ul-Mulk, and the other Amīrs and Maliks, carried the coffin of the deceased Sulṭān to Dehli, and paid their homage to Sulṭān 'Alā'-ud-dīn. They consigned to him the elephants, baggage and the other paraphernalias of sovereignty. This state of affairs continued for a year, but by the decree of God, the Sulṭān fell ill, and it went on increasing till on the 5th Jamādī-ul-Auwal (Sunday, the 8th March, 1394 A.D.) he died.

Khwājā-i-Jahān made vizir.

The death of the Sulṭān.

Verse.

Except the blood of the sovereigns there is nothing on this plate (*i.e.*, world),
Except the dust of the Beautiful there is nothing in this desert (*i.e.*, world).

His rule lasted for one month and sixteen days. *God knows the truth!*

Account of Sulṭān Maḥmud Nāṣir-ud-dīn Shāh.[1]

Accession of Sulṭān Maḥmūd, 23rd March, 1394 A.D.

Sulṭan Maḥmud Nāṣir-ud-dīn was the youngest son of Sulṭān Muḥammad Shāh. On the death of 'Alā'-ud-dīn, most of the Amīrs and Maliks, who were in possession of feudal lands on the west, *viz.*,

---

[1] JNS reads ذکر سلطان محمود شاه : MBL, MBM read سلطان محمود ناصر الدین شاه ; Elliot agrees with JNS.

Ghālib Khān, the Amīr of Sāmāna, Rāi Kamāl-ud-dīn Main, Mūbārak Khān Halājaun,[1] Khawāṣ Khān, the Amīr of Indri and Karnāl, having come out of the city (Dehli) and encamping themselves at Jawārbāg wanted to go back to their respective *aḳṭā's* without an interview (with the Sulṭān). This information reaching Khwājā-i-Jahān, he succeeded in bringing the Amīrs within the city and making them pay homage to Sulṭān Maḥmūd. On the 20th Jamādi-ul-Auwal (Monday, the 23rd March) of the aforesaid year (796 H., 1394 A.D.), the Sulṭān took the title of Nāṣir-ud-dīn Maḥmūd Shāh and ascended the throne in the auspicious palace, with the unanimous consent of the Amīrs, Maliks, grandees, priests, chiefs and holy persons.

Conferment of posts and titles on the Amirs.

The post of vizir was bestowed upon Khwājā-i-Jahān; Muḳarrab-ul-Mulk became Muḳarrab Khān and was nominated the heir-apparent; 'Abdul Rashid Sultānī was given the title of Sa'dat Khān, and made the master of ceremonies. Malik Sārang became known as Sārang Khān[2] and was entrusted with the fief of Dibālpur Malik Daulat Yar, the Dabir, was honoured with the title of Daulat Khān. He received the office of *'Imād-ul-Mulk* and became *'Ariẓ-i-Mamālik*. The affairs of the feudal lands[3] of Hindustān were far from satisfactory[4] owing to the turbulence of the base infidels. The title of Sulṭān-ul-Sharḳ was conferred upon Khwājā-i-Jahān, and the affairs of Hindustān from Ḳanauj to Behar devolved upon him.

Conferment of Ḳanauj to Behar on Khwājā-i-Jahān, who became Sulṭān-Sharḳ.

Khwāja-i-Jahān punishes the infidels of Etāwah, Kol, etc.

In the month of Rajab, 796 H. (May, 1394 A.D.), *May its dignity increase*, Khwājā-i-Jahān was ordered off towards Hindustān with twenty well-equipped elephants. Having punished the infidels of Etawah, Kol, Khor, Kambal[5] and the environs of Ḳanauj, he proceeded to Jaunpur, and brought under his sub-

---

[1] Elliot, Malājūn.

[2] JNS reads. ملک سارنگ خان خطاب کردند.

[3] MBL کار اقطاع : MBM and JNS اقطاعات.

[4] MBL and JNS ضعیف پزیرفته بود.

[5] MBL کهور و کنبل : MBM کهوره کنبل : JNS agrees with MBM. Elliot, Kahūra-Kanil.

jection the fiefs, such as Ḳanauj, Karah, Oudh, Sandīlah,[1] Dālmu,[2] Bahraich, Bihar, and Tirhut. Most of the infidels were extirpated, and those fortresses that had been destroyed by them were restored. The Most High God conferred strength and victory upon the Muslims. The Rāi of Jājnagar and the king of Lakhnauti, who used to send elephants every year to Dehli, now presented Khwājā-i-Jahān with elephants.

Sārang Khān sent to Dibalpur against Shaikhā Khōkhar.

About the same time, Sārang Khān was despatched to Dibālpur for annexing the territory and suppressing the rebellion of Shaikhā Khōkhar. In the month of Sha'bān (June) of the aforesaid year (796 H., 1394 A.D.), Sārang Khān set out for Dibālpur. He recruited and disciplined the soldiers of Dibālpur and confiscated the territory.

Sārang Khān marched against Shaikhā Khōkhar and defeated him.

In the month of Ẕil Ka'da, 796 H. (Aug.-Sep., 1394 A.D.), Rāi Juljain[3] Bhatti and Rāi Daud Kamāl Main, having taken the army of Multān with them forded Sataldar near the village of Tirhāra,[4] and Beah near Dohāli,[5] and approached Lahore. Learning that Sārang Khān was proceeding against him, Shaikhā Khōkhar drew up his army, plundered the suburbs of Dibālpur and laid siege to Ajodhan. It so transpiring that, Sārang Khān having devastated Bhandoit[6] was making a descent, Khōkhar left Ajodhan at night and reached Lahore. On the second day, the parties prepared themselves for action and made a forward advance. The engagement took place at Sāmuthala,[7] at a distance of 12 *kuroh* from Lahore. The Almighty conferred victory on Sārang Khān; meeting with reverses, Shaikhā Khōkhar retired towards Lahore, and in the night he fled towards the mountain of Jamun[8]

---

[1] MBM سندیه : JNS سندیله : MBL شدیده. Elliot, Shadīdah.

[2] Badaoni, Malūta. Ranking, p. 349, f.n. 2, Dalmūr.

[3] MBL ذو العجي : JNS and MBM جلجين.

[4] MBL برهاره : MBM ترهاره : JNS ستاره : Elliot, Tirhara.

[5] MBM and MBL دوهالي : JNS ددهالي. Elliot, Duhālī.

[6] MBM and MBL بهندويت : JNS بهدوئی. Elliot, Hindupat.

[7] JNS ساهو تهله : MBL and MBM ساموتهله : Elliot, Samuthala. Ranking, Samothala.

[8] MBL and JNS read جمون : MBM جون. Elliot, Jud. Badaoni, Jamūn.

with his wife and children. On the next day, Sārang Khān conquered the fortress of Lahore, and having placed at Lahore[1] his brother Kandhu with the title of 'Adil Khān he returned to Dibālpur.

The Sulṭān marches to Bianah.

In the month of Sha'bān of the said year (796 H., June, 1394 A.D.), the Sulṭān took his way to Bianah, taking along with him Sa'dat Khān: Mukarrab Khān was left in the city with some elephants and royal attendants. When the Sulṭān approached Gwālior, Malik 'Alā'-ud-dīn Dahārwāl and Mubārak Khān,[2] the son of Malik Rāju, and Malo, the brother of Sārang Khān, formed a conspiracy against Sa'dat Khān. Getting information of this, the latter caught hold of 'Alā'-ud-dīn and Mubārak Khān, and killed them. Malo took to his heels and sought refuge with Mukarrab Khān in Dehli. The Sulṭān, too, made his return, and reached near Dehli. Mukarrab Khān went forth to meet him and received eminence. But, on account of fear and dread that had taken hold of him, he made his return to the city, and laid the foundation of hostility. On the next day, the Sulṭān and Sa'dat Khān, having collected and made ready the amīrs, maliks, and the elephants, reached the gate leading to the *maidan*. Mukarrab Khān went on fighting from the fortress. This state of affairs continued for a period of three months, till at length the partisans of the Sulṭān took him into the city in the month of Muḥarram, 797 H. (Oct.-Nov., 1394 A.D.). But the elephants, foot, and all the paraphernalia of sovereignty were suffered to remain in the hands of Sa'dat Khān. The presence of the Sulṭān strengthened the position of Mukarrab Khān, who, on the next day, collected the people of the city—from the soldiers to the rabble, and issued out of the city-gate for war. When this news reached Sa'dat Khān, he, too, drew up his men in the maidan. Between the two an engagement took place, in which Mukarrab Khān being worsted returned to the city, and its inhabitants suffered a great deal. But Sa'dat Khān having failed to seize the fortress, retraced his steps, and encamped himself at *Ḥauẓ-i-khāṣ*. As the conquest of the fort of Dehli was beyond the reach of pos-

---

1 MBL کوهور : JNS لاهور.

2 MBL مبارک خان و پسر ملک : JNS and MBM omit و. Elliot reads, Mubārak Khān, son of Malik Rāju.

sibility and the rainy season was near, Sa'dat Khān, perforce, raised the siege and proceeded to Firozābād. He came into agreement with the nobles, who were on his side, regarding the enthronement at Firozābād of one of the sons of Firoz Shāh. *May the blessing of God be on his tomb, and May he dwell in paradise!* Nusrat Khān bin Fateh Khān bin Firoz Shāh,[1] the late Sultān, was taken out of Mewāt, and was installed with the title of Nāsir-ud-dīn Nusrat Shāh in the palace at Firozābād in the month of Rabī'-ul-auwal (Dec.-Jany.) of the aforementioned year (797 H., 1394-95 A.D.). But he was a mere puppet,[2] and Sa'dat Khān wielded the authority.

Nusrat Khān was set upon the throne with the title of Nasir-ud-dīn Nusrat Shāh.

Soon afterwards, some of the slaves of Firoz Shāh and some of the elephant-keepers attached themselves to Sultān Nāsir-ud-dīn. Sa'dat scented no danger. They placed Sultān Nāsir-ud-dīn on an elephant, and gathered round him. Being off his guard, Sa'dat Khān could offer no opposition, he left the palace through the door leading to the seraglio; some of his soldiery joined him and some foolishly dispersed in every direction; Sa'dat Khān entered Dehli with his own party and visited Mukarrab Khān. After a few days, Mukarrab Khān treacherously killed him.

Sa'dat Khān leaves the palace and is killed.

The amirs and maliks who remained at Firozābād, such as, Muhammad Muzaffar,[3] Shahāb Nāhir, Fazl Allah Balkhi, the slaves of Firoz Shāh joined the Sultān, and renewed[4] their homage to the throne.[5] Muhammad Muzaffar became the *vizir*, and was named Tātār Khān. Shahāb Nāhir became Shahāb Khān, and Fazl Allah Balkhi received the title Kutlugh Khān. Malik Almās Sultānī received the command of the royal slaves.[6]

Conferment of titles and posts on Amirs.

---

[1] MBL نصرت خان بن فروز خان : JNS illegible. Elliot, Nusrat Khān, son of Fath Khān, son of Sultān Firoz Shāh.

[2] MBL طریق نمونه پیش داشتند : JNS and MBM پیش نداشته بردند.

[3] JNS and MBM read محمد مظفر وزیر و شهاب ناهر و ملک فضل الله. Elliot agrees with JNS and MBM.

[4] MBL بیت تازه کردند : JNS and MBM بیعت کردند.

[5] Elliot, "pledged their faith to him".

[6] عهدهٔ داریٔ بندگان خاص.

Two Sulṭāns—one at Dehli and the other at Firozābād: disorder in the country.

There were two kings,[1] one at Dehli and the other at Firozābād Muḳarrab Khān secured Bāhādur Nāhir and his adherents, and placed him in charge of the fortress of old Dehli. Malo received the designation of Iḳbāl Khān and (the command of) the fortress of Siri. At length, there ensued conflict every day between Dehli and Firozābād. The Musalmans shed blood of their own relations, but neither of the parties could gain mastery. The districts between Doāb, Sambal,[2] Pānipath, Jhajar and Rohtak remained in the possession of Sulṭān Nāṣir-ud-dīn ; to Sulṭān Maḥmud belonged nothing else except the above mentioned fortresses.[3] The Amīrs and Maliks of the empire set themselves up as rulers, and levied taxes and tribute. This state of things lasted for three months. There was a struggle between Dehli and Firozābād every day ; sometimes, the latter came off victorious and besieged the fort of Dehli, and on occasions Firozābād was besieged and plundered by Dehli.

Enmity between Sārang Khān and Khiẓr Khān.

Under these circumstances, there happened, in the year 798 H. (1395-96 A.D.), an enmity between Sārang Khān and *Masnad-i-Āla* Khiẓr Khān, the amir of Multān. A fierce contest took place between the two. At last, some of the slaves of Malik Mardān Bhatti[4] went over to the side of Sārang Khān.[5] The district of Multān came under the jurisdiction of Sārang Khān. In the month of Ramẓān, 799 H. (May-June, 1397 A.D.), Sārang Khān collected a large army and proceeded towards Sāmāna. Ghālib Khān, the amīr of Sāmāna, shut himself up in the fortress and put forth resistance, but losing all power of opposition and meeting with

---

[1] Badaoni (Ranking, 351) writes, they "were like two kings in the game of chess".

[2] JNS and MBM read سنبل : Badaoni (Ranking) Sanbhal; Elliot, Sambhal; MBL reads سيپنتهه : Tab-i-Akb. reads دواب پاني پت و سون‌پت و رهتک و جهجر.

[3] Badaoni (Ranking, *ibid.*) writes, "....a few old ruined forts such as Dihlī and Sīrī and the rest, remained in the hands of Sulṭān Maḥmūd, and from that time forward this proverb became a common expression : The rule of the Lord of the world is from Dihli to Pālam".

[4] Elliot, Malik Mardān Bhattī ; Ranking (352), Malik Marwān.

[5] JNS and MBL read آخر بعضی غلامان ملک مردان بهتی دادند : MBM reads بعضی ا: غلامان ملک مردان مهي دادند : Tab-i-Akb. reads غلامان بهتی با سارنگ خان بپیوستند.

reverses, he went to Panipath with a small cavalry and footmen, and joined Tātār Khān. When this news transpired to Nusrat Shāh, he despatched Malik Almas, the commandar of the slaves, with ten elephants and a small army to Tātār Khān with orders to march against Sāmāna and driving out Sārang Khān place Sāmāna on Ghālib Khān.

Flight of Sārang Khān. Sāmāna entrusted upon Ghālib Khān.

On the 15th Muharram, 800 H. (Monday, the 8th Oct., 1397 A.D.) a battle was fought between them at Kohlah.[1] The Almighty God conferred victory on Tātār Khān. Sārang Khān fled towards Multān, and Tātār Khān entrusted Sāmāna upon Ghālib Khān.[2] In company with Rāi Kamāl-ud-din Main,[3] Tātār Khān ran in pursuit of Sārang Khān as far as Talwandi,[4] whence he retraced his steps.

Advent of Pir Muhammad, the grandson of Timur.

In the month of Rabī'-ul-auwal, 800 H. (Nov.-Dec., 1397 A.D.), Pir Muhammad, the daughter's son[5] of Timur,[6] the King of Khorāsān, having crossed the river Sindh[7] with a large force, laid siege to the fort of Uchch. 'Ali Malik, who was in charge of the place (Uchch) on behalf of Sārang Khān (the fief-holder of Dibalpur) held out for a month, when the Khān sent out Malik Tāj-ud-dīn, his nāib or deputy, along with the other amīrs and a contingent of 4,000 horsemen[8] in aid of 'Alī Malik. At the news of Tāj-ud-dīn's approach, Pir Muhammad withdrew the siege and fell upon the enemy's reinforcement at Tarmtamah,[9] on the bank of the Beāh. They could not withstand such an unexpected attack; many were killed, while some threw themselves into the river and

---

1 MSS. read کوهله Tab-i-Akb. reads کوتله. Ranking, "the village of Kotla": Elliot, Kūtila.

2 MBL reads تاتار خان سارنگ خان مذکور را تار تار کرده سامانه بحوالهٔ غالب خان کرد : JNS and MBM read تاتار خان سامانه را بحوالهٔ.

3 Badaoni, Kamal-ud-dīn Mubīn.

4 Ranking, Tilaundī.

5 JNS and MBL نبیسهٔ. MBM نشه.

6 Badaoni reads, Amir Timur Gūrgān King of Khorāsān, "Kurkān or Gūrgān stands for son-in-law or for a prince who is allied by marriage with some mighty monarch." Amir Timur was called Timur Gūrgān, because he married the daughter of the last Emperor of the Mongol dynasty.

7 River Sindh refers to the Indus.

8 MBL adds after this و عدکیان آن دیار : JNS and MBM omit this.

9 MSS. read ترمتمه. In Elliot, IV, p. 33, *Tamtama*.

were carried away. Sustaining defeat, Malik Tāj-ud-dīn, with a small force at his command, retreated to Multān. Pir Muḥammad followed him there in pursuit. Sārang Khān dared not oppose him in the field and was compelled to take refuge in the fortress. For six months the siege continued ; at last on the 19th Ramẓān, 800 H., Wednesday, the 5th June, 1398 A.D., provisions running short, Sārang Khān held out the olive branch and visited Pir Muḥammad. The Khān was clapped into prison along with his family, dependents, army and the people of the city, while the victor took possession of Multān, where he stationed his army.[1]

Compact between Iḳbāl and Sulṭān Nāṣir-ud-dīn, and the former's treachery.

In the month of Shawwāl, 800 H. (June-July, 1398 A.D.), Iḳbāl Khān[2] leagued himself with Sulṭān Nāṣir-ud-dīn and a compact was made between the two, at the tomb of the chief of the saints Ḳutub ul-Huḳ-wa-us-Shara'-wa-ud-dīn.[3] Sulṭān Nāṣir-ud-dīn was seated on an elephant and brought to Jahānpanāh.[4] Sulṭān Maḥmud, Muḳarrab Khān and Bahādur Nāhir shut themselves up in the fortress of old Dehli. On the third day, Iḳbāl Khān fell upon the unwary Sulṭān Nāṣir-ud-dīn, who being thus taken unawares quitted Jāhānpanāh with his elephants and a small contingent. Iḳbāl went in his pursuit, and took hold of the elephants[5] belonging to the fugitive. Nāṣir-ud-dīn marched to Firozābād and thence, with his attendants and relatives having crossed the Jaun (Jamuna), went to his Vizir Tātār Khān. Firozābād was then taken possession of by Iḳbāl. Subsequently, daily contests between Muḳarrab Khān and Iḳbāl Khān took place for two months. At length, owing to the intercession of the *amīrs*, reconciliation was effected between them. Muḳarrab Khān made an entry into Jāhānpanāh with Sulṭān Maḥmud and Iḳbāl remained at Siri. All on a sudden, Iḳbāl accompanied by his own men, threw a cordon round the house of Mukarrab and treacherously slew him. Though he refrained from doing

Iḳbāl took the management of the State.

---

1 MBL adds طعمهٔ ماهیان دریا شدند.

2 Was in charge of Siri ; his original name was "Malu".

3 JNS and MBM read نظام الحق etc.

4 MSS. and Elliot read Jahān-panāh : Ranking (354) reads Jahān-numā.

5 MBL reads پیلان نامدار : JNS and MBM omit نامدار.

any personal injury to Sulṭān Maḥmud, yet he took to himself the management of the State and kept the Sulṭān as a puppet.[1]

Ikbāl marched against Tātār Khān, and the latter's flight to Gujrat.

In Ẓil Ka'da, 800 H. (July-Aug., 1398 A.D.), Iḳbāl set out for Panipath against Tātār Khān. When the latter received this intelligence, he left his baggage and elephants in the fort of Panipath and proceeded towards Dehli with a strong force. Iḳbal besieged Panipath, conquered it in two or three days, and finally laid his hands on the elephants, horses and the baggage of Tātār, who in his turn had also attacked Dehli but failed in his attempt to take it. The capitulation of Panipath made Tātār give up the siege (of Dehli), and he fled with his army to his father in Gujrat. Iḳbāl returned victoriously to Dehli laden with elephants, horses and the spoils of war. Malik Naṣir-ul-Mulk, a relation of Tātār Khān, was given the title of 'Adil Khān for his co-operation with Iḳbāl Khān[2] and was, besides, rewarded with lands in the Doāb, while the latter was engaged in carrying on the affairs of the State.

Timur's invasion.

In the month of Safar, 801 H. (Oct.-Nov., 1398 A.D.), report was given currency to that Amīr Timur, the king of Khorāsān, having plundered Talumba[3] had encamped his army at Multān and put to the sword all the soldiers of Sārang Khān that had been imprisoned by the Amīr's grandson. For this reason Sārang Khān was at his wit's end. Timur set off to Bhatnir[4] and having made Juljain Bhatti[5] (the commandant of the fort) a prisoner, killed the people who had been besieged. From thence he proceeded to Sāmāna where the inhabitants of Dibalpur, Ajodhan and Sarsuti had repaired to in fear of

---

[1] MBL adds نقش دیوار بر طریق نمونه مي داشت.

[2] MBL adds لشکر تشیدن سونی حصار پاني پته او گفته بود ; JNS and MBM omit this.

[3] The word is طدن in the JNS : MBL and MBM طلنبه ; Badaoni (355), Tulumba. In Elliot, *ibid.*, 34, *Talina*. Talumba or (Tulumba) is situated at the junction of the Jhelam and the Chinab.

[4] JNS read بهنیر ; MBM and JNS بستنیر. Elliot, *Bhatnir*, *ibid.* Badaoni, Bhat.

[5] In Elliot, *Kulchain*, *ibid.* In JNS and MBM we have رای جلجین بهني ; MBL ذولجي ; Ferishta, Khilji ; Ranking, Jaljin.

the invader. Some of them were made captive and a large number received the glory of martyrdom. The victor then forded Jaun (Jamuna) and made an entry into the Doāb, most parts of which he harried. He halted at Loni [1] and killed all the prisoners that were taken (from the tract) between the Sindh and the Ganges, totalling 50,000 men, more or less, *God alone knows the truth*. The inhabitants of the towns and the villages, Muslims and Hindus [2] alike, got funky and ran away, some to the mountains, some to the desert,[3] some towards the rivers and some again to the fort of Dehli. In Jāmādi-ul-auwal, 801 H. (Jany.-Feb., 1399 A.D.), Timur crossed the Jaun, came to Fīrozābād, and on the day following put himself at the top of *Ḥauẓ-i-khāṣ*. In the *maidan* Iḳbāl with his elephants came *vis-à-vis*; at the first onset the Khān met with his defeat. Some of his elephants fell in the hands of the Amīr's men, so with the remaining elephants he returned to the city through thousand and one difficulties.[4] Still, during the retreat, most of

The sack of Dehli.

the inhabitants of the city and the army were stamped out under foot, and heaps of dead were left. At sundown, Iḳbāl Khān and Sulṭān Maḥmud [5] leaving behind them their ladies and children, emerged out of the city. The latter took his way to Gujrat and the former crossed the Jaun and went over to Baran.[6] Next day, Timur promised safety to the inhabitants and exacted ransom from them. On the fourth day, he ordered that all the inhabitants of the city should be imprisoned and his mandate was carried out. *We belong to Allah, and we resign ourselves to His decree.*[7]

A few days after, *Masnad 'Ali* Khiẓr Khān, *May his tomb be*

The sack of Lahore.

sanctified, who had taken refuge in the mountains of Mewāt in fear of the invader, Bahādur

---

1 In Elliot, *Loni, ibid.* MBL نمولي : MBM نموني : Tab-i-Akb. لوني : In JNS تموني : "Loni" is seven miles N.N.W. of Dehli (Ishwari Pd's *Mediæval India*, p. 307, f.n. 3. Ranking, 356, f.n. 1).

2 JNS read جهود (Jew), referring to non-Muslims. MBL and MBM هنود.

3 In JNS چول is copyist's error for جول, desert.

4 The word is حيله meaning fraud : here translated as "difficulty".

5 MBM omits محمود : JNS and MBL retain it.

6 Bulandshahr.

7 This sentence is omitted in JNS.

Nāhir, Mubārak Khān and Zirak Khān were honoured with an interview, but save Khizr Khān all were enchained. Timur took to the skirts of the hills on his way back from Dehli. Khizr Khān was permitted to go and to him the invader addressed thus—"Having conquered Dehli, I bestow it upon you."[1] On his way, those who remained in the mountains were also imprisoned. Reaching Lahore, the Amir sacked the city and made Shaikhā Khōkhar,[2] who due to his enmity with Sārang Khān had ere long joined Timur and acted as his guide, a prisoner along with his wife, children and those who had taken shelter with him. The victor bestowed upon Khizr Khān the fiefs of Multān and Dibālpur and despatched him there. He then marched via Kabul *en route* Samarkand, his capital.

Timur bestows Dehli upon Khizr Khān.

After the departure of Timur, the vicinity of Dehli, and all those places which his army had passed through, were visited with pestilence and famine. Many died of sickness and many of hunger. For a couple of months Dehli presented a scene of desolation and woe. In the month of Rajab, *May its dignity increase*, Sultān Nāṣir-ud-dīn Nuṣrat Shāh grandson of Sultān Firoz, who having failed to resist Ikbāl Khān had made his way to the Doāb, now advanced to Mirat with a small force and was joined by 'Adil Khān, who brought with him four elephants and an army. Nuṣrat Shāh tactfully brought him under his control and took hold of the elephants. The people of the Doāb who had been set free from the Mughals, began to rally, and Nāṣir-ud-dīn entered Firozābād with 2,000 cavalry. Dehli, though ruined and desolate, came to his power. Shahāb Khān came from Mewāt with ten elephants and a number of adherents: from the Doab came Malik Almās who joined Nāṣir-ud-din. Thus, when a large army collected round him, Nāṣir-ud-din despatched Shahāb Khān to Baran against[3] Ikbāl Khān.

India after Timur's return, 1399–1414 A.D. State of the country.

Rajab, 801 H., Mar.-Apr., 1399 A.D. Nāṣir-ud-din Nuṣrat Shāh came out from Doāb and his contest for the throne.

---

[1] MBL and MBM omit this sentence. JNS retains it. Badaoni (359) also mentions this incident.

[2] MBM کہوکہبر :

[3] MBL برای قلع و قمع : MBM omits و قمع ; JNS agrees with MBM.

But a party of Hindu footmen fell upon Shahâb Khân and put him to death on the way: the Khân's followers dispersed and the elephants were abandoned.[1] Receiving this news, Iḳbâl rushed hotfoot to the place of the occurrence and captured the elephants.

Growth of Iḳbâl's power.

Iḳbâl's power and dignity continued increasing every day and forces collected round him from all directions, while Sulṭân Nâṣir-ud-dīn grew weaker and weaker.

Rabi'-ul-auwal, 801 H. Death of Nuṣrat. Dehli under Iḳbâl. His capital Siri.

In the month of Rabī'-ul-auwal (Nov.-Dec.), Iḳbâl left Baran and paced his way to Dehli with an army. Nuṣrat evacuated Firozâbâd and proceeded to Mewât, where he breathed his last.[2] Dehli thus came into the possession of Iḳbâl who took up his abode at Siri. Some of the inhabitants of the city who had escaped the Mughals came back and renewed their habitations. In a short time Siri became populated.

Dehli re-populated.

Extent of territory under Iḳbâl.

The districts in the Doâb and the fiefs in the vicinity (of the capital) belonged to Iḳbâl, while the outlying parts of the kingdom that (formerly) remained in the possession of the *amīrs* and the *maliks* were kept by them. Thus, Gujrat and its neighbouring countries were under Zafar Khân Wajīb-ul-Mulk[3]; Multân, Dibalpur and parts of Sind were held by *Bandagi Masnad-i-'Ali* Khizr Khân, *May his tomb be sanctified*; Mahobâ and Kâlpi (were placed) under Maḥmud Khân, son of Malik Zâdâh Firoz; the fiefs on the side of Hindustan, e.g., Ḳanauj, Oudh, Karah, 'Dalmau,'[4] Sandilah, Bahraich, Bihâr and Jaunpur under Khwâja-i-Jahân; Dhar under Dilawar Khân; Sâmâna under Ghâlib Khân; Biânah under Shams Khân Auḥadi. The territories of Dehli were parcelled out into so many portions.

The possession of the Amirs.

---

1 MBL and MBM read پیلان پیکار واهی ماندند : JNS واهی ماندند.

2 MBL and MBM omit "where he breathed his last".

3 Elliot, JNS and MBM read وجیب الملک : MBL reads وجیه الملک.

4 JNS and MBL دلمؤ ; MBM دلموء.

Rabī'ul-auwal, 802 H. Iḳbāl to Biānah and his success.

In Rabī'-ul-auwal, 802 H. (Nov., 1399 A.D.) Iḳbāl Khān marched towards Biānah against Shams Khān who was at the town of Nuh-o-Batal.[1] A battle followed, in which victory was awarded to Ikbāl. The vanquished was reduced to beat a retreat leaving a couple of elephants in the hands of the victors, who, thence proceeded against Katehar,[2] where having exacted money and servitude from Rāi Har Sing,[3] returned to Dehli.

To Katehar.

Death of Khwāja-i-Jahān: succeeded by Malik Mubārak Ḳaranful

After the death of Khwāja-i-Jahān at Jaunpur in that year, Malik Mubārak Ḳaranful[4] succeeded to his titles and took the designation of Mubārak Shāh. All the districts came under his possession.

Iḳbal to Hindustan, his success against Rai Sabir, Jamādī-ul-auwal 803 H., Dec., 1400 A.D.

In Jamādī-ul-auwal, 803 H. (Dec.-Jany., 1400-1401 A.D.) Ikbāl set out for Hindustan and was met by Shams Khān, the amīr of Biānah, and Mubārak Khān Bahādur Nāhir. He took them along with him, and in the same month[5] reached Pattiāli[6] on the banks of the *Āb-i-Siyāh*.[7] Here he encountered the accursed Sabir[8] and the other infidels who came with a numerous army. On the day following, an engagement took place in which

---

1 Elliot, Nuh-o-Batal, IV, p. 37. MBL and MBM نوه و بتل : JNS نوه و پتل. Ranking (359), Nūh and Patal.

2 MBL کهتیره . JNS کتهیهر : MBM کتهیر : By Kaīthar or Katehr is meant Rohilkhand.

3 In Elliot, Rai Sing. JNS and MBL هر سنگهه : MBM رای سنکهه : Rai Harsing was Rāi of Etāwah.

4 The MSS. read ملک مبارک قرنفل : Elliot omits قرنفل : Ranking (360) reads Malik Mubarak Ḳarnḳal.

5 JNS جمادی لاول : MBM جماد الاول : MBL جمادي آلاخر : Elliot agrees with JNS and MBM.

6 Ranking (*ibid.*), Baitālī ; Ferishta (Bomb. Text) بتالي.

7 MBL آب بياه : JNS and MBM آب سياه. Badaoni and Elliot agree with JNS and MBM. *Āb-i-Siyāh*, literally "Black water," refers to the Kālinī or the Kālī Naddī, lying between the Jumna and the Ganges. Ferishta (Bom. Text) نهر گنگ.

8 سبير in the MSS. In Elliot, Rai Sir, *ibid.*, 37. Badaoni agrees with Elliot, but Ferishta reads "Rai Sanīr", which Briggs translates as "Ray of Serinagar".

God, the Defender of the Muhammadan religion, conferred victory upon Ikbāl. The turbulent infidels were defeated and subdued. Ikbāl gave them a chase to Etāwah, killing many and imprisoning a large number. *Praise be to God on this account.*[1] He then proceeded to Kanauj when Sultān-ul Shark Mubārak Shāh also came up from Hindustan. Between the two forces intervened the Ganges which neither of the parties could ford. The battle went on for two months till the belligerents retraced their way homewards. During the course of his march Ikbāl scented treachery and put Shams Khān and Mubārak Khān to death.

Ikbāl to Kanauj: his unsuccessful, encounter with Mubārak Shāh.

The same year, Taghi Khān Turkbāchā Sultāni,[2] the son-in-law of Ghālib Khān, the amīr of Sāmāna, collected a huge force and went towards Dibālpur against *Masnad-i-'Ali* Khizr Khān, *May his tomb be exalted.* When Khizr heard of this, he prepared himself for action and set off towards Ajodhan with a large contingent. A battle was fought on the banks of the Dahinda on the 9th Rajab, *May its dignity be exalted*, 803 H. (Wed., 23rd Feb., 1401 A.D.). Khizr came out with flying colours and Taghi Khān (Turkbāchā Sultāni) retired to the town of Bhuhar[3] and was killed by Ghālib Khān and the other amīrs.

Turkbāchā marched against Khizr Khān and the latter's victory at Dahinda, 9th Rajab, 803 H.

In 804 H. (1401-1402 A.D.) Sultān Mahmud issued out from Dhār and proceeded to Dehli. Ikbāl came forth to give him a reception and the Sultān went to the imperial[4] palace in Jāhānpanāh.[5] But as the reins of government were in the hands of Ikbāl, ill-will[6] sprang up between the two.

Sultān Mahmud came out of Dhār, 804 H., 1401-1402 A.D. and marched to Kanauj.

---

1 JNS omits this line.

2 Elliot, Taghī Khān Turkchi Sultānī: Ranking, "Turkbacha Sultani".

3 The word is بہوہر in JNS; in Elliot, Assuhar, *ibid.*, 38. MBL ابہوہر: MBM اسوہر. Ranking, Bhūhar.

4 The words are در کوشک همایون میان جهان پناه: Elliot translates it thus: "Humayun palace in Jahan panah." IV, 38.

5 This name was given to the central portion of the triple Citadel of Dehli connecting old Dehli with Siri. It was situated in the midst of the inhabited city, and had thirteen gates.

6 In the JNS نغلق: is mis-spelt for نفاق.

Accompanied by Iḳbāl, Maḥmud marched to Ḳanauj. In that year Sulṭān Mubārak Shāh died, and his younger brother Ibrāhim succeeded him under the title of Sulṭān Ibrāhim. At the approach of Sulṭān Maḥmud and Iḳbāl Khān, Ibrāhim came out to meet them with a large army. When the two forces neared each other and a fight was impending, the Sulṭān left Iḳbāl in the lurch on pretence of hunting to join Ibrāhim. The latter paid him no attention, so he drew off and went to Ḳanauj. Here he drove out Shāh-Zādāh Hariwī,[1] who held the place for Mubārak Shāh and took possession of the place. Iḳbāl went back to Dehli and Ibrāhim to Jaunpur. At Ḳanauj, the people of every description—the poor and the wealthy—co-operated with Sulṭān Maḥmud; the slaves and the dependents who were lying pell-mell, rallied round him. To sum up, the Sulṭān was content with the *aḳṭā'* of Ḳanauj.

Sulṭān Ibrāhim succeeded Sulṭān Mubarak on the latter's death.

In Jamādī-ul-auwal, 805 H. (Nov.-Dec., 1402 A.D.), Iḳbāl marched against Gwālior, which had been treacherously wrested from the hands of the Musalmans during the invasion of the Mughals by the accursed Bar Singh,[2] who was followed after his death, by his son Biram Deo. The fort being impregnable nothing could be effected against it, and so Iḳbāl returned after plundering the country, to Dehli. Next year, he again marched against it. Biram Deo[3] sallied out of his garrison and a battle was fought at Dholpur.[4] Meeting with defeat, Biram fled back into the fortress. A large number of the infidels were put to the sword. When night came on, Biram evacuated the fort (of Dholpur) and retreated to Gwālior. Iḳbāl made a pursuit of the infidels, and having ravaged their territory, which was situated in a desert, returned to Dehli.

Iḳbāl marched to Gwālior and laid it waste, Jamādi-ul-auwal 805 H., 1402 A.D.

Iḳbāl's second invasion of Gwālior, 806 H. 1403 A.D. Battle of Dholpur.

In 806 H. (1403-1404 A.D.), Tātār Khān, the son of Ẕafar Khān, the Amir of Gujrat, having treacherously confined his father and

---

[1] Elliot, Malik-zādāh Harbūī: Badaoni, "Shāh-zādāh Fatḥ Khān of Herāt."

[2] Badaoni, Har Singh; Ferishta and Elliot, Nur Singh.
MSS. and Tab-i-Akb. read بر سنگه.

[3] MBM and JNS read پسر بيرم خان.

[4] MBM حصار دهولپور.

Tātār Khān, son of Zafar Khān, the Amir of Gujrat, adopts the title of Sulṭān Nāṣir-ud-dīn Muḥammad Shāh.

then sending him off to Asāwal,[1] adopted the title of Sulṭān Nāṣir-ud-dīn Muḥammad Shāh. He then collected a large army and led it against Dehli. But while he was on his way, Shams Khān administered poison to him, and he fell a victim to it on the same day. Alas! what a treachery of the world!! Such an emperor, a valiant champion, kind and merciful, was killed in the twinkling of an eye. His holy spirit was despatched to Dar-ul-Islam (*i.e.*, paradise). In fine that emperor, of disposition commendable and qualities angelic, was assassinated.[2] During the night Zafar Khān was brought out of Asāwal with reinforcements.

Ikbāl's march to Etawah 807 H., 1404-1405 A.D.

In 807 H. (1404-1405 A.D.), Iḳbāl marched the army to Etāwah which was laid siege to by Rāī Sabir,[3] Rāi of Gwālior, Rāī Jālbāhar[4] and the other *rayāns.* The turbulent infidels held out for four months; at last, they negotiated for peace, and made a present of four elephants belonging to the Raja of Gwālior to the victor.

To Kanauj, Shawwāl 807 H., April, 1405 A.D.

In the month of Shawwāl (Apr.), Iḳbāl left Etāwah for Ḳanauj and fought with the Sulṭān Maḥmud. The fort being strong and its conquest remote, Iḳbāl raised the siege and went back to Dehli. As the Sulṭān had reared him (Iḳbāl) up, he (Sulṭan) overlooked his (Iḳbal's) actions, because,

Verse.

Dost thou know why the water does not immerse the log of wood?
For, it is ashamed to plunge that which it nourished.[5]

---

1 JNS and MBM اساول : MBL بهروج. Elliot and Badaoni read, Asāwal (Ahmadabad).

2 The lines from "Alas...... assassinated" is to be found in MBL, JNS and MBM omit them.

3 In Elliot (p. 39), Rāi Sarwar.

4 In Elliot, *ibid.*, and Tab-i-Akb., Rāi Jālhār.

5 The lines from "As the Sulṭān........nourished" are found in MBL: JNS and MBM make no mention of these lines.

To Sāmāna, Muharram 808 H., June-July, 1405 A.D.

In Muḥarram, 808 (June-July, 1405) Iḳbāl marched to Sāmāna. Bairam Khān Turkbācha fled to the mountains of Har Hor[1]; Iḳbāl encamped at the city of Arubar,[2] situated in the mountains of Har Hor. At length, Makhdum-Zādah Sheikh 'Alam-ud-dīn, the grandson of Hazrat Kutub-ul Kitāb-ul 'Alam Sa'iyid Jalāl-Huk ul-Sharā'-ud-dīn Bokhāri,—*May God be pleased with him* nterceded (between tne contending parties) and Bairam Khān came to Iḳbāl Khān, and the former was granted an interview. From thence Iḳbāl proceeded towards Multān. When he reached Talwandi, Rāi Kamāl-ud-din Main[3] arrived. Here he imprisoned Bairam Khān, Rāi Da'ud Kamāl Main, Rāi Hinu Juljain Bhatti.[4] On the third day, he skinned Bairam Khān and carried the rest with him as prisoners.[5] On his arrival at the bank of Dahinda, near the district of Ajodhan,[6] *Bandagi Masnad-i-'Ālā* Khizr Khān, *May his tomb be sanctified*, opposed him with a numerous army.[7] It was manifest that, the army that had broken the pledge was befriended by ruin, for, it is the fair sex, who break their compact.

To Multān.

---

[1] MBL هر هور : JNS and MBM هل هور : In Elliot, Badhnor, IV, 40 : Tab-i-Akb., بد هور.

[2] MBL اروبر : JNS and MBM رو پر : In Elliot, Arubar, *ibid.*; Badaoni, Rupar, in the Ambala Dist., 40 miles North of Ambala city on the south bank of the Sutlej.

[3] JNS and MBM, Kamāl-ud-uin. Badaoni, Rāi Kamāl-ud-din Mubin: Briggs, Kumal Khan Mye. MBL reads Rāi Kamāl Main.

[4] In Elliot, Rāī Hīmū (son of) Khul chain Bhatti : JNS رای هنود جلجیی : MBM رای عینو جلجین. Ferishta, Ray Hubboo, the son of Ray Rutty.

[5] JNS and MBM read سیوم روز پوست بهرام خان کشید و ایشان را بسته برابر خویش برد : MBL reads سیوم روز اقبال خان شکسته عهد پوست آن شبر غران یعني بهرام خان کشید - دیگر آن را بسته و غل در گردن کرده برابر خویش برد.

[6] Ajodhan (or Ajudhan) the ancient name of Pākpattan. Lat. 30° 20′ 40″ N. Long. 73° 25′ 50″ E. It was known as Pāk Pattan or the Ferry of the Pws, from Sheikh Farīd-ud-dīn Ganj Shakkar who is buried there. See Ranking, p. 362, f.n. 2 nd 3.

[7] JNS and MBM read لشکر های قاهرهٔ مقابل اقبال خان آمد : MBL reads لشکرهای قاهرهٔ و حشم و خدم که هر همه شیران صعرکه و مودانِ محاربه بودند مقابل اقبال خان آمد.

Verse.

If there be one woman or there are thousands,
Seldom are they faithful to their agreement.[1]

Battle between Iḳbāl and Khizr Khān, 19th Jamādi-ul-auwal, 808 H. Thurs., 12 Nov., 1405 A.D. Defeat of the former.

On the 19th Jamādī-ul-auwal, 808 H., the two armies met, when Iḳbāl meeting with reverses at the first charge withdrew and was chased. Iḳbāl's horse was wounded and so he could not escape.[2] His horse got stuck in the mire and his enemies overtook him; Iḳbāl attempted to stretch forth his hands and legs: but he[3] was slain; his head was severed from his body and sent to Fatḥpur.

Sulṭān Mahmud took possession of Dehli. Jamādi-ul-ākhir, 808 H., Nov.-Dec., 1405 A.D.

Daulat Khān, Ikhtiār Khān and the other amirs, sent a deputation from Dehli to Sulṭān Mahmud insisting on him to undertake the government. In the month of Jamādī-ul-ākhir of the above year, the Sulṭān left Ḳanauj with a small retinue, came to Dehli and (re)ascended the throne. The family of Iḳbāl was taken out of Dehli and sent to the district of Kol. But the good-natured Emperor did not cause any affliction to his family and attendants.[4] The governorship of the Doāb was conferred upon Daulat Khān; Ikhtiār Khān received the palace of Firozābād (in gift); Iḳlim Khān Bahādur Nāhir[5] made an offering of two elephants to the Sulṭān. In the month of Jamādī-ul-auwal,

Sulṭān Mahmud to Ḳanauj. Jamādi-ul-auwal, 809 H., Oct.-Nov., 1406 A.D.

809 H. (Oct.-Nov., 1406 A.D.), the Sulṭān marched against Ḳanauj and sent Daulat Khān with an army to Sāmāna. At the approach of Sulṭān Mahmud to Ḳanauj, Sulṭān Ibrāhim crossed the Ganges and presented a bold front. After

---

[1] The lines from, "It was manifest ...... agreement," are to be read in MBL and not in JNS or MBM.

[2] In the MS. we have:—اسپ اقبال زخمي شد بيرون امدن نتوانست. Elliot gives the sense as—"Ikbal's horse fell upon him and wounded him so that he could not escape."

[3] The lines from "his horse got stuck .....legs" are to be found in MBL, JNS and MBM omit them.

[4] This line is to be read in MBL and not in JNS or MBM.

[5] In Elliot Iḳlim Khān, *ibid.*, 41. MBL اقليم خان : MBM اقلام : JNS agrees with MBM.

some time Sulṭān Ibrāhim retired to Jaunpur and Sulṭān Maḥmud retraced his way to Dehli. On the homeward march the Sulṭān's army dispersed—his men going towards their respective fiefs. Receiving intelligence of this circumstance, Ibrāhim turned round and came to Ḳanauj. Malik Mahmud Tarmati,[1] who had been left in command by Sulṭān Maḥmud, was besieged at Ḳanauj. This state of affairs continued for four months. At last, receiving no relief, Tarmatī was forced to surrender and seek an interview. Ḳanauj was entrusted to Ikhtiār Khān, the grandson of Malik Daulatyār Kambal.[2]

Ibrāhim to Dehli, Jamādi-ul-auwal, 810 H., Oct.-Nov., 1407 A.D.

Sulṭān Ibrāhim, having passed the rainy season at Ḳanauj, worked his way to Dehli in Jamādī-ul-auwal,[3] 810 H. Nuṣrat Khān Gurg-Andāz[4], Tātār Khān, the son of Sārang Khān, and Malik Marḥabā, the slave of Iḳbāl Khān, deserted Sulṭān Maḥmud and joined Sulṭān Ibrāhim. Asad Khān Lodī was invested at Sambhal (by Ibrāhim). On the second day, the conquest of Sambhal being effected, it was bestowed upon Tātār Khān. From thence, the victor moved onwards to Dehli by fording the Jaun at Kicha[5] in the vicinity of the city (Dehli).[6] Information reached him that, Ẓafar Khān after his conquest of Dhar,[7] made Alb Khān, the son of Dilāwar Khān, a prisoner, and was bound for Jaunpur. Sulṭān Ibrāhim left Marḥaba at Baran with a small battalion, and returned by the ford of Kicha on his way to Jaunpur.[8] In Ẓil-Ḳa'da,[9]

---

1 JNS and MBM read ملک محمود ترمتي : MBL محمود ملک ترمتي. Elliot, Mahmūd Tarmatī. Badaoni, Malik Maḥmud Tarmati.

2 MBL and MBM read كنبله : JNS كنبلي : Ranking (363) Malik Daulatyār Kanpila. Elliot, Ikhtiyār Khān, grandson of Malik Yār Khān Kampila.

3 MBL omits mentioning the month.

4 Ranking, Nuṣrat Khān Karkandāz: Elliot, Garg-andāz.

5 MBL كهجه : MBM كيجه : JNS كيجهه : Badaoni and Elliot, Kicha.

6 JNS and MBM read نزديک سهر کنارهٔ : MBL reads نزديک کناره آب جون در گذر کيجه فرود آمد.

7 In central India, Lat. 23° 36′ N. Long. 75° 4′ E.

8 In central India, between Lat. 25° 23′ 45″ and 26° 12′ N. Long. 82° 10′ and 83° 7′ 45″ E. Sulṭān Ibrahim built at Jaunpur the Atala Masjid out of the materials of a Hindu temple built by Jai Chand.

9 MBL omits Ẓil-Ḳa'da.

of the aforesaid year (Mar.-Apr., 1408 A.D.), Sulṭān Maḥmud left Dehli for Baran and Malik Marḥaba gave him battle, but the latter, being defeated at the first onset, made off and was pursued by the Sulṭān's army and ultimately done to death. The Sulṭān then continued his way to Sambhal,[1] but before he reached the banks of the Ganges, Tātār Khān left his garrison behind (Sambhal) and ran away to Ḳanauj. Sambhal was entrusted to Asad Khān Lodi [2] and the Sulṭān came back to his capital.

Sulṭā. Maḥmud moves to Baran. Zil-Ḳa'da, 810 H., Mar.-April, 1408 A.D.

Daulat Khān, who had been sent against Sāmāna,[3] which on the death of Bahrām Khān had passed to Bairam Khān Turkbāchā, was opposed by the latter. On 11th Rajab,[4] *May its dignity increase,* 809 H. (Wed., 22nd Dec., 1406 A.D.), a battle was fought between the two at a distance of two kuroh [5] from Sāmāna, in which Daulat Khān came off victorious. Bairam meeting with reverses retired to Sirhind, but after a short time, he co-operated with the victor. Previous to this, Bairam had promised fealty to *Masnad-i-'Ālā* Khizr Khān, so, when the latter heard of the fall of Sāmāna, he set out with a large army against Daulat Khān. At Khizr's approach to Fatḥābād,[6] Daulat retreated across the Jaun. The *amirs* and the *maliks* of his party sought an interview with Khizr Khān. The district of Hiṣār Firoza was bestowed upon Ḳawām Khān; Sāmāna and Sannām were taken away from Bairam Khān and were entrusted to *Maj-*

Daulat Khān opposed by Bairam Khān Turkbāchā and the former's success. Rajab, 809 H., Dec.-Jany., 1406-1407 A.D.

March of Khizr against Daulat—the latter's defeat and his retreat.

---

1 In Rohilkhund, 23 m. S.W. of Moradābād.

2 Ranking, Basad Khan; Elliot, simply "Asad Khān."

3 25 m. S.W. of Hānsī and 100 miles eastward of Dehli.

4 MBL بتاریخ ماه رجب. Tab-i-Akb. and Elliot give the same date. Ferishta read 810 H. Badaoni gives 812 H.

5 Kuroh, a road measure of about two miles. In Elliot "kos" instead of kuroh.

6 JNS and MBM فتح آباد: MBL فتح پور. Ranking and Elliot Fatḥābād.

dis-i-'Alā Zirak Khān; the fief of Sirhind[1] and some other *perganahs* were given to Bairam Khān. Khizr returned to Fathpur. In the possession of Sultān Mahmud remained some of the territories in the Doab, the fief of Rohtak and other places.

Possessions of Sultān Mahmud.

In Rajab, *May its dignity increase*, 811 H. (Nov.-Dec., 1408 A.D.), Sultān Mahmud marched towards Hisār Firoza and besieged Kawām Khān in the fort. At length, good sense having dawned upon him, Kawām sent his son to the Sultān for service. Mahmud then returned to his capital viā Dhātrath.[2] Khizr Khān, on hearing what had happened, marched quickly to Fathābād and chastised those who had joined the Sultān. On 11th Ramzān of the aforesaid year (Mon., 28th Jany 1409 A.D.) Khizr Khān sent Malik-ul-Shark Malik Tuhfa with a powerful army against Dhātrath. Fath Khān with his family made his way to the Doab. Those who remained there were plundered and imprisoned. *Bandagi-Masnad-i-'Ālā* (Khizr Khān) then proceeded to Dehli viā Rohtak. Sultān Mahmud and Ikhtiār Khān were hemmed in, the former at Siri and the latter at Firozābād. Due to the scanty supply of provisions, *Masnad-i-'Ālā* crossed the Jaun and came to the Doab, but meeting with opposition (at this place), he recrossed the river and proceeded to Fathpur.

Mahmud's investment of Hisār Firoza. Rajab, 811 H., Nov.-Dec., 1408 A.D.

Sultān Mahmud besieged at Siri by Khizr.

In 812 H.[3] (1409-10 A.D.), Bairam Khān Turkbāchā turned against *Masnad-i-'Ālā* and made an interview with Daulat Khān. At this, *Bandagi-Masnad-i-'Ālā* marched his army to Sirhind. Bairam sent out his family into the mountains and himself proceeded with his forces to join Daulat Khān at the ford of Jaun. *Masnad-i-'Ālā* ran in his pursuit, and encamped on the bank of the river Jaun. Losing all hope, vanquished and distressed,

Khizr's march against Bairam: the latter's submission.

---

1 MBL سیهرند : JNS and MBM read سرهند.

2 M3L دهار ترهت : JNS and MBM دها ترتهه. Elliot, Dhātrath.
MBL تاختن میان دوآب دهار ترهت نامرد کرد.
JNS and MBM تاختن دهاترتهه نامرد.

3 MBL در شهور اثنی عشر.
MBM and JNS در سنه اثنی عشر.

Bairam went over to *Masnad-i-'Ālā* and was restored to his possessions. The victor then returned to Fathpur. During this year, Sultān Mahmud remained in Dehli and undertook no further incursion.

Khizr's march to Rohtak, submission of Idris.

In 813 H. (1410-11 A.D.), *Masnad-i-'Ālā* picked his way to Rohtak and besieged Malik Idris. Fighting continued for six months, but at length being hardly pressed, Idris despatched a large sum of money as a tribute and his son as hostage. *Masnad-i-'Ālā* returned by way of Sāmāna to Fathpur. After the departure of *Masnad-i-'Ālā*, Sultān Mahmud marched towards Katehar,[1] where having enjoyed himself in hunting for some time, he came back to the capital. The affairs of the government was at its lowest ebb; the Sultān paid no attention to the affairs of the state and threw himself into amusement and merry-making.

The affairs of the state.

Khizr to Rohtak, Narnol, Mewāt and Dehli.

In 814 H. (1411-12 A.D.), *Masnad-i-'Ālā* again took his way to Rohtak. Malik Idris and Mubariz Khān, his brother, were permitted to kiss the (royal) feet at Hānsi and bestowed with numerous favours. Thence, having ravaged Narnol, which was in the possession of Iklim Khān Bahādur,[2] he arrived in Mewāt,[3] harried Tijārah, Sarhath,[4] Kharol and most of the places in Mewāt, and going back to Dehli, laid siege to Siri. Sultān Mahmud presented an opposition from that fortress (Siri). Ikhtiār Khān, who was in charge of Firozābād on behalf of Sultān Mahmud, joined *Masnad-i-'Ālā*. The latter marched to the entrance of Siri and encamped at Firozābād. The district of the Doāb and the environments of Dehli passed under his control.

---

1 MBL كيتهر : MBM كيهير : The word is كهير in JNS. In Elliot, Katehr. IV, 43. Ranking (365), Kaithar.

2 In Elliot, Iklīm khān and bahādur Nāhir: Tab-i-Akb. agrees with Elliot. Ferishta, Iklīm Khān and Bahādur Khān.

3 The province of Mewāt (or Miwāt) called after the Meos, a tribe claiming the Rajput origin, lay south of Dehli, and in Mughal times formed part of the Ṣoubah of Agrah. Its most famous towns were Narnol, Ulwar, Tijārah and Rewārī. The province of Mewāt included part of the British Districts of Muttra, Gurgāon, a considerable portion of Ulwar and some of Bharatpur. The history of Mewāt merges from the year 1775 in that of Ulwar and Bharatpur.

4 سرهته in the manuscripts. In Elliot, Sarath, *ibid.*, 44.

In Muharram, 815 H. (Apr. May, 1412 A.D.), provisions running short, (Khizr) went to Fathpur[1] viâ Panipath.[2] In Jamâdī-ul-auwal of the aforesaid year (Aug.-Sep., 1412 A.D.), Sultân Mahmud marched towards Katehar, and after passing some days there a-hunting, returned to Dehli. On his way, the Sultân was struck down with illness in Rajab, *May its dignity increase* (Oct.-Nov., 1412 A.D.), and breathed his last[3].

Death of Sultân Mahmud, Rajab 815 H., 1412 A.D. He reigned for 20 years and 2 months.

Hemistich.

God is eternal and the sovereignty of the country belongs to Him.[4]

He reigned, through all these disasters and vicissitudes, for a period of 20 years and two months. *Allah knows the truth!*

After his death, the *amīrs, maliks* and the servants of the Emperor paid their homage to Daulat Khân. Mubâriz Khân and Malik Idris revolted against *Masnad-i-'Ālā* and joined Daulat. In that year, *Bandagi-Masnad-i-'Ālō* remained in Fathpur, and did not proceed to Dehli.

In Muharram, 816 H., Daulat Khân made his way to Katehar, where Rai Har Singh and other *rāis* sought an interview with him. On reaching Pattiâli[5] he was also befriended by Mahabat Khân, the amir of Badâōn. It transpired that, Sultân Ibrâhim had surrounded Kâdir Khân, the son of Mahmud Khân, and a fight had taken place between the two. Being not in command of sufficient force, Daulat Khân refrained himself from opposing Sultân Ibrâhim.

March of Daulat to Katehar. Muharram, 816 H., Apr.-May, 1413 A.D.

---

1 In Elliot, Firozpur, *ibid.* Badaoni, Fathpur.

2 53 miles north of Dehli. Lat 29° 23′ N. Long 77° 1′ 10″ E.

MBL and MBM بانيپتة.

JNS باني پتهه. Elliot, Panipat.

3 Tab-i-Akb. and Ferishta give Zil-Ka'da; Badaoni does not state the month: Elliot reads Rajab. Ferishta is not clear as to the year in which Mahmud died.

4 This hemistich is found in MBL and MBM and not in JNS.

5 Badaoni, Baitâlī.

In Jamādī-ul-auwal of the same year (July-Aug., 1413 A.D.), *Masnad-i-'Ālā* took his army out of Dehli and reached Ḥiṣār Firozā, where the amirs and the maliks of the country promised him co-operation. Malik Idris was enclosed in the fort of Rohtak and *Masnad-i-'Ālā* went to Mewāt. Jalāl Khān, nephew (brother's son) of Iḳlim Khān,[1] Bahādur Nāhir, waited upon him. Returning from that place, he went to Sambhal and laid it waste. In the month of Ẕil-ḥijjah, of the above year (Feb.-March, 1414 A.D.), he marched against Dehli and placed himself at its entrance gate. The siege of Dehli[2] continued for four months. Subsequently, Malik Lonā and the friends and attendants of Daulat conspired together and took hold of the entrance of the *Naubat Khānā* (bandstand). Finding his situation hopeless, Daulat Khān begged for quarter[3] and sought an interview. *Masnad-i-'Ālā* condoned his faults and having consigned Daulat to the care of Ḳawām Khān sent him off to Ḥiṣār Firoza. He then took possession of Dehli on the 17th Rabī'-ul-auwal, 817 H.[4] (Wed., 6th June, 1414 A.D.).

March of Khizr to Hiṣār Firoza, Rohtak, Mewāt and Sambhal, Jamādī-ul-auwal, 816H.

Khizr to Dehli. Ẕil-ḥijjah, 816 H.

Accession of Khizr to the throne of Dehli. 17th Rabī'-ul-auwal, 817 H., 6th June, 1414 A.D.

---

1 JNS and MBM اقليم خان. MBL اولا، خان.

2 In the MS. the word is دولت خانه.

3 In JNS اما is the copyist slip for امان.

4 MBL simply writes در ماه ربيع اول : MBM reads در هفتم ماه ربيع اول : JNS writes ماه در هفدهم etc. Badaoni agrees with JNS. In Elliot (p. 45) the date is 8th Rabī'-ul-auwal. (Forishta, Vol. 1, p. 505) gives the date as 15th Rabī'-ul-auwal.

THE HOUSE OF SA'IYIDS.

n account of Bandagi Rāyāt-i-'Ālā[1] Khizr Khān,[2] Let the blessing of God be on his tomb, and may he dwell in paradise ![3]

Khizr Khān's lineage and character.

Khizr Khān was the son of Malik-ul-Shark Malik Sulaimān, who was adopted in childhood and brought up by Malik Naṣir-ul-Mulk Mardān[4] Daulat.[5] But the story runs that, he was the son of a

---

1 Service of the exalted (or imperial standards).

2 Khizr Khān is the first of the four kings constituting the Sa'iyid house which is verily regarded as the fourth dynasty of the kings of Dehli.

Native historians trace the family of Khizr to that of the Prophet of Arabia, and they accordingly style him and his successors *Sādāt*, which is the plural of *sa'iyid*, meaning the chief of the family of Muḥammad. What the nature of consanguinity of Khizr to the Prophet's family was, Yaḥiyā, the author of *Tārīkh-i-Mubārakshāhi*, does not tell us. Relying on the reported evidence of Jalālu-ud-din Bokhāry, the head of the Sa'iyids, in favour of Khizr's pretension to the honour of his being a member of the Prophet's family, Yaḥiyā calls him a *Sa'iyid*.

It is interesting to notice how the aforesaid author, like the other native chroniclers, give no title of *Bādshāh* or *Sulṭān* to Khizr. To compensate for this apparent absence of any regal title, some curious appellations were called into requisition. Thus, the expression *Masnad-i-'Ālā*, signifying "the exalted throne" has been invariably made use of so long Khizr did not ascend the throne; but after his accession the title undergoes an alteration to *Rayat-i-'Ālā* meaning "exalted standard". Niẓām-ud-din Aḥmed, the author of *Tabāḳāt-i-Akbarī*, and Al-Badaoni of *Muntakhab-ul-Tawārikh*, prefer the designations of *Rāyāt-i-'Ālā* and *Masnad-i-'Ālā* respectively. This prevalence of unanimity among the Indian historians in depriving Khizr of the usual honorifics assigned to rulers, give some support to the proposition that, he made no pretension to be more than a deputy of Timur with whom he had not imprudently cast in his lot. It has been alleged that, Khizr gave out in public that he held the government for Timur. The coins were struck and the *khuṭba* read in the name of the "noble Tartarian," after whose death, the name of his successor Shāh Rukh was used; and to the latter, occasional tribute was despatched at his capital Samarkand. Further, the supposition, that Khizr deprived himself of the common nomenclature befitting an independent ruler on the ground that this measure would disarm the jealousy which the nobles of the late government would have felt towards him, and that it would bring them to submission instead of preventing them from submitting to his authority, may not be entirely without any foundation.

3 و جعل الجنة مثواه (*May he dwell in paradise*) has been omitted in JNS.

4 Badaoni read Marwān.

5 JNS reads پسر ملک الشرق ملک سلیمان را ملک نصیرالمک مردان دولت در حال

Sa'iyid. (Once) when refreshment was served before *Bandagi Makhdum*, the chief and the progenitor of the Sa'iyids, Jalāl-ul-Hukwa-ul-Sharā'-wa-ud-din Bokhārī, *May God be pleased with him!* who came for advice in the house of Malik Mardān Daulat, Malik Sulaimān was ordered (by his adoptive father) to wash the hands of the guest. The latter said that, he (Malik Sulaimān) was a Sa'iyid zādāh,[1] and (as such) was unfit for such a work as that. Thus, when *Bandagi Makhdum*, the head of the Sa'iyids, bore testimony to Sulaimān's being a *Sa'iyid*, there remained no doubt about his pedigree. Another proof of his *Sa'iyid* origin is, that he was generous, brave, gentle, kind,[2] humble, true to his promise[3] and temperate; these are all the virtues which were conspicuous in Hazrat Mustafā (the Prophet)[4]—*with him be peace!* and were manifest in his nature of laudable attributes.

Multān successively under Malik Mardān, Malik Sheikh, his son, Sulaimān and Khizr.

To sum up, on the death of Malik Mardān Daulat, the fief of Multān devolved upon Malik Sheikh, his son, and soon after the latter's demise, to Malik Sulaimān, who also expiring in a short time, the country along with its dependencies and suburbs fell upon *Bandāgī-i-Bandgān Rāyāt-i-'Ālā, May the Almighty God make him supreme!* from the late Sultān Firoz Shāh. God, the Almighty, had selected him (Khizr) for great work and excessive prosperity and his exalted stateliness waxed from day to day. In fine the incidents of his campaigns and successes before he completed the subjugation of *Dār-ul-mulk* Dehli by the Grace of the All-Powerful God, have been previously related.

خضر خان پسر ملک الشرق ملک سلیمان MBL reads, : طفلگي پسر کرده پرورده بود بود - ملک نصیر الملک مردان دولت در حال طفلگي پسر کرده پرورده (بود).

1 MBL بندگي مخدوم بزبان مبارک فرمودند که این سیو زاده است.
MBM فرمود که سیو است. JNS : بندگي مخدوم فرمود که این سیو است

2 JNS and MBM omit it : MBL retains it.

3 MBL reads مقبول القول و صادق الواد : JNS and MBM omit مقبول القول.

4 MBL reads اوصاف و پرهیزگار و متدین علما و غریب نواز بود و این خصایل و این مجموم اوصاف حضرت. JNS and MBM read حضرت : حضرت

On the 15th Rabī'-ul-auwal, 817 H. (Mon., the 4th June, 1414 A.D.), *Rāyāt-i-'Ālā* made an entry into the fort of Siri, and his army encamped in the palace of Sulṭān Maḥmūd. The inhabitants of the city, who during the course of late events[1] had become ruined and indigent,[2] were rewarded with gifts, pensions and proper allowances. The fortune of Khizr gave them rest and happiness.[3] Malik-ul-Shark Malik Tuḥfa[4] obtained the designation of Tāj-ul-Mulk and the vizirate. Sa'iyid Sālim,[5] the chief of the sa'iyids, received the *akṭa'* (fief), and *shikk* (district) of Sahāranpur.[6] All the affairs (of the state) were set in order. Malik 'Abdur Rahim, adopted son of late Malik Sulaimān, got the title of 'Alā'-ul-Mulk and the *akṭā'* and *shikk* of Multān and Fatḥpur.[7] Malik Sarup[8] became the governor of the city[9] and the vicegerent. Malik Khair-ud-dīn Khāni was appointed the muster-master,[10] Malik Kālū, the keeper of the elephants,[11] and Malik Dā'ud, the secretary.[12] The district in the Doāb[13] was

Khizr's entry into Siri. Allowances to ruined inhabitants and bestowal of offices and fiefs on Amirs.

---

1 MBL حوادثات ماضیه : JNS and MBM حوادث ماضیه.

2 MBL مستاصل و مقل حال و فقیر و حقیر و بی نوا : JNS and MBM omit حقیر و بی نوا.

3 MBL و مرفه الحال الاستبصال . JNS مرفه الحال.

4 Badaoni, Malik Naho.

5 Sa'iyid Salīm was the chief of the fraternity known as the Sa'iyid family of Bārha, whose ancestors seem to have settled in Muzaffarnagar in the Meerut Division of U.P. In course of time they became daring military leaders and helped the emperors on all services of danger. During the seventeenth and eighteenth centuries they shouldered their way to great eminence and filled many important offices about the court.

6 Saharanpur, a district in the Meerut Division of the United Provinces, lying between 29° 34′ and 30° 24′ N. and 77° 7′ and 78° 12′ E., forms the northernly portion of the Doāb or alluvial plain between the Ganges and Jumna.

7 Fatḥpur, in Multān district, Punjab; fifty miles south-east of Multān. Lat. 29° 4, Long. 72° 10′.

8 In Tab-i-Akb. and in Elliot IV, Malik Sarwar: MBL and MBM read سروب : JNS صروپ.

9 شحنه شهری و نائب غیبت.

10 عارض ممالک.

11 شحنه پیل.

12 نائب شغل دبیری.

13 The name Doāb, meaning "two rivers", is commonly applied to the land between the confluence of two rivers, but especially to the tract between the

entrusted to Ikhtiār Khān. The slaves of the *ci-devant* Sulṭān were confirmed in the *pergannahs*, villages and the fiefs which they enjoyed in the late reign (Sulṭān Maḥmūd). They were despatched to their *pergannahs*; the affairs of the state were set to rights.

Tāj-ul-Mulk ravages Katehar (first expedition): submission of its ruler Rai Har Singh.

In 817 H. (1414-15 A.D.), Malik-ul-Shark Tāj-ul-Mulk[1] was sent off with an army to Hindustan,[2] while Khizr himself remained in Dehli. The former crossed the river Jaun and reached Ahār[3]; (then) having forded the Ganges[4] he went to Katehar,[5] plundered and devastated the territory of the infidels. Rāi Har Singh fled to the mountains of Anwāla[6] and feeling himself distressed at the advent of the Muhammadans, he paid them taxes, tribute and money.[7] Mahābat Khān, the *amīr* of Badāōn,[8] also had an interview with Malik Tāj-ul-Mulk. Thence pursuing the course of (the river) Rahab, he came to the ford Sargdawāri[9] and crossed the Ganges; brought to book the

---

Ganges and the Jumna in the United Provinces, extending from the Sivāliks (a range of hills in Northern India, running parallel to the Himālayas for about 200 miles from the Beah to the Ganges) to the junction of the two rivers at Allahabad.

1 According to Badaoni Tāj-ul-Mulk's former name was Malik Naho; but according to Ferishta his name was Malik Tuḥfa.

2 The name implies the "place of the Hindus"; it has been applied to a vaguely-defined area. In Muhammadan histories the term is used for that area which comprises the east of the Punjab and Rājputāna and the greater part of the United Provinces.

3 In the Bulandshahr district, between Bulandshahr and Morādābād: Lat. 28° 27′, Long. 78° 18″, MBL reads قصبه لاهار : JNS and MBM اهار.

4 Badaoni writes that he crossed the Ganges at the ford of Pirāhā (Ranking, 377).

5 MBM كتهير : MBL كيتهر : JNS كتهيمر.

Identified with the present province of Rohilkhand. See Elliot, IV, 49 in 3.

6 MBL كشتي انواله : MBM گهتي انوله : Tab-i-Akb. درۀ آنوله : JNS كهتي آنوله : Elliot (47) has "mountains of Anwala". Identified with Aonla, Aounlah or Aonla-ganj, a town in Bareilly district. Lat. 28° 16′ 25″, Long. 79° 12′ 25″.

7 محصول و مال و خدمتي.

8 Badāōn district, south-western district of the Bareilly division, United Provinces.

9 The three MSS. read سرگدوار : Tab-i-Akb. reads سرگدواري : In Elliot, IV, 47, Sarg-dwari: Badaoni (p. 275) سرکهدواری ; it is located in Farrukhābād district.

infidels of Khorah[1] and Kampil[2] and proceeded to Parham[3] viâ Sakina.[4] Hasan Khân, the *amir* of Râpri[5] and Malik Hamza,[6] his brother, joined Malik Tâj-ul-Mulk. Râi Sabir[7] did homage to him; the infidels of Gwâlior, Seori and Chandwâr[8] paid taxes and tribute and put their heads under the yoke of obedience. He (Tâj-ul-Mulk) wrested Jalesar[9] from the unbelievers of Chandwâr, handed it over to the Musalmans, who formerly owned it and placed his own agents there. From that place he took the course of the black river[10] and inflicting penalty on the infidels of Etâwah returned to Dehli.

Submission of Gwâlior, Seori and Chandwâr. Occupation of Jalesar.

In 818 H. (1415-16 A.D.), (Khizr Khân) conferred upon the noble and illustrious prince Malik-ul-Shark Malik Mubârak who was best suited to sovereignty, proper authority, (in addition to) the districts of Fîrozpûr,[11] Sirhind and all the *aktâ's* of Bairam Khân, the deceased. (Further) he put him in command of all the western countries, and appointed Malik Sadhû Nâdira, *naib* or deputy of Shâhzâdah Mu'azm. After the affairs

Crown-prince Mubârak bestowed with Fîrozpur, Sirhind, etc.

---

1 MBL کهور : MBM and JNS کهوره : In Elliot, Khur; Badaoni, Kahwar identified with modern Shamsabad in the Farrukhâbâd district in U. P.; 18 m. north-west of Fategarh town. Badaoni, p. 276, says:—کهور که حالا بشمساباد مشهور است.

2 Tab-i-Akb. کنپله : In Elliot, Kambil; in Badaoni, *ibid.* کنپله. Kampil is in Farrukhâbâd district, Lat. 27° 37′, Long. 79° 1′.

3 MBM and MBL بارهم : JNS پارهم : Tab-i-Akb. بادهم : In Elliot, Bâdham. In Badaoni پادهم.

4 MBL سکنه : MBM سکینه : JNS سکینهه : In Badaoni سکینه between Kampila and Rapri, 12 m. south-east of Etawah town.

5 In Mainpuri district (in Agra division) situated on the left bank of Jamuna, about 44 m. south-west of Mainpuri. Its founder was Râpur Sen. Cf. Hunter's Gaz. of Ind., XI, 511.

6 Badaoni reads Malik Hamra.

7 In Badaoni, 276, رای سر.

8 Situated on the Jamuna, a few miles below Agra.

9 MBL and JNS جلیسر. MBM reads جانیسر; 38 m. east of Muttra: in Etawah district, Lat. 27° 28′, Long. 78° 20′ 30″.

10 MBL reads آب بیاه : JNS and MBM آب سیاه, Badaoni agrees with JNS and MBM. Refers to *Kâli Nadi*, a tributary of the Ganges—the chief river in the district of Etawah in Agra division. *Kâli Nadi* is a corruption of *Kâlindi*.

11 *Fîrozpur* or *Ferozepore*, a district in the Julundhur division of the Punjab.

of the country had been put into order, the Prince returned with Malik Sadhū Nādira, Zirak Khān, the *amir* of Sāmānā [1] and the other *amīrs* and *maliks*, to Dehli in the month of Ẓil-ḥijjah (Feb., 1416 A.D.).

Tāj-ul-Mulk to Bianah, Gwālior, Kampila and Patiāli.

In 819[2] H. (1416-17 A.D.), Rāyāt-i-'Ālā despatched Tāj-ul-Mulk with a large force to Bianah and Gwālior. On his reaching the confines of Bianah, Malik Karim-ul-Mulk, brother of Shams Khān Auḥadi, came to wait on him. From thence, he continued his way to Gwālior, which he sacked, and having exacted money and servitude from (the Rai of) Gwālior and the other *rāis*, he crossed the Jaun opposite Chandwār, and wended his way to Kampila and Patiālī.[3] Rai Har Singh, the lord of Katehar,

Submission of Har Singh of Katehar.

swore fealty, so, after realising money and subjection, Tāj-ul-Mulk went back to Dehli. Malik Sadhū Nādira,[4] who had been ordered to Sirhind[5] as the agent of Prince Mu'aẓm (Mubārak), was assassinated in Jamādī-ul-auwal (June-July, 1414 A.D.) by some of the Turkbāchās of the family of Bairam Khān and Sirhind was taken possession of by them. Rāyāt-i-'Ālā sent Malik Dā'ud, the secretary and Zirak Khān to put down the miscreants. The Turkbāchās took to their heels across the Sutlej[6] and resorted to the mountains, where the Imperialists, too, went in their pursuit. This state of affairs continued for a couple of months; (but) as the mountains were impregnable, the royalists wheeled round. In the meantime, it was reported in the month of Rajab (Aug.-Sept., 1416 A.D.), *May its dignity increase!* that, Sulṭān Aḥmad of Gujrat[7] had

---

1 In Patiāla State, Punjab, situated 85 cosses on the west of Dehli.

2 MBL در شهور سنه تسع عشر و ثما نمائه : JNS, MBM and Elliot omit و .در شهور

3 In Badaoni, 236, بيتالي; In Etawah district, situated in Lat. 27° 41′, Long. 79° 4′; 44 m. north-west of Fategarh.

4 Ferishta, p. 509, calls him Mullik Ladho.

5 Tract in the Punjab, consisting of the north-eastern portion of the plain which intervenes between the Jamuna and Sutlej rivers.

6 MBL ستلدر : JNS ستلج.

7 MBL سلطان احمد بادشاه عرصهٔ گجرات. JNS and MBM سلطان احمد ضابط گجرات.

come and invested Nāgor.[1] [2]Rāyāt-i-'Ālā set out for Nāgor and passed through Tonk[3] and Todah.[4] On being informed of this, Sulṭān Aḥmad of Gujrat retreated towards Dhār.[5] Then Khizr Khān proceeded to the new city Jhāin[6] and Iliyās Khān, the *amir* of that place, obtained the eminence of kissing the feet (of the Emperor). Having put down the rebellion of that country, Khizr came to Gwālior and besieged its *amīr*. As the fort was exceptionally strong, it could not be conquered; so, accepting money and revenue from Gwālior, the Sulṭān proceeded to Bianah, where Shams Khān Auḥadi, too, offered him money and homage. After this, he picked his way to Dehli.

The Sulṭān to Nāgor, Gwālior and Bianah.

His return to the Capital.

In 820 H. (1417-18 A.D.), it transpired that Ṭūghān Ra'īs and some of the Turkbāchās, who murdered Sādhū, had rebelled. Zirak Khān, the *amīr* of Sāmāna, was sent out with a big force to suppress the rebellion. As the (imperial) army neared Sāmāna, Ṭūghān and sundry other Turkbāchās, who had laid siege to Malik Kamāl Badhan, the representative of Khān-zādah Mu'aẓm in Sirhind,[7] raised the siege and retired to the mountains. Zirak Khān gave them a chase so far as Pail,[8] compelled Ṭūghān to pay a fine, and to expel the Turkbāchā murderers from his own camp, as well as to give up his son as a hostage. Zirak Khān despatched both

Rebellion of Ṭughān Ra'īs and the Turkbāchās.

Their retreat and submission.

---

[1] A town in Jodhpur State, Rajputana, situated 75 miles north-east of Jodhpur, in lat. 27° 11′ 15″, long. 73° 46′ 15″. In Briggs, Bagore (I, 509).

[2] MBL reads این خبر پیش رایات اعلی گذشت.
JNS and MBM omit this line.

[3] In Rajputana, lat. 26° 10′, long. 75° 56′.

[4] In Jaipur State, Rajputana, 63 miles south by west from Jaipur, lat. 26° 4′, long. 75° 39′.

[5] Capital of Dhar State, Central India Agency. Lat. 22° 36′, long. 75° 20′.

[6] JNS—شهر نو اجهاین.
The *Tabakat-i-Akbari* calls it :— شهر نو عروس جهاین.
Badaoni, جهاین : Ranking (379), Chhāin : Ferishta (Bom. Edn.), جالور Ferishta (Tr. by J. Briggs, vol. I, p. 509), "*Jalwar*".

[7] MBM and MBL سیهرند.

[8] MBM باید : MBL بابل : Tab-i-Akb. پایل : JNS پایل : Pāil may be identified with *Baila* or *Byla* in Dehra Dūn district on a high mountain. Lat. 30° 45′, Long. 77° 47′. In Elliot, p. 49, Bail; Ferishta *ibid.*, I, 510, Pail.

the hostage and the amount (realised from Ṯūghān Ra'īs) to Dehli and himself withdrew to Sāmāna.

Tāj-ul-Mulk sent against Rāi Har Singh of Katehar (second expedition).

In 821 H. (1418-19 A.D.), *Rāyāt-i-'Ālā* sent Malik Tāj-ul-Mulk with a numerous army to put down the rebellion of Har Singh[1] of Katehar. When the force went across the Ganges, Har Singh laid waste Katehar and receded to the forests of Anwālā[2] which was twenty-four kuroh[3] in circumference. The army of Islām encamped[4] in the forest, and Har Singh being enclosed therein had to fight. With the assistance of Almighty God, the army of Islām came off with flying colours and all the furniture, baggage, arms and horses fell a prey to the victor. Har Singh retired to the mountains of Kumāyūn. Next day, some 20,000 cavalry were sent in pursuit of the fugitive, whilst Tāj-ul-Mulk remained there (Anwālā) with his troops and requisites. The royal forces waded through the river Rahab and followed up the enemy to the hills of Kumāyūn. Har Singh emerged from the mountains and on the fifth day, the Imperial army returned, having laid hold on a large plunder. Thence, Tāj-ul-Mulk passing along the vicinity of the district of Badāōn came near the bank of the Ganges and went across it at Bijlānā.[5] Mahābat Khān, the *amīr* of Badāōn,[6] was permitted to go, while Tāj-ul-Mulk continued his way to Etāwah, which he overran. Rāi Sabir, the chief of Etāwah, was hemmed in, till peace was effected on his rendering tribute and homage. From that place the victor returned in triumph to Dehli in the month of Rabi'-ul-ākhir (821[7] H.) (May-June, 1418 A.D.). He then placed before *Rāyāt-i-'Ālā* the money and tribute which he had exacted of the Rāi and was (in return) encompassed with special favours.

Latter's defeat.

First expedition against Etāwah. Rāi Sabir, the ruler of Etāwah, renders tribute.

---

1 Ferishta, *ibid*, Nūr Sing. Badaoni, p. 287 (Bibliotheca Indica series) has Harsing Deo (هرسنگ دیو).

2 MBL آنواله. MBM انوله.

3 In Elliot, *ibid.*, 24 kos.

4 MBL نداول کرد. JNS and MBM نزول کرد.

5 MBM بحلانه: JNS and MBL بجلانه: Identified with Bijnaur (or Bijnor), a town in Bijnaur district, in the Berilly Div., U.P. Lat. 29° 22′ 36″. Long. 78° 10′ 32″

6 In Badaoni, *ibid.*, مهابت خان حاکم بداون.

7 Elliot writes 822 H.

Khiẕr to Katehar, Kol, Rahab and Sambhal.

In the year 821 H. (1418-19 A.D.), Rāyāt-i-'Ālā advanced to Katehar.[1] Chastising the recalcitrants of Kol,[2] he scoured the forests of Rahab and Sambhal[3] and overthrew their refractory inhabitants. From thence, in the month of Ẕil-ḳa'da (Nov.-Dec.), he marched to Badāōn[4] and crossed the Ganges near Pattiali.[5] Overcome with terror at the approach of Khiẕr, Mahābat undertook preparations for standing a siege.

To Badāōn.

In the month of Ẕil-ḥijjah (Dec.-Jany., 1418-19 A.D.), Khiẕr Khān invested Badāōn, and Mahābat held out for about six months. When victory was imminent, news arrived that some of the *amirs* and *maliks*, such as Ḳawām Khān, Ikhtiār Khān and the attendants of Maḥmud Shāh, who having been overpowered by Daulat Khān had joined Rāyāt-i-'Ālā,[6] formed a conspiracy against the latter. Whereupon he (Khiẕr) raised the siege of Badāōn and retired to Dehli. On the way, by the banks of the Ganges, on the 20th Jamādī-ul-auwal, 822 H. (Wed., 14th June, 1419 A.D.) having seized Ḳawām Khān, Ikhtiār Khān, and the partisans of Sulṭān Mahmud, Khiẕr put them to death for their conspiracy, and then returned to Dehli with successive marches.

Khiẕr retires to Dehli.

About this time, news arrived of a swindler, who took upon himself the appellation of Sārang Khān. It transpired that, a certain individual had appeared in the mountains of Bājwāra,[7] a dependency of Jālandhar,[8] and had given

Rebellion of an impostor who called himself Sārang Khān.

---

[1] MBL کتهر.

[2] Identified with *Koil* in Aligarh district, United Provinces.

[3] JNS سنبهل : MBL and MBM read نبهل : In Morādābād Dist., U.P., 22 miles S.W. of Morādābād town. Lat. 28° 35′ 5″, Long. 78° 36′ 30″ : west of Srinagar. Lat. 34° 11′, Long. 74° 47′.

[4] Ferishta states (Briggs, I, p. 510) that, the Sulṭān after having laid waste the country of Sambal and Katehar returned to his capital, and after remaining at Dehli only a few days, moved towards Badāōn.

[5] Badaoni, Baitāli. [6] JNS is here illegible.

[7] باجوارة in Hoshiārpur district, Punjab. Ferishta (*ibid.*, page 511) reads Machiwara; Niẕām-ud-din Aḥmed (Tabaḳāt-i-Akbari), and Badaoni, *ibid.*, p. 288, make it Bājwāra. JNS reads مردی در کوه باجوارة اعمال (؟ جالندهر).

[8] Jullundur, division of the Punjab; between lat. 30° 56′ 30″—32° 59′ and long. 75° 6′ 30″—77° 49′ 15″.

himself out to be Sārang Khān. Some foolish and ignorant people joined forces with him. The Sultān bestowed the fief of Sirhind upon Malik Sultān Shāh Lodi[1] and deputed him to suppress the insurrection. In the month of Rajab, July-Aug. (1419 A.D.), Malik Sultān Shāh proceeded with his forces to Sirhind.[2] The *soi-disant* Sārang, with his rustic adherents, sallied forth from Bājwāra, and when he neared Sutlej,[3] the inhabitants of Rupar[4] joined hands with him. In the month of Shā'bān (Aug.-Sep., 1419 A.D.) the forces neared each other near Sirhind. In the conflict that took place, Malik Sultān Shāh Lodi won the laurels, and Sārang the deceiver, retired to Lahori,[5] one of the dependencies of Sirhind. Khwājā 'Alī Indarābi,[6] the amir of Jhath,[7] with his followers had an interview with Sārang. Likewise, did Zirak Khān, the *amīr* of Sāmāna, and Tughān Ra'is Turkbāchā of Jālandhar co-operate with Malik Sultān Shāh. At the approach of the Malik's army to Sirhind, the aforesaid Sārang ran away to Rupar.[8] Khwāja 'Alī deserted Sārang for Zīrak Khān. The following day, when the victorious forces ran in pursuit of the pretender to Rupar, the latter withdrew to the mountains. Here (Rupar), the royal army encamped. In the

Sultān Shāh Lodi deputed against the rebel.

Defeat of the insurgent.

---

1 Ferishta gives him the name of Islām Khān. MBM is here erroneous. It reads کوته اندیش امرا لودي را اقطاع سیهرند.

2 MBL ملک سلطانشه بهرام همچون بهرام چوبین در ماه رجب رجب قدره سنة سلطانشه در ماه MBM and JNS المذکور بالشکر خاصهٔ خویش در سرهند رفت - رجب سنه etc.

3 MBL and MBM ستلرر.

4 JNS روپر : MBM ارو بر : MBL ارو بر : In Umballa district, Punjab; situated on the south bank of the Sutlej, 43m. north of Umballa City.

5 MBL reads لهوري : MBM طرسري : JNS لهرسري : In Elliot (page 51) Tarsari. In Tabakāt-i-Akbari, Lahori. Badaoni (*ibid.*) states that Sārang Khān, meeting with reverses, fled to the hills (بکوهستان در آمد). Ferishta, p. 511, supports Badaoni.

6 MBL مازنداراني : MBM ماريدارالي : Tab-i-Akb. اندراني : JNS reads خواجه علي مار بندراني : we have adopted Elliot, vol. iv, page 51.

7 MBL جهت : MBM جهته : JNS makes it چهت : Jat in Gurgāon district, Punjab, 48m. south-west of Delhi.

8 MBL ازوبر.

meantime, Malik Khair-ud-dīn Khānī was (also) sent with a force to quell the rebellion of Sārang. In the month of Ramzān (Sep.-Oct.) Malik Khair-ud-dīn reached Rupar, and there the forces united, and marched into the mountains in pursuit of the impostor. Sārang Khān's followers were vanquished and helpless, but as the mountains were not easy of conquest the victorious army went back after some time. Malik Khair-ud-dīn Khānī took his way to the capital, and Zirak Khān went to Sāmāna, leaving Sultān Shāh Lodī[1] with a force in possession of the thanah Rupar. So the (royal) army was dispersed.

Tāj-ul-Mulk sent against Etāwah (second expedition) 823 H., 1420 A.D.; its ruler besieged.

In Muharram, 823 H. (Jany.-Feb., 1420 A.D.), the aforesaid Sārang Khān joined Malik Tūghān Ra'is Turk-bāchā, when Tūghān treacherously got the former into his power, made him a prisoner, and later put him to death.[2] That year *Rāyāt-i-'Ālā* remained in the capital and sent away Malik Tāj-ul-Mulk with a strong contingent against Etāwah. Marching through the town of Baran,[3] this army came into the country of Kōl, and after extirpating the rebels in that quarter, it moved to Et...h and there destroyed the village of Dehli, one of the strongholds of the unbelievers. It then marched against Etāwah and besieged Rai Sabir,[4] who sued for peace and paid his annual revenue and tribute. The victorious army (then) proceeded to the country of Chandwār, which it plundered and laid waste. From thence it passed on to Katehar,[5] where Rāi Harsing, its chief, paid revenue and tribute. Triumphant and victorious, Malik Tāj-ul-Mulk then returned to the capital. In the month of Rajab (July-Aug., 1420 A.D.), news arrived that, Tughān Ra'is had for the second time raised the

Tāj-ul-Mulk returns to Dehli via Chandwār and Katehar.

---

1 MBM سلطانشه کودی.

2 On discovering that his colleague possessed a large quantity of jewels, Mullick Tughan caused Sarang Khan to be assassinated. Ferishta, 511.

3 In Bulandshahr district.

4 In Elliot (52), Rai Sarwar; and Saru in Tabakat-i-Akbari. Ferishta (ibid., p. 512) calls him Soomur Ray. Badaoni (p. 288) has Rāi Sīr. Ranking (380), Rāi Sipar.

5 MBL کتهیر. MBM کایتهر.

Second rebellion of Tughān and his failure.

standard of insurrection, and that, having laid siege to the fort of Sirhind, pillāged the tract lying between Mansurpur [1] and Pāil. *Rāyāt-i-'Ālā* again sent Malik Khair-ud-dīn Khāni with a powerful force to coerce the rebel. The latter proceeded to Sāmāna. From thence, the joint forces of *Majlis-i-'Āli* Zirak Khān and Malik Khair-ud-dīn ran after the insurgent, who being apprised of their approach, crossed the Sutlej [2] near Ludhiānā [3] and stood facing the Imperialist from the other side of the river. But the waters were at a low ebb, and the royal force went across. Meeting with reverses, Ṭūghān ran away to the territory of Jasrath Khokhar. The *akṭā'* belonging to the fugitive was bestowed upon Zirak Khān, and Malik Khair-ud-dīn wheeled round to Dehli.

Rāyāt-i-'Ālā to Mewāt.

Capitulation of Mewāt. Jamadi-ul-awal, 824. May-June, 1421.

In the year 824 H. (1421 A.D.), *Rāyāt-i-'Ālā* set out towards Mewāt. Some of the Mewātis were besieged in the *kotlah* (fortress) of Bahādur Nāhir, while sundry others, extended their hands of fellowship to Khizr Khān. *Rāyāt-i-'Ālā* encamped himself near the *kotlah* and the people of Mewāt offered him resistance. The fortress capitulated at the first onset [4] and the besieged retired towards the mountains. Having razed the fortress to the ground, Khizr took his way to Gwālior. Meanwhile, on the 8th Muḥarram, 824 H.[5] (Mon., 13th Jany., 1421 A.D.), Malik Tāj-ul-Mulk breathed his last, and the office of *vizir* and the affairs of the state were entrusted to *Malik-ul-Shark* [6] Malik Sikandar, the eldest son of the deceased. Reaching Gwālior, *Rāyāt-i-'Ālā* invested the chief of the place, ravaged the country and returned to Etāwah, exacting tribute from the Gwālior raja. Rāi Sabir,

Death of Tāj-ul-Mulk, 8th Muḥarram, 824 H., 13th Jany., 1421 A.D. Siege of Gwālior.

---

[1] MBL منصور و بابل : MBM منصور ،بود و مایل : JNS منصور بود و پایل, In Patiala State, Punjab.

[2] MBL اب ستلدر : MBM لب ستلدر : JNS ستلج. [3] MBM and MBL لدهانه.

[4] MBL and MBM read . هم در حملهٔ الاول حصار کوتله شد : JNS جمادی الاول هم در

[5] In Elliot, the date is 7th Muḥarram.
MBL ملک الشرق سکندر.

[6] The title denoted "The lord of the East (or Hindustan)," synonymous with a tract between Benares and Oudh, where the Hindus remained unsubdued.

the ruler of Etāwah was dead, and his son made his submission and consented to pay tribute and accept servitude. The auspicious *Rāyāt-i-'Ālā* falling sick during the campaign, returned to Dehli, where he passed away on the 17th Jamādi-ul-auwal, 824 H. (Tues., 20th May, 1421 A.D.).

Rāyāt-i-'Ālā returns from Etāwah and breathes his last, 17th Jamādi-ul-auwal, 824 H., May 20, 1421 A.D.

Verse

Every evening is followed by the morning.[1]
At last there comes an end to every labour.[2]

May God, the Great and the Glorious, immerse the pure soul (of the deceased sovereign) in the (ocean of) divine mercy: and may He, also, in the name of *Naib-ul-Mukhtār* (Prophet Muhammad) and his descendants who are immaculate,—keep the memory of the *Bādshāh*, the refuge of the world, everlasting till the end of the universe and the cessation of the progeny of Adam!

Account of Sultān-i-'Azam—wa-Khudāigān-i-Mu'azm—Mu'iz-ud-duniyā—wa-ud-din Mubārak Shāh, May his kingdom and sovereignty be eternal and may his command and dignity be most high!

Three days prior to his approaching death, on the 17th Jamādi-ul-auwal, 824 A.H.[3] (Tuesday, 20th May, 1421 A.D.), Khizr Khān, *May the blessing of God be on his tomb!* nominated his worthy and favourite son[4] heir-apparent, and made him sit on the imperial throne with the approbation of all the *Amirs* and *Māliks*. After the death of *Rāyāt-i-'Ālā*, the people in general made a fresh acknowledgment of obedience (to the new successor). The *Amīrs* and *Māliks*, the prelates and chiefs, the judges and all those who were given an office in the reign of the defunct

Accession of Mubārak Shāh, 17th Jamādī-ul-auwal, 824 A.H., May, 1421 A.D.

---

[1] JNS and MBM read از سرهر شامگهي چاشتي است : MBL reads از پس هر شام گهی. etc.

[2] آخر برداشت فرو داشتی است : lit. every ascent is followed by a descent.

[3] JNS and MBL هفدهم : MBM نوزدهم In Elliot (IV, 53), 18th *Jamādī-ul auwal*; In Badaoni, 821 A.H. Ferishta says "three days after his death".

[4] JNS and MBM read فرزند شایشته و خلف بایشته : MBL reads خلق بایسته : بایسته literally means, necessary: requisit

Khizr Khân, *May he have a good resting place!* were confirmed in their (respective) offices, fiefs, *parganas*, villages,[1] pensions and allotments: the new Sultân even increased them of his own accord.[2]

Distribution of fiefs and emoluments to nobles and people.

The fiefs in the districts of Ḥiṣâr Firoza and Hânsi[3] were taken from Mâlik Rajab Nâdir,[4] and entrusted to *Malik-ul-shark* Mâlik Badah, the Sultân's nephew.[5] Mâlik Rajab obtained the fief of the district of Dibalpur.[6] News now arrived that, Jasrath Shaikhâ Khokhar[7] and Ṭūghân Ra'is had raised the standards of rebellion.

Rebellions of Jasrath Shaikhā Khokhar and Ṭūghān Ra'is.

The cause of Ṭūghân's resistance to authority was, that a year previous to this incident, in the month of Jamâdī-ul-auwal, 823 A.H. (May-June, 1420 A.D.), Sulṭân 'Alī,[8] King of Kashmir, who took his cohorts to Thatha,[9] had on his way back been opposed by Jasrath, when the Sulṭân's army was driven pell-mell,[10] a portion being still in Thatha, and a part only came out.[11] Incapable of sustaining the attack, it made a stampede: Sulṭân 'Alī was made captive, and his baggage and provisions were plundered. Excited with victory and exultant at the strength of his battalion, an imprudent rustic that he was, Jasrath displayed (symptoms of)

---

1 MBL دیه و وظیفهٔ معدود تعین داشت : MBM یه و قطیعه و معدود داشت : JNS دیه و وظیفه و معدود داشت.

2 ماورای آن خاصه خویش زیادهٔ گردانیده.

3 MBL اقطاع شق فیروز آباد و هانسي ; JNS and MBM شق حصار فیروزهٔ و هانسي Ḥiṣâr Firoza and Hânsi, in the Punjab; the former between Lat. 28° 36′—29° 49′ and Long. 75° 16′—76° 22′. Hansi in Ḥisar Division.

4 MBL رجب نادرهٔ . JNS and MBM رجب نادر. Elliot, Malik Rajab Nâdir.

5 JNS has ملک بدهٔ برادر زادهٔ : Ferishta reads Mâlik Badr.

6 Ferishta says that, Mâlik Rajab obtained Dipalpur and the Punjab. Dipalpur, in Montgomery district, Punjab, Lat. 30° 37′, Long. 73° 38′.

7 The Khokhars (کهوکهر) sometimes written as (کهکهر) is a totally distinct race from the Gakhars: they style their chief as *Rae* as well as Sulṭân: Badaoni, (289) says:—جسرت کهوکهر بن شیخا کهوکر : Ferishta says, Jusrut brother of Sheikha Gukkar.

8 In Ferishta, Ally Shah.

9 Thatha or Tatta (Thato) in Karachi district, Sind, Bombay.

10 Badaoni says جسرت کهوکر غافل ساخته درون کهانتی شکست داد.

11 JNS and MBL read چیزی درون در و چیزی بیرون آمدهٔ : MBM omits در.

intoxication and fool-hardiness, and began cherishing imaginary visions of the conquest of Dehli.[1] Being informed of the death of Khizr Khān,[2] he went across the Beāh[3] (Beas) and Sutlej[4] with a column of cavalry and infantry and fell upon Rāi Kamāl-uḍ-dīn Main[5] at Talwandi.[6] Rāi Firoz was constrained to betake himself to the desert.[7] Jasrath next ravaged the territory from Ludhiānā[8] to Rupar[9] on the Sutlej. A few days after, he crossed the Sutlej again and led his army to Jālandhar.[10] Zirak Khān was invested in the fort of Jālandhar, and Jasrath having encamped on the bank of Benī,[11] at a distance of three *kuroh* from the town,[12] made a false negotiation for peace.[13] At length, agreement was arrived at between the contending parties on terms that, the fort was to be given up and left over under the care of Ṭughān,[14] that Majlis-i-'Āli Zirak Khān was to take a son of Ṭughān to Dehli,[15] and that Jasrath was to send an embassy (to His Majesty) and return home.

---

1 JNS and MBM read جسرت مذکور مردی کوتاہ اندیش و روستلی بود برباد شد و مشتی حشرات کرد خویش جمع دید ماخولیا دهلي در سر او افتادند : MBL reads اندیشه and گرد in place of اندیش and کرد respectively, and adds شہر before دهلي .

2 بندگی رایات اعلی .

3 JNS کوارا آب بیاہ : MBL گذارا لب بیاہ.

4 MBL ستلدر . JNS ستلج.

5 MBM and JNS کمال الدین مین : MBL کمال مین.
Badaoni reads Kamāl-ud-dīn Mubīn.

6 20 miles S.S.W. of Ludhiana.

7 MSS. read جول : Tab-i-Akb., جون : Elliot reads "desert": Badaoni simply writes "Rāi Firoz fled before him".

8 MBL and MBM لدزمانه : JNS لدمانه .

9 MSS. read اروبر : Rupar, a subdivision of Ambāla, district Punjab: Between 30° 45′ and 31° 13′ N. and 76° 19′ and 76° 44′ E,: 50 miles N.E. of Ludhiana.

10 It was the original capital of the Rajput kingdom of Katoch.

11 MBL کنارۂ آب بیسي موازنۂ سه کروهي از لشکر جسرتهه مذکور نزول فرمود : JNS کنارہ آب بیني جسرتهه مذکور با کل جمعیت : MBM جسرتهه سه کروهي از قصبه کنارہ آب بیني نزول کرد.

12 MBM آب بیني ; MBL بیسي ; JNS بیلی ; In Elliot Beni: Badaoni has سرمنی .

13 مذاکرۂ اصلاح درمیان آورد .

14 Ferishta says Jasrath appointed Ṭughān as the general-in-chief of his troops.

15 یک نفر پسر طوغان مذکور برابر کردہ در حضرت برد .

Accordingly, on the 2nd Jamādī-ul-ākhir, 824 A.H. (Wed., 4th June, 1421 A.D.), Zīrak Khān emerged out of the fort of Jālandhar and encamped on the bank of the Benī, at a distance of about three *kuroh* from the army of Jasrath: next day, Jasrath with the whole of his *entourage* ready (to receive him) approached Zīrak Khān, but he (Jasrath) broke the sanctity of contract, and under proper escort carried him off a prisoner over Sutlej to Ludhiānā.[1] Then, on the 20th Jamādī-ul-ākhir (Sunday, 22nd June, 1421 A.D.), he left the place by successive marches for Sirhind, where he arrived in the middle of the rainy season. Mālik Sultān Shāh Lodī,[2] the Amīr of Sirhind, was besieged in the fort of Sirhind,[3] and although Jasrath put forth best efforts to take the fortress he failed, as God guarded it. When the statement of affairs supplemented by a request for succour from Sultān Shāh Lodī reached the Sultān,[4] he left the city (Dehli) in spite of the rainy season in the month of Rajab (July, 1421 A.D.),[5] and made for Sirhind; with successive marches he reached Kohilā,[6] near Sāmānā,[7] when Jasrath hearing of his advance raised the siege on the 27th Rajab (Monday, the 28th July) and fell back to Ludhiānā. He released Zīrak Khān,[8] who went to Sāmānā and joined the King. The Dehli army now advanced towards Ludhiānā, where Jasrath having forded the Sutlej[9] encamped in front of the victorious army, (on the other bank of the

Jasrath imprisons Zirak, Governor of Jālandhar, and besiege Sultān Shāh at Sirhind.

---

1 MBL and MBM لدرمانه ; JNS لدهيانه .

2 Ferishta says Islām Khān.

3 Sirhind (or Fetehgarh), in Patiāla State, Punjab, situated in 30 88′ N. and 76° 27′ E. The spelling Sirhind is modern, and due to a fanciful derivation from *Sir-hind*, the "head of India" due to its strategic position. Sahrind is said to mean the "lion forest", but one tradition assigns its foundation to Sāhir Rao, a ruler of Lāhore. Imp. Gaz., Punjab, II. 309 *et seq.*

4 خداوند عالم پناه .

5 بتاریخ ماه رجب .

6 JNS كوهلي : MBL and MBM كوهله : Elliot, Kohila: May be identified with mod. *Koi* or *Khoi*, a village in Patiala State, Punjab, 48 miles south of Ludhiānā.

7 Sāmāna, in Patialā State, Punjab, 17 miles south-west of Patiala town.

8 مسند عالی زیرکخان : Ferishta is of opinion that Zirak Khān contrived to effect his escape: Badaoni states جسرتهه زیرکخان را گدار گذاشت .

9 MBL ستلدر : Badaoni, Ludhiānā river.

river). As Jasrath had secured all the boats on the river, he retarded the progress of his adversaries across the stream. For forty days they fought with each other, remaining posted in their respective places. But with the appearance of Canopus the waters subsided, and the Sulṭān mo.ed to Kabulpur. Jasrath, too, keeping himself to the river bank made a *pari passu* progress. On the 11th Shawwāl (Thurs., 9th Oct.) *Khudāwana-i-'Ālm* sent Mālik Sikandar Tuḥfā, *Majlis-i-'Ālī* Zīrak Khān,[1] *Malik-ul-Shark* Maḥmud Ḥasan,[2] Mālik Kālū, and other Amīrs with strong reinforcements and six elephants to cross the river higher up at Rupar.[3] They forded the river in the morning, and, on the same day, *Khudāwand-i-'Ālm* (with the main body of the army) advanced to the place where his *avant-courier* had crossed the stream before. Keeping himself to the river bank, Jasrath made a parallel move. When the tidings that the Imperialists had crossed the river reached him, Jasrath in a fit of nerve stationed himself at a distance of four *kuroh* from the ford. Crossing the river with his baggage, attendants and elephants, the Sulṭān approached the rebel, who without making any show of resistance took to his heels. The King's forces pursued the enemy closely, capturing all their equipage and slaying many a horse and footmen. Jasrath beat a hasty retreat towards Jālandhar with his brave cavalry,[4] and on the day following, he crossed the Beāh. At the advent of the victorious army near the Beāh, the fugitive ran precipitately towards the Rāvī. In chase of the enemy, the Sulṭān crossed the Beāh at the base of the hills and reached the Rāvī near Bhowā.[5] Jasrath crossed Jānhāo[6] and entered Tilhar,[7] situated in the mountains. Rāi Bhim,[8] the chief of Jammu, was

---

1 مجلس عالی زیرکخان .   2 ملک الشرق محمود حسن .

3 MBL and MBM اروبر : JNS روپر .

4 با سواران جرارة : Elliot has "with some light horse".

5 JNS بهوهر : MBL and MBM بهووة .

6 MBL and MBM جانهاو ! JNS جانوهاو ; Badaoni چهناؤ ; The river Chinab is meant. Ranking (383), "crossed the river Chināb".

7 MBL and MBM read تیکمر ; JNS تیلهر ; Tabakat-i-Akbari has Thankar ; Badaoni تیلهر ; Ferishta, Beosul (mod. Bisauli, a town in Kashmir State, Punjab, situated (on the Rāvi).

8 JNS reads رای بهیلم : MBL and MBM agree with JNS. Tab-i-Akb. رای.

honoured with an interview by the Sulṯān [1] and received the eminence of being appointed as (a Imperial) guide.[2] The Rāi went across Jānhāo, and demolished Tilhar which was Jasrath's strongest place, imprisoning many of those who had sought refuge there. Safely and securely laden with booty, the Sulṯān, then found his way to Lāhore.

Reconstruction of Lāhore by the Sulṯān, and its bestowal upon Mahmud Hasan.

In the month of Muḥarram, A.H. 825 (Dec.-Jany., 1420-21 A.D.), the shade of the blessed fortune and the shadow of the Imperial umbrella [3] fell upon the deserted city of Lāhore, which was bereft of any living soul, save the inauspicious owls which had made it their abode. After a time, the Sulṯān turned his attention to the restoration of the city,[4] and under his royal favour building was reconstructed. He stayed there encamped by the side of Rāvī for nearly a month, engaged in repairing the fort and the gates. When the repair work was brought to a completion, the fief of Lāhore was bestowed upon Malik-ul-Shark Maḥmud Ḥasan, and a contingent of two thousand horses [5] was placed under him. Having made suitable arrangements for the upkeep of the army and the fort,[6] His Majesty returned to *Dār-ul-Mulk* Dehli.[7]

Jasrath's advance against Lāhore and his defeats.

In Jamādī-ul-auwal [8] (Apr.-May) of the aforesaid year (825 A.H., 1421 A.D.), Jasrath Shaikhā crossed the Jānhāo and the Rāvī with a large body of infantry and cavalry and proceeding to the auspicious Mubārakābād Lāhore [9] encamped near the tomb of Sheikh-ul-Mushaekh Sheikh Ḥasīn Zanjānī. On the

---

1 شرف پا بیوس مشرف گشت .   2 پیشوا شده .

3 سایه همایون دولت و ظل چتر سلطنت خداوند عالم پناه .

4 بعد مدتی معلوم روی به‌آباداني آورده .

5 MBM and MBL دو هزار : JNS reads هزار سوار : In Elliot (IV, 56), 2,000 horses.

6 JNS استعداد لشگري و حصار گيري مهيا كرده سپرد : MBL ميما و مهنا كرده.

7 JNS بيردو خود بدولت طرف دارالملک دهلی بار گشت, should be بردة خود etc.

8 MBL, MBM and Elliot, Jamādī-ul-ākhir. JNS جمادی لاول.

9 شهر میمون مبارکاباد لاهور: The "happy city" of Lāhore was called *Mubārakābād* after its restorer, the Sulṯān.

11th Jamādī-ul-ākhir (Tues., 2nd June), the two forces opposed each other in the mud fort.[1] By the grace of God and the prosperity of the Emperor, the refuge of the world, Jåsrath was overthrown.[2] The triumphant army, in pursuit of the fugitives, issued out of the mud fort, but did not advance very far, so that, the contestants kept to their respective positions. Next day, Jasrath sacked all those places.[3] Being powerless,[4] Jasrath ran towards the Rāvī on the th (Sunday, 7th June), of the aforesaid month, collected the wise men of the spot, and fell back the next day, one *kuroh*[5] off Lāhore. On the 21st of the month (Friday, 12th June), an engagement took place in the mud fort, when the Royalists by the Grace of God, and the prosperity of the Sulṭān came out victorious, and gave chase to the retiring force. Jasrath returned to his army.[6] In this way did the battle continue outside the fort for a month and five days, but at last, Jasrath losing his heart made off towards Kālānor.[7] Rāi Bhīm, who had come to the fort of Kālānor for rendering aid to the royal forces, excited the enmity of Jasrath (against him),[8] and when the latter approached Kālānor, fighting went on between them but neither side could claim a victory. Ultimately peace was declared in the month of Ramẓān (Aug.-Sep., 1422 A.D.). Jasrath then retired to the banks of the Beāh in order to mobilise his forces from the Khokhars, who had been friendly to him. Sikandar Tuḥfā now arrived (from Dehli) with an innumerable army at the ford of Būhī[9]

---

1 حصار خام.

2 Badaoni (200) says—بعد پنج ماه جسرت...لاهور در امور... تا یک ماه هر روز بقصد گرفتن شهر حمله میکرد و آخر الامر به مقصود نرسیده باز گشته...

3 Elliot reads "Jasrath held his ground." The Text runs—روز دیگر جسرتهه مذکور همانجا تاخت.

4 فرو دست.

5 JNS and MBM یک کروهي : MBL سه کروهي : Elliot "one *Kos*".

6 JNS جسرتهه مذکور باز گشت هم در پردهٔ خویش نزول کرده. MBL در پردهٔ خویش MBM نزد خویش.

7 On the Kirrān in the Gurudaspur district, Punjab, 17 miles west of Gurudāspur town. Here Akbar ascended the throne.

8 Jasrath attacked Rāi Bhīm for having betrayed his retreat to the King.

9 Badaoni says Puhi (پوهي): Ferishta, Lū'ī (لوئی): Ranking (384 f.n. 1). Ponī.

to join forces with Malik Maḥmūd Ḥasan, who had been deputed before by the Emperor against Jasrath. Failing in constant persistence,[1] Jasrath fled across the Rāvī and Jānhāo with his followers, and proceeded to the hills of Tilhar.[2] Malik-ul-Shark Sikandar crossed the Beāh at the ford of Būhī, and on the 12th Shawwāl (Tues., 29th Sep., 1422 A.D.), he arrived at the auspicious city of Lāhore. Malik Maḥmūd Hasan met him at a distance of three *kuroh* outside the fort.

Previous to this, Malik Rajab, Amīr of Dībālpur,[3] Malik Sulṭān Shāh Lodī, Amīr of Sirhind, and Rāi Fīroz Main joined Malik Sikandar. The aforesaid army proceeded along the Rāvī, and forded that river between Kālānor and the town of Bhoh.[4] On reaching the frontiers of Jammū,[5] they were joined by Rāi Bhīm. Afterwards, some of the Khokhars, who fell asunder from Jasrath at the bank of Jānhāo were worsted, and the royal army retraced their way to the happy city, Mubārakābād. In the meantime, His Majesty issued firmāns[6] that, Malik-ul-Shark Maḥmūd Ḥasan should go to the fief of Jālandhar, and having got ready[7] (his followers), should return and join him. Malik Sikandar[8] was entrusted with the civil administration of the auspicious city, and in obedience to the royal mandate, he proceeded with an army to the fort. The Emperor having recalled Maḥmūd Ḥasan and the other *Amīrs*, removed Malik Sikandar from the *vizirate* and appointed Malik-ul-Shark Sarwar-ul-Mulk in his stead, as the governor of the city. The son of the latter succeeded him in the office of governor.

---

1 طاقت مقاومت نبود.

2 Badaoni says Tilwārā.

3 Dipālpur (Dibālpur, Debālpur) in Montgomery, district Punjab, 30° 40′ N, 73° 32′ E, a place of historical importance, and identified by Cunningham with Daidala of Ptolemy.

4 JNS بهوهر ; MBL and MBM بهوه.

5 MSS. read حد جمون.

6 فرمان عالی همایون.

7 مستعد شده.

8 ملک سکندر تهانهٔ شهر میمون نگاهدارد.
MBL کنهیر. MBM کهنبیر. JNS agree with MBM.

In the year 826 A.H. (1422-23 A.D.), His Majesty, the refuge of the world, drew up his forces and resolved upon marching against Hindustān. In the month of Muḥarram (Dec.-Jany., 1422-23 A.D.), he entered the territory of Katehar,[1] and exacted revenue and taxes. Meanwhile, Mahābāt Khān, *Amīr* of Badāōn[2] who had been in great fear of the late Emperor, Khiẓr Khān,[3] *May his tomb be sanctified !*, was honoured with an interview and special favours. The Sulṭān then crossed the Ganges and ravaged the territory of the Rāthors,[4] putting a large number of the turbulent infidels to the sword. For some time the Imperialists encamped on the Ganges, and then His Majesty left Mubāriz, Zirak Khān and Kamāl Khān with a detachment at the fort of Kampilah[5] to suppress the Rāthors. The son of Rāi Sabīr, who had joined His Majesty, and had moved about in his suite, now took alarm and went off. Malik-ul-Shark Malik Khair-ud-dīn Khāni[6] was sent after him with a vast army, but he failed to overtake the refugee. Khair-ud-dīn, however, laid waste the territory (of the Rāi) and descended upon Etāwah. The Sulṭān, too, with successive marches led his army to Etāwah, where the turbulent infidel had thrown himself into the fort. The son of Rāi Sabīr,[7] being worn out submitted at last, and promised to pay him as of old, revenue and also to render him services.[8] The Sulṭān returned victorious to Dehli in

The Sulṭān's expeditions against Katehar, Rāthor and Etāwah.

---

1 In the early Muhammadan period the tract now known as Rohilkhand or the Barelly Division of the United Provinces, was called Katehar. It was named after their inhabitants, the Katehriyā Rajputs who, as the tribal traditions point out, came from Benares or Tirhut, in the 13th and 14th centuries.

2 Badāyun of Badāōn, is a district in the United Provinces. It became an important post in the northern boundary of the Sulṭānate of Dehli, and its governors were chosen from distinguished soldiers who had constantly to face revolts of the turbulent Katehriyā Rajputs. Acc. to Ferishta it was Mahābāt Khān who had been entrusted with a commission against the tribe of Rathor Rajputs.

3 Badaoni says مهابت خان بداوني كد باخضر خان باغي شده بود.

4 The Rāthors are a clan of Rajputs. Badaoni writes در نواحي كهور عرف شمساباد ولايت پنواران (؟) را تاخت.

5 JNS كنبل : MBL and MBM كنبل : In Farrukhābād district, United Provinces, 27° 35′ N. 79° 14′ E. In Mahābhārat, it was the capital of South Panchala, under King Drupada.

6 ملک الشرق ملک خیر الدین خانی.

7 راي سبير : Elliot, Rāī Sarwar.

8 Ferishta says "the Raja's son was delivered as a hostage for his father's future good conduct into the king's hands."

Jamādī-ul-ākhir, 826[1] A.H. (Apr.-May, 1423 A.D.). From Jālandhar came Malik Maḥmud Ḥasan with a large body of followers to wait upon His Majesty, and he was received with great distinction. The office of *'Ariẓ-i-Mamālik*[2] was taken from Malik Khair-ud-dīn Khāni and given to Malik-ul-Shark Maḥmud Ḥasan. Worthy, righteous and trustworthy, Maḥmud Ḥasan assiduously took to the affairs of the State, and his dignity was on the increase. In Jamādī-ul-auwal (Apr.-May), of this same year, a battle was fought between Jásrath Shaikha and Rāī Bhīm,[3] in which the latter was slain, and a large number of his horses and arms fell a prey to Jasrath.

Battle between Jasrath and Rāi Bhīm; the latter slain.

On ascertaining the death of the Rāi, the victor united a small force of the Mughals with his own,[4] and sacked Dibālpur and Lāhore. Malik Sikandar, who was on the alert. immediately ran after Jasrath. and the latter retreating crossed the Jānhāo. Meanwhile, news arrived of the death of Malik 'Alā'-ul-Mulk,[5] *Amīr* of Multān.

It was rumoured that, Sheikh 'Ali,[6] the vice-gerent of the prince and the son of Sar'atmash,[7] was moving forward from Kābul with a large army to make an incursion into Bhakhar[8] and Siwistān. To stem the tide of Mughal invasion and suppress

The invasion of Sheikh 'Ali, the Mughal.

---

1 JNS and MBM read Jamādī-ul-ākhir. MBL, Jamādī-ul-auwal. Elliot agrees with JNS and MBM.

2 عهدهٔ عارض ممالک : *'Ariẓ-i-Mamālik* is the officer through whom petitions are presented to the Sulṭān: Elliot has "Pay Master of the Forces." Ferishta, "Bukshy of the forces."

3 MSS. read بهیلم : Elliot, Bhīm.

4 JNS ماخیش : copyist's error for باخیش : Ferishta says "Jasrath formed an alliance with "Ameer Shaik Ally, a Mughal chieftain in the service of Shaikh Mirza, governor of Kabul."

5 MBL ملک علاء الدین که علاء الملک : JNS and MBM ملک علاء الملک.

6 JNS and MBM شیخ علي نایب امیرزاده پسر سرعتمش : MBL رغتمش : Elliot, Shaikh 'Ali, lieutenant son of the prince the Sar-'atmash. Jasrath raised an army of 12,000 Gukkurs.

7 Ferishta is of opinion that Sheikh 'Ali was prevailed upon to make the incursion by way of creating a diversion, in order that, by drawing off the King's forces from the capital, for the defence of Sindh, his own views on Dehli might be facilitated.

Badaoni makes no mention of Shaikh 'Ali's invasion.

8 In Dera Ismail, district Punjab: situated on the left bank of the Indus; Lat. 31° 37′ 43″, Long. 71° 5′ 52″.

the outbreak, His Majesty placed the districts of Multān and Siwistān under the charge of Malik-ul-Sharḳ Malik Maḥmud Ḥasan, and sent him with a big army, and with all his family and dependents to Multān. Reaching Multān, he restored order among the populace. and bestowed upon each of them suitable rewards, pensions and allowances. The people of the place preserved a tranquil mind and became happy; the inhabitants of the city and the country led a quiet and secure existence. Maḥmuḍ Ḥasan renovated the fortress at Multān that had been damaged in the struggles with the Mughals, and assembled an army around him.

In the meantime, news came to His Majesty that, Alb Khān, Amīr of Dhār had led his army to Gwālior.[1] The Sulṭān hastened thither with a big army, and on his reaching the district of Bianah,[2] the son of Auḥad Khān,[3] Amīr of Bianah, who having assassinated Mubārak Khān, his paternal uncle, raised the banner of insurrection, laid waste the fort of Bianah, and retired to the brow. The Emperor struck his camp at the base of the said hill, and after a time, being hard pressed the rebel paid his revenue and tribute, and put his neck into the collar of obedience. Rāyāt-i-'Ālā then, moved towards Gwālior against Alb Khān.[4] This chief had secured the (usual) fords of the Chambal,[5] and the royal army passed over the said stream by another (new) ford. Mālik Maḥmud Ḥasan and sundry other nobles, such as, the Mewatis,[6]

The Sulṭān proceeded to Gwālior against Alb Khān.

The unsuccessful revolt of the Amir of Bianah.

---

[1] Badaoni writes (291):—الب خان حاکم دهلي بقصد تنبه رای گواليار و عزم تسخير آن ديار آمد. Ferishta calls him Sulṭān Hooshung of Malwa.

[2] Bianah or Biāna, in Bharatpur State, Rajputana, and 50 miles south-west of Agra.

[3] Ameer Khān, the son of Wahid Khān, governor of Bianah (Ferishta); Badaoni reads Shams Khān Auḥadī.

[4] Tabaḳat-i-Akbari has Alf Khān and Alaf Khān. Both are errors for Ulugh Khān.

[5] MBL چهنبل; MBM جيتل; JNS البغان کناره آب جيتک کدرها گرفته فرود آمده بود: Chambal, one of the principal tributaries of the Jamuna, is a river of central India. It rises in Malwa and joins the Jamuna 40 miles below Etāwah.

[6] ميوان: Mewat, an ill-defined tract lying south of Dehli, include the Br. districts of Muttra, Gurgaon, most of the Alwar and a little of Bharatpur states. It takes its name from the Meos, who appear to have been originally same as the *Mināe*

and Nuṣrat Khān, who were the leaders of the victorious army,[1] plundered the baggage of Alb Khān, and brought many of his men, horse and foot as prisoners before the Sulṭān. Taking into account that both parties were Musalmans, His Majesty spared the prisoners' lives and set each of them free. Next day, Alb Khān despatched envoys to make overtures to the King. Learning that Alb Khān was reduced to a state of weakness and compulsion, and disapproving any further design (of hostility) against his co-religionists, the Sulṭān consented to make peace on condition of Alb Khān sending in tribute and retiring from Gwālior. On the following day Alb Khān forwarded his gifts to the Emperor and turned his way towards Dhar. The King stationed himself for some time on the banks of the Chambal, levying contributions upon the infidels according to old custom, after which he safely returned to his capital, laden with booty, in Rajab, 827 A.H. (May-June, 1424 A.D.), and took to administration.

Sulṭān's second expedition to Katehar and Mewat.

In the month of Muḥarram, 828 A.H.[2] (Nov.-Dec., 1424 A.D.), the Sulṭān moved towards Katehar.[3] When he reached the banks of the Ganges, Rāi Har Singh[4] joined the Sulṭān and was honoured with great compassion, but as he had put off paying his quota of tribute for three years, he was detained for a few days.[5] In short, the royal forces went across the Ganges, took the rebels of those parts to task, and continued their progress

---

of Rajputana. The origin of the name "Meo" is disputed, some deriving it from Mewat, which is said to be the Sanskrit *Mīnā-vati*, rich in fish while the Meos derive it from *Maheo*, a word used in driving cattle. Throughout the period of Muhammadan rule the Meos were the Ishmaelites of their own country and of the upper Doab, and harried again and again by the Kings of Dehli from 1259 to 1527. During the troubled times of Timur's invasion, Bahādur Nāhar founded the subdivision of the Mewatīs called *Khān-zādahs*, members of which for many years ruled Mewat. Imp. Gaz., U.P., I, 223. The MSS. read—محمود حسن و بعضی امرا دیگر چنانچه میوان و نصرت خان.

1 یارة.

2 Badaoni says 827 A.H. سبع و عشرین و ثمانمایه.

3 JNS and MBM کتهیهر : MBL کتهیر : Badaoni writes Kumāon and Kaithar.

4 Ferishta says Nursingh. Tab-i-Akb. reads Nursingh.

5 Here JNS is illegible, eaten up by worms. MBL and MBM read او را موقوف سه سال و چند روز در قید افتاد. Tab-i-Akb. کردة مدتی داشتند :

to the hills of Kumāyūn. Here they halted for some time, but when the weather became sultry, they retired homewards along the banks of the Rahab.[1] Crossing the Ganges near Kampil[2] they made for Ḳanauj, but owing to a severe famine having broken out in the cities of Hindustān, the Imperialists moved no further.

Information relating to the insurrection of the Mewātis reaching the Sulṭān, he set out with successive marches against Mewāt, and carried fire and sword through their country.[3] The Mewātis deserted their country[4] and took refuge in Jahrah, their *point d'appui*. This retreat being invulnerable and the provisions running short, the Sulṭān laden with booty, retired to his capital where he arrived in the month of Rajab (May-June, 1425 A.D.). The Amīrs and Māliks were permitted leave, and His Majesty abandoned himself to amusement and pleasure.

Sulṭān's third expedition to Mewāt: submission of Jallu and Ḳaddū.

The following year, 829 A.H. (1425-26 A.D.), the Sulṭān proceeded to Mewāt when Jallu and Ḳaddū,[5] grandsons of Bahādur Nāhir, and several Mewātis who had co-operated with them having laid waste their own territories, retreated to the hills of Andwar. After a siege lasting for several days when the Imperialists pressed hard, the besieged evacuated Andwar and made off to the mountains of Alwar.[6] The Emperor levelled the fort of Andwar in the dust, and hastened to Alwar. On his approach, Jallu and Ḳaddū shut themselves in the fort, and the victorious army followed them.[7]

---

[1] JNS reads آب رهپ.

[2] MBL قصبۀ کنبل : MBM قصبۀ کنگ : JNS قصبه کنپل.

[3] Badaoni writes "reduced the fortresses of Indor and Alwar.

[4] MBL کل ولایت را خراب کرده : MBM کل خلق را خراب. : JNS agrees with MBM. Elliot, "Having driven off all the population." Tab-i-Akb., "Having laid waste and depopulated their country."

[5] جلو و قدو, for Julal and Kuddur, to which "Khan" was usually suffixed. In Ferishta we get Jullu and Kudroo. Badaoni gives no name. In JNS the second و should be omitted after قدو in the line جلو و قدر و نیسگان بهادر ناهر, as its existence would imply the existence of the grandsons of Bahadur Nāhir other than Jallu and Kaddū. The text in MBM is erroneous; it reads خلق و قدو بنکان بهادر.

[6] Alwar or Ulwar, in Rajputana, bet. lat. 27° 4′ 28° 13′ and long. 76° 7′ 77° 14′..

[7] JNS لشکر منصور متواتر دهوره کرد. دهوره, a copyist's error for دهو ره. Ferishta is more precise when he says,...... "the grandsons of Bahadur Nāhir, retreated to the hills of Alwar, and defended the passes with much obstinacy."

At last, being reduced to a state of deep depression, they begged for mercy and were granted with quarter.[1] [2] Subsequently, Kaddū was exalted with the eminence of being permitted to kiss the feet (of His Majesty), [3] but as he was on the point of running away towards the mountains he was captured and committed to custody. The powerful lord and the centre of the universe[4] (i.e., the Sulṭān) ravaged Mewāt, and its adjacent territories and fo. a time took up his quarters there, but owing to the scarcity of supplies he retraced his steps to Dehli, where he arrived in the month of Sha'bān (June-July, 1426 A.D.).

The Sulṭān to Bianah via Mewāt: submission of Muḥammad Khān: Bianah conferred upon Mukbil.

Next year, in Muḥarram,[5] 830 A.H. (Nov.-Dec., 1426 A.D.), the King proceeded to Bianah, and coerced the Mewātis on the way. Muḥammad Khān, s of Auḥad Khān, Amīr of Bianah, shut himse up in the fort. He destroyed the city, retired to the fortress situated on the summit of the mountains, and held out for sixteen days.[6] On the 2nd Rabī'-ul-ākhir (Fri., 31st Jany., 1427 A.D.), the royalist faced Muhammad Khān; accompanied by his numerous army and the notable veterans, the Sulṭān made an ascent on the hill by a pathway situated in its rear.[7] Getting wind of this (incident), the son of Auḥad Khān lost his power of resistance and went *hors de combat* inside the fortress.[8] Discerning his rank unsteady and the fortress in confusion,[9] Muḥammad Khān gave up offering resistance and having come outside his strongholds

[1] Tabakat-i-Akbari and Ferishta relate that they (Jallu and Kaddū) were imprisoned.

[2] In Elliot (pp. 62-63) the portions that follow have been taken from *Tabakat-i-Akbari* as the pages of the MS. used by Elliot were lost at this place.

[3] Some folios are missing in MBM. The lines from "But as he was on the point of running away" to "It now reached the ears of the Emperor" in page 215 are omitted in the text.

[4] خدايگان گيتي مدار.

[5] Elliot, 11th Muharram.

[6] بقوت كوه با لشكر منصور محاربه ميكرد.

[7] JNS پشت در راه كوه : MBL and MBM پشت دروازهٔ كوه بالا.

[8] Ferishta relates that, owing to the desertion of part of the garrison, Muḥammad Khān had to surrender.

[9] JNS قلعه خللي ديد : MBL در قلعهٔ خود تخلّلي ديد.

with a turban round his neck kissed the dust.[1] The Sulṭān, the centre of the universe and the just, and in habits like Naushirwan, promised him safety, the Khān (in return) offered whatever hard cash, valuable goods, arms, furnitures and cattle he had stored in the fort to the victor[2] who remained there for a few days (more). By the order of the Sulṭān, the family and dependents of Muḥammad Khān were taken out of the fort, despatched to Dehli and allowed to live in the palace of *Jahān-panah*.[3] The charge of the fief of Bianah was handed over to Mukbil Khān, a slave of the Sulṭān, and the vice-gerency of the said district and *parganah* Sikri[4] was vested on Malik Khair-ud-dīn Tuḥfa.

The Sulṭān marched against Gwālior and accepted submission of its Rāi.

His Majesty then proceeded to Gwālior On his arrival the Rāī of Gwālior, Thankir[5] and Chandwār made their submission and paid tribute as of old. At the desire of his friends, the Sulṭān safely returned to Dehli, laden with booty and reached his palace in the month of Jamādī-ul-ākhir[6] (Mar.-Apr., 1427 A.D.). He then changed the territory of Maḥmud Ḥasan,[7] giving him charge of Ḥiṣār Firozā and transferring Multān to Malik-ul-sharḳ Rajab Nādir. Shortly after, Muḥammad Khān seceded from the Sulṭān, and effected his escape to Mewāt with his wife and children. Some of his attendants who had been dispersed rejoined him. It transpired that, Malik Mukbil had

---

1 دست و پای کم کرده بضرورت دستار در گلو انداخته و پای از سر ساخته از درون برون امد بشرف خاکبوس مشرف گشت.
Ferishta states, "with a rope about his neck (he) was led into the royal presence."

2 JNS reads - انچه از جنس نقود و نفایس اسباب واسلحه و رخت و گاو درون قلعه داشت بوجه نعل بهای اسپان لشکر منصور پیش گردانید.

3 JNS جهان نمای : MBL and MBM جهان پناه : Badaoni, Jahān Numāh.

4 Later became known as Fatehpur; now a district in the Allahabad Division, United Provinces, lying between 25° 25′ and 26° 16′ N. and 80° 14′ and 81° 20′ E. According to tradition, the Rājās of Argal held a large part of the district as tributaries of the Kanauj Kingdom before the Muhammadan conquest. Nothing definite is known of the history of the district during the early Muhammadan period when it formed a part of the Kingdom of Korah.

5 MSS. have تهنگیر. Elliot, Bhangar.

6 In Elliot, Jamādī-ul-auwal.

7 JNS and MBL read اقطاع از ملک الشرق ملک محمود حسن تحویل شد.

set out with his whole force for Mahr Mahāwan,[1] leaving Malik K̲hair-ud-dīn Tuḥfa in the fort and the *Khiṭṭā* of Bianah empty (of soldiers). Reposing trust in the inhabitants and the chiefs of (that) country,[2] (Muḥammad K̲hān) went to Bianah with a small force, when he was joined by the people of the *Khiṭṭā* and the country. Subsequently, the fort (Bianah) capitulated and the soldiers that had been stationed there were withdrawn to Dehli. The Emperor[3] took Bianah from Malik Muḳbil, and entrusted it to Malik Mubāriz with orders to suppress the rebellion of Muḥammad K̲hān. At the advent of the Imperialists, the rebel retired into the fort, and Malik Mubāriz took possession of Bianah and its adjacent countries. Entrusting the defence of the place to some of his followers, Muḥammad K̲hān ran away to join Sulṭān Ibrāhim S̲harḳī.[4] The Sulṭān summoned Malik Mubāriz to his presence for advice,[5] and in the month of Muḥarram, 831 A.H. (Oct.-Nov., 1427 A.D.), he ordered his army off to Bianah.

The Sulṭān to Kalpi against Ibrāhim S̲harḳi.

On the way, there came an epistle from Ḳādir K̲hān, the ruler of Kalpi,[6] communicating the approach of S̲harḳī, at which the powerful lord and the centre of the universe, made a change of front and went out to meet the invader. It got wind that, S̲harḳī having laid waste *Bhūngāon*,[7] was working his way to Badāōn. The Sulṭān[8] forded the Jaun (Jamuna) at Nūh-

---

1 MBL مهر مهاون : JNS agrees with MBL. Tab-i-Akb. and Elliot مهاون (Mahāwan). Mod. Mahaban, in Muttra district, United Provinces, near the left bank of the Jumna, 27° 27′ N. and 77° 45′ E.

2 بر اعتماد سکان خطه و مقدمان ولایت .

3 خداوند عالم .

4 S̲harḳī was at that time advancing with an army against Kalpi.

5 JNS—ملک مبارز را نیز برای مصلحتی (؟) در حضرت طلب شد. Elliot reads, "to account for the escape of Muḥammad K̲hān."

6 In Jālaun district, United Provinces. Lat. 26° 8′ N. and Long. 79° 45′ E.

7 MBL reads بهو کانور : JNS reads بهیون کانون ; Badaoni has بهون کانور ; Elliot, Bhūkanū. Ranking (386), Bhūngāon, 9¼ miles east from Mainpuri at the junction of Agra and Grand Trunk Roads.

8 حضرت اعلی .

Patal,[1] sacked Chartolī[2] and from thence, he led his army to Atrolī.[3]

Advent of Mukhtass Khān and his defeat.

It now reached the ears of the Emperor[4] that, Mukhtass Khān,[5] brother of Sharkī, had arrived at Etāwah with a large contingent and numerous elephants. Upon this, the King detached from the main body Malik-ul-Shark Mahmud Hasan[6] with 10,000 brave and experienced horsemen and sent him against Mukhtass Khān. Mahmud Hasan and his battalion descended upon the place where the army of Sharkī had pitched their camps. When the Khān was apprised of this news he fell back on his brother, but Mahmud Hasan halted there for some time more with the object of making a night attack upon the adversaries. As the latter were on the look-out, he returned and rejoined the Dehli army. Sharkī, too, advanced along the banks of *Ab-i-siyāh*[7] to Burhānabād, in district Etāwah. To meet his enemy, the Sultān evacuated Atrolī and pitched his camp at Mabin Kotāh,[8] where the belligerents remained only a short distance apart. Discerning the valour of the Emperor, and the strength and vastness of his army, Sharkī retired to Rapri[9] in the month of Jamādī-ul-auwal (Feb.-Mar., 1428 A.D.). There he crossed the Jaun at Gudrang,[10] and marching on towards Bianah, he encamped on the river of Katehar.[11] In pursuit of the

---

1 JNS نوه بتل : MBL نوه و پتل : Badaoni, Nūh Patal.

2 MBL خرتولي : JNS چرتولي ; Badaoni, جرتولي (Jartauli): Elliot, Haroli.

3 In Aligarh district, United Provinces, 16 miles from Aligarh town ; Elliot's translation from Tabakat-i-Akbari here ends.

4 بندگي رايات اعلى .

5 Elliot calls him Mokhlis Khān.

6 ملك الشرق محمود حسن .

7 JNS and MBM كنارهٔ اب سياه گرفته : MBL كنارهٔ لب بياه. Badaoni has آب سياه عرف كالي پاني ; Ferishta, Kaly Nye, referring to Kāli Nadī, properly Kālindi, a river in United Provinces, rising in Muzaffarnagar.

8 MBL بابن‌كوته : MBM بابن‌كوته : Tab-i-Akb. مالي كوته : JNS has مابين كوته : Badaoni simply كوته : Ferishta, Malykota ; and Elliot, Pāyin Kotāh.

9 Ferishta says Rabery. Rāpri, in Shikohābād *tahsil* of Mainpuri district, United Provinces, has always been important as commanding one of the crossing of the Jumna.

10 JNS reads گرزيک : MBL and MBM گدرنگ .

11 JNS and MBM اب كنتهر : Badaoni has آب كيتهر : MBL آب كنبهير . Elliot and Badaoni, "river of Katehr." Tab-i-Akb. كنار كيتهر.

retreating force, the powerful lord and the centre of the universe, crossed the Jaun with successive marches at Chandwār and halted at a distance of four *kuroh* from the enemy. The vanguard of the Imperial army made constant raids upon their opponents, carrying off prisoners, cattle and baggage. This state of things continued for twenty[1] days, the belligerents remaining at a short distance from each other. Drawing out his equipage, footmen and cavalry, S͟harḳī presented a bold front on the 7th Jamādī-ul-āk͟hir[2] (Wed., 24th Mar., 1428 A.D.). His Majesty, Malik-ul-S͟harḳ Sarwarul Mulk[3] the vizir, Sa'iyid-us-Sādāt Sa'iyid Sālim[4] and several other prominent chiefs remained in the camp in safety, while some others were sent against the enemy, such as, Malik-ul-S͟harḳ Malik Maḥmud Hasan, K͟hān-i-'Aẓam Fāth K͟hān, son of Sulṭān Muẓaffar, Majlis-i-'Āli Zirak K͟hān, Malik-ul-S͟harḳ Malik Sulṭān S͟hāh, who received of late the title of Islām K͟hān, Malik Chaman,[5] the grandson of K͟hān-i-Jahān, Malik Kālū K͟hanī, master of elephants, Malik Aḥmad Tuḥfā and Malik Muḳbil K͟hān. The action commenced at noon and continued till sun-down, and when night fell[6] the combatants withdrew to their respective encampments. Neither side retreating, fighting continued till the end.[7] There were many wounded on the side of S͟harḳī, so that, when on the next day, he saw the strength of the royal forces, he marched off towards the Jaun. On the 17th Jamādī-ul-āk͟hir (Sat., 3rd Apr., 1428 A.D.), he forded (the river) at Gudrang,[8] made his way to Rāprī and from thence retraced his steps to his own country. The Emperor pursued him to Gudrang, but the contending party being Muhammadan, he

---

1 MBM and JNS, 20 days: MBL, 22 days.

2 MBL, JNS and MBM read هفتم ماه: Elliot has 17th: Ferishta says 17th Jamad-us-sany.

3 MBL ملک سرور الملک.

4 MBL سید عالم سالم.

5 MBL ملک چمن : MBM ملک حمیں : JNS ملک حیمن.

6 The author here indulges in a verbose style:— از میان یکدیگر مقاتله محاربه نیم روز تا وقت شام رفت هم در عین قتال بودند که سلطان سپهر از ناحیت نیم روز در حدود شام تاخت وبمنزل عین حمیهٔ (؟) عزم نزول پرداخت جهان روشن در چشمها شان تاریک نمود.

7 آن وقت بر بساط مقاومت بازی قایم ماند.

8 MBM and MBL گدرنگه : JNS کذرنکه.

refrained himself from any further chase. He then took his way to Hath Kant,[1] and after exacting customary tribute from the Rāī of Gwālior and the other Rāīs, moved in the direction of Bianah along the course of the Chambal.[2] Mahmud Khān Auhadi, who had befriended Sharkī, being frightened out of his wits, shut himself up in the fortress, situated at the summit of the hill.[3] The Emperor laid siege to the fortress that was excessively lofty and most impregnable. Nevertheless, it was due to the prosperity of His Majesty, the centre of the universe, that the low born tribe suffered losses, and their vanity disappeared before the fury of the victorious forces[4]; their hands were powerless against the assailants and their feet unable to flee. The siege, thus continued for a week; at length, they allowed the invaders to claim the victory and sought for mercy. Full of clemency and pity for the Musalmans, the Sultān, *May God make him supreme!* forebore to punish Muhammad Khān and granted him forgiveness; firmāns were issued to the soldiery ordering them to evacuate the fort.

The Sultān to Gwālior and Bianah.

On the 26th Rajāb (Tuesday, 11th May, 1428 A.D.), Mahmud Khān marched out with his attendants and went off towards Mewāt. *Bandagi-Rāyāt-i-'Ālā* remained there for some time to set in order the wasted city, and with a view to the administration and upkeep of the district of Bianah he appointed as its governor Malik-ul-Shark Malik Mahmud Hasan, who had exhibited bravery and loyalty in the government and the defence of the frontiers, and was successful in the accomplishment of many great duties. He had thus signalised the opening years of the Sultān's rule[5] by waging a war against Jasrath Shekha Khokhar; (again) when he held the command at Lāhore, he had made a stand against the Sheikh-zādah, the deputy of

The Sultān at Bianah.

---

1 MBL هتبکانت : JNS هتبکانون : MBM هتبکانت : Tab-i-Akb. هشتکانت : Badaoni has ستگانه : Forishta, Hulkant : Elliot, Hathkant.

2 MBM جیتل.

3 JNS بالای قلعه کوه : MBL and MBM omit کوه.

4 MSS. have باد عرور ایشان از آتش قهر لشکر منصور فرو نشست.

5 MBL and MBM چنانچه در مبدأ حال جلوس با جسرتهه.

شیخا محاربه کرده : JNS reads مبران جلوس.

the Prince of Khorāsān,[1] and hindered him from making an ingress to Multān. He was now appointed as the commandant of the said fort (of Bianah) with its adjoining territories. The *akta'* of Bianah and all its dependencies were placed under his control.

Mahmud Hasan was appointed commandant of Bianah.

At the desire of his well-wishers, His Majesty worked homewards along the bank of the Jaun (Jamuna), and reaching the capital on the 15th Sha'bān, 831 A.H. (Sunday, May 30, 1428 A.D.), took up his residence in Sīrī. Then he bade farewell to the *Amīrs* and *Māliks* to their fiefs, and gave himself up to pleasure and merry-making.

The Sultān's return to Dehli.

This prayer went up to the Eternal Sultān,[2] the Everlasting and Durable Sovereign, *May His dignity be glorified and His magnificence be exalted*, that this Emperor (Mubārak Shāh), in rank equal to Solomon[3], be kept permanent till the end of this world and the progeny of Adam be in existence, on the imperial seat and on the throne of the country. *Accept this, Oh Lord of the Universe!*

Invocation of blessing by Yahiya Sirhindi, the author.

In the opinion of this humble supplicant[4] (the author) few words, in accordance with the customary invocation of blessing made by the authors and writers[5] (of histories and chronicles), be (also) said in favour of the Emperor, the protector of the universe, towards the close of this work. Though neither a single rose from the thousands in the garden of the Emperor and the rose garden of

---

1 با شیخ زادهٔ نایب شاهزادهٔ خراسان : Elliot reads, "the Prince-Deputy of the Sultān of Khorāsān." The personage referred to is the general of Shah Rukh.

2 JNS reads از درگاه سلطان ازل بادشاه لم یزل ولا یزال جلت قدرته و علت عظمته درخواست آمد.

MBM: از درگاه سلطان ازل و بادشاه لم یزل جلت قدرته و علت کلمته MBL از درگاه از پادشاه لم یزل.

3 No name is more famous in the east than Solomon, the son of David. It is said that not only mankind, and animals, but even the elements and the Genii were under his obedience. His throne was magnificent beyond idea.

4 دعا گوی

5 اصحاب انشا و ارباب املا.

his youth has blossomed forth, nor a single story out of the thousand tales about his wars and conviviality has the nightingale of his (i.e., author's) nature sung,[1] this work, perforce, has now been brought to a finish. If the petitioner continues to exist, he deems it proper that, the future victories, the acts of valour and stories instrumental to the everlasting prosperity of the sovereign should be annually preserved and incorporated in this book. *May it so please the Almighty God, who helps to bring everything to an end and easily encompass it!*[2]

Kaddū punished: Sarwar-ul-Mulk sent to Mewāt.

In the month of Shawwāl of the aforesaid year (July-Aug., 1428 A.D.), (the Sulṭān) imprisoned and then put to death Malik Kaddū Mewātī for his having lent countenance to Sharki and exchanging presents and envoys with him.[3] Malik Sarwar-ul-Mulk was ordered off with an army to Mewāt to coerce the rebels and confiscate their territory. Having laid waste most of their towns and villages that flourished in the desert, he retired to the mountains.[4] Jalāl Khān, brother of Malik Kaddū, and the other chiefs, viz., Ahmad Khān, Malik Fakhr-ud-dīn, Malik 'Alī and their relations, collected all their horsemen and foot-soldiers within the fort of Andwar.[5] When Malik Sarwar-ul-Mulk encamped

---

1 هزار دستان طبعم : MBM omits it.

2 It is apparent how Yaḥiyā wanted to finish off his work with usual eulogies and benedictions upon his patron. Thus he concluded his account with the events happening in 1427 A.D., when the Sulṭān returned to his Capital from the punitive expeditions against the rulers of Gwalior and Mewāt. But on second thought, for reasons best known to himself—it might be as he has himself admitted that the work unless continued would remain incomplete, or that, he recovered from his illness which had probably led to a temporary cessation of his writing with little prospect of continuing it—he took up the thread of his narrative and put off the conclusion.

3 MBI. ملک قدو میوا : MBM قدو و میوا : JNS illegible: reads like قدو و ملو: Elliot IV, 66, "Afterwards he had him (Kaddu) put to death." There is no reference of Mallu.

4 بعضی قصبات و قریات ایشان که در صحرای آبادان بودند بتمام خراب گشته درون کوه آمد.

In Elliot, "the inhabitant of the city" have been made the subject.

5 The three MSS. read اندور : In Elliot and Ferishta, Alwar.

himself near the above fort, the besieged, failing to offer resistance, held out the olive branch under the pledge of sending contributions to His Majesty.[1] In conformity to the peace clause, Malik Sarwar-ul-Mulk having exacted revenue, tribute and hostages paced his way back to the capital with his forces.

Siege of Kalānor by Jasrath and the march of Sikandar Tuḥfa against him: Jasrath's success.

In the month of Ẓīl-ḳa‘da, 831 H. (Aug.-Sep., 1428), the report went that, Jasrath Khokhar had besieged Kalānor. Malik-ul-Sharḳ Malik Sikandar Tuḥfā, Amir of Lāhore, marched towards Kalānor to give relief to the besieged. Jasrath quitted his position at Kalānor and moved on a few *Kuroh*; a conflict took place between him and Sikandar, from which, by the decree of the Most High God, Jasrath came out triumphant. Courting defeat, Malik Sikandar fell back on Lāhore, while Jasrath on his way through Kalānor crossed the Beāh near Jālandhar and sacked the place. Impregnable as the fort of Jālandhar was, the invader failed to take it, and retreated to Kalānor carrying off the men of the locality.

Jasrath defeated by Sikandar Tuḥfa and the Rāi of Kalānor.

Being apprised of this event, the Sulṭān ordered Majlis-i-‘Ālī Zirak Khān, *amir* of Sāmāna, and Islām Khān, *amir* of Sirhind,[2] to proceed with their army in aid of Malik Sikandar. But before they arrived at the "happy city" of Lāhore, Malik-ul-Sharḳ Malik Sikandar had marched out to Kalānor, and there uniting with his own forces all the horse and foot belonging to Rāi Ghālib Kalānori, he ran after Jasrath and met him near Kāngra, on the bank of the Beāh. Jasrath, who was prepared for action, drew up his forces, and the fight commenced. By the Grace of Most High God, the forces of Islām came off with flying colours and Jasrath's army was destroyed. Dispersed and defeated and leaving behind him the spoils of war that had been secured at Jālandhar, Jasrath made his retreat towards Tilhar[3] and re-

---

[1] .که مال بر غریق گرو امکان در حضرت فرستند

[2] MBL and MBM سیهرند;

[3] MBL reads تیهکهر: JNS and MBM تیلهر.

garded the defeat as a gain. Malik-ul-Shark Malik Sikandar[1] then returned to Lāhore, the auspicious city.

Mahmud Hasan suppress the rebels of Bianah.

In the month of Muharram, 832 H. (Oct.-Nov., 1428 A.D.), Malik-ul-Shark Malik Mahmud Hasan[2] having suppressed the infidels of Bianah who having joined with Mahmud Khān Auhadi had fomented rebellion,[3] quitted that district and went to Dehli to pay his respects to His Majesty, the blessed and the powerful. He was honoured with the eminence of kissing the feet (of the Emperor) and became the recipient of extreme favour and the fief of Hisār Firoza.[4]

The Sultān marched to Mewāt: submission of the Mewātis.

Subsequently, Bandagī Rāyāt-i-'Ālā resolved upon marching into the mountains of Mewāt and pitched his camp at the top of *Hauz-i-khās*. The *amīrs* and *maliks* came from the four winds and joined the Sultān. Marching forward, the Sultān proceeded to Hindwārī,[5] and halted there for some time. Jalāl Khān Mewāti and the other Mewātis being subjected to a great stress promised to pay, as of old, tribute and taxes, while some of them were granted the honour of paying homage.

Multān restored to Mahmud Hasan.

In Shawwāl (July-Aug., 1429 A.D.), Rāyāt-i-'Ālā, laden with spoils of war, found his way to Dehli. He did not launch into any further campaign that year. The same year, tiding came of the demise of Malik Rajab Nādir, *amir* of Multān; the fief of Multān was restored to Malik-ul-Shark Mahmud Hasan, who received the title of 'Imād-ul-Mulk[6] and was sent to Multān with a numerous army.

---

1 In JNS the presence of و between Malik-ul-Shark and Malik Sikandar is due to copyist's mistake.

2 In JNS the و between Malik-ul-Shark and Malik Mahmud Hasan should be deleted.

3 The text in JNS is defective: it runs—

ملک الشرق وملک محمود حسن فسدۀ کفار ولایت بیانه با که محمود خان
اوحدي جمع شدۀ بنیاد نهاد بودند فرو نشاندۀ از خط بیانه برای پابوسي حضرت
در شهر آمد ٭

4 In Badaoni (I, 293) the fortress of Firozah. Ranking, 387.

5 MBM هندواري : JNS and MBL مهندواري : Elliot, Hindwārī.

6 "Pillar of the State", *i.e.*, minister.

The Sulṭān marched against Gwālior and Hathkānt.

In the year 833 H. (1429-30 A.D.), Bandagī Rāyāt-i-'Ālā led his army by successive marches to Gwālior via Bianah. Inflicting penalty on the offenders of Gwālior, he passed over to Hathkānt.[1] The Rāi of Hathkānt was defeated and he made away to the mountains of Jālbahār.[2] His territory was harried and most of the unbelievers of that country were made prisoners. From thence the army proceeded to Rāpri,[3] and the fief of Rāpri was taken from the son of Ḥasan Khān and made over to Malik Ḥamza.[4] Richly laden with plunder, the Sulṭān then safely returned to the capital in the month of Rajab of the abovementioned year (Mar.-Apr., 1430 A.D.). During the march Sa'iyid Sālim was struck with illness and he died. His remains was placed in a cofin, carried to Dehli with promptness and interred there. To sum up, for thirty years was Sa'iyid Sālim in the service of the late Khizr Khān,[5] *May his tomb be sanctified*, owning several fiefs and *parganas* in the Doab, besides the fort of Tabarhindah[6] (Sirhind). Rāyāt-i-'Ālā had also bestowed upon him the *khiṭṭa* of Sarsuti[7] and the *akṭā'* of Amroha.[8] A covetous man as the defunct Sa'iyid was, he had in the course of time amassed a huge sum of money and made a good stock of grain and other commodities in Tabarhindah.[9]

Death of Sa'iyid Sālim. His career.

---

1 MBL هتهیکانت : MBM هتنکانت : JNS reads هته کانون : Ferishta, Hulkant: Elliot, Hathkānt. Hatkant is said by Abūl Fazl to be the chief town of Bhadāwar, a district S. E. of Agra.

2 MBL, JNS and MBM جالبهار : Elliot IV, 68, Jalhār.

3 Ferishta has Rabery : MBL and MBM رابری : JNS راپری : Badaoni, Rāpri.

4 JNS and MBM بعوالۀ ملک همزه : MBL adds پسر before ملک عمزه : Badaoni writes, "having taken the Rāpri dist. from the son of Ḥasan Khān gave it to Malik Ḥamza."

5 The text in MBM is erroneous. It reads, سالم مرحوم مغفور خضر خان.

6 اقطاعات و پرگنات خارج قلع تبهنده درمیان دواب : Badaoni (294) has اقطاع تبرهند داشت.

7 Sarsuti or Sirsa, a district in Ḥiṣar Division, Punjab, between the rivers Sutlej and Ghaghar.

8 In Moradabad District.

9 Modern Bhatinda (also known as Gobindgarh) situated in Patiala State, Punjab. It appears in the early Muhammadan historians as Batrinda, often incorrectly transposed into Tabarhindh. In the early Muhammadan period the country round formed an important fief of the Dehli empire.

Following his demise, the *aktā's* and *parganas* that he possessed were distributed among his sons, the eldest of whom received the title of Sa'iyid Khān and the youngest that of Shujā'-ul-Mulk.

Insurrection of Pulād Turkbāchā.

In the month of Shawwāl (June-July, 1430 A.D.), Pulād Turkbāchā, a slave of Sa'iyid Sālim, came near Tabarhindah at the instigation of Sa'iyid's sons, and there stirred up an insurrection. Rāyat-i-'Ālā took into custody the sons of the late Sa'iyid and sent Malik Yusuf Sarup[1] and Rāi Hīnū Bhattī[2] to allure Pulād to their side and to lay hold on the late Sa'iyid's wealth.

His treachery and success.

When they gained access to the fort of Tabarhindah, Pulād, on the very first day, sought a conference[3] and offered terms of peace. He sent them provisions and lulled them into security,[4] but on the following day, he emerged out of the fortress with his adherents, and made a sortie. Being informed of this perfidy and fraud, Malik Yusuf and Rāi Hīnū took the field. Though the royalists were covered with iron, yet by the decree of God, they had to yield the palm to the infamous Pulād and were scattered like drops at the first onset. The victor pursued the vanquished to the distance of a *farsang*.[5] The imperial forces made their way to the district of Sarsuti, and whatever baggage tents, cash and goods they possessed fell a prey to Pulād.

The Sulṭān marched against Pulād; latter besieged in Tabarhindah.

On receiving intimation of this news, Rāyat-i-'Ālā became thoughtful; he then set out in person for Tabarhindah, and after a prolonged march reached Sarsuti, where the *amīrs* and *maliks* of the vicinity leagued with him. Pulād made vast preparations for standing the siege, and gathering strength and reinforcements, fortified himself in Tabarhindah.[6]

---

[1] In Badaoni, Malik Yusuf Sarwar: Elliot has Yusuf Sarup.

[2] MBL, JNS and MBM read رای هبنو: Badaoni has Hansu Bhatti; Ferishta, Rai Hubbu. Elliot agrees with Badaoni.

[3] مذاکرهٔ ملاقات کرد.

[4] بی غم گردانید.

[5] Equivalent to about 18,000 ft. in length.

[6] استعداد حصار گیری بسیار داشت بدان مستحکمی و تقویت در حصار محصر گشت.

Majlis-i-'Ālī Zīrak Khān, Malik Kālū,[1] keeper of the elephants,[2] Islām Khān and Kamāl Khān threw a cordon round the fort. Malik-ul-Shark 'Imād-ul-Mulk, *amīr* of Multān, was summoned (by the Sultān) to advise upon the suppression of Pulād's insurrection. In the month of Zīl-hijjah (Aug.-Sep., 1430 A.D.), 'Imād-ul-Mulk left his army in Multān, and hastened[3] to Sarsutī with a small following, where he was honoured with the royal interview. But before this, Pulād had expressed himself that, he had reliance on the promise and protection of 'Imād-ul-Mulk[4] and that if the latter would accompany him, he would put his neck in the collar of obedience and make himself eminent by the glory of kissing the feet (of His Majesty). To win over[5] Pulād, Rāyāt-i-'Ālā sent 'Imād-ul-Mulk to Tabarhindah. Out came Pulād from his shelter, and he had an interview with 'Imād-ul-Mulk and Malik Kālū in front of the gate.[6] An agreement and a stipulation were arrived at on terms that, on the next day,[7] Pulād would emerge out of the fort, and pay his respects to *Bandagi Rāyāt-i-'Ālā*. But as Pulād suspected 'Imād-ul-Mulk of deep designs[8] and got frightened of his army, he determined to hold out. Malik-ul-Shark 'Imād-ul-Mulk returning to His Majesty was sent back to Multān,[9] in the month of Ṣafar,

'Imād-ul-Mulk sent for negotiation; his failure.

---

1 MBL زیرک خان و ملک و ملکه کالو.

2 MBL شحنه : MBM and JNS شحنۀ پیل.

3 جراره. Elliot reads جریده.

4 MBL قول دوست را ست ملک اعماد الملک : MBM قول و دست راس ملک : JNS قول و دست ملک اعتماد.

5 بری ترغیب.

6 A lacuna occurring in Elliot's Manuscript the portions that follow have been taken by the editor of Elliot's papers from Tabakat-i-Akbari.

7 The lines "Pulād would emerge........provisions of the people of the locality" (p. 228) are missing in MBM.

8 MBL ترسانیده : JNS میان لشکر کسی او را بترسانیده میان لشکر.. Ferishta writes, "One of 'Imād-ul-Mulk's attendants being acquainted with Pulād, hinted to him privately, that though 'Imād-ul-Mulk was a man of honour and would certainly adhere to his promise, yet the king might not be so scrupulous."

9 Ferishta (I, 524) writes, "the king finding the reduction of the place would occupy time, and thinking so large an army unnecessary for the siege, permitted 'Imād-ul-Mulk to return to his Government at Multān."

Badaoni says (p. 294):—

او بعد از طلب امان از حسار بیرون آمد — عمادالملک را دید باز اعتماد نکرد و ترسیده بحصار رفت و جنگها کرد ٭

834 H. (Oct.-Nov., 1430 A.D.), while the latter safely set out for Dehli leaving orders for Khān-i-'Azam Islām Khān, Kamāl Khān,[1] and Rāi Firoz Main to carry the investment of Tabarhindah.[2] Malik-ul-Shark 'Imād-ul-Mulk, returning to Tabarhindah, instructed the aforesaid *amīrs* and *maliks*, and himself carried on the siege to such a length that not a soul could emerge out of the fort, and thus, when the siege was firmly established,[3] he retired with successive marches to Multān. Pulād offered resistance for six months. Some time prior to this, Pulād had despatched his servants to Sheikh 'Alī Mughal[4] at Kabul soliciting his assistance in return for ready money and goods. Leaving Kabul with a big army, Sheikh 'Alī came in aid of Pulād in the month of Jamādī-ul-akhīr (Feb.-Mar., 1431 A.D.), near 'Ain-ud-dīn Khokhar at Talwārā, on the bank of the Jilum. Amīr Muzaffar and Khājekā, the nephews of Khokhar, collected a numerous army from Seor and Sakunat[5] and co-operated with the prince From thence, the prince took with him the people of Seor and the Khokhars, and proceeded to Tabarhindah.[6] On the way, Malik Abu-l-Khair Khokhar, too sought an interview with him. Malik 'Ain-ul-Mulk and Malik Abu-l-Khair Khokhar were appointed to act as his guides. He proceeded along the Beāh, and passing through the district of Kasur[7] forded the Beāh at Būhī. He then ravaged the country of Rāi Firoz.[8] With a view to bring together his companions, the Rāi left the environs of Tabarhindah without leave

Ali Mughal came in aid of Pulād.

---

[1] In Ferishta, Kaly Khān.

[2] MBL تبرهنده : JNS بتهنده.

[3] MBL قضيۀ محاصرۀ استحکام پذيرفت : JNS قصبه محاصره.

[4] MBL شيخ علي مغل : JNS شيخ زاده علي مغل : In Elliot (70), Shaikh 'Ali Beg: Ferishta (524), Amīr Shaikh 'Alī: Badaoni (294), Shaikh 'Alī Mughal, Governor of Kabul.

[5] JNS reads سيور و سکرنت : MBL سلونت.

[6] Elliot has, "In the month of Jamādi-ul-auwal Shaikh 'Alī went to Tabarhindh"

[7] 34 m. south-east of Lāhore.

[8] Ferishta writes, "(Sheikh 'Alī) ravaged the country of those chiefs who held estates in the Punjab, and who were conducting the siege of Surhind (Tabarhindh)"

from the other *amirs* and marched out.[1] Sheikh 'Alī was at a non-plus.[2] When he came within ten *kuroh* distance from Tabarhindah, Islām Khān, Kamāl Khān and the other *amirs* raised the siege and retired to their own homes. At the approach of Sheikh 'Alī, Pulād issued out of Tabarhindah, and making an interview with him, paid the stipulated amount of two lacs of tankas. Sheikh 'Alī left Tabarhindah, carrying with him the ladies and the children of Pulād, and devastated on the way most of the territories of Rāi Firoz. He, then, crossed the Sutlej[3] at Tirhānah, imprisoned the inhabitants of the tract from Jalandhar to Jaran[4]- -Manjhur,[5] and returned along the banks of the Beāh. Crossing the Beāh in the month of Rajab (Mar.-Apr., 1431 A.D.), *May God increase its dignity*,[6] he marched to Lāhore, where Malik-ul-Shark Malik Sikandar, its *amir*, offered him the usual customary annual tribute and gave him a send-off. Thence, passing through Kasur, he halted at Tilwārā[7] opposite Dibalpur, the renowned city.[8] He desolated the country[9] in the course of twenty days that he stayed there.[10] Being informed of the return of Sheikh 'Alī and of his having devastated the territory of Rāi Firoz and the *akta'* of Jālandhar, Malik-ul-Shark 'Imād-ul-Mulk advanced with a strong force to a distance o

The royalists retired at the advent of Sheikh 'Alī.

---

1 This fact is not mentioned in Elliot (70).

2 شيخ علي مذكور خيرة تر گشت.

3 MBL ستلدر. JNS ستلج.

4 MBL جارب : JNS جارن : Mod. Zira, in Firozpur dist. Punjab, Lat. 30° 5' Long. 75° 2' 45".

5 MBL and JNS منجهور : Elliot, Makhjahur. Mod. Makhu in Firozpur dis Lat. 31° 6', Long. 75° 5'.

6 رجب قدرة.

7 MBL تلوارة شهر لوهبر. JNS تلوارة شهر لاهور.

8 JNS and MBM در تلوارة شهر لاهور : MBL omits شهر لاهور.

9 زراعت آن ديار را ... .. خراب ساخت.

10 Ferishta (525) says "40,000 Hindus were computed to have been massacred besides a great number carried away prisoners."

forty *kuroh*, and took up his quarters at Ṭalumba.[1] Terror-stricken, Sheikh 'Alī returned along the Rāvī to Talumba and there deeming himself unsafe moved to Khatibpur.[2] Rāyat-i-'Ālā sent letters patent to 'Imād-ul-Mulk ordering him to leave Ṭalumba and go to Multān, in order to avoid an encounter with Sheikh 'Alī. On the 24th Sha'bān (Mon., 7th May, 1431 A.D.), he proceeded accordingly to Multān. Being emboldened at[3] the relinquishment of Tabarhindah by the *amīrs* and the *maliks*, and at his successful sack of the country, Sheikh 'Alī, fearless of the violence and perfidy of the fraudulent sphere, crossed the Rāvī at Khatibpur, went towards Multān, which was desolate owing to the drying up of the Rāvī, and destroying the habitations on either banks of the Jilum, came to a distance of ten *kuroh* from Multān. Malik-ul-Shark Imād-ul-Mulk, had despatched Malik Sulṭān Shāh Lodi[4] to serve as a piquet. Sheikh 'Alī Mughal advanced with his forces, and the opponents meeting each other, the battle commenced. At last, Lodi was killed; of his soldiers, some died in the battle and some[5] retired to Multān. On the 3rd Ramẓān[6] (Tues., 15th May, 1431 A.D.), the holy month, Sheikh 'Alī occupied Khasruābād,[7] and on the following day,[8] collecting all his forces and making them ready for war, he went near the *namāzgah* (the place of worship) in Multān.[9] 'Imād-ul-Mulk, too, prepared himself for action, and presented a front. Some of his foot had marched ahead; being worn out in the orchards, his

Advance of 'Imād-ul-Mulk and the flight of Sheikh 'Alī to Talban and Khatibpur.

Occupation of Khasruābād by Sheikh 'Alī: his advance to Multān.

---

1 MBL and MBM طلبنهه : JNS تلبن : Badaoni طلبنه : Tab-i-Akb. طلنبه. Elliot and Ferishta, Toolumba: modern Ṭalambha, 52 m. north-east of Multān.

2 MBL and MBM خوطپور : JNS reads خطبور : Badaoni خوطپور : Tab-i-Akb. خطيب پور. Ferishta and Elliot, Khatibpur.

3 مغرور برباد شده بود.

4 MBL ملک سليمان شه لودي : JNS سلطانشه. Tab-i-Akb. agrees with JNS.

5 MBL بعضی باز گشته : JNS omits باز گشته.

6 Ferishta, 4th Ramẓān.

7 Ferishta and Elliot, Khairābād. Badaoni, Khasruābād.

8 Elliot has 25th Ramẓān.

9 JNS reads نزدیک نمازگاه خطه ملتان : Elliot " against the gates of Multān."

army failed to come back to the fort, and was compelled to retire to Khasruâbâd. Every day his soldiers took away by force the cattle and provisions of the people of the locality, and of those living on the banks of the Jilum.[1] With all his equipage and retinue ready for war, Sheikh 'Alī advanced against the gâtes of Multân on the 25th of the month (Wed., 6th June). The army of 'Imâd-ul-Mulk, and the people inhabiting the city made a sally. In the conflict which ensued in the garden, the assailants lost the goods, cattle and ladder[2] that they brought with them. Defeated and subdued, the infantry returned to its sphere of influence.[3] On Friday, the 27th of the same month (8th June, 1431 A.D.), they returned and opened a fresh assault. Dismounting his horsemen in order to push through the gates of the city, 'Imâd-ul-Mulk fell upon his enemy with his horse and foot, and the latter unable to withstand his attack made off. Some were put to the sword, while some succeeded in falling back to the main body. Being routed again that day, they did not venture to make any further assault upon the place.

'Imād-ul-Mulk defeated Sheikh 'Alī.

As a matter of fact, when these transactions were reported to Râyât-i-'Âlâ, he sent Majlis-i-'Ālī Khân-i-'âzam Fath Khân,[4] son of Sulṭân Muzaffar Gujrâti, Majlis-i-'Ālī Zirak Khân, Malik Kâlu, keeper of the elephants, Khân-i-'âzam Islâm Khân,[5] Malik Yusuf Sarwar-ul-Mulk, Khân-i-'âzam Kamâl Khân, Râi Juljain Bhatti[6] with a large following to reinforce 'Imâd-ul-Mulk. On the 26th Shawwâl (Sat., 7th July) of the abovementioned year (834 H., 1431 A.D.), the (aforesaid) *amīrs* and *maliks* reached the khiṭṭa of Multân, and there remained encamped for some time.[7] They proceeded on Friday, the

Reinforcements sent to 'Imād-ul-Mulk.

---

[1] The extract from Tabakat-i-Akbari in Elliot here terminates.

[2] JNS reads جنس گاوسیر و نردبان : MBI گلو سر. [3] دایرهٔ خویش.

[4] MBL مجلس عالي خان خان اعظم : JNS مجلس خان اعظم فتح‌خان.

[5] JNS خان اعظم اپ لام خان : MBL خان اعظم اسلام خان.

[6] MBL هینو نولجي بهتي : MBM هنبو جلجین بهتي : JNS has رای هنیو جلجین بهتي : Elliot; Râi Hansu Khūl Chain : Tab-i-Akb. هنو بهتي :

[7] In JNS مقام ساختن : should be مقام ساختند.

3rd Ẕīl-ḳa'da (13th July, 1431 A.D.), and approaching the prayer-house, made an attempt to enter the *kotlah* (fortress) of 'Alā'-ul-Mulk. Being informed of this, Sheikh 'Alī drew up all his cavalry and infantry in battle array, and met his adversaries. The royal forces were also ready for the encounter. 'Imād-ul-Mulk was in the centre; Majlis-i-'Ālī Fath Khān, Malik Yusuf and Rāi Hinu[1] on the right; Majlis-ī-'Ālī Zirak Khān, Malik Kālū, Khān-i-'āẕam Islām Khān and Khān-i-'āẕam Kamāl Khān on the left. Catching sight of the imperialists, Sheikh 'Alī dispersed in confusion from a distance, and when the former opened the assault, the latter made a stampede, and so hasty was his retreat that he durst not look behind. While endeavouring to escape, several of the chiefs were put to the sword. Sheikh 'Alī with the remnant of his army took shelter in the fortification, which had been raised round the baggage. When the victorious army approached the fortification, the enemy being unable to resist them made their way to the Jilum,[2] in which many were drowned, and many, at the divine order, reached the army of Fira'wn,[3] and of the survivors some were killed and some imprisoned. Receiving a wound, Hājī Kār[4] perished among the drowned. Sheikh 'Alī and Amir Muẕaffar safely crossed the stream, and retired with a small cavalry to Seor,[5] their arms, baggage and equipments fell into the hands of the victors. Such a dire calamity never befell any army in any previous occasion, or in any other reign. Those who took to the water were drowned, and those who participated in the engagement were killed; neither flight nor fight availed to save them. [6]So that thou wouldst say, each and all entered, suddenly and by chance, the orifice of death. "*For him we are, and to Him we return!*"

Defeat of Sheikh 'Alī and his retreat.

---

1 MBL and JNS رای هنبو.

2 MBL and MBM جمله در آب جیلم در آمدند : JNS آب جیلم غرق شوند.

3 JNS بفرعون آلهي بلشكر فرعون رسيدند : MBL and MBM فرعون بفرمان آلهي : فرعون means Pharaoh; in general, any cruel tyrant.

4 MBL حاجبکار : JNS حاجیکار.

5 JNS and MBM read سیور : MBL سور : Badaoni has شیور : Tabaḳat-i-Akbari, Shor; Ferishta, Shewar; Ranking, Shīwar.

6 The lines, "So that thou wouldst say......wind", have been left out in Elliot's History.

Author's remark on the insecurity of Time and Fortune.

It is evident to all having exact knowledge and strong experience that, the active Heavens and Time, the great charmer, display curious[1] feats out of the bi-coloured sheets and the multi-coloured veils before the vain[2] and the short-sighted!

Couplet.

Ugly in appearance[3] is this world full of deceptive colour,
Each morning it appears with captivating decorations!

Let it not be concealed from the eye of observation of every intelligent man that, one from inadvertence of youth ought neither be misled by this coquetting harridan (i.e., the world) who has a semblance of a girl of fourteen, nor should he put his trust upon the flattery and fraud of this deceptive assassin, nor should he pin his faith[4] upon this whore![5] What valiant champions of kingdom and Emperors seated on the throne of sovereignty hath she not removed from their capitals and thrones, and enclosed them in the biers![6] Many a young damsel from the garden of elegance[7] and bride from the meadow of beauty[8] hath she taken out of their spring season, (youth) and hath dealt upon them whirlwind-like blows of autumn and imprisoned them in the dust of destruction!

Distich.

Each atom that thou observeth in the dust,
So many Solomons blown away by the wind!

---

1 JNS باز گونه بازیها : MBL باز گونه کونه بازیها : MBM هر گونه بازیها.

2 JNS and MBM مردم دراز امل : MBL دراز امد.

3 JNS and MBM مکرة طلعتي است : MBL طلعتس.

4 MBM and MBL اعتبار باید گرفت : JNS اعتبار نباید گرفت.

5 JNS قحبه دلاله : MBL قحبه لا : MBM قحبه ولا.

6 JNS از تختگاه تخت بخت بتخته تابوت : MBL از تختگاه تخت بتخته چوب تابوت : MBM agrees with JNS.

7 JNS چند نوبران باغ لطافت : MBL و خندهای نوبرانِ باغ ظرافت : MBM agrees with JNS.

8 JNS راغ طرافت : MBL راغ لطافت : MBM لطافت را.

To return to our story: [1] Malik-ul-Sharḳ 'Imād-ul-Mulk *alia* Malik Maḥmud Ḥasan, and other *amirs* ran in pursuit of Sheikh 'Ali to Seor on the 4th Zil-ḳa'da (Sat., 14th July, 1431 A.D.), Amīr Muẓaffar [2] made preparations for standing the siege in the fort of Seor and to fight it out. Defeated and discouraged, Sheikh 'Alī retired to Kabul with few adherents. In the meantime, the imperialists in pursuance to the royal mandate, gave up the siege of Seor, and took their way to the capital.

Flight of Sheikh 'Alī.

It was for this reason that, Multān was taken from Malik Maḥmud Ḥasan,[3] and bestowed upon Malik Khair-ud-dīn Khanī in fief. But this act of transfer was imprudent and inconsiderate as some insurrection broke out in Multān, an account of which will be given in the subsequent pages.[4]

Multān bestowed upon Khair-ud-din; Its consequences.

In the month of Rabī'-ul-auwal, 835 H. (Nov.-Dec., 1431 A.D.) it was made known to the Sulṭān that Malik Sikandar Tuḥfa had taken the route of Jālandhar. Jasrath Shaikha Khokhar came down with a strong detachment from the hills,[5] and having forded the Jilum, the Rāvī and the Beāh approached Jālandhar on the bank of the Benī.[6] Malik Sikandar was unwary, but he encountered the enemy with a small following. At the first onset, he met with defeat, and by divine pre-ordination and the inevitable decree of God, his horse[7] having got stuck in the mire he was carried into captivity by Jasrath. Some (of Sikandar's men) were slain in the battle, and some retreated

Jasrath advanced to Jālandhar, defeated and imprisoned Sikandar Tuḥfa.

---

1 JNS and MBM باز ایم برسر قصهٔ : MBL omit سر.

2 "Nephew of Sher 'Ali"—Tābaḳāt-i-Akbari.

3 Ferishta writes that the king becoming zealous of the popularity of 'Imād-ul-Mulk called him to court.

4 JNS کیفیت بسباق در قلع اید MBL : که کیفیت سیاق و در اخر سیاق اوراق مشرع اوراق مشرع : MBM کیفیت سباق و در آخر سباق اوراق مشرع.

5 MBL از کوه تیکهر : MBM تیلهر : JNS simply از کوه. Elliot. "mountains of Telhar.

6 JNS has بینی : MBL and MBM بیني : Elliot, Par[illegible].

7 JNS and MBL پای اسپ او : MBM پای او.

to Jālandhar. Jasrath carried off Sikandar and some others who had been made prisoners with him, and marched in triumph to Lāhore to which fortress he laid siege. Sa'iyid Najm-ud-dīn, lieutenant of Sikandar and Malik Khushkhabr his slave, held the fort and offered battle. The strife continued day to day. Meanwhile, Sheikh 'Alī brought together a party of accursed wretches, and ravaged the environs of Multān. He made prisoners the people of Khatībpūr[1] and of several other villages on the bank of the Jilum as he descended that river. On the 17th Rabī'-ul-auwal (Fri., 23rd Nov., 1431 A.D.), he reached Talumba, and on the pretext of making peace with its people, he put them to death and kept their chiefs prisoners. He then permitted his detestable followers to get possession of the fort. The day following, the whole of the Muslims became captive in the hands of the impure, irreligious and imprudent heretics.[2] Though many good men of the locality were prelates, *Sa'iyids* and ķāzis, neither any respect for the Musalman religion, nor the fear of God could restrain that accursed, cruel and inauspicious-faced wretch! Young women and children were carried off from their families and dragged to his house. Of the people, some were made food for the unsparing sword, and some let off. The fortified and the strong fortress of Talumba was levelled to the ground. * * May God, glorified be his name! Uproot the foundation of the accursed (infidel) in the manner resembling (the saying of God) "*I have raised to the dust their high mansions*",[3] and may He keep in perpetuity, so long the world exists, the ruler of the Muslims and their religion! * *[4]

Jasrath advanced to Lāhore.

Sack of Multān by Sheikh 'Alī: His atrocities.

Meanwhile, Pulād Turkbachā marched out of Tabarhindah with his retinue and devastated the country of Rāi Firoz. When the Rāi was informed of this, he encountered the invader with his infantry and cavalry, and a conflict ensued. By God's decree, the

Rāi Firoz defeated and slain by Pulād.

---

[1] MBL and MBM خوطيپور : MS. has خطبور : in Badaoni خوطپور.

[2] MBL omits "in the hands of ...... heretics." JNS and MBM retain it.

[3] JNS جعلنا عاليها و سافلها. The insertion of, is due to the copyist's error.

[4] The portion within the asterisk is omitted in Elliot.

Rāi met with his death; Pulād severed off the Rāi's head and carried it to Tabarhindan. A good many horse and an ample supply of grain fell in the hands of Pulād. On receipt of this information, *Bandagī Hazrat Rāyāt-i-'Ālā* (the Emperor) took the route of Multān and Lāhore on Jamadī-ul-auwal[1] (Jany.-Feb., 1432 A.D.), and appointed Malik Sarwar[2] as an advanced guard to put down the rebellion. At the approach of the army (royal) to Sāmāna, the infamous and depraved Jasrath raised the siege of the fort, and retreated to the hills of Telhar,[3] carrying with him Malik Sikandar. Sheikh 'Alī also, in fear of the imperialists, fell back on Bartot.[4] *Malik-ul-Shark* Shams-ul-Mulk was deprived of the fief of Lāhore[5]; and it devolved upon *Khān-i-'Azam* Nusrat Khān *Gurg-andāz*.[6] Malik Sarwar brought the family of Shams-ul-Mulk out of Lāhore, and sent them to the capital. Thus the fort of Lāhore and the *aktā'* of Jālandhar came under the control of Nusrat Khān.

The Sultān set out against Pulād; latter raise the siege of Multān.

Lāhore and Jālandhar bestowed upon Nusrat Khān.

In the month of Zīl-hijjah (July-Aug., 1432 A.D.) of the year, Jasrath appeared with a large army from the hills and advanced to Lāhore; a battle took place between him and Nusrat Khān, in which the former being defeated turned on his heels. *Bandagī Rāyāt-i-'Ālā* (the Sultān) encamped himself near Panipath on the bank of the Jaun. Thence, in the month of the auspicious Ramzān (May, 1432 A.D.), he ordered off *Malik-ul-Shark* Imād-ul-Mulk with strong reinforcements to

Re-appearance of Jasrath, his defeat and flight. The Sultān's return.

---

[1] In Ferishta, 1st Jamadi-ul-auwal.

[2] JNS ملک سروپ: In Ferishta, Survur-ul-Mulk; Badaoni reads ملک یوسف سرور الملک.

[3] JNS and MBM تیلهر: MBL تیکهر.

[4] MBL باربوت: JNS and MBM بارتوت: In Ferishta (p. 527), Kabul; Badaoni writes—جسرت بجانب ... کوه پایه و شیخ علي نیز بجانب ولایت خود رفت.

[5] Badaoni writes Jālandhar.

[6] کرگ انداز: It may be read both as کرگ انداز and گرگ انداز: کرگ and گرگ mean rhinoceros and wolf respectively: Briggs reads the epithet *Goorg andaz* and says that it was so given to the chiet, probably, from his having personally got the better of a wolf. Badaoni writes گرگ انداز.

Bianah and Gwālior for coercing the rebellious infidels. The Sultān, with the appearance of fortunate aspect of constellation, safely made his way to the capital.

The Sulṭān march against Sāmāna. Muharram, 836 H. (Aug.-Sept., 1432 A.D.)

In Muharram, 836 H. (Aug.-Sept., 1432 A.D.), the Sulṭān marched from the capital to Sāmāna to punish the disaffected people of the neighbourhood. He, then, proceeded to Panipath with a strong detachment. Meanwhile, intelligence was brought to him that *Makhdumā-i-Jahān* (the crown mother) was taken ill. On the receipt of this intelligence, the Sulṭān immediately returned to the capital, with a few horse, leaving his army and baggage in charge of the *amirs* and *maliks* (at Panipath). A few days after his return his mother died. After performing her funeral obsequies, he remained for ten days in the capital, and then rejoined his army.

Malik Sarwar despatched to Tabarhindah against Pulād.

The Sulṭān ordered Malik Sarwar to proceed with a contingent against Tabarhindah, which was ably defended by Pulād Turkbāchā, who made an ample provision of grain and other requisites which he had secured from the country of Rāi Firoz. The fort was invested and operations were begun. When the preparation was complete, Malik Sarwar-ul-Mulk[1] placed *Majlis-i-'Ālī* Zirak Khān, Islām Khān and Kahūn Rāj in command and proceeded with a few escort to effect a union with *Rāyāt-i-'Ālā* at Panipath.

Lāhore and Jālandhar bestowed upon Kākā Lodī, who was defeated by Jasrath.

The Sulṭān, the refuge of the world, having laid aside the intention of proceeding on his intended expedition, took the fiefs of Lāhore and Jālandhar from Nuṣrat Khān, and bestowed them upon Malik Allah-dād Kākā Lodī.[2] When Malik Allah-dād reached Jālandhar, Jasrath who was prepared and ready (for action), crossed the Beāh and came to Bājwāra.[3] A battle followed, in which Almighty God conferred victory on the former, and the latter, being worsted, retired to the mountains of Kothī.[4]

---

[1] MBL ملک سروپ سرور الملک : JNS and MBM omit سروپ.

[2] Badaoni, *ibid.*, Allāh-dad Kālu Lodi.

[3] There was a gap at this place in Elliot's MS.: Bājwārrah, 25 miles N.E. of Jālandhar, and 1½ m. east of Hoshiārpur.

[4] Badaoni simply writes—بکوه پایه رفت : MSS. read کوتهی.

In the month of Rabī'-ul-auwal (Oct.-Nov.) of the year (836 H., 1432 A.D.), the Sulṭān marched his army to the hills of Mewāt, and with successive marches arrived at Tā'orū.[1] Jalāl Khān Meo, on receipt of this news, shut himself up with a large army in the fortress of Andwar,[2] one of the strongest citadels belonging to the Mewātis. Next day, the Sulṭān undertook preparations for its assault, but before his forces drew near, Jalāl Khān set fire to the fort, came out of it and set out towards Kotlāh. Most part of the provisions, materials and grain, which the Rāi had kept in stock in prospect of the siege, fell into the hands of the royalists. *Rāyāt-i-Ālā* moved onwards, and having encamped himself at Tajārāh devastated the greater part of Mewāt. Failing to hold his own against the victors, Jalāl Khān tendered his submission on promise of paying usual revenue and taxes; he abandoned his rash proceedings and was pardoned. Malik 'Imād-ul-Mulk, also, joined the Sulṭān at Tajārāh with a strong force composed of horse and foot from Bianah. Rāyāt-i-'Ālā, *May God increase his dignity*, then sent Malik Kamāl-ul-Mulk,[3] and all the *amirs* and *maliks* from Tajārāh to bring the infidels of Gwālior and Etāwah to a coerced obedience, and he himself returned with an escort to the capital, where he arrived in the month of Jamādi-ul-auwal (Dec.-Jany., 1432-33 A.D.).

The Sulṭān to Mewāt; Submission of Jalāl Khān.

Kamāl-ud-din sent against Gwālior and Etāwah

After he (the Sulṭān) had sojourned in the capital for a few days, advices were received that Sheikh 'Alī was advancing with a numerous army against the *amirs* who had invested Tabarhindah. The Sulṭān became thoughtful, for he apprehended, lest these *amīrs*, alarmed at the news should abandon the siege, as it had been done before. Malik-ul-Sharq Malik 'Imād-ul-Mulk was sent to bring relief to the *amīrs* and consequent to his arrival at Tabarhindah, they were emboldened and strengthened. In fine, Sheikh 'Alī advancing

Sheikh 'Alī invests Lāhore.

1 MBM, MBL تاؤرو : JNS reads تاو رور : In Elliot, Tāoru : Tabakat-i-Akbari, Nadir

2 MBL اندور : MBM and JNS اندرو.

3 MBL and MBM كمال الملک : JNS كمال الدين : In Elliot, Malik Kamāl-ul-

rapidly from Seor[1] entered the country on the banks of the Beāh, and having taken many prisoners from Sāhniwāl and other places, went to the auspicious city of Lāhore. Malik Yusuf Sarwar,[2] Malik Ismā'il, nephew of *Majlis-i-'Ālī* Zirak Khān, and Malik Rājā, son of Bahār Khān[3] had been left in charge of the fort of Lāhore. The fort was laid siege to, and the fight commenced. The people of the city (Lāhore) were off their guard; consequently, Malik Yusuf and Malik Ismā'il left the city by night and fled. Sheikh 'Alī despatched a force in their pursuit. Many of the horsemen fell under the attack of the accursed pursuers, and many were taken prisoners, including Malik Rājā. On the following day, the accursed Sheikh 'Alī[4] made all the Musalmans of the city, both men and women, prisoners. This vile, irreligious fellow had no better object or occupation than that of ravaging the seats of Islām and of making the Musalmans captive. "*Oh God! assist those who helped the religion of the Prophet, and disgrace those who discredited his religion!*" God, the Most High and the Helper of the Muslim religion, increased the malevolence of that accursed fellow. As a matter of fact, after making prisoners of the men of Lāhore, Sheikh 'Alī remained there for some time, and renovated (the ramparts of) the fortress[5] which had been damaged at places. Then leaving about 2,000 men, horse and foot behind, with the means of standing a siege, he marched towards Dībālpūr. Malik Yusuf Sarwar-ul-Mulk was about to abandon the fort of Dībālpūr and flee, as he had abandoned that of Lāhore, but *Malik-ul-shark* 'Imād-ul-Mulk at Tabarhindah, being informed of his intention, sent *Malik-ul-umarā'* Malik Aḥmad, his brother, with a large army, to hold the fort of Dībālpūr. Before this, Sheikh 'Alī had made his escape through a thousand and one difficulties from Malik-ul-shark and the dread of that chief still ruled in his heart, so he was unable to go to Dībālpūr.

---

[1] MSS. سیور : Badaoni شیور : Ferishta, Shewar: Elliot and Tabakat-i-Akbari, Shor.

[2] MBL یوسف سروپ : MBM یوسف سروت : JNS agrees with MBM: Elliot, Sarwar; Badaoni, Malik Yūsuf Surūru-Mulk.

[3] MBL بهار خان : JNS پهار خار، : Elliot, Bihār Khān.

[4] In JNS آن ملعون مقهور شده (؟) یعني شیخ علي : شده is copyist's mistake.

[5] بازار سر عمارت کرد.

The Sultān proceed to Sāmāna and Talwandī.

In Jamādi-ul-akhir (Jany.-Feb., 1433 A.D.), Mubārak Shāh received intelligence of the conduct of the vanquished. Fierce and brave, the Sultān unhesitatingly marched his numerous soldiers to Sāmāna. There, he waited some days for *Malik-ul-shark* Kamāl-ul-Mulk. When that chief, with the force at his command, joined the Sultān, the latter left Sāmāna, and proceeded *vîa* Sannām to Talwandī (belonging to) Rāi Fīroz Maīn, where he encamped. *Malik-ul-shark* 'Imād-ul-Mulk and Islām Khān Lodī who had been sent to Tabarhindah, (here) joined *Rāyāt-i-Ālā* (the Sultān).[1] Giving orders to the other *amīrs* not to evacuate the fort,[2] the Sultān hastened on, and forded at Būhī.[3] When the enemy heard of these movements, he was at his wits' end and took to flight. The royal forces reached the vicinity of Dībālpūr, and crossing the Beāh, encamped on the bank of the Rāvī, when the accursed foe had already crossed the Jilum. *Malik-ul-shark* Sikandar Tuhfa now received the title of *Shams-ul-Mulk*, with the fiefs of Dībālpūr and Jālandhar. Despatching a strong force against the enemy who was invested in the fort of Lāhore,[4] the Sultān safely proceeded to the fort of Seor, which was in the possession of the enemy,[5] and went across the Rāvī near Ṭalambha,[6] sending *Malik-ul-shark* in pursuit of the foe (Sheikh 'Alī). But the latter fled precipitately without casting a look behind, and a large number of horse and much baggage and goods which he had got in boats, fell into the hands of the forces of Islām. Amīr Muzaffar, nephew of Sheikh 'Alī, was in command of the fort of Seor,[7] and he defended the place for a whole month; being worn out at last, he opened

Dībālpūr and Jālandhar upon Sikandar Tuhfa.

Retreat of Sheikh 'Alī.

---

[1] در رکاب علی آمرده پیوستند*.

[2] تا از گرد حصار دور نشوند.

[3] MS. بوهي : Badaoni (297), پوهي : Elliot (77), Pohī.

[4] There is a Lacuna in JNS : the text reads : جالندهر یافت محصر بودند نامرد کرده.

[5] آن مقهور.

[6] MBL and MBM طلنبه : JNS طلبنه : Elliot, Tulamba.

[7] Ferishta, Muzaffar Khān.

negotiations for peace. In the month of Ramẕān (Apr.-May, 1433 A.D.), *May it have blessing!* he gave his daughter to the king's son [1] and paid a large tribute. In the month of S̲hawwāl (May-June, 1433 A.D.), the accursed (Mug̲hals) who had been besieged in Lāhore capitulated to *Malik-ul-s̲hark* S̲hams-ul-Mulk, and the latter took possession of the fort. *When the expedition of Seor came to a successful issue and Lāhore was conquered, the Emperor, the refuge of the world, took his way to Dehli. The same month,

Submission of Muzaffar, nephew of S̲heik̲h 'Alī.

Sulṭān's pilgrimage to Multān.

the triumphant Sulṭān, attended by his brave and numerous soldiers, went on a pilgrimage to (the tombs of) great and holy persons near Multān. At the renowned city of Dībālpūr, he left in charge of *Malik-ul-s̲hark* Kamāl-ul-Mulk, his elephants, foot soldiers, equipage and the other necessaries. After the completion of the pilgrimage to the holy saints and the management of public affairs in those tracts in the course of few days, the Sulṭān contented and happy, quickly returned to Dībālpūr, and made a halt for some time.

Conferment of the fort of Lāhore upon S̲heik̲h 'Alī.

Apprehensive of the vanquished S̲heik̲h 'Alī, and in accordance with the principles of sovereignty and the time-honoured principles of war and peace, His Majesty conferred (the fort ?) Lāhore and Dībālpūr upon him (the vanquished S̲heik̲h 'Alī ?) [2] with experienced and tried warriors.* [3] As *Malik-ul-s̲hark* 'Imād-ul-Mulk had been successful in the discharge of duties entrusted to him, the *aḳṭā's* of Lāhore and Jālandhar were taken from Malik S̲hams-ul-Mulk and given to the former. Bianah was conveyed from Malik 'Imād-ul-Mulk to S̲hams-ul-Mulk. Leaving his elephants and horses, his army, baggage and followers, in charge of *Malik-ul-s̲hark* Kamāl-ul-Mulk, the Sulṭān, with all speed, returned to

Lāhore and Jālandhar given to 'Imād-ul-Mulk; Sikandar Tuḥfa got Bianah in exchange for Lāhore which was given to 'Imād-ul-Mulk.

---

[1] Ferishta writes, "he gave his daughter to the king."

[2] The Text runs:—

از اندیشه شیخ علي مقهور حصار لاهور و دیبالپور خواست تابمبارزي ستوده و بهادران جنگ آزموده بر قانون جهانداری و قاعدهٔ حلالخواري ميان همگنان علم و در صف هیجا ثابت قدم باشد بحواله او گردانیده باز گردد ٭

Badaoni writes:—

از ملاحظهٔ شیخ علي اقطاع لاهور و دیبالپور را بملک الشرق عماد الملک داد ٭

[3] The portion within the asterisk is omitted in Elliot.

Dehli on the day of 'Īd.[1] The *amīrs* and *maliks* of Dehli, all the retinue and the bāzār people received the eminence of kissing the feet of His Majesty, the refuge of the world. Attended by felicity, happiness and a daily-increasing royal train, the Sulṭan reached Dehli in an auspicious moment.[2]

Sulṭān returns to Dehli.

On the 1st Ẕīl-ḥijjah (July-Aug., 1433 A.D.), *Malik-ul-Sharḳ* Kamāl-ul-Mulk arrived (in Dehli) with his army. The duties of *Dīwān* and *Vizir* were not effectively discharged by Sarwar-ul-Mulk so he was divested of *Kār-i-ashrāf*. As *Malik-ul-Sharḳ* Kamāl-ul-Mulk had proved himself trustworthy, useful and loyal, the *Kār-i-ashrāf* was transferred to him, and the office of *Vizir* was conferred upon Sarwar-ul-Mulk. Both carried on the affairs of the state in concert, but they did not hit off well. The officers (of the state) consulted Kamāl on state matters,[3] so Sarwar-ul-Mulk's thoughts turned towards blood. The previous deprivation of Dībālpūr rankled like a thorn in his heart.* * *[4] In the garden of Fortune, no other rose blossomed forth except that unfortunate rose, and that incautious fellow now resolved upon[5] effecting some revolution in the state. Some villainous infidels, such as, the sons of Kāngu and Kājo Khatrī, whose families since the days of their fore-fathers had been patronised and protected by the royal house, and each of whom had been the possessors of large attendants, vast territory and great power, some treacherous Muslims also, like Miran Ṣadr,[6] the *nāib-i-'āriẓ-i-mamālik*, Ḳāẓī Abdus Ṣamad, the Royal Chamberlain,[7] leagued with him, and made deliberations together.[8] They did not find an

Kamāl became Dīwān and Sarwar the Vizir.

Saṛwar-ul-Mulk brought about a revolution: was joined by Khatris, Miran Ṣadr and Abdus Ṣamad.

---

1 Badaoni writes, 'Id-i-Ḳurbān.

2 JNS reads با دولت و کبکۀ روز افزون بوقت سعد و وقت میمون درون در آمد.

3 اصحاب مناصب و دیوان وزارت در همه کارها رجوع اوردند.

4 This portion has been omitted in Elliot.

5 از قلب بی تدبیر درین تدبیر شد.

6 Elliot (78), Mirān Shahib: Badaoni (p. 268) and Ferishta (p. 529), Mirān Sadr.

7 MSS. read خاص حاجب: In Elliot, Khān Hajib.

8 درین خوض بودند و استدعا مي نمودند.

opportunity; but, neither any fear of God nor the shame of man restrained them from vain thoughts and foolish deed.

Foundation of Kharābābad or Mubārakābād.

To sum up, the Emperor, the refuge of the world, had determined to construct a city on the banks of the Jaun, and on the 17th Rabī'-ul-auwal, 837 H. (Sunday, 1st Nov., 1433 A.D.), he laid the foundation of a city at *Kharābābād-i-duniya*, and named that ill-omened city Mubārakābād.[1] Little did the Sulṭān know how shaken was the strong foundation of his (existence), and how it (his life) had turned its face towards departure.[2] Much of his time and care he devoted to the completion of this work of construction. In the aforesaid month, advices were received of the reduction of the

Reduction of Tabarhindah; Pūlād killed.

fort of Tabarhindah by the *amirs* who had been sent against it, and of the death of the evil Pūlād whose head had been cut off and sent to Sulṭān through Mirān Ṣadr. Next day, the Sulṭān marched out on pretence of hunting, to settle and bring order in Tabarhindah. Soon after, he returned in good health and spirits to Mubārakābād. The travellers from Hindustan brought intelligence of a war having broken out between Sulṭān Ibrāhim and Alb Khān,[3] on account of

War between Ibrāhim (Sharḳi) and Alb Khān of Kālpi.

Kālpi. Previous to this, His Majesty had decided to march his army there; and on hearing this intelligence, his course was decided. Orders were sent forth in every direction to the *amirs* of the capital and the *maliks* of every country, to collect their army with all speed, and to reinforce the Emperor. Like the stars round the moon a big force was collected[4] round the Emperor; in

March of the Sulṭān.

the month of Jamadi-ul-akhīr (Jany.-Feb., 1434 A.D.), the Sulṭān in conformity to the desire of

---

[1] Elliot, Oct. 31, 1435 A.D.

JNS reads—شهری خراب آباد دنیا بنیاد نهاد و ان صهر شوم مبارک باد نام نهاد

Badaoni, p. 298, writes—شهری بنا کرد و مبارک آباد که در معنی خرابا باد بود نام نهاد

"He founded a city which he called Mubārakābād, but which in reality, was Kharābābād (ruined city)."

[2] نمیدانست که بنیادش سخت سست گشته و مي خواهد که روي به انهدم آرد.

[3] "He was the governor of Kalpi and he had obtained the title of Sulṭān Ho..shing": Badaoni.

[4] JNS لشکر کثیر گرد بادشاه چو ستارة بر گردة ماه؟ . . .

the nobles and the grandees, set out (for Hindustan) with the royal paraphernalia and the victorious banner, and encamped for a few days at the *chautrah* (raised square place) of Shīrgāh.

Verse.

Not aware was he of the pre-ordination of Fate,
It drew a line of policy on the page of pleasure.[1]

Bereft of ceremony and escorted by few attendants the Emperor, the refuge of the world, made his way to Mubārakābād to witness the progress of the building.[2] The vile Sarwar-ul-Mulk, who was awaiting an opportunity, set to work the wicked infidels and the treacherous Miran Ṣadr, lest his secret machinations should be disclosed. A time of privacy was what his plans required.

Assassination of the Sulṭān, 9th Rajab, 837 H. 19th Feb., A.D. 1434[3].

On Friday, the 9th Rajab, *May God increase its dignity*, 837 H. (Fri., 19th Feb., 1434 A.D.), the Sulṭān reached Mubārakābād with only a few escort, and was preparing for Juma' prayers,[4] when Miran Ṣadr craftily removed the *amīrs* who were on guard, and like a cunning fox and a blood-thirsty jackal, brought his wretched infidels armed and mounted on horse on pretence of leave-taking. Sadhāran[5] Kāngū stood with his party outside the door to prevent any outside relief. The Emperor, possessor of the world and fierce in hunting lions, having entire confidence in them, paid no heed to these preparations; he had been exceedingly kind and generous to these foes of God and enemies of himself. Suddenly, rushed out from the ambush the evil-destined Sidh Pal,[6] the grandson of the accursed Kaju, and dealt with his sword such a ruthless blow upon the royal cypress and the bouquet of youth, (the Emperor), that his water of life flowed upon the dust of death. Each

---

[1] JNS خطی مشت : MBL and MBM خط مشیت.

[2] بادشاہ عالم پناہ کاہ بیکاہ ؟ بجہت جہد عمارت شہر.

[3] Elliot, 19th Jany.

[4] Ferishta writes, "The King went to worship at a mosque lately built in the new city."

[5] MBL and JNS سدھارن.

[6] MBL سدھپال : MBM سدھیپال : JNS سدھیبال : Badaoni سدۂ پال : Elliot, Sidhu Pal: Ferishta, Sid Pal.

of those irreligious mad fellows, such as Rānu the black, his assistants and confederates, at the sight of whose vileness even the Black-Demon is repugnant, and before whose noise the sound of hell wait with anxiety, (then rushed out) martyred the righteous Emperor with their dagger and javelin. "*For Him we are and to Him we return!*"

A discourse on the mutability of the worldly things.

[1] It is perfectly apparent to those having true knowledge and insight of truth, that this cruel sphere breaks the bond of sincerity, and the discordant time fails to redeem his pledge of assistance. Firstly, like one given to drinking, it sometimes bestows, without rhyme or reason, gifts upon people devoid of ability secondly, like an infant, who is not ashamed of what it does, it takes back the gift (from its recipient) for no fault of the latter. Every chief who wants to wax strong and powerful is hurled in the dust of ignominy, and those who are after honour and dignity are reduced to the dirt of impurity.

Verse.

Who shall long for this worldly wealth![2]
To whom has it been faithful so that it may be to us!

The aim of this composition and the use of such figurative expressions are to show that, men of wealth and possessors of dignity and retinue, ought neither be deceived by this deceptive dominion and the faithless world, nor they be outwitted by the favour and the connection of this perfidious sphere, nor should trust it for reasons mentioned above. *Those with eyes should take lesson!*

Verse.

Those things, that they have said in Shahnāmās,
Of Rustum,[3] the brass bodied and Isfandiyār;
That the Masters of country should take note,
"The world is the memorial of most people.

---

[1] The portion that follows is not to be found in Elliot.

[2] JNS دولت گیتي : MBL and MBM صحبت گیتي.

[3] *Rustam zāl*, Rustum, the son of Zal, was the most renowned hero among the Persians, and was said to have been a general under *Cai caus*, and his successor *Cai Khosrou*, whilst others place him in the reign of *Khishtasp* (Darius Hystaspes).

The sovereignty of late Mubārak Shāh extended for a period of over thirteen years, three months and sixteen days. *God knows the truth!*

An account of Sulṭān-ul 'Ahad-ul Zamān[1] Muḥammad Shāh, May his empire and sovereignty endure for ever, and may his command and dignity be exalted!

Character of Muḥammad Shāh.

Muḥammad Shāh (bin Farid Shāh bin Khiẓr Khān[2] was) an affable and kind sovereign, with every laudable quality: in nature praiseworthy, perfect in accomplishments and devoid of unlaudable traits in character.[3] Over his august forehead was manifest the mark[4] of sovereignty, and his fortunate countenance diffused divine splendour.[5]

His accession, 9th Rajab, 837 H., 19th Feb., 1434 A.D.

When Mubārak Shāh, the august Sulṭān and martyr, *May the blessing of God be on his tomb and may he ever dwell in Paradise!*[6] received the eminence and glory of martyrdom, the mischievous infidels and the depraved Miran Ṣadr came near Sarwar-ul-Mulk and enlightened him on the event. Sarwar-ul-Mulk and his associates were filled with delight and vain-glory. Later on, with the assent of the *amirs, maliks, imāms,* Sa'īyids, grandees, people, *ulemas* and Ḳāẓis, the Sulṭān ascended the throne when an auspicious constellation was in the ascendant, on Friday, the 9th

---

Rustam was one of the twelve champions of Persia, called "*duwazdeh rokh*". His single combat with Isfandiyar, the son of Darius Hystaspes, of the first dynasty of Persian kings, is highly celebrated in the East. It lasted for two days: when finding the *brazen body* of his antagonist had a magic charm against arrows, he killed him with the blow of a mace. Rustam was afterwards put to death by Bahaman or Ardeshir Dirazdest (Artaxerxes Longimanus), son of Isfandiyar.

1 The Sulṭān of the age and time.

2 JNS reads ذکر سلطان العهد و الزمان محمد شاه بن خضر خان برادر زاده و پسر خوانده مبارک شاه بود خلد الله ملکه و سلطانه و علی امده و شانه بادشاهی حلیم و کریم, etc.

MBL and MBM write محمد شاه بن فرید شاه بن خضر شاه بادشاهی حلیم و کریم, etc.

3 همه خصایل محمود (؟ نا محمود) از طبع گزیده او مفقود. 4 آثار بادشاهي.

5 MBL reads انوار فضل الهي و اسرار نامتناهي: JNS and MBM omit اسرار نا متناهي.

6 JNS and MBM omit "May he dwell in Paradise": MBM reads it.

Rajab, *May its dignity be exalted!* 837 H. (19th Feb., 1434 A.D.).

Attitude of Sarwar-ul-Mulk.

Although, Sarwar-ul-Mulk had tendered fealty to him he showed self-importance and head-strongness,[1] so much so, that he took possession of the cash, treasure-troves, royal studs, elephants and the armoury. The title of *Khān-i-Jahān* was conferred upon him, and that of *Mu'īn-ul-Mulk* upon Mirān Ṣadr. The wretched unbelievers became self-conceited and vain, and their motives were actuated by self-interest: at length, they got their deserts.[2]

Kamāl-ul-Mulk wanted to take vengeance on the murderers.

In fine, Malik-ul-Shark Kamāl-ul-Mulk,[3] worthy of a proper khānate and royalty[4] went inside the city with all the *amirs*, *maliks*, baggage, elephants, infantry and attendants and[5] made an acknowledgment of obedience. He wanted to exact retribution for the murder of Mubārak Shāh, his own patron, from the conceited and vain infidels, vile Sarwar-ul-Mulk, traitor Mirān and their confederates, and friends, but could not get an opportunity for action. Ultimately, this important affair was brought about by the Divine Providence, the Generous King, from the hands of Asaf[6] the second, the chosen of God, the Warrior in the field of bravery,[7] the Chief Traveller in (the path of) dispute, brought to pass this difficult task with such celerity and easiness[8] as has never been related in any (other) tale or history. Although, Rustam of the romance, out of revenge for Siavesh,[9] laid waste the house

---

1 خود را درمیان دیده خودرای کردن گرفت.

2 Text runs آخر لامر دیدند انچه دیدند و یافتند انچه.

3 He was the deputy Vizir: Ferishta calls him Kaly Khān.

4 که در خود خاني و سزاوار جهانباني است.

5 بیعت کرد : بیعت properly to agree with, to receive a promise or pledge for the settling of a bargain.

6 *Asaf* or *Asāf* (*Ben Berkhiya*), a great man supposed by the Arabians to have been Solomon's grand vizir. He is said to have obtained from God the highest degree of perfection, and is therefore constantly supposed by the Muslims as a model of excellence.

7 JNS سردار زندگان نزاعت : MBL سردار وزندگانی بداعت : MBM سردار و زندگان نزاعت.

8 بدین زودی کاری و بدین آساني دشواری بد آید.

9 JNS سیا و حبش an error for سیاوش, father of great Cyrus.

of Afrasiyab,[1] nevertheless, it took a long time and required no small effort on his part for the consummation of the desired result. A detailed account as to how the retribution was made has been related later on in general terms.

Sarwar-ul-Mulk captured attendants of Mubārak Shāh.

To return to our narrative; on the day following, Sarwar-ul-Mulk called for some of the attendants of Mubārak Shāh, each of whom was a person of rank and dignity, on the pretence of exacting fealty (from them). He placed them under confinement, and put Malik Surā, the *amīr* of Kōh, to death in the maidan: Malik Karmchand,[2] Malik Mukbil, Malik Fatūh,[3] Malik Bīrā were (also) shut up. That unprincipled traitor did his level best in uprooting the family of Mubārak Shāh; he (further) laid his hands on the *aktā's* and parganas of the country: some of the *aktā's*, (such as) Bianah, Amroha,[4] Narnol,[5] Kuhram, and some parganas in the Doāb, he conferred upon Sidhpal, Sadhāran and their kins-

Elevation of Hindu conspirators.

men. Rānu, the Black, the slave of Sidhpal[6] was ordered off to Bianah with a big force and the whole of his family to obtain possession of the *shikk* Bianah.[7] In the month of Sha'bān (Mar.-Apr., 1434 A.D.) he approached Bianah (Wed., 24th Mar., 1434 A.D.), and on the 12th of the month he entered it. Halting there for the night,

Rānū sent to Bianah, opposed by Yusuf Khān Auhadi and killed by the latter.

that incautious (fellow) wanted to seize the fort, (belonging to) the great Sultān.[8] Next day, with all his equipage and retinue well equipped and made ready, that unsuccessful infidel rode onwards. When Yusuf Khān Auhadi received

---

[1] Afrasiyab appears to have been rather a family surname, like the Pharaoh's, the Ptolemys' or the Cæsar's. Rustam being one of the generals of the great Cyrus, the defeat of Afrasiyāb must have happened above 150 years after the conquest of Persia by the first of that name. The first Afrasiyāb is much celebrated in Persian poetry. Scythian or Turk by birth, he invaded Persia, killed its King Nuzar, and reigned there for 12 years, about seven centuries before the Christian era; but was afterwards driven beyond the Oxus by a famous chief, called *zalzer* (or golden hair).

[2] In Elliot, Malik Makhdum.

[3] MS. فتوح : In Elliot (81), Malik Kanauj.

[4] In Moradabad district, U.P.

[5] In Patiāla State, Punjab.

[6] Ferishta writes, "Ranu, a slave of the Vizier" (Sarwar-ul-Mulk).

[7] In Bharatpur State, Rajputana. 50 m. S.-W. of Agra.

[8] JNS مي خواست كه قلع سلطان كسير(؟ كبير) آ اب (؟ ان) بى تدبير قابض شود .

an intimation of this, he drew up his forces from Hindwan,[1] and suddenly made himself ready for an encounter with a large number of foot and horse. Near the *ḥaẓira* (mausoleum) of the Prince, the opponents drew up their respective forces in battle array, and the conflict took place. The treacherous, wicked and vile infidels lost their power of remaining (in the battle-field) and at the very first onset they made a stampede. The accursed Rānu, the Black, and many others were made food for the unsparing sword. The impure head of the unlucky fellow was cut off the body and hung up at the entrance. The whole of his family, the females and the young children, became prisoners in the hands of the army of Islām. The Most High God, the Protector of the Islāmic religion, conferred victory upon Yusuf Khān and rendered him assistance in taking a bloody vengeance for the assassination of Mubārak Shāh on the dirty and depraved fellow (Rānu).

To sum up, when the evil disposition of Sarwar-ul-Mulk and the malefactions of the defeated infidels was rumoured in the country, several *amīrs* and *maliks*, who had been brought up and raised to honour by the late Rāyat-i-'Ālā Khiẓr Khān, now went into rebellion. The inconsiderate Sarwar-ul-Mulk set about giving them counsel, and fomented strife and disturbances. It was reported that, (the following Amīrs, such as,) Malik Allah-dād Kākā Lodi,[2] *amīr* of Sambhal and Ahār,[3] Miyan Chaman,[4] the holder of Badāōn and grandson of late Khān Jahān, Amir 'Alī Gujrāti,[5] Amir Kik[6] Turkbacha were bent upon making opposition.[7] Malik-ul-Shark Kamāl-ul-Mulk, Khān

Revolt of Amirs.

---

1 MBL هندوت : JNS and MBM هندوان : Hindaun, in Jaipur State, Rajputana, 71 m. S.-W. of Agra and 20 miles South of Bianah.

2 Tab-i-Akb., Kakā Lodi : Badaoni, Kalā Lodi.

3 20 m. N.-E. of Bulandshahr.

4 In Ferishta (533), Malik Joomun : Tab-i-Akb. ملک چمن : Badaoni agree with Tab-i-Akb.

5 Ferishta, Meer Ally Guzrāti.

6 MBL and JNS امیر کیک : *Ibid.*, Ameer Khān Toork : In Elliot (81), Kambal Turkbāchā.

7 JNS ملک الله داد کاکا لودي امیر سنبل و اهار و میان چمن مقطع خطه بدانون نبسه خانجهان مرحوم و امیر علي گجراتي و امیر کیک ترک بچه بسمع او رسانیدند : که اختلاف و اختلال شود : MBL reads که اختلاف ملک الله داد, etc. : MBM که اختلاف و اختلال ملک الله داد .

Badaoni writes (p. 301):

و دیگر امرا از برای انتقام مبارک جمعیت بسیار سر کرده جانب دهلي روان شدند

i-'Azam Sa'iyid Khān, son of Sa'iyid Sālim, were appointed to bring the rebels to obedience, and Malik Yusuf, the son of Sarwar-ul-Mulk and Sadhāran[1] Kangu went along with them. In the month of the holy Ramzan (April-May) (Kamāl) wheeled his column into line, and marching out encamped himself at the top of *Hauz-i-Rāni*.[2] A few days after, he marched his forces and halted on the banks of the Jaun, and crossing the river at Kīchā,[3] he reached and halted at Baran, intent upon his schemes of retribution. Gaining intelligence of the approach of the victorious army (Kamāl), Malik Allah-dād, desirous as he was to avoid an action, attempted to cross the Ganges for some other place; but when he was enlightened as to Malik-ul-Shark Kamāl-ul-Mulk's real intention of exacting a full revenge, he was reassured[4] and encamped at Ahār. At this, Malik Sarwar-ul-Mulk sent out Malik Hoshiyār, his slave,[5] under the pretence of assisting Malik-ul-Shark Kamāl-ul-Mulk.[6] Soon after this, Malik Chaman also drew up his forces from Badāōn by way of attending to[7] Malik Allah-dād, and joined him at Ahār. Malik Yusuf and Hoshiyār and Sadhāran who were terror-stricken, (now) became more pusillanimous and found themselves reduced to straits.[8] Perplexed and ill-at-ease, like the ball tossed from post to pillar and throwing the ball of bravery out of their hands, they fled headlong to the capital in fear of the victorious army. On the last day of the holy Ramzan (Apr.-May), of the year (837 H., 1434 A.D.), Malik Allah-dād, Miyān Chaman and

Kamāl-ul-Mulk, 'Azam Khān, Yusuf and Kangu sent against the rebel.

Kamāl encamps at Baran.

Retreat of the insurgents.

---

1 Ferishta, Sadnun : MBL and JNS کنکو : MBM کیکو : Tab-i-Akb. کانکو .

2 MBL حوض راني : MBM رابي : JNS حوض رابي : Elliot has simply "hauz".

3 MBM کیحیة : JNS کحة : MBL کیچهة .

4 بربن تقویت .

5 Badaoni writes نایب خود .

6 "But in reality, to ascertain his treachery, and watch over the safety of Yusuf." Elliot, IV, 82. "But in reality with secret instructions to watch his motions." Ferishta, I, 534. Badaoni : "Under pretence of reinforcing Kamāl-ul-Mulk, as a spy into their army."

7 بر سبیل اهتمام .

میدان مقاومت تنگ دیدند .

the other *amīrs* who had joined them, went over to Kamāl-ul-Mulk. When a considerable force had, with great pomp, collected round him, on the 2nd Shawwāl (Wed., 12th May), he (Kamāl) crossed (the Ganges) at the ford of Kicha. Being informed of this, Sarwar-ul-Mulk, although in reduced circumstances, made preparations for standing a siege.[1] Next day, came out the King of the Heavens having unsheathed his sword, the Sun, from the scabbard, the spheres that is (ever) contrary to agreement. Malik-ul-Shark Kamāl, the sun of the sphere of dominion, drew out his dagger of retribution and faced his adversaries. He encamped his army in the plain and the orchards. The wretched infidels and the scoundrel Hoshiyār, accompanied by a group of associates and well-wishers sallied forth and participated in the battle. When the belligerents came *vis-à-vis*, the malcontents suffered defeat; and became[2] discomfited. Distressed and afflicted in mind and body at the defeat, they retired to the fortifications. Those who were short-sighted, unsheathed their dagger of boasting, and indulged themselves in vain talks; laying aside their arms they fell upon the imperialists.[3] Many were put to the sword, and many were made prisoners. Next day, (Kamāl-ul-Mulk) issued out of the groves and pressing on, encamped near the fortress of Siri. Most of the *amīrs* and *maliks* of the surrounding country united forces with him. In the month of Shawwāl (May-June, 837 H., 1434 A.D.), the fortress was so closely blockaded that no one could come out of it. In spite of the repeated assaults made by the besiegers and several breaches in the fortifications, the garrison, owing to the impregnability of the fortress held out for three months. In the month of Zil-hijjah, of the year (July-Aug., 837 H., 1434 A.D.), Zirak Khān, *amīr* of Sāmāna, breathed his last, and his fiefs were bestowed upon Mahmud Khān, the eldest son

Sarwar-ul-Mulk stood a siege against Kamāl.

Kamāl encamps near Siri; its investment continued for three months.

Demise of Zirak Khān of Sāmāna.

---

[1] "Sarwar-ul-Mulk took post in the citadel of Siri," Ferishta, *ibid.*

[2] MSS. have: چون یکدیگرا روی با روی شوند روی به انهزام آوردند پشت تقویت ایشان و جمع پریشان از بدیکشان چنان شکسته خورد.

[3] کسانی که کوتاه اندیشي تیغ زبان لاف دراز کرده و گزاف مي گفتند سپرد ران افگندند و بی سپر سواران (?) لشکر منصور گشتند.

of the deceased. To sum up all, although His Majesty kept up a show of alliance with the besieged, he was desirous of taking revenge for the murder of K͟hān-i-s͟hahīd Mubārak S͟hāh, but found no opportunity. The garrison, in their turn, were apprehensive lest the Emperor gaining an opportunity[1] should betray them. Thus, each became suspicious of the other.

Sarwar-ul-Mulk was killed while attempting to murder the Sulṭān.

On the 8th Muḥarram, 838 H.[2] (Sat., 14th August, 1434 A.D.), the traitor Sarwar-ul-Mulk, and the sons of perfidious Miran Ṣadr broke into the royal apartments one by one with designs upon the Emperor,[3] intending to send him down in the fire of violence.[4] The Sulṭān, the refuge of the world, being ready and on the alert, managed the affair with skill[5] and dealt a blow from the dagger of punishment upon the traitors. The treacherous Sarwar-ul-Mulk was done to death with the blows of the sword and dagger, and the sons of Miran Ṣadr were taken prisoners and slain in front of the *darbār*. When the wretched infidels were informed of this, they shut themselves up in the fortress and made preparations for war. The Emperor conveyed this information to Malik-ul-S͟hark̤ Kamāl-ul-Mulk, directing him to come into the city with a party of his followers. Accompanied by other *amīrs* and *maliks*

Death of Sidhpal.

Malik-ul-S͟hark̤ entered (the city) by the Bag͟h-dād gate. Sidhpal, the accursed, set fire to his own house, making his wife and children fuel for hell.[6] He then came out and died while fighting. Sadhāran Kāngu and the other *Khatris*[7] who had been pinioned were led off to the tomb[8] of *K͟hān-i-s͟hahīd* Mubārak S͟hāh and driven to death. Malik Hos͟hiyār and Mubārak, the Kotwal, were taken captive and decapitated in front

---

1 بوقت فرصت و هنگام خلوت.

2 In Ferishta (1. 535), 840 H.: Badaoni writes 838 H.

3 با خاطر بر مکر باندیشه غدر.

4 This part of the sentence has been wrongly transcribed by the copyist in JNS.

5 کار از حدعایت و از فرط نهایت گذاشت.

6 زن و فرزند خود را هیزم دوزخ گردانید.

7 Ferishta, Katris.

8 MS. خطیرة: so has Badaoni; Elliot, *Khatira.*

of the Red gate. In fine, on the next day, Malik-ul-Shark Kamāl-ul-Mulk and all the *amīrs* and *maliks* who waited outside (the city) took the oath of allegiance [1] to the Sulṭān, the refuge of the world, and concurring with one another and with the people in general they enthroned him (Muḥammad Shāh). Malik-ul-Shark Kamāl-ul-Mulk received the Vizirate and the appellation of Kamāl Khān. Malik Chaman was dubbed Ghāzī-ul-Mulk, and the fiefs of Amrohā and Badāōn were confirmed on him.

Amīrs and maliks offer allegiance to the Sulṭān.

And in return were conferred with titles, etc.

Malik Allah-dād refused the title of Khān for himself,[2] but obtained the title of Dariya Khān for his brother. Malik Khūnraj Mubārak Khāni[3]. was named Ikbāl Khān and was confirmed in the fiefs of Ḥiṣar Firozā. All the *amīrs* and *maliks* were favoured with high dignity and rich gifts; and every person who held offices or fiefs, or villages or grants, or pensions received confirmation, and even an increase of their possessions.[4] The eldest son of Sa'iyid Sālim was entitled *Majlis-i-'Ālī* Sa'iyid Khān, and the younger one Shujā'-ul Mulk. Malik Madh 'Alam,[5] his sister's son, was entitled 'Alā'-ul-Mulk, and Malik Rukn-ud-dīn was designated Naṣir-ul-Mulk. They also received golden girdles, ranks drums and fiefs. Malik-ul-Shark Ḥājī Shudanī was made governor of the capital.[6]

When the administration of the kingdom was put in order, the Sulṭān determined on going to Multān. In the month of Rabī'-ul-ākhir (Nov.-Dec.), of the year[7] 838 H. (1434 A.D.), he encamped at the *chabutrā* of Mubārakpur,[8] and issued *farmāns* to the *amīrs* and *maliks* ordering them to appear before him with their forces ready. Malik-ul-Shark (Imād-ul-Mulk) made his allegiance, and received

The Sulṭān marched to Multān.

---

1 بیعت کردند.

2 هیچ خطاب خاني التزام نمود : Badaoni (p. 303) writes هیچ خطاب قبول نبرد.

3 MBL and MBM کمون راج : JNS ملک کهنبو راج مبارک : Elliot (84), Malik Khūnrāj Mubarak Khāni.

4 ماوراء آن زیادت خاصه خویش تعین کردن فرمود.

5 MBL and MBM ملک مدہ عالم ملک بدہ : Elliot reads Malik Madh 'Alam.

6 شحنه شهر دار الملک.

7 Badaoni has 840 H.

8 MBL and MBM چبوترہ : JNS در چوترہ مبارکپور : Badaoni (303) در مبارکپور.

(in return) valuable presents and great honours. (When) Malik-ul Shark approached the Sulṭān, most of the *amīrs* and *maliks* who delayed their coming[1] now came to His Majesty. Majlis-i-'Ālī Islām Khān, Mahmud Khān, son of Zirak Khān, Khān-i-'Azam Asad Khān, Kamāl Khān,[2] Mahmud Khān, son of Naṣrat Khān, Yusuf Khān Auhadi, Ahmad Khān, grandson of Bahādur Khān Mewātī, Iḳbal Khān, *amīr* of Ḥiṣār Fiıozā, and Amīr 'Ālī Gujrātī were honoured with marks of favour and *God knows the truth.*[3]

THE END.

---

[1] MBM and the MS. used by Elliot terminate here.

[2] MBL writes کمال خان نبسهٔ بهادر خان مِوه اقبال خان امیر حصار فیروزه, etc.

MBL ends with 8th Rajab, Wed., 23rd July. تمت الکتاب مبارکشاهی بعون الملک الّهي هشتم ماه رجب رجب قدره سبع و خمسین و تسعمائه (957 H.=1550 A.D.) المجرت و النّبویة.

JNS ends with تمت الکتاب مبارکشاهی تصنیف شیخ یحی رهندي بوقت ظهر تاریخ بیست و یکم رمضان المبارک, 21st Ramzan, سنه ۱۰۳۸ (1038 H.=1628 A.D.) تمام شد.

[3] MBL and JNS come to a close here.

INDEX OF TĀRIKH-Ī-MUBĀRAK SHĀHĪ.

THE NUMBERS REFER TO THE PAGES; *n*. STANDS FOR FOOTNOTE.

A

B

C

D

G

I

K

L

R

T

Z